Grant Allen

The evolution of the idea of God : an inquiry into the origins of religions

Grant Allen

The evolution of the idea of God : an inquiry into the origins of religions

ISBN/EAN: 9783337261429

Printed in Europe, USA, Canada, Australia, Japan

Cover: Foto ©Lupo / pixelio.de

More available books at **www.hansebooks.com**

THE EVOLUTION OF THE IDEA
OF GOD

NEW SCIENTIFIC BOOKS

PIONEERS OF EVOLUTION FROM THALES TO HUXLEY. By EDWARD CLODD. With Portraits in Photogravure of Darwin, Huxley, Mr. A. R. WALLACE, and Mr. Herbert Spencer. 5s. *net*. [Second Edition.

THE SUBCONSCIOUS SELF IN ITS RELATION TO EDUCATION AND HEALTH. By LOUIS WALDSTEIN, M.D. 3s. 6d.

THE EVOLUTION OF THE IDEA OF GOD

AN INQUIRY INTO THE ORIGINS OF RELIGIONS

BY

GRANT ALLEN

AUTHOR OF "PHYSIOLOGICAL ÆSTHETICS" "THE
COLOURS OF FLOWERS" "FORCE
AND ENERGY" ETC

LONDON: GRANT RICHARDS 1897

BUTLER & TANNER,
THE SELWOOD PRINTING WORKS,
FROME, AND LONDON.

PREFACE

Two main schools of religious thinking exist in our midst at the present day: the school of humanists and the school of animists. This work is to some extent an attempt to reconcile them. It contains, I believe, the first extended effort that has yet been made to trace the genesis of the belief in a God from its earliest origin in the mind of primitive man up to its fullest development in advanced and etherealised Christian theology. My method is therefore constructive, not destructive. Instead of setting out to argue away or demolish a deep-seated and ancestral element in our complex nature, this book merely posits for itself the psychological question, " By what successive steps did men come to frame for themselves the conception of a deity ? "—or, if the reader so prefers it, " How did we arrive at our knowledge of God ? " It seeks provisionally to answer these profound and important questions by reference to the earliest beliefs of savages, past or present, and to the testimony of historical documents and ancient monuments. It does not concern itself at all with the validity or invalidity of the ideas in themselves; it does but endeavour to show how inevitable they were, and how man's relation with the external universe was certain *a priori* to beget them as of necessity.

In so vast a synthesis, it would be absurd to pretend at the present day that one approached one's subject entirely *de novo*. Every enquirer must needs depend much upon the various researches of his predecessors in various parts of his field of enquiry. The problem before us divides itself into three main portions : *first*, how did men come to believe in many gods—the origin of polytheism ; *second*, how, by elimination of most of these gods, did certain races of men come to believe in one single supreme and omnipotent God—the origin of monotheism ; *third* how, having arrived at that concept, did the most advanced races and civilisations come to conceive of that God as Triune, and to identify one of his Persons with a particular divine and human incarnation—the origin of Christianity. In considering each of these three main problems I have been greatly guided and assisted by three previous enquirers or sets of enquirers.

As to the *origin of polytheism*, I have adopted in the main Mr. Herbert Spencer's remarkable ghost theory, though with certain important modifications and additions. In this part of my work I have also been largely aided by materials derived from Mr. Duff Macdonald, the able author of *Africana*, from Mr. Turner, the well-known Samoan missionary, and from several other writers, supplemented as they are by my own researches among the works of explorers and ethnologists in general. On the whole, I have here accepted the theory which traces the origin of the belief in gods to primeval ancestor-worship, or rather corpse-worship, as against the rival theory which traces its origin to a supposed primitive animism.

As to the *rise of monotheism*, I have been influenced in no small degree by Kuenen and the Teutonic school of Old Testament criticism, whose ideas have been supplemented by later concepts derived from Professor Robertson Smith's admirable work, *The Religion of the Semites*. But here, on the whole, the central explanation I have to offer is, I venture to think, new and original : the theory, good or bad, of the circumstances which led to the elevation of the ethnical Hebrew God, Jahweh, above all his rivals, and his final recognition as the only true and living god, is my own and no one else's.

PREFACE.

As to the *origin of Christianity*, and its relations to the preceding cults of corn and wine gods, I have been guided to a great extent by Mr. J. G. Frazer and Mannhardt, though I do not suppose that either the living or the dead anthropologist would wholly acquiesce in the use I have made of their splendid materials. Mr. Frazer, the author of that learned work, *The Golden Bough*, has profoundly influenced the opinions of all serious workers at anthropology and the science of religion, and I cannot too often acknowledge the deep obligations under which I lie to his profound and able treatises. At the same time, I have so transformed the material derived from him and from Dr. Robertson Smith as to have made it in many ways practically my own; and I have supplemented it by several new examples and ideas, suggested in the course of my own tolerably wide reading.

Throughout the book as a whole, I also owe a considerable debt to Dr. E. B. Tylor, from whom I have borrowed much valuable matter; to Mr. Sidney Hartland's *Legend of Perseus*; to Mr. Lawrence Gomme, who has come nearer at times than anyone else to the special views and theories here promulgated; and to Mr. William Simpson of the *Illustrated London News*, an unobtrusive scholar whose excellent monographs on *The Worship of Death* and kindred subjects have never yet received the attention they deserve, at the hands of unprejudiced students of religion. My other obligations, to Dr. Mommsen, to my friends Mr. Edward Clodd, Professor John Rhys, and Professor York Powell, as well as to numerous travellers, missionaries, historians, and classicists, are too frequent to specify.

Looking at the subject broadly, I would presume to say once more that my general conclusions may be regarded as representing to some extent a reconciliation between the conflicting schools of humanists and animists, headed respectively by Mr. Spencer and Mr. Frazer, though with a leaning rather to the former than the latter.

At the same time it would be a great mistake to look upon my book as in any sense a mere eirenicon or compromise. On the contrary, it is in every part a new and personal work, containing, whatever its value, a fresh and original synthesis of the subject. I would venture to point out as especially novel the two following points: the complete demarcation of religion from mythology, as practice from mere explanatory gloss or guesswork; and the important share assigned in the genesis of most existing religious systems to the deliberate manufacture of gods by killing. This doctrine of the manufactured god, to which nearly half my book is devoted, seems to me to be a notion of cardinal value. Among other new ideas of secondary rank, I would be bold enough to enumerate the following: the establishment of three successive stages in the conception of the Life of the Dead, which might be summed up as Corpse-worship, Ghost-worship, and Shade-worship, and which answer to the three stages of preservation or mummification, burial, and cremation; the recognition of the high place to be assigned to the safe-keeping of the oracular head in the growth of idol-worship; the importance attached to the sacred stone, the sacred stake, and the sacred tree, and the provisional proof of their close connection with the graves of the dead; the entirely new conception of the development of monotheism among the Jews from the exclusive cult of the jealous god; the hypothesis of the origin of cultivation from tumulus-offerings, and its connection with the growth of gods of cultivation; the wide expansion given to the ancient notion of the divine-human victim; the recognition of the world-wide prevalence of the five-day festival of the corn or wine god, and of the close similarity which marks its rites throughout all the continents, including America; the suggested evolution of the god-eating sacraments of lower religions from the cannibal practice of honorifically eating one's dead relations;* and the evidence

---

* While this work was passing through the press a similar theory has

of the wide survival of primitive corpse-worship down to our own times in civilised Europe. I could largely increase this rapid list of what I believe to be the new contributions here made to the philosophy of religious evolution; but I purposely refrain. I think it will be allowed that if even a few of these ideas turn out on examination to be both new and true, my book will have succeeded in justifying its existence.

I put forth this work with the utmost diffidence. The harvest is vast and the labourers are few. I have been engaged upon collecting and comparing materials for more than twenty years. I have been engaged in writing my book for more than ten. As I explain in the last chapter, the present first sketch of the conclusions at which I have at last arrived is little more than provisional. I desire in my present essay merely to lay down the lines of the general theory which after so many years of study I incline to accept. If my attempt succeeds in attracting public attention, I hope to follow it up by several other volumes in which the main opinions or suggestions here set forth may be reinforced and expanded by copious collections of evidence and illustrations. If it fails to arouse public attention, however, I must perforce be satisfied with this very inadequate preliminary statement. I should also like to add here, what I point out at greater length in the body of the work, that I do not hold dogmatically to all or to a single one of the ideas I have now expressed. They are merely conceptions forced upon my mind by the present state of the evidence; and I recognise the fact that in so vast and varied a province, where almost encyclopædic knowledge would be necessary in order to enable one to reach a decided conclusion, every single one or all together of these conceptions are liable to be upset by further research. I merely say, "This is how

been propounded by Mr. Flinders Petrie in an article on "Eaten with Honour," in which he reviews briefly the evidence for the custom in Egypt and elsewhere.

the matter figures itself to me at present, on the strength of the facts now and here known to us."

A few chapters of the book were separately published in various reviews at the time they were first written. They were composed, however, from the outset, as parts of this book, which does not therefore consist of disconnected essays thrown into line in an artificial unity. Each occupies the precise place in the argument for which it was first intended. The chapters in question are those on " Religion and Mythology," and " The Life of the Dead," contributed under the titles of " Practical Religion " and " Immortality and Resurrection " to the *Fortnightly Review*; that on " Sacred Stones," contributed under the same name to the same periodical; and that on " The Gods of Egypt," which originally appeared in the *Universal Review*. I have to thank the proprietors and editors of those magazines for permission to print them in their proper place here. They have all been altered and brought up as far as I could bring them to the existing state of our knowledge with regard to the subjects of which they treat.

In dealing with so large a variety of materials, drawn from all times and places, races and languages, it would be well-nigh impossible to avoid errors. Such as my own care could discover I have of course corrected: for the rest, I must ask on this ground the indulgence of those who may happen to note them.

I have endeavoured to write without favour or prejudice, animated by a single desire to discover the truth. Whether I have succeeded in that attempt or not, I trust my book may be received in the same spirit in which it has been written,—a spirit of earnest anxiety to learn all that can be learnt by enquiry and investigation of man's connection with his God, in the past and the present. In this hope I commit it to the kindly consideration of that small section of the reading public which takes a living interest in religious questions.

CONTENTS.

	PAGE
PREFACE	iii

CHAPTER

I.	CHRISTIANITY AS A RELIGIOUS STANDARD	1
II.	RELIGION AND MYTHOLOGY	20
III.	THE LIFE OF THE DEAD	42
IV.	THE ORIGIN OF GODS	63
V.	SACRED STONES	93
VI.	SACRED STAKES	127
VII.	SACRED TREES	138
VIII.	THE GODS OF EGYPT	154
IX.	THE GODS OF ISRAEL	180
X.	THE RISE OF MONOTHEISM	204
XI.	HUMAN GODS	225
XII.	THE MANUFACTURE OF GODS	247
XIII.	GODS OF CULTIVATION	272
XIV.	CORN- AND WINE-GODS	301
XV.	SACRIFICE AND SACRAMENT	313
XVI.	THE DOCTRINE OF THE ATONEMENT	347
XVII.	THE WORLD BEFORE CHRIST	362
XVIII.	THE GROWTH OF CHRISTIANITY	373
XIX.	SURVIVALS IN CHRISTENDOM	409
XX.	CONCLUSION	434
INDEX		439

THE EVOLUTION OF THE IDEA OF GOD.

CHAPTER I.

CHRISTIANITY AS A RELIGIOUS STANDARD.

I PROPOSE in this work to trace out in rough outline the evolution of the idea of God from its earliest and crudest beginnings in the savage mind of primitive man to that highly evolved and abstract form which it finally assumes in contemporary philosophical and theological thinking.

In the eyes of the modern evolutionary enquirer the interest of the origin and history of this widespread idea is mainly psychological. We have before us a vast and pervasive group of human opinions, true or false, which have exercised and still exercise an immense influence upon the development of mankind and of civilisation : the question arises, Why did human beings ever come to hold these opinions at all, and how did they arrive at them ? What was there in the conditions of early man which led him to frame to himself such abstract notions of one or more great supernatural agents, of whose objective existence he had certainly in nature no clear or obvious evidence ? Regarding the problem in this light, as essentially a problem of the processes of the human mind, I set aside from the outset, as foreign to my purpose, any kind of enquiry into the objective validity of any one among the religious beliefs thus set before us as subject-matter. The question whether there may be a God or gods, and, if so, what may be his or their substance and attributes, do not here concern us. All we have to do in our present capacity is to ask ourselves strictly, What first suggested to the mind of man the notion of deity in the abstract at all? And how, from the early multiplicity of deities which we find to have prevailed in all primitive times among all human races, did the conception of a single great and unlimited deity first take its rise? In other words, why did men ever believe there were gods at all, and why from many gods did they arrive at one? Why from polytheism have the most advanced nations proceeded to monotheism?

To put the question in this form is to leave entirely out of consideration the objective reality or otherwise of the idea itself. To analyse the origin of a concept is not to attack the validity of the belief it encloses. The idea of gravitation, for example, arose by slow degrees in human minds, and reached at last its final expression in Newton's law. But to trace the steps by which that idea was gradually reached is not in any way to disprove or to discredit it. The Christian believer may similarly hold that men arrived by natural stages at the knowledge of the one true God; he is not bound to reject the final conception as false merely because of the steps by which it was slowly evolved. A creative God, it is true, might prefer to make a sudden revelation of himself to some chosen body of men; but an evolutionary God, we may well believe, might prefer in his inscrutable wisdom to reveal his own existence and qualities to his creatures by means of the same slow and tentative intellectual gropings as those by which he revealed to them the physical truths of nature. I wish my enquiry, therefore, to be regarded, not as destructive, but as reconstructive. It only attempts to recover and follow out the various planes in the evolution of the idea of God, rather than to cast doubt upon the truth of the evolved concept.

In investigating any abstruse and difficult subject, it is often best to proceed from the known to the unknown, even although the unknown itself may happen to come first in the order of nature and of logical development. For this reason, it may be advisable to begin here with a brief preliminary examination of Christianity, which is not only the most familiar of all religions to us Christian nations, but also the best known in its origins : and then to show how far we may safely use it as a Standard of Reference in explaining the less obvious and certain features of earlier or collateral cults.

Christianity, then, viewed as a religious standard, has this clear and undeniable advantage over almost every other known form of faith—that it quite frankly and confessedly sets out in its development with the worship of a particular Deified Man.

This point in its history cannot, I think, be overrated in importance, because in that single indubitable central fact it gives us the key to much that is cardinal in all other religions ; every one of which, as I hope hereafter to show, equally springs, directly or indirectly, from the worship of a single Deified Man, or of many Deified Men, more or less etherealised.

Whatever else may be said about the origin of Christianity, it is at least fairly agreed on either side, both by friends and foes, that this great religion took its rise around the personality of a certain particular Galilean teacher, by name Jesus, concerning whom, if we know anything at all with any approach to certainty, we know at least that he was a man of the people, hung on a cross in Jerusalem under the procuratorship of Caius Pontius Pilatus. That kernel of fact—a man, and his death—Jesus Christ and him crucified—is the one almost undoubted historical nucleus round which all the rest of a vast European and Asiatic system of thought and belief has slowly crystallised.

Let us figure clearly to ourselves the full import of these

truths. A Deified Man is the central figure in the faith of Christendom.

From the very beginning, however, a legend, true or false (but whose truth or falsity has no relation whatever to our present subject), gathered about the personality of this particular Galilean peasant reformer. Reverenced at first by a small body of disciples of his own race and caste, he grew gradually in their minds into a divine personage, of whom strange stories were told, and a strange history believed by a group of ever-increasing adherents in all parts of the Græco-Roman Mediterranean civilisation. The earliest of these stories, in all probability—certainly the one to which most importance was attached by the pioneers of the faith—clustered about his death and its immediate sequence. Jesus, we are told, was crucified, dead, and buried. But at the end of three days, if we may credit the early documents of our Christian faith, his body was no longer to be found in the sepulchre where it had been laid by friendly hands : and the report spread abroad that he had risen again from the dead, and lived once more a somewhat phantasmal life among the living in his province. Supernatural messengers announced his resurrection to the women who had loved him : he was seen in the flesh from time to time for very short periods by one or other among the faithful who still revered his memory. At last, after many such appearances, more or less fully described in the crude existing narratives, he was suddenly carried up to the sky before the eyes of his followers, where, as one of the versions authoritatively remarks, he was " received into heaven, and sat on the right hand of God "—that is to say, of Jahweh, the ethnical deity of the Hebrew people.

Such in its kernel was the original Christian doctrine as handed down to us amid a mist of miracle, in four or five documents of doubtful age and uncertain authenticity. Even this central idea does not fully appear in the Pauline epistles, believed to be the oldest in date of all our Christian writings: it first takes full shape in the somewhat later Gospels and Acts of the Apostles. In the simplest and perhaps the earliest of these definite accounts we are merely told the story of the death and resurrection, the latter fact being vouched for on the dubious testimony of "a young man clothed in a long white garment," supplemented (apparently at a later period) by subsequent "appearances" to various believers. With the controversies which have raged about these different stories, however, the broad anthropological enquiry into the evolution of God has no concern. It is enough for us here to admit, what the evidence probably warrants us in concluding, that a real historical man of the name of Jesus did once exist in Lower Syria, and that his disciples at a period very shortly after his execution believed him to have actually risen from the dead, and in due time to have ascended into heaven.

At a very early date, too, it was further asserted that Jesus was in some unnatural or supernatural sense "the son of God"—that is to say, once more, the son of Jahweh, the local and national deity of the Jewish people. In other words, his worship was affiliated upon the earlier historical worship of the people in whose midst he lived, and from whom his first disciples were exclusively gathered. It was not, as we shall more fully see hereafter, a revolutionary or purely destructive system. It based itself upon the common conceptions of the Semitic community. The handful of Jews and Galileans who accepted Jesus as a divine figure did not think it necessary, in adopting him as a god, to get rid of their own preconceived religious opinions. They believed rather in his prior existence, as a part of Jahweh, and in his incarnation in a human body for the purpose of redemption. And when his cult spread around into neighboring countries (chiefly, it would seem, through the instrumentality of one Paul of Tarsus, who had never seen him, or had beheld him only in what is vaguely called "a vision") the cult of Jahweh went hand in hand with it, so that a sort of modified mystic monotheism, based on Judaism, became the early creed of the new cosmopolitan Christian church.

Other legends, of a sort familiar in the lives of the founders of creeds and churches elsewhere, grew up about the life of the Christian leader; or at any rate, incidents of a typical kind were narrated by his disciples as part of his history. That a god or a godlike person should be born of a woman by the ordinary physiological processes of humanity seems derogatory to his dignity—perhaps fatal to his godhead : * therefore it was asserted—we know not whether truly or otherwise—that the founder of Christianity, by some mysterious afflatus, was born of a virgin. Though described at times as the son of one Joseph, a carpenter, of Nazareth, and of Mary, his betrothed wife, he was also regarded in an alternative way as the son of the Hebrew god Jahweh, just as Alexander, though known to be the son of Philip, was also considered to be the offspring of Amon-Ra or Zeus Ammon). We are told, in order to lessen this discrepancy (on the slender authority of a dream of Joseph's), how Jesus was miraculously conceived by the Holy Spirit of Jahweh in Mary's womb. He was further provided with a royal pedigree from the house of David, a real or mythical early Hebrew king ; and prophecies from the Hebrew sacred books were found to be fulfilled in his most childish adventures. In one of the existing biographies, commonly ascribed to Luke, the companion of Paul, but supposed to bear traces of much later authorship, many such marvellous stories are recounted of his infantile adventures : and in all our documents, miracles attest his supernatural powers, while appeal is constantly made to the fulfilment of supposed predictions (all of old Hebrew origin) as a test and credential of the reality of his divine mission.

* On this subject, see Mr. Sidney Hartland's *Legend of Perseus*, vol. i, *passim*.

We shall see hereafter that these two points—the gradual growth of a myth or legend, and affiliation upon earlier local religious ideas—are common features in the evolution of gods in general, and of the God of monotheism in particular. In almost every case where we can definitely track him to his rise, the deity thus begins with a Deified Man, elevated by his worshippers to divine rank, and provided with a history of miraculous incident, often connected with the personality of preexistent deities.

In the earlier stages, it seems pretty clear that the relations of nascent Christianity to Judaism were vague and undefined : the Christians regarded themselves as a mere sect of the Jews, who paid special reverence to a particular dead teacher, now raised to heaven by a special apotheosis of a kind with which everyone was then familiar. But as the Christian church spread to other lands, by the great seaports, it became on the one hand more distinct and exclusive, while on the other hand it became more definitely dogmatic and theological. It was in Eygpt, it would seem, that the Christian Pantheon (if I may be allowed the expression in the case of a religion nominally monotheistic) first took its definite Trinitarian shape. Under the influence of the old Egyptian love for Triads or Trinities of gods, a sort of mystical triune deity was at last erected out of the Hebrew Jahweh and the man Jesus, with the aid of the Holy Spirit or Wisdom of Jahweh, which had come to be regarded by early Christian minds (under the influence of direct divine inspiration or otherwise) as a separate and coordinate person of this composite godhead. How far the familiar Egyptian Trinity of Osiris, Isis, and Horus may have influenced the conception of the Christian Trinity, thus finally made up of Father, Son, and Holy Ghost, we shall discuss at a later stage of our enquiry ; for the present, it may suffice to point out that the Græco-Egyptian Athanasius was the great upholder of the definite dogma of the Trinity against opposing (heretical) Christian thinkers ;

and that the hymn or so-called creed known by his name (though not in all probability of his own composition) bears the impress of the mystical Egyptian spirit, tempered by the Alexandrian Greek delight in definiteness and minuteness of philosophical distinction.

In this respect, too, we shall observe in the sequel that the history of Christianity, the most known among the religions, was exactly parallel to that of earlier and obscurer creeds. At first, the relations of the gods to one another are vague and undetermined; their pedigree is often confused and even contradictory; and the pantheon lacks anything like due hierarchical system or subordination of persons. But as time goes on, and questions of theology or mythology are debated among the priests and other interested parties, details of this sort get settled in the form of rigid dogmas, while subtle distinctions of a philosophical or metaphysical sort tend to be imported by more civilised men into the crude primitive faith. The belief that began with frank acceptance of Judaism, *plus* a personal worship of the Deified Man, Jesus, crystallised at last into the Catholic Faith in one God, of three persons, the Father, the Son, and the Holy Ghost.

Quibbles are even made, and discussions raised at last as to the question whether Father and Son are "of one substance" or only "of like substance"; whether the Holy Ghost proceeds from the Father and the Son, or from the Father only; and so on *ad infinitum.*

It was largely in other countries than Judæa, and especially in Gaul, Rome, and Egypt, too, as I believe, that symbolism came to the aid of mysticism: that the cross, the tau, the labarum, the fish, the Alpha and Omega, and all the other early Christian emblems were evolved and perfected; and that the beginnings of Christian art took their first definite forms. Such forms were especially to a great extent evolved in the Roman catacombs. Christianity, being a universal, not a local or national, religion, has adopted in its course many diverse elements from most varied sources.

Originally, it would seem, the Christian pantheon was almost exclusively filled by the triune God, in his three developments or "persons," as thus rigorously conceived by the Alexandrian intelligence. But from a very early time, if not from the first dawn of the Christian cult, it was customary to reverence the remains of those who had suffered for the faith, and perhaps even to invoke their aid with Christ and the Father. The Roman branch of the church, especially, accustomed to the Roman ancestor-worship and the Roman reverence for the Dii Manes, had its chief places of prayer in the catacombs, where its dead were laid. Thus arose the practice of the invocation of saints, at whose graves or relics prayers were offered, both to the supreme deity and to the faithful dead themselves as intercessors with Christ and the Father. The early Christians, accustomed in their heathen stage to pay respect and even worship to the spirits of their deceased friends, could not immediately give up this pious custom after their conversion to the new creed, and so grafted it on to their adopted religion. Thus the subsidiary founders of Christianity, Paul, Peter, the Apostles, the Evangelists, the martyrs, the confessors, came to form, as it were, a subsidiary pantheon, and to rank to some extent almost as an inferior order of deities.

Among the persons who thus shared in the honours of the new faith, the mother of Jesus early assumed a peculiar prominence. Goddesses had filled a very large part in the devotional spirit of the older religions: it was but natural that the devotees of Isis and Pasht, of Artemis and Aphrodite, should look for some corresponding object of feminine worship in the younger faith. The Theotokos, the mother of God, the blessed Madonna, soon came to possess a practical importance in Christian worship scarcely inferior to that enjoyed by the persons of the Trinity themselves—in certain southern countries, indeed, actually superior to it. The Virgin and Child, in pictorial representation, grew to be the favourite subject of Christian art. How far this particular development of the Christian spirit had its origin in Egypt, and was related to the well-known Egyptian figures of the goddess Isis with the child Horus in her lap, is a question which may demand consideration in some future treatise. For the present, it will be enough to call attention in passing to the fact that in this secondary rank of deities or semi-divine persons, the saints and martyrs, all alike, from the Blessed Virgin Mary down to the newest canonised among Roman Catholic prelates, were at one time or another Living Men and Women. In other words, besides the one Deified Man, Jesus, round whom the entire system of Christianity centres, the Church now worships also in the second degree a whole host of minor Dead Men and Women, bishops, priests, virgins, and confessors.

From the earliest to the latest ages of the Church, the complexity thus long ago introduced into her practice has gone on increasing with every generation. Nominally from the very outset a monotheistic religion, Christianity gave up its strict monotheism almost at the first start by admitting the existence of three persons in the godhead, whom it vainly endeavoured to unify by its mystic but confessedly incomprehensible Athanasian dogma. The Madonna (with the Child) rose in time practically to the rank of an independent goddess (in all but esoteric Catholic theory) : while St. Sebastian, St. George, St. John Baptist, St. Catherine, and even St. Thomas of Canterbury himself, became as important objects of worship in certain places as the deity in person. At Milan, for example, San Carlo Borromeo, at Compostella, Santiago, at Venice, St. Mark, usurped to a great extent the place of the original God. As more and more saints died in each generation, while the cult of the older saints still lingered on everywhere more or less locally, the secondary pantheon grew ever fuller and fuller. Obscure personages, like St. Crispin and St. Cosmas, St. Chad and St. Cuthbert rose to the rank of departmental or local patrons, like the departmental and local gods of earlier religions. Every trade, every guild, every nation, every province, had its peculiar saint. And at the same time, the theory of the Church underwent a constant evolution. Creed was added to creed—Apostles', Nicene, Athanasian, and so forth, each embodying some new and often subtle increment to the whole mass of accepted dogma. Council after council made fresh additions of articles of faith—the Unity of Substance, the Doctrine of the Atonement, the Immaculate Conception, the Authority of the Church, the Infallibility of the Pope in his spiritual capacity. And all these also are well-known incidents of every evolving cult : constant increase in the number of divine beings ; constant refinements in the articles of religion, under the influence of priestly or scholastic metaphysics.

Two or three other points must still be noted in this hasty review of the evolution of Christianity, regarded as a standard of religion ; and these I will now proceed to consider with all possible brevity.

In the matter of ceremonial and certain other important accessories of religion it must frankly be admitted that Christianity rather borrowed from the older cults than underwent a natural and original development on its own account. A priesthood, as such, does not seem to have formed any integral or necessary part of the earliest Christendom : and when the orders of bishops, priests, and deacons were introduced into the new creed, the idea seems to have been derived rather from the existing priesthoods of anterior religions than from any organic connexion with the central facts of the new worship. From the very nature of the circumstances this would inevitably result. For the primitive temple (as we shall see hereafter) was the Dead Man's tomb ; the altar was his gravestone ; and the priest was the relative or representative who continued for him the customary gifts to the ghost at the grave. But the case of Jesus differs from almost every other case on record of a Deified Man in this—that his body seems to have disappeared at an early date ; and that, inasmuch as his resurrection and ascension into heaven were made the corner-stone of the new faith, it was impossible for worship of his remains to take the same form as had been taken in the instances of almost all previously deified Dead Persons. Thus, the materials out of which the Temple, the Altar, Sacrifices, Priesthood, are usually evolved (as we shall hereafter see) were here to a very large extent necessarily wanting.

Nevertheless, so essential to religion in the minds of its followers are all these imposing and wonted accessories that our cult did actually manage to borrow them ready-made from the great religions that went before it, and to bring them into some sort of artificial relation with its own system. You cannot revolutionize the human mind at one blow. The pagans had been accustomed to all these ideas as integral parts of religion as they understood it : and they proceeded as Christians to accommodate them by side-issues to the new faith, in which these elements had no such natural place as in the older creeds. Not only did sacred places arise at the graves or places of martyrdom of the saints; not only was worship performed beside the bones of the holy dead, in the catacombs and elsewhere ; but even a mode of sacrifice and of sacrificial communion was invented in the mass,—a somewhat artificial development from the possibly unsacerdotal Agape-feasts of the primitive Christians. Gradually, churches gathered around the relics of the martyr saints : and in time it became a principle of usage that every church must contain an altar—made of stones on the analogy of the old sacred stones ; containing the bones or other relics of a saint, like all earlier shrines ; consecrated by the pouring on of oil after the antique fashion ; and devoted to the celebration of the sacrifice of the mass, which became by degrees more and more expiatory and sacerdotal in character. As the saints increased in importance, new holy places sprang up around their bodies; and some of these holy places, containing their tombs, became centres of pilgrimage for the most distant parts of Christendom; as did also in particular the empty tomb of Christ himself, the Holy Sepulchre at Jerusalem.

The growth of the priesthood kept pace with the growth of ceremonial in general, till at last it culminated in the mediæval papacy, with its hierarchy of cardinals, archbishops, bishops, priests, and other endless functionaries. Vestments, incense, and like accompaniments of sacerdotalism also rapidly gained ground. All this, too, is a common trait of higher religious evolution everywhere. So likewise are fasting, vigils, and the ecstatic condition. But asceticism, monasticism, celibacy, and other forms of morbid abstinence are peculiarly rife in the east, and found their highest expression in the life of the Syrian and Egyptian hermits.

Lastly, a few words must be devoted in passing to the rise and development of the Sacred Books, now excessively venerated in North-western Christendom. These consisted in the first instance of genuine or spurious letters of the apostles to the various local churches (the so-called Epistles), some of which would no doubt be preserved with considerable reverence; and later of lives or legends of Jesus and his immediate successors (the so-called Gospels and the Acts of the Apostles). Furthermore, as Christianity adopted from Judaism the cult of its one supreme divine figure, now no longer envisaged as Jahweh, the national deity of the Hebrews, but as a universal cosmopolitan God and Father, it followed naturally that the sacred books of the Jewish people, the literature of Jahweh-worship, should also receive considerable attention at the hands of the new priesthood. By a gradual process of selection and elimination, the canon of scripture was evolved from these heterogeneous materials: the historical or quasi-historical and prophetic Hebrew tracts were adopted by the Church, with a few additions of later date, such as the Book of Daniel, under the style and title of the Old Testament. The more generally accepted lives of Christ, again, known as Evangels or Gospels ; the Acts of the Apostles ; the epistles to the churches ; and that curious mystical allegory of the Neronian persecution known as the Apocalypse, were chosen out of the mass of early Christian literature to form the authoritative collection of inspired writing which we call the New Testament. The importance of this heterogeneous anthology of works belonging to all ages and systems, but confounded together in popular fancy under the name of the Books, or more recently still as a singular noun, the Bible, grew apace with the growth of the Church : though the extreme and superstitions adoration of their mere verbal contents has only been reached in the debased and reactionary forms of Christianity followed at the present day by our half-educated English and American Protestant dissenters.

From this very brief review of the most essential factors in the development of the Christian religion as a system, strung loosely together with a single eye to the requirements of our present investigation, it will be obvious at once to every intelligent reader that Christianity cannot possibly throw for us any direct or immediate light on the problem of the evolution of the idea of God. Not only did the concept of a god and gods exist full-fledged long before Christianity took its rise at all, but also the purely monotheistic conception of a single supreme God, the creator and upholder of all things, had been reached in all its sublime simplicity by the Jewish teachers centuries before the birth of the man Jesus. Christianity borrowed from Judaism this magnificent concept, and, humanly speaking, proceeded to spoil it by its addition of the Son and the Holy Ghost, who mar the complete unity of the grand Hebrew ideal. Even outside Judaism, the selfsame notion had already been arrived at in a certain mystical form as the "esoteric doctrine" of the Egyptian priesthood; from whom, with their peculiar views as to emanations and Triads, the Christian dogmas of the Trinity, the Logos, the Incarnation, and the Holy Ghost were in large part borrowed. The Jews of Alexandria, that eastern London, formed the connecting link between Egyptian heathenism, Hellenic philosophy, and early Christianity; and their half-philosophical, half-religious ideas may be found permeating the first writings and the first systematic thought of the nascent church. In none of these ways, therefore, can we regard Christianity as affording us any direct or immediate guidance in our search for the origin and evolution of the concepts of many gods, and of one God the creator.

Still, in a certain secondary and illustrative sense, I think we are fully justified in saying that the history of Christianity, the religion whose beginnings are most surely known to us, forms a standard of reference for all the other religions of the world, and helps us indirectly to understand and explain the origin and evolution of these deepest among our fundamental spiritual conceptions.

Its value in this respect may best be understood if I point out briefly in two contrasted statements the points in which it may and the points in which it may not be fairly accepted as a typical religion.

Let us begin first with the points in which it may.

In the first place, Christianity is thoroughly typical in the fact that beyond all doubt its most central divine figure was at first, by common consent of orthodox and heterodox alike, nothing other than a particular Deified Man. All else that has been asserted about this particular Man—that he was the Son of God, that he was the incarnation of the Logos, that he existed previously from all eternity, that he sits now on the right hand of the Father—all the rest of these theological stories do nothing in any way to obscure the plain and universally admitted historical fact that this Divine Person, the Very God of Very God, being of one substance with the Father, begotten of the Father before all worlds, was yet, at the moment when we first catch a glimpse of him in the writings of his followers, a Man recently deceased, respected, reverenced, and perhaps worshipped by a little group of fellow-peasants who had once known him as Jesus, the son of the carpenter. On that unassailable Rock of solid historical fact we may well be content to found our argument in this volume. Here at least nobody can accuse us of " crude and gross Euhemerism." Or rather the crude and gross Euhemerism is here known to represent the solid truth. Jesus and his saints—Dominic, Francis, Catherine of Siena—are no mere verbal myths, no allegorical concepts, no personifications of the Sun, the Dawn, the Storm-cloud. Leaving aside for the present from our purview of the Faith that one element of the older supreme God—the Hebrew Jahweh,—whom Christianity borrowed from the earlier Jewish religion, we can say at least with perfect certainty that every single member of the Christian pantheon—Jesus, the Madonna, St. John Baptist, St. Peter, the Apostles, the Evangelists—were, just as much as San Carlo Borromeo or St. Thomas of Canterbury or St. Theresa, Dead Men or Women, worshipped after their death with divine or quasi-divine honours. In this the best-known of all human religions, the one that has grown up under the full eye of history, the one whose gods and saints are most distinctly traceable, every object of worship, save only the single early and as yet unresolved deity of the Hebrew cult, whose origin is lost for us in the mist of ages, turns out on enquiry to be indeed a purely Euhemeristic god or saint,—in ultimate analysis, a Real Man or Woman.

That point alone I hold to be of cardinal importance, and of immense or almost inestimable illustrative value, in seeking for the origin of the idea of a god in earlier epochs.

In the second place, Christianity is thoroughly typical in all that concerns its subsequent course of evolution ; the gradual elevation of its central Venerated Man into a God of the highest might and power; the multiplication of secondary deities or saints by worship or adoration of other Dead Men and Women; the growth of a graduated and duly subordinated hierarchy of divine personages; the rise of a legend, with its miracles and other supernatural adjuncts; the formation of a definite theology, philosophy, and systematic dogmatism; the development of special artistic forms, and the growth or adoption of appropriate symbolism; the production of sacred books, rituals, and formularies; the rise of ceremonies, mysteries, initiations, and sacraments; the reverence paid to relics, sacred sites, tombs, and dead bodies; and the close connexion of the religion as a whole with the ideas of death, the soul, the ghost, the spirit, the resurrection of the body, the last judgment, hell, heaven, the life everlasting, and all the other vast group of concepts which surround the simple fact of death in the primitive human mind generally.

Now, in the second place, let us look wherein Christianity to a certain small extent fails to be typical, or at least to solve our fundamental problems.

It fails to be typical because it borrows largely a whole ready-made theology, and above all a single supreme God, from a pre-existent religion. In so far as it takes certain minor features from other cults, we can hardly say with truth that it does not represent the average run of religious systems; for almost every particular new creed so bases itself upon elements of still earlier faiths; and it is perhaps impossible for us at the present day to get back to anything like a really primitive or original form of cult. But Christianity is very far removed indeed from all primitive cults in that it accepts ready-made the monotheistic conception, the high-water-mark, so to speak, of religious philosophising. While in the frankness with which it exhibits to us what is practically one half of its supreme deity as a Galilean peasant of undoubted humanity, subsequently deified and etherealised, it allows us to get down at a single step to the very origin of godhead ; yet in the strength with which it asserts for the other half of its supreme deity (the Father, with his shadowy satellite the Holy Ghost) an immemorial antiquity and a complete severance from human life, it is the least anthropomorphic and the most abstract of creeds. In order to track the idea of God to its very source, then, we must apply in the last resort to this unresolved element of Christianity—the Hebrew Jahweh—the same sort of treatment which we apply to the conception of Jesus or Buddha ; —we must show it to be also the immensely transfigured and magnified ghost of a Human Being ; in the simple and forcible language of Swinburne, " The shade cast by the soul of man."

Furthermore, Christianity fails to be typical in that it borrows also from pre-existing religions to a great extent the ideas of priesthood, sacrifice, the temple, the altar, which, owing to the curious disappearance or at least unrecognisability of the body of its founder (or, rather, its central object of worship), have a less natural place in our Christian system than in any other known form of religious practice. It is quite true that magnificent churches, a highly-evolved sacerdotalism, the sacrifice of the mass, the altar, and the relics, have all been imported in their fullest shape into developed Christianity, especially in its central or Roman form. But every one of these things is partly borrowed, almost as a survival or even as an alien feature, from earlier religions, and partly grew up about the secondary worship of saints and martyrs, their bones, their tombs, their catacombs, and their reliquaries. Christianity itself, particularly when viewed as the worship of Christ (to which it has been largely reduced in Teutonic Europe), does not so naturally lend itself to these secondary ceremonies ; and in those debased schismatic forms of the Church which confine themselves most strictly to the worship of Jesus and of the supreme God, sacerdotalism and sacramentalism have been brought down to a minimum, so that the temple and the altar have lost the greater part of their sacrificial importance.

I propose, then, in subsequent chapters, to trace the growth of the idea of a God from the most primitive origins to the most highly evolved forms; beginning with the ghost, and the early undeveloped deity: continuing through polytheism to the rise of monotheism; and then returning at last once more to the full Christian conception, which we shall understand far better in detail after we have explained the nature of the yet unresolved or but provisionally resolved Jehovistic element. I shall try to show, in short, the evolution of God, by starting with the evolution of gods in general, and coming down by gradual stages through various races to the evolution of the Hebrew, Christian, and Moslem God in particular. And the goal towards which I shall move will be the one already foreshadowed in this introductory chapter,—the proof that in its origin the concept of a god is nothing more than that of a Dead Man, regarded as a still surviving ghost or spirit, and endowed with increased or supernatural powers and qualities.

CHAPTER II.

RELIGION AND MYTHOLOGY.

AT the very outset of the profound enquiry on which we are now about to embark, we are met by a difficulty of considerable magnitude. In the opinion of most modern mythologists mythology is the result of "a disease of language." We are assured by many eminent men that the origin of religion is to be sought, not in savage ideas about ghosts and spirits, the Dead Man and his body or his surviving double, but in primitive misconceptions of the meaning of words which had reference to the appearance of the Sun and the Clouds, the Wind and the Rain, the Dawn and the Dusk, the various phenomena of meteorology in general. If this be so, then our attempt to derive the evolution of gods from the crude ideas of early men about their dead is clearly incorrect; the analogy of Christianity which we have already alleged is a mere will o' the wisp; and the historical Jesus himself may prove in the last resort to be an alias of the sun-god or an embodiment of the vine-spirit.

I do not believe these suggestions are correct. It seems to me that the worship of the sun, moon, and stars, instead of being an element in primitive religion, is really a late and derivative type of adoration; and that mythology is mistaken in the claims it makes for its own importance in the genesis of the idea of a God or gods. In order, however, to clear the ground for a fair start in this direction, we ought, I think, to begin by enquiring into the relative positions of mythology and religion. I shall therefore devote a preliminary chapter to the consideration of this important subject.

Religion, says another group of modern thinkers, of whom Mr. Edward Clodd is perhaps the most able English exponent, "grew out of fear." It is born of man's terror of the great and mysterious natural agencies by which he is surrounded. Now I am not concerned to deny that many mythological beings of various terrible forms do really so originate. I would readily accept some such vague genesis for many of the dragons and monsters which abound in all savage or barbaric imaginings—for Gorgons and Hydras and Chimæras dire, and other manifold shapes of the superstitiously appalling. I would give up to Mr. Clodd the Etruscan devils and the Hebrew Satan, the Grendels and the Fire-drakes, the whole brood of Cerberus, Briareus, the Cyclops, the Centaurs. None of these, however, is a god or anything like one. They have no more to do with religion, properly so called, than the unicorn of the royal arms has to do with British Christianity. A god, as I understand the word, and as the vast mass of mankind has always understood it, is a supernatural being *to be revered and worshipped*. He stands to his votaries, on the whole, as Dr. Robertson Smith has well pointed out, in a kindly and protecting relation. He may be angry with them at times, to be sure; but his anger is temporary and paternal alone: his permanent attitude towards his people is one of friendly concern; he is worshipped as a beneficent and generous Father. It is the origin of gods in this strictest sense that concerns us here, not the origin of those vague and formless creatures which are dreaded, not worshipped, by primitive humanity.

Bearing this distinction carefully in mind, let us proceed to consider the essentials of religion. If you were to ask almost any intelligent and unsophisticated child, "What is religion?" he would answer offhand, with the clear vision of youth, "Oh, it's saying your prayers, and reading your Bible, and singing hymns, and going to church or to chapel on Sundays." If you were to ask any intelligent and unsophisticated Hindu peasant the same question, he would answer in almost the self-same spirit, "Oh, it is doing poojah regularly, and paying your dues every day to Mahadeo." If you were to ask any simple-minded African savage, he would similarly reply, "It is giving the gods flour, and oil, and native beer, and goat-mutton." And finally if you were to ask a devout Italian contadino, he would instantly say, "It is offering up candles and prayers to the Madonna, attending mass, and remembering the saints on every festa."

And they would all be quite right. This, in its essence, is precisely what we call religion. Apart from the special refinements of the higher minds in particular creeds, which strive to import into it all, according to their special tastes or fancies, a larger or smaller dose of philosophy, or of metaphysics, or of ethics, or of mysticism, this is just what religion means and has always meant to the vast majority of the human species. What is common to it throughout is Custom or Practice: a certain set of more or less similar Observances: propitiation, prayer, praise, offerings: the request for divine favours, the deprecation of divine anger or other misfortunes: and as the outward and visible adjuncts of all these, the altar, the sacrifice, the temple, the church; priesthood, services, vestments, ceremonial.

What is not at all essential to religion in its wider aspect —taking the world round, both past and present, Pagan, Buddhist, Mohammadan, Christian, savage, and civilised— is the ethical element, properly so called. And what is very little essential indeed is the philosophical element, theology or mythology, the abstract theory of spiritual existences. This theory, to be sure, is in each country or race closely related with religion under certain aspects; and the stories told about the gods or God are much mixed up with the cult itself in the minds of worshippers; but they are no proper part of religion, strictly so called. In a single word, I contend that religion, as such, is essentially practical : theology or mythology, as such, is essentially theoretical.

Moreover, I also believe, and shall attempt to show, that the two have to a large extent distinct origins and roots : that the union between them is in great part adventitious : and that, therefore, to account for or explain the one is by no means equivalent to accounting for and explaining the other.

Frank recognition of this difference of origin between religion and mythology would, I imagine, largely reconcile the two conflicting schools of thought which at present divide opinion between them on this interesting problem in the evolution of human ideas. On the one side, we have the mythological school of interpreters, whether narrowly linguistic, like Professor Max Müller, or broadly anthropological, like Mr. Andrew Lang, attacking the problem from the point of view of myth or theory alone. On the other side, we have the truly religious school of interpreters, like Mr. Herbert Spencer, and to some extent Mr. Tylor, attacking the problem from the point of view of practice or real religion. The former school, it seems to me, has failed to perceive that what it is accounting for is not the origin of religion at all—of worship, which is the central-root idea of all religious observance, or of the temple, the altar, the priest, and the offering, which are its outer expression—but merely the origin of myth or fable, the mass of story and legend about various beings, real or imaginary, human or divine, which naturally grows up in every primitive community. The latter school, on the other hand, while correctly interpreting the origin of all that is essential and central in religion, have perhaps underestimated the value of their opponents' work through regarding it as really opposed to their own, instead of accepting what part of it may be true in the light of a contribution to an independent but allied branch of the same enquiry.

In short, if the view here suggested be correct, Spencer

and Tylor have paved the way to a true theory of the Origin of Religion : Max Müller, Lang, and the other mythologists have thrown out hints of varying value towards a true theory of the Origin of Mythology, or of its more modern equivalent and successor, Theology.

A brief outline of facts will serve to bring into clearer relief this view of religion as essentially practical—a set of observances, rendered inevitable by the primitive data of human psychology. It will then be seen that what is fundamental and essential in religion is the body of practices, remaining throughout all stages of human development the same, or nearly the same, in spite of changes of mythological or theological theory ; and that what is accidental and variable is the particular verbal explanation or philosophical reason assigned for the diverse rites and ceremonies.

In its simplest surviving savage type, religion consists wholly and solely in certain acts of deference paid by the living to the persons of the dead. I shall try to show in the sequel that down to its most highly evolved modern type in the most cultivated societies, precisely similar acts of deference, either directly to corpses or ghosts as such, or indirectly to gods who were once ghosts, or were developed from ghosts, form its essence still. But to begin with I will try to bring a few simple instances of the precise nature of religion in its lowest existing savage mode.

I might if I chose take my little collection of illustrative facts from some theoretical writer, like Mr. Herbert Spencer, who has collected enough instances in all conscience to prove this point ; but I prefer to go straight to an original observer of savage life and habit, a Presbyterian missionary in Central Africa —the Rev. Duff Macdonald, author of *Africana*—who had abundant opportunities at the Blantyre Mission for learning the ideas and practice of the Soudanese natives, and who certainly had no theoretic predisposition towards resolving all religious notions into the primitive respect and reverence for the dead or the worship of ancestors.

Here, in outline, but in Mr. Macdonald's own words, are the ideas and observances which this careful and accurate investigator found current among the tribes of the heart of Africa. "I do not think," he says, "I have admitted any point of importance without having heard at least four natives on the subject. The statements are translations, as far as possible, from the *ipsissima verba* of the negroes."

The tribes he lived among "are unanimous in saying that there is something beyond the body which they call spirit. Every human body at death is forsaken by this spirit." That is the almost universal though not quite primitive belief, whose necessary genesis has been well traced out by Mr. Herbert Spencer, and more recently in America with great vigour and clearness by Mr. Lester Ward.

"Do these spirits ever die?" Mr. Macdonald asks. "Some," he answers, "I have heard affirm that it is possible for a troublesome spirit to be killed. Others give this a direct denial. Many, like Kumpama, or Cherasulo, say, 'You ask me whether a man's spirit ever dies. I cannot tell. I have never been in the spirit-world, but this I am certain of, that spirits live for a very long time.'"

On the question, "Who the gods are?" Mr. Macdonald says:

"In all our translations of Scripture where we found the word GOD we used *Mulungu;* but this word is chiefly used by the natives as a general name for spirit. The spirit of a deceased man is called his Mulungu, and all the prayers and offerings of the living are presented to such spirits of the dead. It is here that we find the great centre of the native religion. The spirits of the dead are the gods of the living.

"Where are these gods found? At the grave? No. The villagers shrink from yonder gloomy place that lies far beyond their fields on the bleak mountain side. It is only when they have to lay another sleeper beside his forefathers that they will go there. Their god is not the body in the grave, but the spirit, and they seek this spirit at the place where their departed kinsman last lived among them. It is the great tree at the verandah of the dead man's house that is their temple; and if no tree grow here they erect a little shade, and there perform their simple rites. If this spot become too public, the offerings may be defiled, and the sanctuary will be removed to a carefully-selected spot under some beautiful tree. Very frequently a man presents an offering at the top of his own bed beside his head. He wishes his god to come to him and whisper in his ear as he sleeps."

And here, again, we get the origin of nature-worship:

"The spirit of an old chief may have a whole mountain for his residence, but he dwells chiefly on the cloudy summit. There he sits to receive the worship of his votaries, and to send down the refreshing showers in answer to their prayers."

Almost as essential to religion as these prime factors in its evolution—the god, worship, offerings, presents, holy places, temples—is the existence of a priesthood. Here is how the Central Africans arrive at that special function:

"A certain amount of etiquette is observed in approaching the gods. In no case can a little boy or girl approach these deities, neither can anyone that has not been at the mysteries. The common qualification is that a person has attained a certain age, about twelve or fourteen years, and has a house of his own. Slaves seldom pray, except when they have had a dream. Children that have had a dream tell their mother, who approaches the deity on their behalf. (A present for the god is necessary, and the slave or child may not have it.)

"Apart from the case of dreams and a few such private matters, it is not usual for anyone to approach the gods except the chief of the village. He is the recognised high priest who presents prayers and offerings on behalf of all that live in his village. If the chief is from home his wife will act, and if both are absent, his younger brother. The natives worship not so much individually as in villages or communities. Their religion is more a public than a private matter."

But there are also further reasons why priests are necessary. Relationship forms always a good ground for intercession. A mediator is needed.

"The chief of a village," says Mr. Macdonald, "has another title to the priesthood. It is his relatives that are the village gods. Everyone that lives in the village recognises these gods; but if anyone remove to another village he changes his gods. He recognises now the gods of his new chief. One wishing to pray to the god (or gods) of any village naturally desires to have his prayers presented through the village chief, because the latter is nearly related to the village god, and may be expected to be better listened to than a stranger."

A little further on Mr. Macdonald says:

"On the subject of the village gods opinions differ. Some say that every one in the village, whether a relative of the chief or not, must worship the forefathers of the chief. Others say that a person not related to the chief must worship his own forefathers, otherwise their spirits will bring trouble upon him. To reconcile these authorities we may mention that nearly everyone in the village is related to its chief, or if not related is, in courtesy, considered so. Any person not related to the village chief would be polite enough on all public occasions to recognise the village god: on occasions of private prayer (which are not so numerous as in Christendom) he would approach the spirits of his own forefathers.

"Besides, there might be a god of the land. The chief Kapeni prays to his own relatives, and also to the old gods of the place. His own relatives he approaches himself; the other deities he may also approach himself, but he often finds people more closely related and consequently more acceptable to the old gods of the land."

The African pantheon is thus widely peopled. Elimination and natural selection next give one the transition from the ghost to the god, properly so called.

"The gods of the natives then are nearly as numerous as their dead. It is impossible to worship all ; a selection must be made, and, as we have indicated, each worshipper turns most naturally to the spirits of his own departed relatives ; but his gods are too many still, and in farther selecting he turns to those that have lived nearest his own time. Thus the chief of a village will not trouble himself about his great-great-grandfather : he will present his offering to his own immediate predecessor, and say, 'O father, I do not know all your relatives, you know them all, invite them to feast with you.' The offering is not simply for himself, but for himself and all his relatives."

Ordinary ghosts are soon forgotten with the generation that knew them. Not so a few select spirits, the Cæsars and Napoleons, the Charlemagnes and Timurs of savage empires.

"A great chief that has been successful in his wars does not pass out of memory so soon. He may become the god of a mountain or a lake, and may receive homage as a local deity long after his own descendants have been driven from the spot. When there is a supplication for rain the inhabitants of the country pray not so much to their own forefathers as to the god of yonder mountain on whose shoulders the great rain-clouds repose. (Smaller hills are seldom honoured with a deity.)"

Well, in all this we get, it seems to me, the very essentials and universals of religion generally,—the things without which no religion could exist—the vital part, without the ever-varying and changeable additions of mere gossiping mythology. In the presents brought to the dead man's grave to appease the ghost, we have the central element of all worship, the practical key of all cults, past or present.

On the other hand, mythologists tell us nothing about the origin of prayer and sacrifice : they put us off with stories of particular gods, without explaining to us how those gods ever came to be worshipped. Now, mythology is a very interesting study in its own way : but to treat as religion a mass of stories and legends about gods or saints, with hardly a single living element of practice or sacrifice, seems to me simply to confuse two totally distinct branches of human enquiry. The Origin of Tales has nothing at all to do with the Origin of Worship.

When we come to read Mr. Macdonald's account of a native funeral, on the other hand, we are at once on a totally different tack ; we can understand, as by an electric flash, the genesis of the primitive acts of sacrifice and religion.

"Along with the deceased is buried a considerable part of his property. We have already seen that his bed is buried with him ; so also are all his clothes. If he possesses several tusks of ivory, one tusk or more is ground to a powder between two stones and put beside him. Beads are also ground down in the same way. These precautions are taken to prevent the witch (who is supposed to be answerable for his death) from making any use of the ivory or beads.

"If the deceased owned several slaves, an enormous hole is dug for a grave. The slaves are now brought forward. They may be either cast into the pit alive, or the undertakers may cut all their throats. The body of their master or their mistress is then laid down to rest above theirs, and the grave is covered in.

"After this the women come forward with the offerings of food, and place them at the head of the grave. The dishes in which the food was brought are left behind. The pot that held the drinking-water of the deceased and his drinking-cup are also left with him. These, too, might be coveted by the witch, but a hole is pierced in the pot, and the drinking calabash is broken.

"The man has now gone from the society of the living, and he is expected to share the meal thus left at his grave with those that have gone before him. The funeral party breaks up; they do not want to visit the grave of their friend again without a very good reason. Anyone found among the graves may be taken for a cannibal. Their friend has become a citizen of a different village. He is with all his relatives of the past. He is entitled to offerings or presents which may come to him individually or through his chief. These offerings in most cases he will share with others, just as he used to do when alive."

Sometimes the man may be buried in his own hut.

"In this case the house is not taken down, but is generally covered with cloth, and the verandah becomes the place for presenting offerings. His old house thus becomes a kind of temple. . . . The deceased is now in the spirit-world, and receives offerings and adoration. He is addressed as 'Our great spirit that has gone before.' If anyone dream of him, it is at once concluded that the spirit is 'up to something.' Very likely he wants to have some of the survivors for his companions. The dreamer hastens to appease the spirit by an offering."

So real is this society of the dead that Mr. Macdonald says:

"The practice of sending messengers to the world beyond the grave is found on the West Coast. A chief summons a slave, delivers to him a message, and then cuts off his head. If the chief forget anything that he wanted to say, he sends another slave as a postscript."

I have quoted at such length from this recent and extremely able work because I want to bring into strong relief the fact that we have here going on under our very eyes, from day to day, *de novo*, the entire genesis of new gods and goddesses, and of all that is most central and essential to religion—worship, prayer, the temple, the altar, priesthood, sacrifice. Nothing that the mythologists can tell us about the Sun or the Moon, the Dawn or the Storm-cloud, Little Red Riding Hood or Cinderella and the Glass Slipper, comes anywhere near the Origin of Religion in these its central and universal elements. Those stories or guesses may be of immense interest and importance as contributions to the history of ideas in our race ; but nothing we can learn about the savage survival in the myth of Cupid or Psyche, or about the primitive cosmology in the myth of the children of Kronos, helps us to get one inch nearer the origin of God or of prayer, of worship, of religious ceremonial, of the temple, the church, the sacrifice, the mass, or any other component part of what we really know as Religion in the concrete. These myths may be sometimes philosophic guesses, sometimes primitive folk-tales, but they certainly are not the truths of Religion. On the other hand, the living facts, here so simply detailed by a careful, accurate, and unassuming observer, strengthened by the hundreds of similar facts collected by Tylor, Spencer, and others, do help us at once to understand the origin of the central core and kernel of religion as universally practised all the world over.

For, omitting for the present the mythological and cosmological factor, which so often comes in to obscure the plain religious facts in missionary narrative or highly-coloured European accounts of native beliefs, what do we really find as the underlying truths of all religion ? That all the world over practices essentially similar to those of these savage Central Africans prevail among mankind ; practices whose affiliation upon the same primitive ideas has been abundantly proved by Mr. Herbert Spencer ; practices which have for their essence the propitiation or adulation of a spiritual being or beings, derived from ghosts, and conceived of as similar, in all except the greatness of the connoted attributes, to the souls of men. " Whenever the [Indian] villagers are questioned about their creed," says Sir William Hunter, " the same answer is invariably given : ' The common people have no idea of religion, but to do right [ceremonially] and to worship the village god.'"

In short, I maintain that religion is not mainly, as the mistaken analogy of Christian usage makes us erroneously call it, Faith or Creed, but simply and solely Ceremony, Custom, or Practice. And I am glad to say that, for early Semitic times at least, Professor Robertson Smith is of the same opinion.

If one looks at the vast mass of the world, ancient and modern, it is quite clear that religion consists, and has always consisted, of observances essentially similar to those just described among the Central African tribes. Its core is worship. Its centre is the God—that is to say, the Dead Ancestor or Relative. The religion of China is to this day almost entirely one of pure ancestor-cult. The making of offerings and burning of joss-paper before the Family Dead form its principal ceremonies. In India, while the three great gods of the mystical Brahmanist philosophy are hardly worshipped in actual practice at all, every community and every house has its own particular gods and its own special cult of its little domestic altar.

"The first Englishman," says Sir William Hunter, "who tried to study the natives as they actually are, and not as the Brahmans described them, was struck by the universal prevalence of a worship quite distinct from that of the Hindu deities. A Bengal village has usually its local god, which it adores either in the form of a rude unhewn stone, or a stump, or a tree marked with red-lead. Sometimes a lump of clay placed under a tree does duty for a deity, and the attendant priest, when there is one, generally belongs to one of the half-Hinduised low-castes. The rude stone represents the non-Aryan fetish; and the tree seems to owe its sanctity to the non-Aryan belief that it forms the abode of the ghosts, or gods, of the village."

Omitting the mere guesswork about the fetish and the gratuitous supposition, made out of deference to the dying creed of Max-Müllerism, that ancestor-worship must necessarily be a "non-Aryan" feature (though it exists or existed in all so-called Aryan races), this simple description shows us the prevalence over the whole of India of customs essentially similar to those which obtain in Central Africa and in the Chinese provinces.

The Roman religion, in somewhat the same way, separates itself at once into a civic or national and a private or family cult. There were the great gods, native or adopted, whom the State worshipped publicly, as the Central African tribes worship the chief's ancestors ; and there were the Lares and Penates, whom the family worshipped at its own hearth, and whose very name shows them to have been in origin and essence ancestral spirits. And as the real or practical Hindu religion consists mainly of offering up rice, millet, and ghee to the little local and family deities or to the chosen patron god in the Brahmanist pantheon, so, too, the real or practical Roman religion consisted mainly of sacrifice done at the domestic altar to the special Penates, *farre pio et saliente mica*.

I will not go on to point out in detail at the present stage of our argument how Professor Sayce similarly finds ancestor-worship and Shamanism (a low form of ghost-propitiation) at the root of the religion of the ancient Accadians ; how other observers have performed the same task for the Egyptians and Japanese ; and how like customs have been traced among Greeks and Amazulu, among Hebrews and Nicaraguans, among early English and Digger Indians, among our Aryan ancestors themselves and Andaman Islanders. Every recent narrative of travel abounds with examples. Of Netherland Island I read, "The skulls of their ancestors were treasured for gods ;" of the New Hebrides, "The people worshipped the spirits of their ancestors. They prayed to them, over the kava-bowl, for health and prosperity." In New Caledonia, "Their gods were their ancestors, whose relics they kept up and idolised." At Tana, "The general name for gods seemed to be *aremha ;* that means a *dead man*, and hints," says the Rev. George Turner, with pleasing frankness, "alike at the origin and nature of their religious worship." When the chief prayed, he offered up yam and fruits, saying, "Compassionate father, here is some food for you; eat it. Be kind to us on account of it." Those who wish to see the whole of the evidence on this matter marshalled in battle array have only to turn to the first volume of Mr. Herbert Spencer's *Principles of Sociology*, where they will find abundant examples from all times and places gathered together in a vast and overwhelming phalanx.

What concerns us in this chapter a little more is to call attention by anticipation to the fact that even in Christianity itself the same primitive element survives as the centre of all that is most distinctively religious, as opposed to theological, in the Christian religion. And I make these remarks provisionally here in order that the reader may the better understand to what ultimate goal our investigation will lead him.

It is the universal Catholic custom to place the relics of saints or martyrs under the altars in churches. Thus the body of St. Mark the Evangelist lies under the high altar of St. Mark's, at Venice; and in every other Italian cathedral, or chapel, a reliquary is deposited within the altar itself. So well understood is this principle in the Latin Church, that it has hardened into the saying, "No relic, no altar." The sacrifice of the mass takes place at such an altar, and is performed by a priest in sacrificial robes. The entire Roman Catholic ritual is a ritual derived from the earlier sacerdotal ideas of ministry at an altar, and its connection with the primitive form is still kept up by the necessary presence of human remains in its holy places.

Furthermore, the very idea of a church itself is descended from the early Christian meeting-places in the catacombs or at the tombs of the martyrs, which are universally allowed to have been the primitive Christian altars. We know now that the cruciform dome-covered plan of Christian churches is derived from these early meeting-places at the junction of lanes or alleys in the catacombs ; that the nave, chancel, and transepts indicate the crossing of the alleys, while the dome represents the hollowed-out portion or rudely circular vault where the two lines of archway intersect. The earliest dome-covered churches were attempts, as it were, to construct a catacomb above ground for the reception of the altar-tomb of a saint or martyr. Similarly with the chapels that open out at the side from the aisles or transepts. Etymologically, the word chapel is the modernised form of *capella*, the arched sepulchre excavated in the walls of the catacombs, before the tomb at which it was usual to offer up prayer and praise. The chapels built out from the aisles in Roman churches, each with its own altar and its own saintly relics, are attempts to reproduce above ground in the same way the original sacred places in the early Christian excavated cemeteries. We will recur to this subject at much greater length in subsequent chapters.

Thus Christianity itself is linked on to the very antique custom of worship at tombs, and the habit of ancestor-worship by altars, relics, and invocation of saints, even revolutionary Protestantism still retaining some last faint marks of its origin in the dedication of churches to particular evangelists or martyrs, and in the more or less disguised survival of altar, priesthood, sacrifice, and vestments.

Now, I do not say ancestor-worship gives us the whole origin of everything that is included in Christian English minds in the idea of religion. I do not say it accounts for all the cosmologies and cosmogonies of savage, barbaric, or civilised tribes. Those, for the most part, are pure mythological products, explicable mainly, I believe, by means of the key with which mythology supplies us ; and one of them, adopted into Genesis from an alien source, has come to be accepted by modern Christendom as part of that organised body of belief which forms the Christian creed, though not in any true sense the Christian religion. Nor do I say that ancestor-worship gives us the origin of those ontological, metaphysical, or mystical conceptions which form part of the philosophy or theology of many priesthoods. Religions, as we generally get them envisaged for us nowadays, are held to include the mythology, the cosmogony, the ontology, and even the ethics of the race that practises them. These extraneous developments, however, I hold to spring from different roots and to have nothing necessarily in common with religion proper. The god is the true crux. If we have once accounted for the origin of ghosts, gods, tombs, altars, temples, churches, worship, sacrifice, priesthoods, and ceremonies, then we have accounted for all that is essential and central in religion, and may hand over the rest— the tales, stories, and pious legends—to the account of comparative mythology or of the yet unfounded science of comparative idealogy.

Once more, I do not wish to insist, either, that every particular and individual god, national or naturalistic, must necessarily represent a particular ghost—the dead spirit of a single definite once-living person. It is enough to show, as Mr. Spencer has shown, that the idea of the god, and the worship paid to a god, are directly derived from the idea of the ghost, and the offerings made to the ghost, without necessarily holding, as Mr. Spencer seems to hold, that every god is and must be in ultimate analysis the ghost of a particular human being. Once the conception of gods had been evolved by humanity, and had become a common part of every man's imagined universe —of the world as it presented itself to the mind of the percipient—then it was natural enough that new gods should be made from time to time out of abstractions or special aspects and powers of nature, and that the same worship should be paid to such new-made and purely imaginary gods as had previously been paid to the whole host of gods evolved from personal and tribal ancestors. It is the first step that costs : once you have got the idea of a god fairly evolved, any number of extra gods may be invented or introduced from all quarters. A great pantheon readily admits new members to its ranks from many strange sources. Familiar instances in one of the best-known pantheons are those of Concordia, Pecunia, Aius Locutius, Rediculus Tutanus. The Romans, indeed, deified every conceivable operation of nature or of human life ; they had gods or goddesses for the minutest details of agriculture, of social relations, of the first years of childhood, of marriage and domestic arrangements generally. Many of their deities, as we shall see hereafter, were obviously manufactured to meet a special demand on special occasions. But at the same time, none of these gods, so far as we can judge, could ever have come to exist at all if the ghost-theory and ancestor-worship had not already made familiar to the human mind the principles and practice of religion generally. The very idea of a god could not otherwise have been evolved ; though, when once evolved, any number of new beings could readily be affiliated upon it by the human imagination.

Still, to admit that other elements have afterwards come in to confuse religion is quite a different thing from admitting that religion itself has more than one origin. Whatever gives us the key to the practice of worship gives us the key to all real religion. Now, one may read through almost any books of the mythological school without ever coming upon a single word that throws one ray of light upon the origin of religion itself thus properly called. To trace the development of this, that, or the other story or episode in a religious myth is in itself a very valuable study in human evolution : but no amount of tracing such stories ever gives us the faintest clue to the question why men worshipped Osiris, Zeus, Siva, or Venus ; why they offered up prayer and praise to Isis, or to Artemis ; why they made sacrifices of oxen to Capitolian

Jove at Rome, or slew turtle-doves on the altar of Jahweh, god of Israel, at Jerusalem. The ghost-theory and the practice of ancestor-worship show us a natural basis and genesis for all these customs, and explain them in a way to which no mythological enquiry can add a single item of fundamental interest.

It may be well at this point to attempt beforehand some slight provisional disentanglement of the various extraneous elements which interweave themselves at last with the simple primitive fabric of practical religion.

In the first place, there is the mythological element. The mythopœic faculty is a reality in mankind. Stories arise, grow, gather episodes with movement, transform and transmute themselves, wander far in space, get corrupted by time, in ten thousand ways suffer change and modification. Now, such stories sometimes connect themselves with living men and women. Everybody knows how many myths exist even in our own day about every prominent or peculiar person. They also gather more particularly round the memory of the dead, and especially of any very distinguished dead man or woman. Sometimes they take their rise in genuine tradition, sometimes they are pure fetches of fancy or of the romancing faculty. The ghosts or the gods are no less exempt from these mythopœic freaks than other people; and as gods go on living indefinitely, they have plenty of time for myths to gather about them. Most often, a myth is invented to account for some particular religious ceremony. Again, myths demonstrably older than a particular human being—say Cæsar, Virgil, Arthur, Charlemagne—may get fitted by later ages to those special personalities. The same thing often happens also with gods. Myth comes at last, in short, to be the history of the gods; and a personage about whom many myths exist, whether real or imaginary, a personification of nature or an abstract quality, may grow in time to be practically a divine being, and even perhaps to receive worship, the final test of divinity.

Again, myths about the gods come in the long run, in many cases, to be written down, especially by the priests, and themselves acquire a considerable degree of adventitious holiness. Thus we get Sacred Books; and in most advanced races, the sacred books tend to become an important integral part of religion, and a test of the purity of tenets or ceremonial. But sacred books almost always contain rude cosmological guesses and a supernatural cosmogony, as well as tales about the doings, relationships, and prerogatives of the gods. Such early philosophical conjectures come then to be intimately bound up with the idea of religion, and in many cases even to supersede in certain minds its true, practical, central kernel. The extreme of this tendency is seen in English Protestant Dissenting Bibliolatry.

Rationalistic and reconciliatory glosses tend to arise with advancing culture. Attempts are made to trace the pedigree and mutual relations of the gods, and to get rid of discrepancies in earlier legends. The Theogony of Hesiod is a definite effort undertaken in this direction for the Greek pantheon. Often the attempt is made by the most learned and philosophically-minded among the priests, and results in a quasi-philosophical mythology like that of the Brahmans. In the monotheistic or half-monotheistic religions, this becomes theology. In proportion as it grows more and more laboured and definite the attention of the learned and the priestly class is more and more directed to dogma, creed, faith, abstract formulæ of philosophical or intellectual belief, while insisting also upon ritual or practice. But the popular religion remains usually, as in India, a religion of practical custom and observances alone, having very little relation to the highly abstract theological ideas of the learned or the priestly.

Lastly, in the highest religions, a large element of ethics, of sentiment, of broad humanitarianism, of adventitious emotion, is allowed to come in, often to the extent of obscuring the original factors of practice and observance.

We are constantly taught that "real religion" means many things which have nothing on earth to do with religion proper, in any sense, but are merely high morality, tinctured by emotional devotion towards a spiritual being or set of beings.

Owing to all these causes, modern investigators, in searching for the origin of religion, are apt to mix up with it, even when dealing with savage tribes, many extraneous questions of cosmology, cosmogony, philosophy, metaphysics, ethics, and mythology. They do not sufficiently see that the true question narrows itself down at last to two prime factors—worship and sacrifice. In all early religions, the practice is at a maximum, and the creed at a minimum. We, nowadays, look back upon these early cults, which were cults and little else, with minds warped by modern theological prejudices—by constant wrangling over dogmas, clauses, definitions, and formularies. We talk glibly of the Hindu faith or the Chinese belief, when we ought rather to talk of the Hindu practice or the Chinese observances. By thus wrongly conceiving the nature of religion, we go astray as to its origin. We shall only get right again when we learn to separate mythology entirely from religion, and when we recognise that the growth and development of the myth have nothing at all to do with the beginnings of worship. The science of comparative mythology and folk-lore is a valuable and light-bearing study in its own way: but it has no more to do with the origin of religion than the science of ethics or the science of geology. There are ethical rules in most advanced cults: there are geological surmises in most sacred books: but neither one nor the other is on that account religion, any more than the history of Jehoshaphat or the legend of Samson.

What I want to suggest in the present chapter sums itself up in a few sentences thus: Religion is practice, mythology is story-telling. Every religion has myths that accompany it: but the myths do not give rise to the religion: on the contrary, the religion gives rise to the myths. And I shall attempt in this book to account for the origin of religion alone, omitting altogether both mythology as a whole, and all mythical persons or beings other than gods in the sense here illustrated.

CHAPTER III.

THE LIFE OF THE DEAD.

The object of this book, we saw at the beginning, is to trace the evolution of the idea of God. But the solution of that problem implies two separate questions—first, how did men begin to frame the idea of a god at all ; and second, how did they progress from the conception of many distinct gods to the conception of a single supreme God, like the central deity of Christianity and of Islam. In other words, we have first to enquire into the origin of polytheism, and next into its gradual supersession by monotheism. Those are the main lines of enquiry I propose to follow out in the present volume.

Religion, however, has one element within it still older, more fundamental, and more persistent than any mere belief in a god or gods—nay, even than the custom or practice of supplicating and appeasing ghosts or gods by gifts and observances. That element is the conception of the Life of the Dead. On the primitive belief in such life, all religion ultimately bases itself. The belief is in fact the earliest thing to appear in religion, for there are savage tribes who have nothing worth calling gods, but have still a religion or cult of their dead relatives. It is also the latest thing to survive in religion; for many modern spiritualists, who have ceased to be theists, or to accept any other form of the supernatural, nevertheless go on believing in the continued existence of the dead, and in the possibility of intercommunication between them and the living. This, therefore, which is the earliest manifestation of religious thought, and which persists throughout as one of its most salient and irrepressible features, must engage our attention for a little time before we pass on to the genesis of polytheism.

But the belief in continued life itself, like all other human ideas, has naturally undergone various stages of evolution. The stages glide imperceptibly into one another, of course; but I think we can on the whole distinguish with tolerable accuracy between three main layers or strata of opinion with regard to the continued existence of the dead. In the first or lowest stratum, the difference between life and death themselves is but ill or inadequately perceived; the dead are thought of as yet bodily living. In the second stratum, death is recognised as a physical fact, but is regarded as only temporary; at this stage, men look forward to the Resurrection of the Body, and expect the Life of the World to Come. In the third stratum, the soul is regarded as a distinct entity from the body; it survives it in a separate and somewhat shadowy form: so that the opinion as to the future proper to this stage is not a belief in the Resurrection of the Body, but a belief in the Immortality of the Soul. These two concepts have often been confounded together by loose and semi-philosophical Christian thinkers; but in their essence they are wholly distinct and irreconcilable.

I shall examine each of these three strata separately.

And first as to that early savage level of thought where the ideas of life and death are very ill demarcated. To us at the present day it seems a curious notion that people should not possess the conception of death as a necessary event in every individual human history. But that is because we cannot easily unread all our previous thinking, cannot throw ourselves frankly back into the state of the savage. We are accustomed to living in large and populous communities, where deaths are frequent, and where natural death in particular is an every-day occurrence. We have behind us a vast and long history of previous ages;

and we know that historical time was occupied by the lives of many successive generations, all of which are now dead, and none of which on the average exceeded a certain fixed limit of seventy or eighty odd years. To us, the conception of human life as a relatively short period, bounded by a known duration, and naturally terminating at a relatively fixed end, is a common and familiar one.

We forget, however, that to the savage all this is quite otherwise. He lives in a small and scattered community, where deaths are rare, and where natural death in particular is comparatively infrequent. Most of his people are killed in war, or devoured by wild beasts, or destroyed by accidents in the chase, or by thirst or starvation. Some are drowned in rapid rivers; some crushed by falling trees or stones; some poisoned by deadly fruits, or bitten by venomous snakes; some massacred by chiefs, or murdered in quarrels with their own tribesmen. In a large majority of instances, there is some open and obvious cause of death; and this cause is generally due either to the hand of man or to some other animal; or failing that, to some apparently active effort of external nature, such as flood, or lightning, or forest fires, or landslip and earthquake. Death by disease is comparatively rare; death by natural decay almost unknown or unrecognised.

Nor has the savage a great historic past behind him. He knows few but his tribesmen, and little of their ancestors save those whom his parents can remember before them. His perspective of the past is extremely limited. Nothing enables him to form that wide idea of the necessity and invariability of death which to us is so familiar. That "all men are mortal" is to civilised man a truism; to very early savages it would necessarily have seemed a startling paradox. No man ever dies within his own experience; ever since he can remember, he has continued to exist as a permanent part of all his adventures. Most of the savage's family have gone on continuously living with him. A death has been a rare and startling occurrence. Thus the notion of death as an inevitable end never arises at all; the notion of death as due to natural causes seems quite untenable. When a savage dies, the first question that arises is "Who has killed him?" If he is slain in war, or devoured by a tiger, or ripped up by an elephant, or drowned by a stream in spate, or murdered by a tribesman, the cause is obvious. If none of these, then the death is usually set down to witchcraft.

Furthermore, the mere fact of death is much less certain among primitive or savage men than in civilised communities. We know as a rule with almost absolute certainty whether at a given moment a sick or wounded man is dead or living. Nevertheless, even among ourselves, cases of doubt not infrequently occur. At times we hesitate whether a man or woman is dead or has fainted. If the heart continues to beat, we consider them still living; if not the slightest flutter of the pulse can be perceived, we consider them dead. Even our advanced medical science, however, is often perplexed in very obscure cases of catalepsy; and mistakes have occurred from time to time, resulting in occasional premature burials. The discrimination of true from apparent death is not always easy. Vesalius, the eminent anatomist, opened a supposed corpse in which the heart was seen to be still beating; and the Abbé Prévost, who had been struck by apoplexy, was regarded as dead, but recovered consciousness once more under the surgeon's scalpel. Naturally, among savages, such cases of doubt are far more likely to occur than among civilised people; or rather, to put it as the savage would think of it, there is often no knowing when a person who is lying stiff and lifeless may happen to get up again and resume his usual activity. The savage is accustomed to seeing his fellows stunned or rendered unconscious by blows, wounds, and other accidents, inflicted either by the enemy, by wild beasts, by natural agencies, or by the wrath of his tribesmen; and he never knows how soon the effect of such accidents may pass away, and the man may recover his ordinary vitality. As a rule, he keeps and tends the bodies of his friends as long as any chance remains of their ultimate recovery, and often (as we shall see in the sequel) much longer.

Again, in order to understand this attitude of early man towards his wounded, his stricken, and his dead, we must glance aside for a moment at the primitive psychology. Very early indeed in the history of the human mind, I believe, some vague adumbration of the notion of a soul began to pervade humanity. We now know that consciousness is a function of the brain; that it is intermitted during sleep, when the brain rests, and also during times of grave derangement of the nervous or circulatory systems, as when we faint or assume the comatose condition, or are stunned by a blow, or fall into catalepsy or epilepsy. We also know that consciousness ceases altogether at death, when the brain no longer functions; and that the possibility of its further continuance is absolutely cut off by the fact of decomposition. But these truths, still imperfectly understood or rashly rejected by many among ourselves, were wholly unknown to early men. They had to frame for themselves as best they could some vague working hypothesis of the human mind, from data which suggested themselves in the ordinary course of life; and the hypothesis which they framed was more or less roughly that of the soul or spirit, still implicitly accepted by a large majority of the human species.

According to this hypothesis every man consists of two halves or parts, one material or bodily, the other immaterial or spiritual. The first half, called the body, is visible and tangible; the second half, called the soul, dwells within it, and is more or less invisible or shadowy. It is to a large extent identified with the breath; and like the breath it is often believed to quit the body at death, and even to go off in a free form and live its own life elsewhere. As this supposed independence of the soul from the body lies at the very basis of all ghosts and gods, and therefore of religion itself, I may be excused for going at some length into the question of its origin.

Actually, so far as we know by direct and trustworthy evidence, the existence of a mind, consciousness, or "soul," apart from a body, has never yet been satisfactorily demonstrated. But the savage derived the belief, apparently, from a large number of concurrent hints and suggestions, of which such a hypothesis seemed to him the inevitable result. During the daytime he was awake; at night he slept; yet even in his sleep, while his body lay curled on the ground beside the camp-fire, he seemed to hunt or to fight, to make love or to feast, in some other region. What was this part of him that wandered from the body in dreams?—what, if not the soul or breath which he naturally regarded as something distinct and separate? And when a man died, did not the soul or breath go from him? When he was badly wounded, did it not disappear for a time, and then return again? In fainting fits, in catalepsy, and in other abnormal states, did it not leave the body, or even play strange tricks with it? I need not pursue this line of thought, already fully worked out by Mr. Herbert Spencer and Dr. Tylor. It is enough to say that from a very early date, primitive man began to regard the soul or life as something bound up with the breath, something which could go away from the body at will and return to it again, something separable and distinct, yet essential to the person, very vaguely conceived as immaterial or shadowy, but more so at a later than at an earlier period.*

Moreover, these souls or spirits (which quitted the body in sleep or trance) outlived death, and appeared again to survivors. In dreams, we often see the shapes of living men; but we also see with peculiar vividness the images of the departed. Everybody is familiar with the frequent

---

* The question of the Separate Soul has recently received very full treatment from Mr. Frazer in *The Golden Bough*, and Mr. Sidney Hartland in *The Legend of Perseus*.

reappearance in sleep of intimate friends or relations lately deceased. These appearances, I fancy, are especially frequent during the first few months of bereavement, and gradually weaken in frequency and vividness as time goes on. The reason for both sets of phenomena I take to be this: the nervous structures, accustomed to be stimulated in particular combinations by intercourse with the dead friend, miss automatically their wonted stimulation; and being therefore in a highly nourished and unstable state, are peculiarly ready to undergo ideal stimulation in sleep, as we know to be the case with other well-nurtured and underworked nerve-centres. Or, to put it less materially, the brain falls readily into a familiar rhythm. But in course of time the channels atrophy by disuse; the habit is lost; and the dream-appearances of the dead friend grow more and more infrequent. The savage, however, accepts the dream-world as almost equally real with the world of sense-presentation. As he envisages the matter to himself, his soul has been away on its travels without its body, and there has met and conversed with the souls of dead friends or relations.

We must remember also that in savage life occasions for trance, for fainting, and for other abnormal or comatose nervous conditions occur far more frequently than in civilised life. The savage is often wounded and fails from loss of blood; he cuts his foot against a stone, or is half killed by a wild beast; he fasts long and often, perforce, or is reduced to the very verge of starvation; and he is therefore familiar, both in his own case and in the case of others, with every variety of unconsciousness and of delirium or delusion. All these facts figure themselves to his mind as absences of the soul from the body, which is thus to him a familiar and almost every-day experience.

Moreover, it will hence result that the savage can hardly gain any clear conception of Death, and especially of death from natural causes. When a tribesman is brought home severely wounded and unconscious, the spectator's immediate idea must necessarily be that the soul has gone away and deserted the body. For how long it has gone, he cannot tell; but his first attempts are directed towards inducing or compelling it to return again. For this purpose, he often addresses it with prayers and adjurations, or begs it to come back with loud cries and persuasions. And he cannot possibly discriminate between its temporary absence and its final departure. As Mr. Herbert Spencer well says, the consequences of blows or wounds merge into death by imperceptible stages. "Now the injured man shortly 'returned to himself,' and did not go away again; and now, returning to himself only after a long absence, he presently deserted his body for an indefinite time. Lastly, instead of these temporary returns, followed by final absence, there sometimes occurred cases in which a violent blow caused continuous absence from the very first; the other self never came back at all."

In point of fact, during these earlier stages, the idea of Death as we know it did not and does not occur in any form. There are still savages who do not seem to recognise the universality and necessity of death—who regard it on the contrary as something strange and unatural, something due to the machination of enemies or of witchcraft. With the earliest men, it is a foregone conclusion, psychologically speaking, that they should so regard it; they could not form any other concept without far more extended knowledge than they have the means of possessing. To them, a Dead Man must always have seemed a man whose soul or breath or other self had left him, but might possibly return again to the body at any time.

Each of the three stages of thought above discriminated has its appropriate mode of disposing of its dead. The appropriate mode for this earliest stage is Preservation of the Corpse, which eventuates at last in Mummification.

The simplest form of this mode of disposal of the corpse consists in keeping it in the hut or cave where the family dwell, together with the living. A New Guinea woman thus kept her husband's body in her hut till it dried up of itself, and she kissed it and offered it food every day, as though it were living. Many similar cases are reported from elsewhere. Hut preservation is common in the very lowest races. More frequently, however, owing to the obvious discomfort of living in too close proximity to a dead body, the corpse at this stage of thought is exposed openly in a tree or on a platform or under some other circumstances where no harm can come to it. Among the Australians and Andaman Islanders, who, like the Negritoes of New Guinea, preserve for us a very early type of human customs, the corpse is often exposed on a rough raised scaffold. Some of the Polynesian and Melanesian peoples follow the same practice. The Dyaks and Kyans expose their dead in trees. "But it is in America," says Mr. Herbert Spencer, "that exposure on raised stages is commonest. The Dakotahs adopt this method; at one time it was the practice of the Iriquois; Catlin, describing the Mandans as having scaffolds on which 'their *dead live* as they term it,' remarks that they are thus kept out of the way of wolves and dogs; and Schoolcraft says the same of the Chippewas." Generally speaking, at the lowest grades of culture, savages preserve the actual bodies of their dead above ground, either in the home itself, or in close proximity to it. We shall recur later on to this singular practice.

A slight variant on this method, peculiar to a very maritime race, is that described by Mr. H. O. Forbes among the natives of Timurlaut:

"The dead body is placed in a portion of a *prau* fitted to the length of the individual, or within strips of *gabagaba*, or stems of the sago-palm pinned together. If it is a person of some consequence, such as an *Orang Kaya*, an ornate and decorated *prau*-shaped coffin is specially made. This is then enveloped in calico, and placed either on the top of a rock by the margin of the sea at a short distance from the village, or on a high pile-platform erected on the shore about low-tide mark. On the top of the coffin-lid are erected tall flags, and the figures of men playing gongs, shooting guns, and gesticulating wildly to frighten away evil influences from the sleeper. Sometimes the platform is erected on the shore above high-water mark, and near it is stuck in the ground a tall bamboo full of palm-wine; and suspended over a bamboo rail are bunches of sweet potatoes for the use of the dead man's *Nitu*. When the body is quite decomposed, his son or one of the family disinters the skull and deposits it on a little platform in his house, in the gable opposite the fireplace, while to ward off evil from himself he carries about with him the atlas and axis bones of its neck in his *luon*, or *siri-*holder."

This interesting account is full of implications whose fuller meaning we will perceive hereafter. The use of the skull and of the talisman bone should especially be noted for their later importance. For skulls are fundamental in the history of religion.

Cases like these readily pass into the practice of Mummifying, more especially in dry or desert climates. Even in so damp a tropical country as New Guinea, however, D'Albertis found in a shed on the banks of the Fly River two mummies, artificially prepared, as he thought, by removal of the flesh, the bones alone being preserved with the skin to cover them. Here we have evidently a clear conception of death as a serious change, of a different character from a mere temporary absence. So, too, Mr. Chalmers says of the Koiari people in the same island, " They treat their dead after this fashion. A fire is kept burning day and night at the head and feet for months. The entire skin is removed by means of the thumb and forefinger, and the juices plastered all over the face and body of the operator (parent, husband, or wife of the deceased). The fire gradually desiccates the flesh, so that little more than the skeleton is left." But mummification for the most part is confined to drier climates, where it is artificially performed down to a very evolved stage of civilisation, as we know well in Peru and Egypt.

One word must be said in passing as to the frequent habit of specially preserving, and even carrying about the person, the head or hand of a deceased relative. This has been already mentioned in the case of Timurlaut; and it occurs frequently elsewhere. Thus Mr. Chalmers says of a New Guinea baby: "It will be covered with two inches of soil, the friends watching beside the grave; but eventually the skull and smaller bones will be preserved and worn by the mother." Similarly, in the Andaman Islands, where we touch perhaps the lowest existing stratum of savage feeling, "widows may be seen with the skulls of their deceased partners suspended round their necks." The special preservation of the head, even when the rest of the body is eaten or buried, will engage our attention at a later period: heads so preserved are usually resorted to as oracles, and are often treated as the home of the spirit. Mr. Herbert Spencer has collected many similar instances, such as that of the Tasmanians who wore a bone from the skull or arm of a dead relation. He rightly notes, too, that throughout the New World "the primitive conception of death as a long-suspended animation seems to have been especially vivid;" and we find accordingly that customs of this character are particularly frequent among American savages. Thus, to draw once more from his great storehouse, the Crees carried bones and hair of dead relations about for three years; while the Caribs and several Guiana tribes distributed the clean bones among the kinsmen of the deceased. In the Sandwich Islands, also, bones of kings and chiefs were carried about by their descendants, under the impression that the dead exercised guardianship over them.

At this stage of thought, it seems to me, it is the actual corpse that is still thought to be alive; the actual corpse that appears in dreams; and the actual corpse that is fed and worshipped and propitiated with presents.

Ceremonial cannibalism, which will be more fully considered hereafter, appears in this stratum, and survives from it into higher levels. The body is eaten entire, and the bones preserved; or the flesh and fat are removed, and the skin left; or a portion only is sacramentally and reverently eaten by the surviving relations. These processes also will be more minutely described in the sequel.

The first stage merges by gradual degrees into the second, which is that of Burial or its equivalent. Cave-burial of mummies or of corpses forms the transitional link. Indeed, inasmuch as many races of primitive men lived habitually in caves, the placing or leaving the corpse in a cave seems much the same thing as the placing or leaving it in a shed, hut, or shelter. The cave-dwelling Veddahs simply left the dead man in the cave where he died, and themselves migrated to some other cavern. Still, cave-burial lingered on late with many tribes or nations which had for ages outlived the habit of cave-dwelling. Among the South American Indians, cave-burial was common; and in Peru it assumed high developments of mummification. The making of an artificial cave or vault for the dead is but a slight variant on this custom; it was frequent in Egypt, the other dry country where the making of mummies was carried to a high pitch of perfection. The Tombs of the Kings at Thebes are splendid instances of such artificial caves, elaborated into stately palaces with painted walls, where the dead monarchs might pass their underground life in state and dignity. Cave-tombs, natural or artificial, are also common in Asia Minor, Italy, and elsewhere.

During the first stage, it may be noted, the attitude of man towards his dead is chiefly one of affectionate regard. The corpse is kept at home, and fed or tended; the skull is carried about as a beloved object. But in the second stage, which induces the practice of burial, a certain Fear of the Dead becomes more obviously apparent. Men dread the return of the corpse or the ghost, and strive to keep it within prescribed limits. In this stage, the belief in the Resurrection of the Body is the appropriate creed; and though at first the actual corpse is regarded as likely to return to plague survivors, that idea gives place a little later, I believe, to the conception of a less material double or spirit.

And here let us begin by discriminating carefully between the Resurrection of the Body and the Immortality of the Soul.

The idea of Resurrection arose from and is closely bound up with the practice of burial, the second and simpler mode of disposing of the remains of the dead. The idea of Immortality arose from and is closely bound up with the practice of burning, a later and better innovation, invented at the third stage of human culture. During the early historical period all the most advanced and cultivated nations burnt their dead, and, in consequence, accepted the more ideal and refined notion of Immortality. But modern European nations bury their dead, and, in consequence, accept, nominally at least, the cruder and grosser notion of Resurrection. Nominally, I say, because, in spite of creeds and formularies, the influence of Plato and other ancient thinkers, as well as of surviving ancestral ideas, has made most educated Europeans really believe in Immortality, even when they imagine themselves to be believing in Resurrection. Nevertheless, the belief in Resurrection is the avowed and authoritative belief of the Christian world, which thus proclaims itself as on a lower level in this respect than the civilised peoples of antiquity.

The earliest of these two ways of disposing of the bodies of the dead is certainly by burial. As this fact has recently been called in question, I will venture to enlarge a little upon the evidence in its favour. In point of time, burial goes back with certainty to the neolithic age, and with some probability to the palæolithic. Several true interments in caves have been attributed by competent geologists to the earlier of these two periods, the first for which we have any sure warranty of man's existence on earth. But, as I do not desire to introduce controversial matter of any sort into this exposition, I will waive the evidence for burial in the palæolithic age as doubtful, and will merely mention that in the Mentone caves, according to Mr. Arthur Evans, a most competent authority, we have a case of true burial accompanied by neolithic remains of a grade of culture earlier and simpler than any known to us elsewhere. In other words, from the very earliest beginning of the neolithic age men buried their dead; and they continued to bury them, in caves or tumuli, down to the end of neolithic culture. They buried them in the Long Barrows in England; they buried them in the Ohio mounds; they buried them in the shadowy forests of New Zealand; they buried them in the heart of darkest Africa. I know of no case of burning or any means of disposal of the dead, otherwise than by burial or its earlier equivalent, mummification, among people in the stone age of culture in Europe. It is only when bronze and other metals are introduced that races advance to the third stage, the stage of cremation. In America, however, the Mexicans were cremationists.

The wide diffusal of burial over the globe is also a strong argument for its relatively primitive origin. In all parts of the world men now bury their dead, or did once bury them. From the Tombs of the Kings at Pekin to the Pyramids of Memphis; from the Peruvian caves to the Samoyed graveyards, we find most early peoples, most savage peoples, most primitive peoples, once or still engaged in one or other form of burying. Burial is the common and universal mode; burning, exposure, throwing into a sacred river, and so forth, are sporadic and exceptional, and in many cases, as among the Hindus, are demonstrably of late origin, and connected with certain relatively modern refinements of religion.

Once more, in many or most cases, we have positive evidence that where a race now burns its dead, it used once to bury them. Burial preceded burning in preheroic Greece, as it also did in Etruria and in early Latium. The people of the Long Barrows, in Western Europe generally, buried their dead; the people of the Round Barrows who succeeded them, and who possessed a far higher grade of culture, almost always cremated. It has been assumed that burning is primordial in India ; but Mr. William Simpson, the well-known artist of the *Illustrated London News*, calls my attention to the fact that the Vedas speak with great clearness of burial as the usual mode of disposing of the corpse, and even allude to the tumulus, the circle of stones around it, and the sacred *temenos* which they enclose. According to Rajendralala Mitra, whose high authority on the subject is universally acknowledged, burial was the rule in India till about the thirteenth or fourteenth century before the Christian era; then came in cremation, with burial of the ashes, and this continued till about the time of Christ, when burial was dispensed with, and the ashes were thrown into some sacred river. I think, therefore, until some more positive evidence is adduced on the other side, we may rest content with our general conclusion that burial is the oldest, most universal, and most savage mode of disposing of the remains of the dead among humanity after the general recognition of death as a positive condition. It probably took its rise in an early period, while mankind was still one homogeneous species; and it has been dispersed, accordingly, over the whole world, even to the most remote oceanic islands.

What is the origin of this barbaric and disgusting custom, so repugnant to all the more delicate sentiments of human nature ? I think Mr. Frazer is right in attributing it to the terror felt by the living for the ghosts (or, rather, at first the corpses) of the dead, and the fear that they may return to plague or alarm their surviving fellow tribesmen.

In his admirable paper on " Certain Burial Customs as Illustrative of the Primitive Theory of the Soul," Mr. Frazer points out that certain tribes of early men paid great attention to the dead, not so much from affection as from selfish terror. Ghosts or bodies of the dead haunt the earth everywhere, unless artificially confined to bounds, and make themselves exceedingly disagreeable to their surviving relatives. To prevent this, simple primitive philosophy in its second stage has hit upon many devices. The most universal is to bury the dead—that is to say, to put them in a deep-dug hole, and to cover them with a mighty mound of earth, which has now sadly degenerated in civilised countries into a mere formal heap, but which had originally the size and dignity of a tumulus. The object of piling up this great heap of earth was to confine the ghost (or corpse), who could not easily move so large a superincumbent mass of matter. In point of fact, men buried their dead in order to get well rid of them, and to effectually prevent their return to light to disturb the survivors.

For the same reason heavy stones were often piled on the top of the dead. In one form, these became at last the cairn; and, as the ghosts of murderers and their victims tend to be especially restless, everybody who passes their graves in Arabia, Germany, and Spain is bound to add a stone to the growing pile in order to confine them. In another form, that of the single big stone rolled just on top of the body to keep it down by its mass, the makeweight has developed into the modern tombstone. In our own times, indeed, the tombstone has grown into a mere posthumous politeness, and is generally made to do duty as a record of the name and incomparable virtues of the deceased (concerning whom, *nil nisi bonum*); but in origin it was nothing more than the big, heavy boulder, meant to confine the ghost, and was anything but honorific in intention and function.

Again, certain nations go further still in their endeavours to keep the ghost (or corpse) from roaming. The corpse of a Damara, says Galton, having been sewn up in an old ox-hide is buried in a hole, and the spectators jump backwards and forwards over the grave to keep the deceased from rising out of it. In America, the Tupis tied fast all the limbs of the corpse, " that the dead man might not be able to get up, and infest his friends with his visits." You may even divert a river from its course, as Mr. Frazer notes, bury your dead man securely in its bed, and then allow the stream to return to its channel. It was thus that Alaric was kept in his grave from further plaguing humanity; and thus Captain Cameron found a tribe of Central Africans compelled their deceased chiefs to "cease from troubling." Sometimes, again, the grave is enclosed by a fence too high for the dead man to clear even with a running jump; and sometimes the survivors take the prudent precaution of nailing the body securely to the coffin, or of breaking their friend's spine, or even—but this is an extreme case—of hacking him to pieces. In Christian England the poor wretch whom misery had driven to suicide was prevented from roaming about to the discomfort of the lieges by being buried with a stake driven barbarously through him. The Australians, in like manner, used to cut off the thumb of a slain enemy that he might be unable to draw the bow; and the Greeks were wont to hack off the extremities of their victims in order to incapacitate them for further fighting. These cases will be seen to be very luminiferous when we come to examine the origin and meaning of cremation.

Burial, then, I take it, is simply by origin a means adopted by the living to protect themselves against the vagrant tendencies of the actual dead. For some occult reason, the vast majority of men in all ages have been foolishly afraid of meeting with the spirits of the departed. Their great desire has been, not to see, but to avoid seeing these singular visitants; and for that purpose they invented, first of all, burial, and afterwards cremation.

The common modern conception of the ghost is certainly that of an immaterial or shadowy form, which can be seen but not touched, and which preserves an outer semblance of the human figure. But that idea itself, which has been imported into all our descriptions and reasonings about the ghost-beliefs of primitive man, is, I incline to think, very far from primitive, and has been largely influenced by quite late conceptions derived from the cremational rather than the burial level of religious philosophy. In other words, though, in accordance with universal usage and Mr. Frazer's precedent, I have used the word "ghost" above in referring to these superstitious terrors of early man, I believe it is far less the spirit than the actual corpse itself that early men even in this second stage were really afraid of. It is the corpse that may come back and do harm to survivors. It is the corpse that must be kept down by physical means, that must be covered with earth, pressed flat beneath a big and ponderous stone, deprived of its thumbs, its hands, its eyes, its members. True, I believe the savage also thinks of the ghost or double as returning to earth; but his psychology, I fancy, is not so definite as to distinguish very accurately between corpse and spirit. The accurate differentiation of the two belongs rather, it seems to me, to the post-cremational and more spiritual philosophy than to the primary or preservative, and the secondary or inhumational. Anybody who looks at the evidence collected by Mr. Frazer will see for himself that precautions are taken rather against the return of the actual physical body than against the return of the ghost or spirit. Or perhaps, to be more precise, the two are hardly thought of at this early stage in separation or antithesis.

If we look at the means taken to preserve the body after death among the majority of primitive peoples, above the Tasmanian level, this truth of the corpse being itself immortal becomes clearer and clearer. We are still, in fact, at a level where ghost and dead man are insufficiently differentiated. In all these cases it is believed that the dead body continues to live in the grave the same sort of life that it led above ground ; and for this purpose it is provided with weapons, implements, utensils, food, vessels, and all the necessaries of life for its new mansion. Continued sentient existence of the body after death is the keynote of the earliest level of psychical philosophy. First, the corpse lives in the hut with its family: later, it lives in the grave with its forefathers.

But side by side with this naïve belief in the continued existence of the body after death, which survives into the inhumational stage of evolution, goes another and apparently irreconcilable belief in a future resurrection. Strictly speaking, of course, if the body is still alive, there is no need for any such special revivification. But religious thought, as we all know, does not always pride itself upon the temporal virtues of logic or consistency; and the savage in particular is not in the least staggered at being asked to conceive of one and the same subject in two opposite and contradictory manners. He does not bring the two incongruities into thought together; he thinks them alternately, sometimes one, sometimes the other. Even Christian systematists are quite accustomed to combine the incongruous beliefs in a future resurrection and in the continued existence of the soul after death, by supposing that the soul remains meanwhile in some nondescript limbo, apart from its body—some uncertain Sheol, some dim hades or purgatory or "place of departed spirits." The savage is scarcely likely to be more exacting in this matter than our doctors of divinity.

It is the common belief of the second or inhumational stage, then, that there will be at some time or other a "General Resurrection." No doubt this General Resurrection has been slowly developed out of the belief in and expectation of many partial resurrections. It is understood that each individual corpse will, or may, resurge at some time: therefore it is believed that all corpses together will resurge at a single particular moment. So long as burial persists, the belief in the Resurrection persists beside it, and forms a main feature in the current conception of the future life among the people who practise it.

How, then, do we progress from this second or inhumational stage to the third stage with its practice of burning, and its correlated dogma of the Immortality of the Soul?

In this way, as it seems to me. Besides keeping down the ghost (or corpse) with clods and stones, it was usual in many cases to adopt other still stronger persuasives and dissuasives in the same direction. Sometimes the persuasives were of the gentlest type; for example, the dead man was often politely requested and adjured to remain quiet in the grave and to give no trouble. But sometimes they were less bland; the corpse was often pelted with sticks, stones, and hot coals, in order to show him that his visits at home would not in future be appreciated. The ordinary stake and mutilation treatment goes, it is clear, upon the same principle; if the man has no feet or legs of his own, he cannot very well walk back again. But further developments of the like crude idea are to cut off the head, to tear out the heart, to hack the body in pieces, to pour boiling water and vinegar over the dangerous place where the corpse lies buried. Now burning, I take it, belonged originally to the same category of strong measures against refractory ghosts or corpses; and this is the more probable owing to the fact that it is mentioned by Mr. Frazer among the remedies recommended for use in the extreme case of vampires. Its original object was, no doubt, to prevent the corpse from returning in any way to the homes of the living.

Once any people adopted burning as a regular custom, however, the chances are that, *cæteris paribus*, it would continue and spread. For the practice of cremation is so much more wholesome and sanitary than the practice of burial that it would give a double advantage in the struggle for existence to any race that adopted it, in peace and in war. Hence it is quite natural that when at a certain grade of culture certain races happened to light upon it in this superstitious way, those races would be likely to thrive and to take the lead in culture as long as no adverse circumstances counteracted the advantage.

But the superstitions and the false psychology which gave rise at first to the notion of a continued life after death would not, of course, disappear with the introduction of burning. The primitive cremationists may have hoped, by reducing to ashes the bodies of their dead, to prevent the recurrence of the corpse to the presence of the living; but they could not prevent the recurrence of the ghost in the dreams of the survivors; they could not prevent the wind that sighed about the dead man's grave, the bats that flitted, the vague noises that terrified, the abiding sense of the corpse's presence. All the factors that go to make up the ghost or the *revenant* (to use a safe word less liable to misinterpretation) still remained as active as ever. Hence, I believe, with the introduction of cremation the conception of the ghost merely suffered an airy change. He grew more shadowy, more immaterial, more light, more spiritual. In one word, he became, strictly speaking, a ghost as we now understand the word, not a returning dead man. This conception of the ghost as essentially a shade or shadow belongs peculiarly, it seems to me, to the cremating peoples. I can answer for it that among negroes, for example, the "duppy" is conceived as quite a material object. It is classical literature, the literature of the cremating Greeks and Romans, that has familiarised us most with the idea of the ghost as shadowy and intangible. Burying races have more solid doubles. When Peter escaped from prison in Jerusalem, the assembled brethren were of opinion that it must be "his angel." The white woman who lived for years in a native Australian tribe was always spoken of by her hosts as a ghost. In one word, at a low stage of culture the *revenant* is conceived of as material and earthly; at a higher stage, he is conceived of as immaterial and shadowy.

THE CUSTOM OF CREMATION. 63

Now when people take to burning their dead, it is clear they will no longer be able to believe in the Resurrection of the Body. Indeed, if I am right in the theory here set forth, it is just in order to prevent the Resurrection of the Body at inconvenient moments that they take to burning. To be sure, civilised nations, with their developed power of believing in miracles, are capable of supposing, not only that the sea will yield up its dead, but also that burnt, mangled, or dispersed bodies will be collected from all parts to be put together again at the Resurrection. This, however, is not the naïve belief of simple and natural men. To them, when you have burnt a body you have utterly destroyed it, here and hereafter; and we know that mutilation and burning were employed for this very purpose in the case of vampires and other corpses whose total suppression was desirable. Sepoys were blown from the guns in the Indian mutiny for the express reason that, according to the Hindu belief, that method of disposing of them destroyed not only the body but the soul as well— got rid of them entirely. The ordinary human idea is that when you burn a body you simply annihilate it; and on that very account early Christians preferred burial to cremation, because they thought they stood thereby a better chance at the Resurrection. It is true they allowed that the divine omnipotence could make new bodies for the martyrs who were burnt; but for themselves, they seem to have preferred on the average to go on afresh with their old familiar ones.

Naturally, therefore, among cremating peoples, the doctrine of the Resurrection of the Body tended to go out, and what replaced it was the doctrine of the Immortality of the Soul. You may burn the body, but the spirit still survives; and the survival gives origin to a new philosophy of ghosts and *revenants*, a new idea of the inner nature of ghosthood. Gradually the spirit gets to be conceived as diviner essence, entangled and imprisoned, as it were, in the meshes of the flesh, and only to be set free by means of fire, which thus becomes envisaged at last as friendly rather than destructive in its action on the dead body. What was at first a precaution against the return of the corpse becomes in the end a pious duty; just as burial itself, originally a selfish precaution against the pranks and tricks of returning corpses, becomes in the end so sacred and imperative that unburied ghosts are conceived as wandering about, Archytas-wise, begging for the favour of a handful of sand to prevent them from homeless vagabondage for ever. Nations who burn come to regard the act of burning as the appointed means for freeing the ghost from the confining meshes of the body, and regard it rather as a solemn duty to the dead than as a personal precaution.

Not only so, but there arises among them a vague and fanciful conception of the world of shades very different indeed from the definite and material conception of the two earlier stages. The mummy was looked upon as inhabiting the tomb, which was furnished and decorated for its reception like a house; and it was provided with every needful article for use and comfort. Even the buried body was supplied with tools and implements for the ghost. The necessities of the shade are quite different and more shadowy. He has no need of earthly tools or implements. The objects found in the Long Barrows of the burying folk and the Round Barrows of the cremationists well illustrate this primordial and far-reaching difference. The Long Barrows of the Stone Age people are piled above an interment; they contain a chambered tomb, which is really the subterranean home or palace of the body buried in it. The wives and slaves of the deceased were killed and interred with him to keep him company in his new life in the grave; and implements, weapons, drinking-cups, games, trinkets, and ornaments were buried with their owners. The life in the grave was all as material and real as this one; the same objects that served the warrior in this world would equally serve him in the same form in the next. It is quite different with the Round Barrows of the Bronze Age cremationists. These barrows are piled round an urn, which determines the shape of the tumulus, as the chambered tomb and the corpse determine the shape of the earlier Stone Age interments. They contain ashes alone; and the implements and weapons placed in them are all broken or charred with fire. Why? Because the ghost, immaterial as he has now become, can no longer make use of solid earthly weapons or utensils. It is only their ghosts or shadows that can be of any use to the ghostly possessor in the land of shades. Hence everything he needs is burnt or broken, in order that its ghost may be released and liberated; and all material objects are now conceived as possessing such ghosts, which can be utilised accordingly in the world of spirits.

Note also that with this advance from the surviving or revivable Corpse to the immortal Soul or Spirit, there goes almost naturally and necessarily a correlative advance from continued but solitary life in the tomb to a freer and wider life in an underground world of shades and spirits. The ghost gets greatly liberated and emancipated. He has more freedom of movement, and becomes a citizen of an organised community, often envisaged as ruled over by a King of the Dead, and as divided into places of reward and punishment. But while we modern Europeans pretend to be resurrectionists, it is a fact that our current ghostly and eschatological conceptions (I speak of the world at large, not of mere scholastic theologians) have been largely influenced by ideas derived from this opposite doctrine—a doctrine once held by many or most of our own ancestors, and familiarised to us from childhood in classical literature. In fact, while most Englishmen of the present day believe they believe in the Resurrection of the Body, what they really believe in is the Immortality of the Soul.

It might seem at first sight as though a grave discrepancy existed between the two incongruous ideas, first of burying or burning your dead so that they may not be able to return or to molest you, and second of worshipping at their graves or making offerings to their disembodied spirits. But to the savage mind these two conceptions are by no means irreconcilable. While he jumps upon the corpse of his friend or his father to keep it in the narrow pit he has digged for it, he yet brings it presents of food and drink, or slays animals at the tomb, that the ghost may be refreshed by the blood that trickles down to it. Indeed, several intermediate customs occur, which help us to bridge over the apparent gulf between reverential preservation of the mummified body, and the coarse precautions of burial or burning. Thus, in many cases, some of which we shall examine in the next chapter, after the body has been for some time buried, the head is disinterred, and treasured with care in the family oratory, where it is worshipped and tended, and where it often gives oracles to the members of the household. A ceremonial washing is almost always a feature in this reception of the head; it recurs again and again in various cases, down to the enshrinement of the head of Hoseyn at Cairo, and that of St. Denis at the abbey of the same name, to both of which we shall allude once more at a far later stage of our enquiry. For the present, it must suffice to say that the ceremonial and oracular preservation of the head—the part which sees, and speaks, and eats, and drinks, and listens—is a common feature in all religious usages; that it gives rise apparently to the collections of family skulls which adorn so many savage huts and oratories; that it may be answerable ultimately for the Roman *busta* and many other imitative images of the dead, in which the head alone is represented; and that when transferred to the sacred human or animal victim (himself, as we shall hereafter see, a slain god), it seems to account for the human heads hung up by the Dyaks and other savages about their houses, as also for the skulls of oxen and other sacred animals habitually displayed on the front of places of worship, whose last relic is the sculptured oxen's heads which fill the metopes in some Greek and most Roman temples. Much of this, I admit, will be little comprehensible to the reader at the present stage of our argument: but I beg him to bear in mind provisionally this oracular and representative value of the head or skull from this point forth; he will find, as he proceeds, its meaning will become clearer and ever clearer at each successive stage of our exposition.

I ought also to add that between complete preservation of the corpse and the practice of burial there seems to have gone another intermediate stage, now comparatively rare, but once very general, if we may judge from the traces it has left behind it—a stage when all the body or part of it was sacramentally eaten by the survivors as an act of devotion. We will consider this curious and revolting practice more fully when we reach the abstruse problem of sacrifice and sacrament; for the present it will suffice to say that in many instances, in Australia, South America, and elsewhere, the body is eaten, while only the bones are burned or buried. Among these savages, again, it usually happens that the head is cleaned of its flesh by cooking, while the skull is ceremonially washed, and preserved as an object of household veneration and an oracular deity. Instances will be quoted in succeeding chapters.

Thus, between the care taken to prevent returns of the corpse, and the worship paid to the ghost or shade, primitive races feel no such sense of discrepancy or incongruity as would instantly occur to civilised people.

The three stages in human ideas with which this chapter deals may be shortly summed up as corpse-worship, ghost-worship, and shade-worship.

CHAPTER IV.

THE ORIGIN OF GODS.

MR. HERBERT SPENCER has traced so admirably in his *Principles of Sociology* the progress of development from the Ghost to the God that I do not propose in this chapter to attempt much more than a brief recapitulation of his main propositions, which, however, I shall supplement with fresh examples, and adapt at the same time to the conception of three successive stages in human ideas about the Life of the Dead, as set forth in the preceding argument. But the hasty *résumé* which I shall give at present will be fleshed out incidentally at a later point by consideration of several national religions.

In the earliest stage of all—the stage where the actual bodies of the dead are preserved,—Gods as such are for the most part unknown: it is the corpses of friends and ancestors that are worshipped and reverenced. For example, Ellis says of the corpse of a Tahitian chief that it was placed in a sitting posture under a protecting shed; "a small altar was erected before it, and offerings of fruit, food, and flowers were daily presented by the relatives, or the priest appointed to attend the body." (This point about the priest is of essential importance.) The Central Americans, again, as Mr. Spencer notes, performed similar rites before bodies dried by artificial heat. The New Guinea people, as D'Albertis found, worship the dried mummies of their fathers and husbands. A little higher in the scale, we get the developed mummy-worship of Egypt and Peru, which survives even after the evolution of greater gods, from powerful kings or chieftains. Other evidence in abundance has been adduced from Polynesia and from Africa. Wherever the actual bodies of the dead are preserved, there also worship and offerings are paid to them.

Often, however, as already noted, it is not the whole body but the head alone that is specially kept and worshipped. Thus Mr. H. O. Forbes says of the people of Buru: "The dead are buried in the forest in some secluded spot, marked often by a *merang* or grave-pole; over which at certain intervals the relatives place tobacco, cigarettes, and various offerings. When the body is decomposed, the son or nearest relative disinters the head, wraps a new cloth about it, and places it in the Matakau at the back of his house, or in a little hut erected for it near the grave. It is the representative of his forefathers, whose behests he holds in the greatest respect."

Two points are worthy of notice in this interesting account, as giving us an anticipatory hint of two further accessories whose evolution we must trace hereafter; first the grave-stake, which is probably the origin of the wooden idol; and second, the little hut erected over the head by the side of the grave, which is undoubtedly one of the origins of the temple or praying-house. Observe also the ceremonial wrapping of the skull in cloth, and its oracular functions.

Similarly, Mr. Wyatt Gill, the well-known missionary, writes of a dead baby at Boera, in New Guinea: "It will be covered with two inches of soil, the friends watching beside the grave; but eventually the skull and smaller bones will be preserved and worn by the mother." And of the Suau people he says: "Enquiring the use of several small houses, I learned that it is to cover grave-pits. All the members of a family at death occupy the same grave, the earth that thinly covered the last occupant being scooped out to admit the newcomer. These graves are shallow; the dead are buried in a sitting posture, hands folded. The earth is thrown in up to the mouth only. An earthen pot covers the head. After a time the pot is taken off, the perfect skull removed and cleansed—eventually to be hung up in a basket or net inside the dwelling of the deceased over the fire, to blacken in the smoke." In Africa, again, the skull is frequently preserved in such a pot and prayed to. In America, earthenware pots have been found moulded round human skulls in mounds at New Madrid and elsewhere; the skull cannot be removed without breaking the vessel. Indeed, this curious method of preservation in pots seems to be very widespread; we get perhaps a vague hint or reminiscence of its former prevalence in Europe in the story of Isabella and the pot of basil.

The special selection and preservation of the head as an object of worship thus noted in New Guinea and the Malay Archipelago is also still found among many other primitive peoples. For instance, the Andamanese widows keep the skulls of their husbands as a precious possession: and the New Caledonians, in case of sickness or calamities, "present offerings of food to the skulls of the departed." Mr. Spencer quotes several similar examples, a few of which alone I extract from his pages.

"' In the private fetish-hut of King Adólee, at Badagry, the skull of that monarch's father is preserved in a clay vessel placed in the earth.' He 'gently rebukes it if his success does not happen to answer his expectations.' Similarly among the Mandans, who place the skulls of their dead in a circle, each wife knows the skull of her former husband or child, 'and there seldom passes a day that she does not visit it, with a dish of the best cooked food. . . . There is scarcely an hour in a pleasant day, but more or less of these women may be seen sitting or lying by the skull of their child or husband—talking to it in the most pleasant and endearing language that they can use (as they were wont to do in former days), and seemingly getting an answer back.'"

This affectionate type of converse with the dead, almost free from fear, is especially characteristic of the first or corpse-preserving stage of human death-conceptions. It seldom survives where burial has made the feeling toward the corpse a painful or loathsome one, and it is then confined to the head alone, while the grave itself with the body it encloses is rather shunned and dreaded.

A little above this level, Mr. Du Chaillu notes that some of his West African followers, when going on an expedition, brought out the skulls of their ancestors (which they religiously preserved) and scraped off small portions of the bone, which they mixed with water and drank ; giving as a reason for this conduct that their ancestors were brave, and that by drinking a portion of them they too became brave and fearless like their ancestors. Here we have a simple and early case of that habit of "eating the god" to whose universality and importance Mr. Frazer has so forcibly called attention, and which we must examine at full in a subsequent chapter.

Throughout the earlier and ruder phases of human evolution, this primitive conception of ancestors or dead relatives as the chief known objects of worship survives undiluted : and ancestor-worship remains to this day the principal religion of the Chinese, and of several other peoples. Gods, as such, are practically unknown in China. Ancestor-worship also survives in many other races as one of the main cults, even after other elements of later religion have been superimposed upon it. In Greece and Rome, it remained to the last an important part of domestic ritual. But in most cases, a gradual differentiation is set up in time between various classes of ghosts or dead persons, some ghosts being considered of more importance and power than others; and out of these last it is that gods as a rule are finally developed. A god, in fact, is in the beginning at least an exceptionally powerful and friendly ghost—a ghost able to help, and from whose help great things may reasonably be expected.

Again, the rise of chieftainship and kingship has much to do with the growth of a higher conception of godhead; a dead king of any great power or authority is sure to be thought of in time as a god of considerable importance. We shall trace out this idea more fully hereafter in the religion of Egypt; for the present it must suffice to say that the supposed power of the gods in each pantheon has regularly increased in proportion to the increased power of kings or emperors.

When we pass from the first plane of corpse-preservation and mummification to the second plane where burial is habitual, it might seem at a hasty glance as though continued worship of the dead, and their elevation into gods, would no longer be possible. For we saw that burial is prompted by a deadly fear lest the corpse or ghost should return to plague the living. Nevertheless, natural affection for parents or friends, and the desire to ensure their good will and aid, make these seemingly contrary ideas reconcilable. As a matter of fact, we find that even when men bury or burn their dead, they continue to worship them: while, as we shall show in the sequel, even the great stones which they roll on top of the grave to prevent the dead from rising again become in time altars on which sacrifices are offered to the spirit.

In these two later stages of thought with regard to the dead which accompany burial and cremation, the gods, indeed, grow more and more distinct from minor ghosts with an accelerated rapidity of evolution. They grow greater in proportion to the rise of temples and hierarchies. Furthermore, the very indefiniteness of the bodiless ghost tells in favour of an enlarged godship. The gods are thought of as more and more aerial and immaterial, less definitely human in form and nature; they are clothed with mighty attributes; they assume colossal size; they are even identified with the sun, the moon, the great powers of nature. But they are never quite omnipotent during the polytheistic stage, because in a pantheon they are necessarily mutually limiting. Even in the Greek and Roman civilisation, it is clear that the gods were not commonly envisaged by ordinary minds as much more than human; for Pisistratus dressed up a courtesan at Athens to represent Pallas Athene, and imposed by this cheap theatrical trick upon the vulgar Athenians; while Paul and Barnabas were taken at Lystra for Zeus and Hermes. Many similar instances will occur at once to the classical scholar. It is only quite late, under the influence of monotheism, that the exalted conceptions of deity now prevalent began to form themselves in Judaism and Christianity.

Mere domestic ancestor-worship, once more, could scarcely give us the origin of anything more than domestic religion—the cult of the *manes*, the household gods, as distinct from that of the tribal and national deities. But kingship supplies us with the missing link. We have seen in Mr. Duff Macdonald's account of the Central African god-making how the worship of the chief's ancestors gives rise to tribal or village gods; and it is clear how, as chieftainship and kingship widen, national gods of far higher types may gradually evolve from these early monarchs. Especially must we take the time-element into account, remembering that the earlier ancestors get at last to be individually forgotten as men, and remain in memory only as supernatural beings. Thus kingship rapidly reacts upon godship. If the living king himself is great, how much greater must be the ancestor whom even the king himself fears and worships; and how infinitely greater still that yet earlier god, the ancestor's ancestor, whom the ancestor himself revered and propitiated! In some such way there grows up gradually a hierarchy of gods, among whom the oldest, and therefore the least known, are usually in the end the greatest of any.

The consolidation of kingdoms and empires, and the advance of the arts, tell strongly with concurrent force in these directions; while the invention of written language sets a final seal on the godhead and might of great early ancestors. Among very primitive tribes, indeed, we find as a rule only very domestic and recent objects of worship. The chief prays for the most part to his own father and his immediate predecessors. The more ancient ancestors, as Mr. Duff Macdonald has so well pointed out, grow rapidly into oblivion. But with more advanced races, various agencies arise which help to keep in mind the early dead ; and in very evolved communities these agencies, reaching a high pitch of evolution, make the recent gods or kings or ghosts seem comparatively unimportant by the side of the very ancient and very long-worshipped ones. More than of any other thing, it may be said of a god, *vires acquirit eundo*. Thus, in advanced types of society, saints or gods of recent origin assume but secondary or minor importance ; while the highest and greatest gods of all are those of the remotest antiquity, whose human history is lost from our view in the dim mist of ages.

Three such agencies of prime importance in the transition from the mere ghost to the fully developed god must here be mentioned. They are the rise of temples, of idols, and, above all, of priesthoods. Each of these we must now consider briefly but separately.

The origin of the Temple is various ; but all temples may nevertheless be reduced in the last resort either into graves of the dead, or into places where worship is specially offered up to them. This truth, which Mr. Herbert Spencer arrived at by examination of the reports of travellers or historians, and worked up in connection with his *Principles of Sociology*, was independently arrived at through quite a different line of observation and reasoning by Mr. William Simpson, the well-known artist of the *Illustrated London News*. Mr. Simpson has probably visited a larger number of places of worship all over the world than any other traveller of any generation : and he was early impressed by the fact which forced itself upon his eyes, that almost every one of them, where its origin could be traced, turned out to be a tomb in one form or another. He has set forth the results of his researches in this direction in several admirable papers, all of which, but especially the one entitled *The Worship of Death*, I can confidently recommend to the serious attention of students of religion. They contain the largest collection of instances in this matter ever yet made ; and they show beyound a doubt the affiliation of the very idea of a temple on the tomb or grave of some distinguished dead person, famous for his power, his courage, or his saintliness.

The cave is probably the first form of the Temple. Sometimes the dead man is left in the cave which he inhabited when living ; an instance of which we have already noticed among the Veddahs of Ceylon. In other cases, where races have outgrown the custom of cave-dwelling, the habit of cave-burial, or rather of laying the dead in caves or in artificial grottoes, still continues through the usual conservatism of religious feeling. Offerings are made to the dead in all these various caves : and here we get the beginnings of cave-temples. Such temples are at first of course either natural or extremely rude ; but they soon begin to be decorated with rough frescoes, as is done, for example, by the South African Bushmen. These frescoes again give rise in time by slow degrees to such gorgeous works as those of the Tombs of the Kings at Thebes ; each of which has attached to it a magnificent temple as its mortuary chapel. Sculpture is similarly employed on the decoration of cave-temples ; and we get the final result of such artistic ornament in splendid cave-temples like those of Ellora. Both arts were employed together in the beautiful and interesting Etruscan tomb-temples.

In another class of cases, the hut where the dead man lived is abandoned at his death by his living relations, and thus becomes a rudimentary Temple where offerings are made to him. This is the case with the Hottentots, to take an instance at a very low grade of culture. Of a New

Guinea hut-burial, Mr. Chalmers says : " The chief is buried in the centre ; a mat was spread over the grave, on which I was asked to sit until they had a weeping." This weeping is generally performed by women—a touch which leads us on to Adonis and Osiris rites, and to the Christian Pietà. Mr. Spencer has collected several other excellent examples. Thus, the Arawaks place the corpse in a small boat and bury it in the hut ; among the Creeks, the habitation of the dead becomes his place of interment; the Fantees likewise bury the dead person in his own house ; and the Yucatanese "as a rule abandoned the house, and left it uninhabited after the burial." I will not multiply quotations ; it will be better to refer the reader to Mr. Spencer's own pages, where a sufficient number of confirmatory examples are collected to satisfy any but the most prejudiced critic. " As repeated supplies of food are taken to the abandoned house," says Mr. Spencer, "and as along with making offerings there go other propitiatory acts, the deserted dwelling house, turned into a mortuary house, acquires the attributes of a temple."

A third origin for Temples is found in the shed, hut, or shelter, erected over the grave, either for the protection of the dead or for the convenience of the living who bring their offerings. Thus, in parts of New Guinea, according to Mr. Chalmers, " The natives bury their dead in the front of their dwellings, and cover the grave with a small house, in which the near relatives sleep for several months."

"Where house-burial is not practised," says Mr. Spencer, once more, " the sheltering structure raised above the grave, or above the stage bearing the corpse, becomes the germ of the sacred building. By some of the New Guinea people there is a 'roof of atap erected over' the burial-place. In Cook's time the Tahitians placed the body of a dead person upon a kind of bier supported by sticks and under a roof. So, too, in Sumatra, where 'a shed is built over' the grave ; and so, too, in Tonga. Of course this shed admits of enlargement and finish. The Dyaks in some places build mausoleums like houses, 18 feet high, ornamentally carved, containing the goods of the departed—sword, shield, paddle, etc. When we read that the Fijians deposit the bodies of their chiefs in small *enbures* or temples, we may fairly conclude that these so-called temples are simply more-developed sheltering structures. Still more clearly did the customs of the Peruvians show that the structure erected over the dead body develops into a temple. Acosta tells us that ' every one of these kings Yncas left all his treasure and revenues to entertaine the place of worshippe where his body was layed, and there were many ministers with all their familie dedicated to his service.'"

Note in the last touch, by anticipation, one origin of priesthood.

On the other hand, we saw in Mr. Duff Macdonald's account of the Central African natives that those savages do not worship at the actual grave itself. In this case, terror of the *revenant* seems to prevent the usual forms of homage at the tomb of the deceased. Moreover, the ghost being now conceived as more or less freely separable from the corpse, it will be possible to worship it in some place remote from the dreaded cemetery. Hence these Africans " seek the spirit at the place where their departed kinsman last lived among them. It is the great tree at the verandah of the dead man's house that is their temple : and if no tree grow here, they erect a little shade, and there perform their simple rites." We have in this case yet another possible origin for certain temples, and also, I will add by anticipation of a future chapter, for the sacred tree, which is so common an object of pious adoration in many countries.

Beginning with such natural caves or such humble huts, the Temple assumes larger proportions and more beautiful decorations with the increase of art and the growth of kingdoms. Especially, as we see in the tomb-temples and pyramids of Egypt and Peru, does it assume great size and acquire costly ornaments when it is built by a powerful king for himself during his own lifetime. Temple-tombs of this description reach a high point of artistic development in such a building as the so-called Treasury of Atreus at Mycenæ, which is really the sepulchre of some nameless prehistoric monarch. It is admirably reconstructed in Perrot and Chipiez.

Obviously, the importance and magnificence of the temple will react upon the popular conception of the importance and magnificence of the god who inhabits it. And conversely, as the gods grow greater and greater, more art and more constructive skill will constantly be devoted to the building and decoration of their permanent homes. Thus in Egypt the tomb was often more carefully built and splendidly decorated than the house; because the house was inhabited for a short time only, but the tomb for eternity. Moreover, as kings grew more powerful, they often adorned the temples of their ancestors with emulous pride, to show their own greatness. In Egypt, once more, the original part of all the more important temples is but a small dark cell, of early origin, to which one successive king after another in later dynasties added statelier and ever statelier antechambers or porches, so that at last the building assumed the gigantic size and noble proportions of Karnak and Luxor. This access of importance to the temple cannot have failed to add correspondingly to the dignity of the god; so that, as time went on, instead of the early kings being forgotten and no longer worshipped, they assumed ever greater and greater importance from the magnificence of the works in which their memory was enshrined. To the very end, the god depends largely on his house for impressiveness. How much did not Hellenic religion itself owe to the Parthenon and the temple of Olympian Zeus! How much does not Christianity itself owe to Lincoln and Durham, to Amiens and Chartres, to Milan and Pisa, to St. Mark's and St. Peter's! Men cannot believe that the deities worshipped in such noble and dimly religious shrines were once human like themselves, compact of the same bodies, parts, and passions. Yet in the last instance at least we know the great works to be raised in honour of a single Lower Syrian peasant.

With this brief and imperfect notice of the origin of temples, which will indirectly be expanded in later portions of my work, I pass on from the consideration of the sacred building itself to that of the Idol who usually dwells within it.

Where burial prevails, and where arts are at a low stage of development, the memory of the dead is not likely to survive beyond two or three generations. But where mummification is the rule, there is no reason why deceased persons should not be preserved and worshipped for an indefinite period; and we know that in Egypt at least the cult of kings who died in the most remote times of the Early Empire was carried on regularly down to the days of the Ptolemies. In such a case as this, there is absolutely no need for idols to arise; the corpse itself is the chief object of worship. We do find accordingly that both in Egypt and in Peru the worship of the mummy played a large part in the local religions; though sometimes it alternated with the worship of other holy objects, such as the image or the sacred stone, which we shall see hereafter to have had a like origin. But in many other countries, where bodies were less visibly and obviously preserved, the worship due to the ghost or god was often paid to a simulacrum or idol; so much so that "idolatry" has become in Christian parlance the common term for most forms of worship other than monotheistic.

Now what is the origin and meaning of Idols, and how can they be affiliated upon primitive corpse or ghost worship?

Like the temple, the Idol, I believe, has many separate origins, several of which have been noted by Mr. Herbert

Spencer, while others, it seems to me, have escaped the notice even of that profound and acute observer.

The earliest Idols, if I may be allowed the contradictory expression, are not idols at all—not images or representations of the dead person, but actual bodies, preserved and mummified. These pass readily, however, into various types of representative figures. For in the first place the mummy itself is usually wrapped round in swathing-cloths which obscure its features ; and in the second place it is frequently enclosed in a wooden mummy-case, which is itself most often rudely human in form, and which has undoubtedly given rise to certain forms of idols. Thus, the images of Amun, Khem, Osiris, and Ptah among Egyptian gods are frequently or habitually those of a mummy in a mummy-case. But furthermore, the mummy itself is seldom or never the entire man ; the intestines at least have been removed, or even, as in New Guinea, the entire mass of flesh, leaving only the skin and the skeleton. The eyes, again, are often replaced, as in Peru, by some other imitative object, so as to keep up the lifelike appearance. Cases like these lead on to others, where the image or idol gradually supersedes altogether the corpse or mummy.

Mr. H. O. Forbes gives an interesting instance of such a transitional stage in Timor-laut. "The bodies of those who die in war or by a violent death are buried," he says ; "and if the head has been captured [by the enemy], a cocoanut is placed in the grave to represent the missing member, and to deceive and satisfy his spirit." There is abundant evidence that such makeshift limbs or bodies amply suffice for the use of the soul, when the actual corpse has been destroyed or mutilated. Sometimes, indeed, the substitution of parts is deliberate and intentional. Landa says of the Yucatanese that they cut off the heads of the ancient lords of Cocom when they died, and cleared them from flesh by cooking them (very probably to eat at a sacrificial feast, of which more hereafter) ; then they sawed off the top of the skull, filled in the rest of the head with cement, and, making the face as like as possible to the original possessor, kept these images along with the statues and the ashes. Note here the usual preservation of the head as exceptionally sacred. In other cases, they made for their fathers wooden statues, put in the ashes of the burnt body, and attached the skin of the occiput taken off the corpse. These images, half mummy, half idol, were kept in the oratories of their houses, and were greatly reverenced and assiduously cared for. On all the festivals, food and drink were offered to them.

Mr. Spencer has collected other interesting instances of this transitional stage between the corpse or mummy and the mere idol. The Mexicans, who were cremationists, used to burn a dead lord, and collect the ashes ; "and after kneading them with human blood, they made of them an image of the deceased, which was kept in memory of him." Sometimes, as in Yucatan, the ashes were placed in a man-shaped receptacle of clay, and temples or oratories were erected over them. "In yet other cases," says Mr. Spencer, "there is worship of the relics, joined with the representative figure, not by inclusion, but only by proximity." Thus Gomara tells us that the Mexicans having burnt the body of their deceased king, gathered up the ashes, bones, jewels, and gold in cloths, and made a figure dressed as a man, before which, as well as before the relics, offerings were placed. It is clear that cremation specially lends itself to such substitution of an image for the actual dead body. Among burying races it is the severed skull, on the contrary, that is oftenest preserved and worshipped.

The transition from such images to small stone sarcophagi, like those of the Etruscan tombs, is by no means a great one. These sarcophagi contained the burnt ashes of the dead, but were covered by a lid which usually represented the deceased, reclining, as if at a banquet, with a beaker in his hands. The tombs in which the sarcophagi were placed were of two types ; one, the stone pyramid or cone, which, says Dr. Isaac Taylor, "is manifestly a survival of the tumulus"; the other, the rock-cut chamber, "which is a survival of the cave." These lordly graves are no mere cheerless sepulchres; they are abodes for the dead, constructed on the model of the homes of the living. They contain furniture and pottery; and their walls are decorated with costly mural paintings. They are also usually provided with an antechamber, where the family could assemble at the annual feast to do homage to the spirits of departed ancestors, who shared in the meal from their sculptured sarcophagus lids.

At a further stage of distance from the primitive mummy-idol we come upon the image pure and simple. The Mexicans, for example, as we have seen, were cremationists; and when men killed in battle were missing, they made wooden figures of them, which they honoured, and then burnt them in place of the bodies. In somewhat the same spirit the Egyptians used to place beside the mummy itself an image of the dead, to act as a refuge or receptacle for the soul, "in case of the accidental destruction of the actual body." So the Mexicans once more, if one of their merchants died on a journey, were accustomed to make a statue of wood in the shape of the deceased, to which they paid all the honours they would have done to his actual corpse before burning it. In Africa, while a king of Congo is being embalmed, a figure is set up in the palace to represent him, and is daily furnished with food and drink. Mr. Spencer has collected several similar instances of idols substituted for the bodies of the dead. The Roman *imagines* wore masks of wax, which preserved in like manner the features of ancestors. Perhaps the most curious modern survival of this custom of double representations is to be found in the effigies of our kings and queens still preserved in Westminster Abbey.

There are two other sources of idol-worship, however, which, as it seems to me, have hardly received sufficient attention at Mr. Spencer's hands. Those two are the stake which marks the grave, and the standing stone or tombstone. By far the larger number of idols, I venture to believe, are descended from one or other of these two originals, both of which I shall examine hereafter in far greater detail. There is indeed no greater lacuna, I fancy, in Mr. Spencer's monumental work than that produced by the insufficient consideration of these two fruitful sources of worshipful objects. I shall therefore devote a considerable space to their consideration in subsequent chapters; for the present it will suffice to remark that the wooden stake seems often to form the origin or point of departure for the carved wooden image, as well as for such ruder objects of reverence as the cones and wooden pillars so widely reverenced among the Semitic tribes; while the rough boulder, standing stone, or tombstone seems to form the origin or point of departure for the stone or marble statue, the commonest type of idol the whole world over in all advanced and cultivated communities. Such stones were at first mere rude blocks or unhewn masses, the descendants of those which were rolled over the grave in primitive times in order to keep down the corpse of the dead man, and prevent him from returning to disturb the living. But in time they grew to be roughly dressed into slabs or squares, and finally to be decorated with a rude representation of a human head and shoulders. From this stage they readily progressed to that of the Greek Hermæ. We now know that this was the early shape of most Hellenic gods and goddesses; and we can trace their evolution onward from this point to the wholly anthropomorphic Aphrodite or Here. The well-known figure of the Ephesian Artemis is an intermediate case which will occur at once to every classical reader. Starting from such shapeless beginnings, we progress at last to the artistic and splendid bronze and marble statues of Hellas, Etruria, and Rome, to the many-handed deities of modern India, and to the sculptured Madonnas and Pietàs of Renaissance Italy.

Naturally, as the gods grow more beautiful and more artistically finished in workmanship, the popular idea of their power and dignity must increase *pari passu*. In Egypt, this increase took chiefly the form of colossal size and fine manipulation of hard granitic materials. The so-called Memnon and the Sphinx are familiar instances of the first; the Pashts of Syenite, the black basalt gods, so well known at the Louvre and the British Museum, are examples of the second. In Greece, effect was sought rather by ideal beauty, as in the Aphrodites and Apollos, or by costliness of material, as in the chryselephantine Zeus and the Athene of the Parthenon. But we must always remember that in Hellas itself these glorious gods were developed in a comparatively short space of time from the shapeless blocks or standing stones of the ruder religion; indeed, we have still many curious intermediate forms between the extremely grotesque and hardly human Mycenæan types, and the exquisite imaginings of Myron or Phidias. The earliest Hellenic idols engraved by Messrs. Perrot and Chipiez in their great work on *Art in Primitive Greece* do not rise in any respect superior to the Polynesian level; while the so-called Apollos of later archaic workmanship, rigidly erect with their arms at their sides, recall in many respects the straight up-and-down outline of the standing stone from which they are developed.

I should add that in an immense number of instances the rude stone image or idol, and at a still lower grade the unwrought sacred stone, stands as the central object under a shed or shelter, which develops by degrees into the stately temple. The advance in both is generally more or less parallel; though sometimes, as in historical Greece, a temple of the noblest architecture encloses as its central and principal object of veneration the rough unhewn stone of early barbaric worship. So even in Christendom, great churches and cathedrals often hold as their most precious possession some rude and antique image like the sacred Bambino of Santa Maria in Ara Cœli at Rome, or the "Black Madonnas" which are revered by the people at so many famous Italian places of pilgrimage.

Nor do I mean to say that every Idol is necessarily itself a funereal relic. When once the idea of godship has been thoroughly developed, and when men have grown accustomed to regard an image or idol as the representative or dwelling-place of their god, it is easy to multiply such images indefinitely. Hundreds of representations may exist of the self-same Apollo or Aphrodite or Madonna or St. Sebastian. At the same time, it is quite clear that for most worshippers, the divine being is more or less actually confused with the image; a particular Artemis or a particular Notre Dame is thought of as more powerful or more friendly than another. I have known women in Southern Europe go to pray at the shrine of a distant Madonna, "because she is greater than our own Madonna." Moreover, it is probable that in many cases images or sacred stones once funereal in origin, and representing particular gods or ghosts, have been swallowed up at last by other and more powerful deities, so as to lose in the end their primitive distinctness. Thus, there were many Baals and many Ashteroths; probably there were many Apollos, many Artemises, many Aphrodites. It is almost certain that there were many distinct Hermæ. The progress of research tends to make us realise that numberless deities, once considered unique and individual, may be resolved into a whole host of local gods, afterwards identified with some powerful deity on the merest external resemblances of image, name, or attribute. In Egypt at least this process of identification and centralisation was common. Furthermore, we know that each new religion tends to swallow up and assimilate to itself all possible elements of older cults; just as Hebrew Jahwehism tried to adopt the sacred stones of early Semitic heathenism by associating them with episodes in the history of the patriarchs; and just as Christianity has sanctified such stones in its own area by using them sometimes as the base of a cross, or by consecrating them at others with the name of some saint or martyr.

But even more than the evolution of the Temple and the Idol, the evolution of the Priesthood has given dignity, importance, and power to the gods. For the priests are a class whose direct interest it is to make the most of the greatness and majesty of the deities they tend or worship.

Priesthood, again, has probably at least two distinct origins. The one is quasi-royal; the other is quasi-servile.

I begin with the first. We saw that the chief of an African village, as the son and representative of the chief ghosts, who are the tribal gods, has alone the right to approach them directly with offerings. The inferior villager, who desires to ask anything of the gods, asks through the chief, who is a kinsman and friend of the divine spirits, and who therefore naturally understands their ideas and habits. Such chiefs are thus also naturally priests. They are sacred by family; they and their children stand in a special relation to the gods of the tribe, quite different from the relation in which the common people stand; they are of the blood of the deities. This type of relation is common in many countries; the chiefs in such instances are "kings and priests, after the order of Melchizedek."

To put it briefly, in the earliest or domestic form of religion, the gods of each little group or family are its own dead ancestors, and especially (while the historic memory is still but weak) its immediate predecessors. In this stage, the head of the household naturally discharges the functions of priest; it is he who approaches the family ghosts or gods on behalf of his wives, his sons, his dependants. To the last, indeed, the father of each family retains this priestly function as regards the more restricted family rites; he is priest of the worship of the *lares* and *penates;* he offers the family sacrifice to the family gods; he reads family prayers in the Christian household. But as the tribe or nation arises, and chieftainship grows greater, it is the ghosts or ancestors of the chiefly or kingly family who develop most into gods; and the living chief and his kin are their natural representatives. Thus, in most cases, the priestly office comes to be associated with that of king or chief. Indeed, we shall see hereafter in a subsequent chapter that many kings, being the descendants of gods, are gods themselves; and that this union of the kingly and divine characters has much to do with the growth of the dignity of godhead. Here, however, I waive this point for the present; it will suffice for us to note at the present stage of our argument that in a large number of instances the priesthood and the kingship were inherent and hereditary in the self-same families.

"The union of a royal title with priestly duties," says Mr. Frazer in *The Golden Bough*, " was common in ancient Italy and Greece. At Rome and in other Italian cities there was a priest called the Sacrificial King or King of the sacred rites (*Rex Sacrificulus* or *Rex Sacrorum*), and his wife bore the title of Queen of the Sacred Rites. In republican Athens, the second magistrate of the state was called the King, and his wife the Queen; the functions of both were religious. Many other Greek democracies had titular kings, whose duties, so far as they are known, seem to have been priestly. At Rome the tradition was that the Sacrificial King had been appointed after the expulsion of the kings in order to offer the sacrifices which had been previously offered by the kings. In Greece a similar view appears to have prevailed as to the origin of the priestly kings. In itself the view is not improbable, and it is borne out by the example of Sparta, the only purely Greek state which retained the kingly form of government in historical times. For in Sparta all state sacrifices were offered by the kings as descendants of the god. This combination of priestly functions with royal authority is familiar to every one. Asia Minor, for example, was the seat of various great religious capitals, peopled by thousands of

'Sacred slaves,' and ruled by pontiffs who wielded at once temporal and spiritual authority, like the popes of mediæval Rome. Such priest-ridden cities were Zela and Pessinus. Teutonic Kings, again, in the old heathen days seem to have stood in the position and exercised the powers of high priests. The Emperors of China offer public sacrifices, the details of which are regulated by the ritual books. It is needless, however, to multiply examples of what is the rule rather than the exception in the early history of the kingship."

We will return hereafter in another connexion to this ancient relation of kingship with priesthood, which arises naturally from the still more ancient relation of the king to the god.

Where priesthood originates in this particular way, little differentiation is likely to occur between the temporal and the ecclesiastical power. But there is a second and far more potent origin of priesthood, less distinguished in its beginnings, yet more really pregnant of great results in the end. For where the king is a priest, and the descendant of the gods, as in Peru and Egypt, his immediate and human power seems to overshadow and as it were to belittle the power of his divine ancestors. No statue of Osiris, for example, is half so big in size as the colossal figure of Rameses II. which lies broken in huge pieces outside the mortuary temple of the king it commemorates, among the ruins of Thebes. But where a separate and distinct priesthood gets the management of sacred rites entirely into its own hands, we find the authority of the gods often rising superior to that of the kings, who are only their vicegerents: till at last we get Popes dictating to emperors, and powerful monarchs doing humble penance before the costly shrines of murdered archbishops.

The origin of independent or quasi-servile priesthood is to be found in the institution of "temple slaves,"—the attendants told off as we have already seen to do duty at the grave of the chief or dead warrior. Egypt, again affords us, on the domestic side, an admirable example of the origin of such priesthoods. Over the lintel of each of the cave-like tombs at Beni Hassan and Sakkarah is usually placed an inscription setting forth the name and titles of its expected occupant (for each was built during the life-time of its owner), with an invocation praying for him propitious funeral rites, and a good burial-place after a long and happy life. Then follows a pious hope that the spirit may enjoy for all eternity the proper payment of funereal offerings, a list of which is ordinarily appended, together with a statement of the various anniversaries on which they were due. But the point which specially concerns us here is this: Priests or servants were appointed to see that these offerings were duly made; and the tomb was endowed with property for the purpose both of keeping up the offerings in question, and of providing a stipend or living-wage for the priest. As we shall see hereafter, such priesthoods were generally made hereditary, so as to ensure their continuance throughout all time: and so successful were they that in many cases worship continued to be performed for several hundred years at the tomb; so that a person who died under the Early Empire was still being made the recipient of funeral dues under kings of the Eighteenth and Nineteenth Dynasties.

I give this interesting historical instance at some length because it is one of the best known, and also one of the most persistent. But everywhere, all the world over, similar evolutions have occurred on a shorter scale. The temple attendants, endowed for the purpose of performing sacred rites for the ghost or god, have grown into priests, who knew the habits of the unseen denizen of the shrine. Bit by bit, prescriptions have arisen; customs and rituals have developed; and the priests have become the depositaries of the divine traditions. They alone know how to approach the god; they alone can read the hidden signs of his pleasure or displeasure. As intermediaries between worshipper and deity, they are themselves half sacred. Without them, no votary can rightly approach the shrine of his patron. Thus at last they rise into importance far above their origin; priestcraft comes into being; and by magnifying their god, the members of the hierarchy magnify at the same time their own office and function.

Yet another contributing cause must be briefly noted. Picture-writing and hieroglyphics take their rise more especially in connexion with tombs and temples. The priests in particular hold as a rule the key to this knowledge. In ancient Egypt, to take a well-known instance, they were the learned class; they became the learned class again under other circumstances in mediæval Europe. Everywhere we come upon sacred mysteries that the priests alone know; and where hieroglyphics exist, these mysteries, committed to writing, become the peculiar property of the priests in a more special sense. Where writing is further differentiated into hieratic and demotic, the gulf between laity and priesthood grows still wider; the priests possess a special key to knowledge, denied to the commonalty. The recognition of Sacred Books has often the same result; of these, the priests are naturally the guardians and exponents. I need hardly add that side by side with the increase of architectural grandeur in the temple, and the increase of artistic beauty and costliness in the idols or statues and pictures of the gods, goes increase in the stateliness of the priestly robes, the priestly surroundings, the priestly ritual. Finally, we get ceremonies of the most dignified character, adorned with all the accessories of painting and sculpture, of candles and flowers, of incense and music, of rich mitres and jewelled palls,—ceremonies performed in the dim shade of lofty temples, or mosques, or churches, in honour of god or gods of infinite might, power, and majesty, who must yet in the last resort be traced back to some historic or prehistoric Dead Man, or at least to some sacred stone or stake or image, his relic and representative.

Thus, by convergence of all these streams, the primitive mummy or ghost or spirit passes gradually into a deity of unbounded glory and greatness and sanctity. The bodiless soul, released from necessary limits of space and time, envisaged as a god, is pictured as ever more and more superhuman, till all memory of its origin is entirely forgotten. But to the last, observe this curious point: all new gods or saints or divine persons are, each as they crop up first, of demonstrably human origin. Whenever we find a new god added from known sources to a familiar pantheon, we find without exception that he turns out to be—a human being. Whenever we go back to very primitive religions, we find all men's gods are the corpses or ghosts of their ancestors. It is only when we take relatively advanced races with unknown early histories that we find them worshipping a certain number of gods who cannot be easily and immediately resolved into dead men or spirits. Unfortunately, students of religion have oftenest paid the closest attention to those historical religions which lie furthest away from the primitive type, and in which at their first appearance before us we come upon the complex idea of godhead already fully developed. Hence they are too much inclined, like Professor Robertson Smith, and even sometimes Mr. Frazer (whose name, however, I cannot mention in passing without the profoundest respect), to regard the idea of a godship as primordial, not derivative ; and to neglect the obvious derivation of godhead as a whole from the cult and reverence of the deified ancestor. Yet the moment we get away from these advanced and too overlaid historical religions to the early conceptions of simple savages, we see at once that no gods exist for them save the ancestral corpses or ghosts; that religion means the performance of certain rites and offerings to these corpses or ghosts ; and that higher elemental or departmental deities are wholly wanting. Even in the great historical religions themselves, the further back we go, and the lower down we probe, the closer do we come to the foundation-stratum of ghosts or ancestor-gods. And where, as in Egypt, the evidence is oldest and most complete throughout, the more do we observe how the mystic nature-gods of the later priestly conceptions yield, as we go back age by age in time, to the simpler and more purely human ancestral gods of the earliest documents.

It will be our task in the succeeding chapters of this work to do even more than this—to show that the apparently unresolvable element in later religions, including the Hebrew god Jahweh himself, can be similarly affiliated by no uncertain evidence upon the primitive conception of a ghost or ancestor.

CHAPTER V.

SACRED STONES.

I MENTIONED in the last chapter two origins of Idols to which, as I believed, an insufficient amount of attention had been directed by Mr. Herbert Spencer. These were the Sacred Stone and the Wooden Stake which mark the grave. To these two I will now add a third common object of worship, which does not indeed enter into the genesis of idols, but which is of very high importance in early religion—the sacred tree, with its collective form, the sacred grove. All the objects thus enumerated demand further attention at our hands, both from their general significance in the history of religion, and also from their special interest in connexion with the evolution of the God of Israel, who became in due time the God of Christianity and of Islam, as well as the God of modern idealised and sublimated theism.

I will begin with the consideration of the Sacred Stone, not only because it is by far the most important of the three, but also because, as we shall shortly see, it stands in the direct line of parentage of the God of Israel.

All the world over, and at all periods of history, we find among the most common objects of human worship certain blocks of stone, either rudely shaped and dressed by the hand, or else more often standing alone on the soil in all their native and natural roughness. The downs of England are everywhere studded with cromlechs, dolmens, and other antique megalithic structures (of which the gigantic trilithons of Stonehenge and Avebury are the best-known examples), long described by antiquaries as "druidical remains," and certainly regarded by the ancient inhabitants of Britain with an immense amount of respect and reverence. In France we have the endless avenues of Carnac and Locmariaker; in Sardinia, the curious conical shafts known to the local peasants as *sepolture dei giganti*— the tombs of the giants. In Syria, Major Conder has described similar monuments in Heth and Moab, at Gilboa and at Heshbon. In India, five stones are set up at the corner of a field, painted red, and worshipped by the natives as the Five Pandavas. Theophrastus tells us as one of the characteristics of the superstitious man that he anoints with oil the sacred stones at the street corners; and from an ancient tradition embedded in the Hebrew scriptures we learn how the patriarch Jacob set up a stone at Bethel "for a pillar," and "poured oil upon the top of it," as a like act of worship. Even in our own day there is a certain English hundred where the old open-air court of the manor is inaugurated by the ceremony of breaking a bottle of wine over a standing stone which tops a tumulus; and the sovereigns of the United Kingdom are still crowned in a chair which encloses under its seat the ancestral sacred stone of their heathen Scottish and Irish predecessors.

Now, what is the share of such sacred stones in the rise and growth of the religious habit?

It is hardly necessary, I suppose, to give formal proof of the familiar fact that an upright slab is one of the commonest modes of marking the place where a person is buried. From the ancient pillar that prehistoric savages set up over the tumulus of their dead chief, to the headstone that marks the dwarfed and stunted barrow in our own English cemeteries, the practice of mankind has been one and continuous. Sometimes the stone is a rough boulder from the fields; a representative of the big block which savages place on the grave to keep the corpse from rising: sometimes it is an oblong slab of slate or marble; sometimes, and especially among the more advanced races, it is a shapely cross or sculptured monument. But wherever on earth interment is practised, there stones of some sort, solitary or in heaps, almost invariably mark the place of burial.

Again, as presents and sacrifices are offered at graves to the spirits of the dead, it is at the stone which records the last resting-place of the deceased that they will oftenest be presented. As a matter of fact we know that, all the world over, offerings of wine, oil, rice, ghee, corn, and meat are continually made at the graves of chiefs or relations. Victims, both human and otherwise, are sacrificed at the tomb, and their blood is constantly smeared on the headstone or boulder that marks the spot. Indeed, after a time, the grave and the stone get to be confounded together, and the place itself comes to have a certain sacredness, derived from the ghost which haunts and inhabits it.

Four well-marked varieties of early tombstone are recognised in the eastern continent at least, and their distribution and nature is thus described by Major Conder:

"Rude stone monuments, bearing a strong family resemblance in their mode of construction and dimensions, have been found distributed over all parts of Europe and Western Asia, and occur also in India. In some cases they are attributable to early Aryan tribes; in others they seem to be of Semitic origin. They include *menhirs*, or standing stones, which were erected as memorials, and worshipped as deities, with libations of blood, milk, honey, or water poured upon the stones: *dolmens*, or stone tables, free standing—that is, not covered by any mound or superstructure, which may be considered without doubt to have been used as altars on which victims (often human) were immolated: *cairns*, also memorial, and sometimes surrounding menhirs; these were made by the contributions of numerous visitors or pilgrims, each adding a stone as witness of his presence: finally *cromlechs*, or stone circles, used as sacred enclosures or early hypæthral temples, often with a central menhir or dolmen as statue or altar."

There can be very little doubt that every one of these monuments is essentially sepulchral in character. The menhir or standing stone is the ordinary gravestone still in use among us: the dolmen is a chambered tomb, once covered by a tumulus, but now bare and open: the cairn is a heap of stones piled above the dead body: the stone circle is apparently a later temple built around a tomb, whose position is marked by the menhir or altar-stone in its centre. And each has been the parent of a numerous offspring. The menhir gives rise to the obelisk, the stone cross, and the statue or idol; the dolmen, to the sarcophagus, the altar-tomb, and the high altar; the cairn, to the tope and also to the pyramid; the cromlech, or stone circle, to the temple or church in one at least of its many developments.

Each of these classes of monuments, Major Conder observes, has its distinctive name in the Semitic languages, and is frequently mentioned in the early Hebrew literature. The *menhir* is the "pillar" of our Authorised Version of the Old Testament; the *dolmen* is the "altar"; the *cairn* is the "heap"; and the stone circle appears under the names Gilgal and Hazor. The significance of these facts will appear a little later on when I reach a more advanced stage in the evolution of stone-worship.

In the simplest and most primitive stage of religion, such as that pure ancestor-cult still surviving unmixed among the people of New Guinea or the African tribes whose practice Mr. Duff Macdonald has so admirably described for us, it is the corpse or ghost itself, not the stone to mark its dwelling, which comes in for all the veneration and all the gifts of the reverent survivors. But we must remember that every existing religion, however primitive in type, is now very ancient; and it is quite natural that in many cases the stone should thus come itself to be regarded as the ghost or god, the object to which veneration is paid by the tribesmen. In fact, just in proportion as the ghost evolves into the god, so does the tombstone begin to evolve into the fetish or idol.

At first, however, it is merely as the rude unshapen stone that the idol in this shape receives the worship of its votaries. This is the stage that has been christened by that very misleading name fetishism, and erroneously supposed to lie at the very basis of all religion. Here are a few interesting samples of this stage of stone-worship, taken from the very careful Samoan collection of Mr. Turner, of the London Missionary Society:

" Fonge and Toafa were the names of the two oblong smooth stones which stood on a raised platform of loose stones inland of one of the villages. They were supposed to be the parents of Saato, a god who controlled the rain. When the chiefs and people were ready to go off for weeks to certain places in the bush for the sport of pigeon-catching, offerings of cooked taro and fish were laid on the stones, accompanied by prayers for fine weather and no rain. Any one who refused an offering to the stones was frowned upon ; and in the event of rain was blamed and punished for bringing down the wrath of the fine-weather god, and spoiling the sports of the season."

Here, even if one doubts that Saato was a deceased weather-doctor, and that Fonge and Toafa were his father and mother (which I do not care to insist upon), it is at least clear that we have to deal essentially with two standing stones of precisely the same sort as those which habitually mark sepulture.

Of the gods of Hudson's Island, Mr. Turner gives this very interesting and suggestive account:

" Foelangi and Maumau were the principal gods. They had each a temple; and under the altars, on which were laid out in rows the skulls of departed chiefs and people, were suspended offerings of pearl-shell and other valuables. Foelangi had an unchiselled block of stone to represent him—something like a six feet high gravestone. . . . Offerings of food were taken to the temples, that the gods might first partake before anyone else ate anything. . . . Husked cocoanuts were laid down, one before each skull."

And of St. Augustine Island he writes: "At the Temple of Maumau there stood a nine feet high coral sandstone slab from the beach. . . . Meat offerings were laid on the altars, accompanied by songs and dances in honour of the god."

Similarly, about one of the Gilbert Group, Mr. Turner says:

"They had other gods and goddesses, and, as was common in this group, had sandstone slabs or pillars set up here and there among the houses. Before these shrines offerings of food were laid during the day, which the priests took away stealthily by night and made the credulous believe that gods and not mortals had done it. If the stone slab represented a *goddess* it was not placed erect, but laid down on the ground. Being *a lady* they thought it would be cruel to make her stand so long."

In these cases, and in many others, it seems to me clear that the original gravestone or menhir itself is the object of worship, viewed as the residence of the ghost or god in whose honour it was erected. For in Samoa we know that the grave "was marked by a little heap of stones, a foot or two high," and at De Peyster's Island "a stone was raised at the head of the grave, and a human head carved on it"—a first step, as we have already seen, towards the evolution of one form of idol.

Similar instances abound everywhere. Among the Khonds of India, every village has its local god, represented by an upright stone under the big tree on the green, to use frankly an English equivalent. (The full importance of this common combination of sacred stone and sacred tree will only come out at a later stage of our enquiry.) In Peru, worship was paid to standing stones which, says Dr. Tylor, "represented the penates of households and the patron-deities of villages "—in other words, the ghosts of ancestors and of tribal chiefs. "Near Acora," says the Marquis de Nadaillac, "the bodies were placed under megalithic stones, reminding us of the dolmens and cromlechs of Europe. One vast plain is covered with erect stones, some forming circles, some squares, and often covered in with large slabs which entirely closed round the sepulchral chamber." In Fiji the gods and goddesses "had their abodes or shrines in black stones like smooth round milestones, and there received their offerings of food." An immense number of similar instances have been collected by Dr. Tylor and other anthropologists.

But when once the idea of the sacredness of stones had thus got firmly fixed in the savage mind, it was natural enough that other stones, resembling those which were already recognised as gods, should come to be regarded as themselves divine, or as containing an indwelling ghost or deity. Of this stage, Mr. Turner's *Samoa* again affords us some curious instances.

"Smooth stones apparently picked up out of the bed of the river were regarded as representatives of certain gods, and wherever the stone was, there the god was supposed to be. One resembling a fish would be prayed to as the fisherman's god. Another, resembling a yam, would be the yam god. A third, round like a breadfruit, the breadfruit god—and so on."

Now, the word "apparently" used by this very cautious observer in this passage shows clearly that he had never of his own knowledge seen a stone thus selected at random worshipped or deified, and it is therefore possible that in all such cases the stone may really have been one of sepulchral origin. Still, I agree with Mr. Spencer that when once the idea of a ghost or god is well developed, the notion of such a spirit as animating any remarkable or odd-looking object is a natural transition.* Hence I in-

* The whole subject is admirably worked out in *The Principles of Sociology*, § 159.

cline to believe Mr. Turner is right, and that these stones may really have been picked out and worshipped, merely for their oddity, but always, as he correctly infers, from the belief in their connexion with some god or spirit.

Here is another case, also from Polynesia, where no immediate connexion with any particular grave seems definitely implied:

"Two unchiselled 'smooth stones of the stream' were kept in a temple at one of the villages, and guarded with great care. No stranger or over-curious person was allowed to go near the place, under penalty of a beating from the custodians of these gods. They represented good and not malicious death-causing gods. The one made the yams, breadfruit, and cocoanuts, and the other sent fish to the nets.

"Another stone was carefully housed in another village as the representative of a rain-making god. When there was overmuch rain, the stone was laid by the fire and kept heated till fine weather set in."

Further instances (if fairly reported) occur elsewhere. "Among the lower races of America," says Dr. Tylor, summarising Schoolcraft, "the Dakotahs would pick up a round boulder, paint it, and then, addressing it as grandfather, make offerings to it, and pray it to deliver them from danger." But here the very fact that the stone is worshipped and treated as an ancestor shows how derivative is the deification—how dependent upon the prior association of such stones with the tomb of a forefather and its indwelling spirit. Just in the same way we know there are countries where a grave is more generally marked, not by a stone, but by a wooden stake; and in these countries, as for instance among the Samoyedes of Siberia, sticks, not stones, are the most common objects of reverence. (Thus, again, stick-worship is found "among the Damaras of South Africa, whose ancestors are represented at the sacrificial feasts by stakes cut from trees or bushes consecrated to them, to which stakes the meat is first offered.") But here, too, we see the clear affiliation upon ancestor-worship; and indeed, wherever we find the common worship of "stocks and stones," all the analogies lead us to believe the stocks and stones either actually mark the graves of ancestors or else are accepted as their representatives and embodiments.

The vast majority, however, of sacred stones with whose history we are well acquainted are indubitably connected with interments, ancient or modern. All the European sacred stones are cromlechs, dolmens, trilithons, or menhirs, of which Mr. Angus Smith, a most cautious authority, observes categorically, "We know for a certainty that memorials of burials are the chief object of the first one, and of nearly all, the only object apparently." So many other examples will come out incidentally in the course of the sequel that I will not labour the point any further at present. Among the most remarkable instances, however, I cannot refrain from mentioning the great Sardinian sacred stones, which so often occur in the neighbourhood of the *nuraghi*, or ancient forts. These consist of tall conical monoliths, rough and unhewn in the oldest examples, rudely hewn in the later ones, and occasionally presenting some distant resemblance to a human face—the first rough draft of the future idol. "Behind the monolith lies the burial-place, ten to fourteen yards long by one or two in width." These burial-places have been examined by the Abbate Spano.

"He was satisfied that several bodies had been buried together in the same tomb, and that these were therefore family burial-places. When the death of one of the members of the tribe occurred, one of the great transverse stones which covered the long alley built behind the monolith was removed, and then replaced until the time came for another body to claim its place in the tomb. The monolith, called by the Sardinian peasants *pietra dell' altare*, or altar-stone, because they believe it to have been used for human sacrifice, always faces the south or east."

Such a surviving tradition as to the human sacrifices, in an island so little sophisticated as Sardinia, has almost certainly come down to us unbroken from a very early age.

I have already stated that the idol is probably in many cases derived from the gravestone or other sacred stone. I believe that in an immense number of cases it is simply the original pillar, more or less rudely carved into the semblance of a human figure.

How this comes about we can readily understand if we recollect that by a gradual transference of sentiment the stone itself is at last identified with the associated spirit. Here, once more, is a transitional instance from our Polynesian storehouse.

The great god of Bowditch Island "was supposed to be embodied in a stone, which was carefully wrapped up with fine mats, and never seen by any one but the king" (note this characteristic touch of kingly priesthood), "and that only once a year, when the decayed mats were stripped off and thrown away. In sickness, offerings of fine mats were taken and rolled round the sacred stone, and thus it got busked up to a prodigious size; but as the idol was exposed to the weather out of doors, night and day, the mats soon rotted. No one dared to appropriate what had been offered to the god, and hence the old mats, as they were taken off, were heaped in a place by themselves and allowed to rot."

Now the reasonableness of all this is immediately apparent if we remember that the stones which stand on graves are habitually worshipped, and anointed with oil, milk, and blood. It is but a slight further step to regard the stone, not only as eating and drinking, but also as needing warmth and clothing. As an admirable example of the same train of thought, working out the same result elsewhere, compare this curious account of a stone idol at Inniskea (a rocky islet off the Mayo coast), given by the Earl of Roden, as late as 1851, in his *Progress of the Reformation in Ireland:*

"In the south island, in the house of a man named Monigan, a stone idol, called in the Irish 'Neevougi,' has been from time immemorial religiously preserved and worshipped. This god resembles in appearance a thick roll of home-spun flannel, which arises from the custom of dedicating a dress of that material to it whenever its aid is sought; this is sewn on by an old woman, its priestess, whose peculiar care it is. Of the early history of this idol no authentic information can be procured, but its power is believed to be immense; they pray to it in time of sickness; it is invoked when a storm is desired to dash some hapless ship upon their coast; and, again, the exercise of its power is solicited in calming the angry waves, to admit of fishing or visiting the mainland."

Nor is this a solitary instance in modern Europe. "In certain mountain districts of Norway," says Dr. Tylor, "up to the end of the last century, the peasants used to preserve round stones, washed them every Thursday evening, ... smeared them with butter before the fire, laid them in the seat of honour on fresh straw, and at certain times of the year steeped them in ale, that they might bring luck and comfort to the house."

The first transitional step towards the idol proper is given in some rude attempt to make the standing stone at the grave roughly resemble a human figure. In the later Sardinian examples, two conical lumps, representing the breasts, seem to mark that the figure is intended to be female—either because a woman is buried there, or to place the spot under the protection of a goddess. From this rude beginning we get every transitional form, like the Hermæ and the archaic Apollos, till we arrive at the perfect freedom and beauty of Hellenic sculpture. Says Grote, in speaking of Greek worship, "their primitive memorial erected to a god did not even pretend to be an image, but was often nothing more than a pillar, a board, a shapeless stone, or a post [notice the resemblance to ordinary grave-marks] receiving care and decoration from the neighbourhood as well as worship." Dr. Tylor, to whose great collection of instances I owe many acknowledgments, says in comment on this passage, "Such were the log that stood for Artemis in Eubœa; the stake that represented Pallas Athene 'sine effigie rudis palus, et informe lignum;' the unwrought stone (λίθος ἀργὸς) at Hyethos, which 'after the ancient manner' represented Heracles; the thirty such stones which the Pharæans in like fashion worshipped for the gods; and that one which received such honour in Bœotian festivals as representing the Thespian Eros." Such also was the conical pillar of Asiatic type which stood instead of an image of the Paphian Aphrodite, and the conical stone worshipped in Attica under the name of Apollo. A sacred boulder lay in front of the temple of the Trœzenians, while another in Argos bore the significant name of Zeus Kappotas. "Among all the Greeks," says Pausanias, "rude stones were worshipped before the images of the gods." Among the Semites, in like manner, Melcarth was reverenced at Tyre under the form of two stone pillars.

Intermediate forms, in which the stone takes successively a face, a head, arms, legs, a shapely and well-moulded body, are familiar to all of us in existing remains. The well-known figures of Priapus form a good transitional example. "At Tàbala, in Arabia," says Professor Robertson Smith, "a sort of crown was sculptured on the stone of al-Lat to mark her head." Indeed, to the last, the pillar or monolithic type is constantly suggested in the erect attitude and the proportions of the statue among all except the highest Hellenic examples. I may add, that even in Islam itself, which so sternly forbids images of any sort, some traces of such anthropomorphic gravestones may still be found. I noticed in the mosque of Mehemet Ali at Cairo that the headstones of the Vice-regal family were each adorned with a fez and tassel.

It is worth noting that the obelisk, also, doubtless owes its origin to the monolith or standing stone. Whatever fresh sacredness it may later have obtained from the associations of sun-worship, as a solar ray, cannot mask for any wide anthropological enquirer the fact that it is by descent a mere shapeless head-stone, with a new symbolic meaning given to it (as so often happens) in a new religion. The two obelisks which stand so often before Egyptian temples are clearly the analogues of the two pillars of Melcarth at Tyre, and the sacred pair at Paphos, Herapolis, and Solomon's temple. In the same way, the Indian tope and the pyramid are descendants of the cairn, as the great stone-built tombs of the Numidian kings in Algeria seem to be more advanced equivalents of the tumulus or round barrow. And let me clear the ground here for what is to follow by adding most emphatically that the genesis of stone-worship here sketched out precludes the possibility of phallic worship being in any sense a primitive form of it. The standing stone may have been, and doubtless often was, in later stages, identified with a phallus ; but if the theory here advocated is true, the lingam, instead of lying at the root of the monolith, must necessarily be a later and derivative form of it. At the same time, the stone being regarded as the ancestor of the family, it is not unnatural that early men should sometimes carve it into a phallic shape. Having said this, I will say no more on the subject, which has really extremely little to do with the essentials of stone worship, save that on many gravestones of early date a phallus marked the male sex of the occupant, while breasts, or a symbolical triangle, or a mandorla, marked the grave of a woman.

Sometimes, both forms of god, the most primitive and the most finished, the rude stone and the perfect statue, exist side by side in the same community.

"In the legendary origin of Jagannáth," says Sir William Hunter, "we find the aboriginal people worshipping a blue stone in the depths of the forest. But the deity at length wearies of primitive jungle offerings, and longs for the cooked food of the more civilised Aryans, upon whose arrival on the scene the rude blue stone gives place to a carved image. At the present hour, in every hamlet of Orissa, this twofold worship coexists. The common people have their shapeless stone or block, which they adore with simple rites in the open air; while side by side with it stands a temple to one of the Aryan gods, with its carved idol and elaborate rites."

Where many sacred stones exist all round, marking the graves of the dead, or inhabited by their spirits, it is not surprising, once more, that a general feeling of reverence towards all stones should begin to arise—that the stone *per se*, especially if large, odd, or conspicuous, should be credited to some extent with indwelling divinity. Nor is it astonishing that the idea of men being descended from stones should be rife among people who must often, when young, have been shown headstones, monoliths, boulders, or cromlechs, and been told that the offerings made upon them were gifts to their ancestors. They would accept the idea as readily as our own children accept the Hebrew myth of the creation of Adam, our prime ancestor, from "the dust of the ground"—a far less promising material than a block of marble or sandstone. In this way, it seems to me, we can most readily understand the numerous stories of men becoming stones, and stones becoming men, which are rife among the myths of savage or barbarous peoples.

Fernandez de Piedrahita says that the Laches "worshipped every stone as a god, as they said they had all been men." Arriaga tells us the Peruvians paid honour to "very large stones, saying that they were once men." In the American *Report of the Bureau of Ethnology* for 1880, several stories are told of metamorphosis of men into stones from the Iroquois legends. According to Dorman, the Oneidas and Dakotahs claim descent from stones, to which they ascribe animation. An interesting intermediate form, which shows the growth of this idea, is given in Arriaga's statement that the Marcayoc, or idol worshipped in Peru as the patron of the village, " is sometimes a stone and sometimes a mummy ": in other words, it depended upon circumstances whether they reverenced the body itself or the gravestone that covered it. Among the Coast Negroes, when a person dies, a stone is taken to a certain house—the village valhalla—to represent his ghost; and among the Bulloms, women " make occasional sacrifices and offerings of rice to the stones which are preserved in memory of the dead." At Tanna, in the New Hebrides, Mr. Gray, a missionary, found "a piece of sacred ground, on which were deposited the stones in which they supposed the spirits of their departed relatives to reside"; and Commander Henderson, commenting upon a similar case from Vati Island, says these " were the only form of gods the natives possessed, and into them they supposed the souls of their departed friends and relatives to enter." Some of them " had a small piece chipped out on one side, by means of which the indwelling ghost or spirit was supposed to have ingress or egress." Of a third sort, rudely fashioned by hand, Captain Henderson says acutely, " these, it seemed to me, were the beginnings of a graven image—a common stone, sacred as the dwelling-place of an ancestral ghost." *

Classical and Hebrew literature are full of examples of such stones, believed to have been once human. Niobe and Lot's wife are instances that will at once occur to every reader. In Bœotia, Pausanias tells us, people believed Alkmene, the mother of Herakles, was changed into a stone. Perseus and the Gorgon's head is another example, paralleled by the Breton idea that their great stone circles were people, who, in the modern Christianised version of the story, were turned into stone for dancing on a Sunday. (About this Christianisation I shall have a word to say further on; meanwhile, observe the similar name of the Giant's Dance given to the great

* I owe this and several other references to Mr. Spencer's Appendix, as I do some of my previously cited cases to Mr. Lang or Dr. Tylor.

Stonehenge of Ireland.) In the same way there is a Standing Rock on the upper Missouri which parallels the story of Niobe—it was once a woman, who became petrified with grief when her husband took a second wife. Some Samoan gods (or ancestral ghosts) "were changed into stones," says Mr. Turner, "and now stand up in a rocky part of the lagoon on the north side of Upolu."

On the other hand, if men become stones, stones also become men, or at least give birth to men. We get a good instance of this in the legend of Deucalion. Again, by the roadside, near the city of the Panopœans, lay the stones out of which Prometheus made men. Manke, the first man in Mitchell Island, came out of a stone. The inhabitants of the New Hebrides say that "the human race sprang from stones and the earth." On Francis Island, says Mr. Turner, "close by the temple there was a seven-feet-long beach sandstone slab erected, before which offerings were laid as the people united for prayer"; and the natives here told him that one of their gods had made stones become men. "In Melanesia," says Mr. Lang, "matters are so mixed that it is not easy to decide whether a worshipful stone is the dwelling of a dead man's soul, or is of spiritual merit in itself, or whether the stone is the spirit's outward part or organ." And, indeed, a sort of general confusion between the stone, the ghost, the ancestor, and the god, at last pervades the mind of the stone-worshipper everywhere. "The curious anthropomorphic idea of stones being husbands and wives, and even having children," as Dr. Tylor calls it—an idea familiar to the Fijians as to the Peruvians and Lapps—is surely explicable at once by the existence of headstones either to men or women, and the confusion between the mark and the ghost it commemorates.

An interesting side-point in this gradual mixing up of the ghost and the stone, the god and the image, is shown in a gradual change of detail as to the mode of making offerings at the tomb or shrine. On the great trilithon in

Tonga, Miss Gordon-Cumming tells us, a bowl of kava was placed on a horizontal stone. Here it must have been supposed that the ghost itself issued forth (perhaps by night) to drink it, as the serpent which represented the spirit of Anchises glided from the tomb to lick up the offerings presented by Æneas. Gradually, however, as the stone and the ghost get more closely connected in idea the offering is made to the monument itself; though in the earlier stages the convenience of using the flat altar-stone (wherever such exists) as a place of sacrifice for victims probably masks the transition even to the worshippers themselves. Dr. Wise saw in the Himalayas a group of stones "erected to the memory of the petty Rajahs of Kolam," where "some fifty or sixty unfortunate women sacrificed themselves." The blood, in particular, is offered up to the ghost; and "the cup-hollows which have been found in menhirs and dolmens," says Captain Conder, "are the indications of the libations, often of human blood, once poured on these stones by heathen worshippers." "Cups are often found," says a good Scotch observer, "on stones connected with the monuments of the dead, such as on the covering stones of kistvaens, particularly those of the short or rarest form ; on the flat stones of cromlechs; and on stones of chambered graves." On the top of the cairn at Glen Urquhart, on Loch Ness, is an oblong mass of slate-stone, obviously sepulchral, and marked with very numerous cups. When the stones are upright the notion of offering the blood to the upper part, which represents the face or mouth, becomes very natural, and forms a distinct step in the process of anthropomorphisation of the headstone into the idol.

We get two stages of this evolution side by side in the two deities of the Samoyed travelling ark-sledge, "one with a stone head, the other a mere black stone, both dressed in green robes with red lappets, and both smeared with sacrificial blood." In the Indian groups of standing stones, representing the Five Pandavas, "it is a usual practice," says Dr. Tylor, "to daub each stone with red paint, forming, as it were, a great blood-spot where the face would be if it were a shaped idol." Mr. Spencer, I think, hits the key-note of this practice in an instructive passage. "A Dakotah," he says, "before praying to a stone for succour paints it with some red pigment, such as red ochre. Now, when we read that along with offerings of milk, honey, fruit, flour, etc., the Bodo and Dhimáls offer 'red lead or cochineal,' we may suspect that these three colouring matters, having red as their common character, are substitutes for blood. The supposed resident ghost was at first propitiated by anointing the stone with human blood; and then, in default of this, red pigment was used, ghosts and gods being supposed by primitive men to be easily deceived by shams." It is possible, too, that with the process of idealisation and spiritualisation it might be supposed a substitute would please the gods equally well, or that redness generally was the equivalent of blood, in the same way as the Chinese burn paper money and utensils to set free their ghosts for the use of ancestral spirits.

In any case, it is interesting to note that the faces of many Hindu gods are habitually painted red. And that this is the survival of the same ancient custom we see in the case of Shashti, protectress of children, whose proper representative is "a rough stone as big as a man's head, smeared with red paint, and set at the foot of the sacred vata-tree." Like customs survived in Greece down to the classical period. "The faces of the ancient gilded Dionysi at Corinth," says Mr. Lang, quoting Pausanias, "were smudged all over with cinnabar, like fetish-stones in India or Africa." In early South Italy, too, the Priapus-Hermes, who protected the fields, had his face similarly "daubed with minium." Is it possible to dissever these facts from the cannibal banquets of the Aztec gods, where the images had lumps of palpitating human flesh thrust into their lips, and where their faces were smeared with the warm blood of the helpless victims?

Only in one instance, however, have I been able to trace the custom of painting with red directly back to cannibalism, and that is among the man-eaters of the New Hebrides, where, when a man died, and his body was laid out in a piece of thick native cloth, "the face was kept exposed and painted red." I believe with this practice must ultimately be correlated the red-painted faces of the Corinthian Dionysi.

Another point of considerable interest and importance in the evolution of stone worship is connected with the migration of sacred stones. When the Israelites left Egypt, according to the narrative in Exodus, they carried the bones of Joseph with them. When Rachel left her father's tent she stole the family teraphim to accompany her on her wanderings. When Æneas flew from burning Troy, he bore away to his ships his country's gods, his Lares and Penates. All of these tales, no doubt, are equally unhistorical, but they represent what, to the people who framed the legends, seemed perfectly natural and probable conduct. Just in the same way, when stone-worshippers migrate from one country to another, they are likely to carry with them their sacred stones, or at least the most portable or holiest of the number.

Here is a very good illustrative case, once more from that most valuable storehouse, Turner's *Samoa*. The Fijian gods and goddesses we saw, according to Tylor, "had their abodes or shrines in black stones like smooth round millstones, and there received their offerings of food." But on a certain Samoan island, says Mr. Turner, "In a district said to have been early populated by settlers from Fiji, a number of fancy Fijian stones were kept in a temple, and worshipped in time of war. The priest, in consulting them, built them up in the form of a wall, and then watched to see how they fell. If they fell to the westward, it was a sign that the enemy there was to be driven; but if they fell to eastward, that was a warning of defeat, and delay in making an attack was ordered accordingly."

I canot find room here for many detailed instances of similar migrations; but there are two examples in Britain so exceedingly interesting that even in so hasty a notice I cannot pass them by without a brief mention. The inner or smaller stones at Stonehenge are known to be of remote origin, belonging to rocks not found nearer Salisbury Plain than Cumberland in one direction or Belgium in the other. They are surrounded by a group of much larger stones, arranged as trilithons, but carved out of the common sarsen blocks distributed over the neighbouring country. I have tried to show elsewhere that these smaller igneous rocks, untouched by the tool,* were the ancient sacred stones of an immigrant tribe that came into Britain from the Continent, probably over a broad landbelt which then existed where the Straits of Dover now flow; and that the strangers on their arrival in Britain erected these their ancestral gods on the Plain of Amesbury, and further contributed to their importance and appearance by surrounding them with a circle of the biggest and most imposing grey-wethers that the new country in which they had settled could easily afford.

The other case is that of the Scone stone. This sacred block, according to the accredited legend, was originally the ancestral god of the Irish Scots, on whose royal tumulus at Tara it once stood. It was carried by them to Argyllshire on their first invasion, and placed in a cranny of the wall (say modern versions) at Dunstaffnage Castle. When the Scotch kings removed to Scone, Kenneth II. took the stone to his new lowland residence. Thence

---

* So Moses in the legend commanded the children of Israel to build "an altar of whole stones, over which no man hath lift up any iron"; and so of the boulders composing the altar on Mount Ebal it was said, "Thou shalt not lift up any iron tool upon them." The conservatism of religion kept up the archaic fashion for sacred purposes.

Edward I. carried it off to England, where it has ever since remained in Westminster Abbey, as part of the chair in which the sovereigns of Britain sit at their coronation. The immense significance of these facts or tales will be seen more clearly when we come to consider the analogies of the Hebrew ark. Meanwhile, it may help to explain the coronation usage, and the legend that wherever the Stone of Destiny is found " the Scots in place must reign," if I add a couple of analogous cases from the history of the same mixed Celtic race. According to Dr. O'Donovan, the inauguration stone of the O'Donnells stood on a tumulus in the midst of a large plain; and on this sacred stone, called the Flagstone of the Kings, the elected chief stood to receive the white wand or sceptre of kingship. A cylindrical obelisk, used for the same purpose, stands to this day, according to Dr. Petrie, in the Rath-na-Riogh. So, too, M'Donald was crowned King of the Isles, standing on a sacred stone, with an impression on top to receive his feet. He based himself, as it were, upon the gods his ancestors. The Tara stone even cried aloud, Professor Rhys tells us, when the true king placed his feet above it. The coronation stone exists in other countries; for example, in Hebrew history, or half-history, we learn that when Abimelech was mads king it was "by the plain of the pillar that was in Shechem"; and when Jehoash was anointed by Jehoiada, " the king stood by a pillar, as the manner was." In front of the church of Sant' Ambrogio at Milan stands the stone pillar at which the Lombard kings and German emperors took the coronation oath, under the ancient lime-trees which overshadow the piazza.

Now, it is quite true that Mr. Skene, the best authority on Celtic Scotland, rejects this story of the Stone of Destiny in most parts as legendary: he believes the Scone stone to have been merely the sacred coronation-block of the Pictish Kings at Scone, and never to have come from Ireland at all. Professor Ramsay thinks it is a piece of red sandstone broken off the rock of that district of Scotland. Even Professor Rhys (who gives a most interesting account of the Tara Stone) seems to have doubts as to the migration. But, true or not, the story will amply serve my purpose here; for I use it only to illustrate the equally dubious wanderings of a Hebrew sacred stone, at which we will arrive in due time; and one legend is surely always the best possible parallel of another.

In the course of ages, as religions develop, and especially as a few great gods grow to overshadow the minor ancestral Lares and spirits, it often comes about that sacred stones of the older faith have a new religious significance given them in the later system. Thus we have seen the Argives worshipped their old sacred stone under the name of Zeus Kappotas; the Thespians identified theirs with the later Hellenic Eros; and the Megarians considered a third as the representative of Phœbus. The original local sacred stone of Delos has been found on the spot where it originally stood, beneath the feet of the statue of the Delian Apollo. And this, I am glad to see, is Mr. Andrew Lang's view also; for he remarks of the Greek unwrought stones, "They were blocks which bore the names of gods, Hera, or Apollo, names perhaps given, as De Brosses says, to the old fetishistic objects of worship, *after* the anthropomorphic gods entered [I should say, were developed in] Hellas." So, too, in India, the local sacred stones have been identified with the deities of the Hindu pantheon; Mr. Hislop remarks that in every part of the Deccan (where Hinduism is of comparatively late introduction) four or five stones may often be seen in the ryot's field, placed in a row and daubed with red paint, which the peasants call the Five Pandavas; but, says Dr. Tylor, "he reasonably takes these Hindu names to have superseded more ancient appellations." Islam, in like manner, has adopted the Kaaba, the great black stone of the Holy Place at Mecca; and the Egyptian religion gave a new meaning to the pillar or monolith, by shaping it as an obelisk to represent a ray of the rising sun-god.

Sometimes the sanctity of the antique stones was secured in the later faith by connecting them with some legend or episode of the orthodox religion. Thus the ancient sacred stone kept at Delphi—no doubt the original oracle of that great shrine, as the rude Delian block was the precursor of the Delian Apollo—was explained with reference to the later Hellenic belief by the myth that it was the stone which Kronos swallowed in mistake for Zeus: an explanation doubtless due to the fact that this boulder was kept, like Monigan's Irish idol and the Samoan god, wrapped up in flannel; and in the myth, Rhea deceived Kronos by offering him, instead of Zeus, a stone wrapped in swaddling-bands. There is here indeed food for much reflection. The sacred stone of the Trœzenians, in like manner, lay in front of the temple; but it was Hellenised, so to speak, by the story that on it the Trœzenian elders sat when they purified Orestes from the murder of his mother.

In modern Europe, as everybody knows, a similar Christianisation of holy wells, holy stones, and holy places has been managed by connecting them with legends of saints, or by the still simpler device of marking a cross upon them. The cross has a threefold value: in the first place, it drives away from their accustomed haunts the ancient gods or spirits, always envisaged in early Christian and mediæval thought as devils or demons; in the second place, it asserts the supremacy of the new faith; and in the third place, by conferring a fresh sanctity upon the old holy place or object, it induces the people to worship the cross by the mere habit of resorting to the shrine at which their ancestors so long worshipped. Gregory's well-known advice to St. Augustine on this matter is but a single example of what went on over all Christendom. In many cases, crosses in Britain are still found firmly fixed in old sacred stones, usually recognisable by their unwrought condition. The finest example in Europe is probably the gigantic monolith of Plumen in Brittany, topped by an insignificant little cross, and still resorted to by the peasants (especially the childless) as a great place of worship. The prehistoric monuments of Narvia in the Isle of Man have been Christianised by having crosses deeply incised upon them. Other cases, like the Black Stones of Iona, which gave sanctity to that Holy Isle long before the time of Columba, will doubtless occur at once to every reader. With many of the Scotch sculptured stones, it is difficult to decide whether they were originally erected as crosses, or are prehistoric monuments externally Christianised.

I have thus endeavoured briefly to suggest the ultimate derivation of all sacred stones from sepulchral monuments, and to point out the very large part which they bear in the essential of religion—that is to say, worship—everywhere. There is, however, one particular application to which I wish to call special attention, because of its peculiar interest as regards the origin of the monotheistic god of Judaism and Christianity. Hitherto in this chapter, I have intentionally made but very few allusions to the faith and the sacred stones of the Hebrews, because I wished first to give a general view of the whole ramifications and modifications of stone-worship before coming down to the particular instance in which we modern Europeans are most deeply interested. I will now, however, give a brief summary of what seems to me most suggestive and important in the early Semitic stone-cult. These results are no doubt already familiar in outline to most cultivated readers, but it is possible they may appear in a somewhat new light when regarded in connexion with the general history of stone-worship as here elucidatd.

That the Semites, as well as other early nations, were stone-worshippers we know from a great number of positive instances. The stone pillars of Baal and the wooden Ashera cones were the chief objects of adoration in the Phœnician religion. The Stone of Bethel was apparently a menhir: the cairn of Mizpeh was doubtless a sepulchral monument. The Israelites under Joshua, we are told, built a Gilgal of twelve standing stones; and other instances in the early traditions of the Hebrews will be noticed in their proper place later on. Similarly, among the Arabs of the time of Mohammed, two of the chief deities were Manah and Lât, the one a rock, the other a sacred stone or stone idol: and the Kaaba itself, the great black stone of local worship, even the Prophet was compelled to recognise and Islamise by adopting it bodily into his monotheistic religion.

The stone worship of the Semites at large, though comparatively neglected by Professor Robertson Smith, must have played a large part in the religion of that race, from which the Hebrews were a special offshoot. "In Arabia," says Professor Smith, "where sacrifice by fire was almost unknown, we find no proper altar, but in its place a rude pillar or heap of stones, beside which the victim is slain, the blood being poured out over the stone or at its base." To the great orientalist, it is true, the sacred stone or altar, like the sacred tree and the sacred fountain, are nothing more than "common symbols at sanctuaries"; he thinks of them not as gods but merely as representatives of the god, arbitrarily chosen. After the evidence I have already adduced, however, I think it will be seen that this position is altogether untenable; indeed, Dr. Smith himself uses many phrases in this connexion which enables us to see the true state of the case far more clearly than he himself did. "The sacred stones [of the Arabs], which are already mentioned by Herodotus, are called *ansab*, i.e., stones set up, pillars. We also find the name *ghariy*, 'blood-bedaubed,' with reference to the ritual just described [of sacrifice at the *nosb* or sacred pillar]. The meaning of this ritual will occupy us later: meantime the thing to be noted is that the altar is only a modification of the *nosb*, and that the rude Arabian usage is the primitive type out of which all the elaborate altar ceremonies of the more cultivated Semites grew. Whatever else was done in connexion with a sacrifice, the primitive rite of sprinkling or dashing the blood against the altar, or allowing it to flow down on the ground at its base, was hardly ever omitted; and this practice was not peculiar to the Semites, but was equally the rule with the Greeks and Romans, and indeed with the ancient nations generally."

"It is certain," says Professor Smith again, "that the original altar among the Northern Semites, as well as among the Arabs, was a great stone or cairn, at which the blood of the victim was shed." There is no difference, he declares, between the Hebrew altar and the Arabian standing stone. "Monolithic pillars or cairns of stone are frequently mentioned in the more ancient parts of the Old Testament as standing at Sanctuaries, generally in connexion with a sacred legend about the occasion on which they were set up by some famous patriarch or hero. In the biblical story, they usually appear as mere memorial structures without any definite ritual significance; but the pentateuchal law looks on the use of sacred pillars as idolatrous. This is the best evidence that such pillars held an important place among the appurtenances of Canaanite temples; and as Hosea speaks of the pillar as an indispensable feature in the sanctuaries of Northern Israel in his time, we may be sure that by the mass of the Hebrews the pillars of Shechem, Bethel, Gilgal, and other shrines were looked upon, not as mere memorials of historical events, but as necessary parts of the ritual apparatus of a place of worship. . . . From these evidences, and especially from the fact that libations of the same kind are applied to both, it seems clear that the altar is a differentiated form of the primitive rude stone pillar. But the sacred stone is more than an altar, for in Hebrew and Canaanite sanctuaries the altar, in its developed form as a table or hearth, does not supersede the pillar; the two are found side by side at the same sanctuary, the altar as a piece of sacrificial apparatus, and the pillar as a visible symbol or embodiment of the presence of the deity, which in process of time comes to be fashioned and carved in various ways, till ultimately it becomes a statue or anthropomorphic idol of stone, just as the sacred tree or post was ultimately developed into an image of wood."

In spite of much obvious groping in the dark in this and other passages of the *Religion of the Semites*, it is clear that the learned professor recognised at least one central fact—"the sacred stone at Semitic sanctuaries was from the first an object of worship, a sort of rude idol in which the divinity was somehow supposed to be present." Again, he notes that "Jacob's pillar is more than a mere landmark, for it is anointed, just as idols were in antiquity, and the pillar itself, not the spot on which it stood, is called 'the house of God,' as if the deity were conceived actually to dwell in the stone, or manifest himself therein to his worshippers. And this is the conception which appears to have been associated with sacred stones everywhere. When the Arab daubed blood on the *nosb*, his object was to bring the offering into direct contact with the deity; and in like manner the practice of stroking the sacred stone with the hand is identical with the practice of touching or stroking the garments or beard of a man in acts of supplication before him." Elsewhere he says: "So far as evidence from tradition and ritual goes, we can only think of the sacred stone as consecrated by the actual presence of the godhead, so that whatever touched it was brought into immediate contact with the deity." And he quotes a line from an Arab poet in which the Arabian gods are expressly described as "gods of stone."

It is thus clear that sacred stones were common objects of worship with the Semites in general, and also with the Hebrew people in particular. But after the exclusive worship of Jahweh, the local Jewish god, had grown obligatory among the Jews, it became the policy of the "Jehovist" priests to Jehovise and to consecrate the sacred stones of Palestine by bringing them into connex-

ion with the Jehovistic legend and the tales of the Patriarchs. Thus Professor Cheyne comments as follows upon the passage in Isaiah where the prophet mocks the partizan of the old polytheistic creed as a stone-worshipper—
" Among the smooth stones of the valley is thy portion: They, they are thy lot: Even to them hast thou poured a drink offering: Thou hast offered a meat offering:

" The large smooth stones referred to above were the fetishes of the primitive Semitic races, and anointed with oil, according to a widely spread custom. It was such a stone which Jacob took for a pillow, and afterwards consecrated by pouring oil upon it. The early Semites and reactionary idolatrous Israelites called such stones Bethels. . . . i.e., houses of *El* (the early Semitic word for God)*. . . . In spite of the efforts of the 'Jehovist' who desired to convert these ancient fetishes into memorials of patriarchal history, the old heathenish use of them seems to have continued especially in secluded places."

Besides the case of the stone at Bethel, there is the later one (in our narrative) when Jacob and Laban made a covenant, "and Jacob took a stone, and set it up for a pillar. And Jacob said unto his brethren, Gather stones; and they took stones and made an heap: and they did eat there upon the heap." So, once more, at Shalem, he erects an altar called El-Elohe-Israel; he sets a pillar upon the grave of Rachel, and another at the place at Luz where God appeared to him. Of like import is the story of the twelve stones which the twelve men take out of Jordan to commemorate the passage of the tribes. All are clearly attempts to Jehovise these early sacred stones or local gods by connecting them with incidents in the Jehovistic version of the ancient Hebrew legends.

That such stones, however, were worshipped as deities in early times, before the cult of Jahweh had become an exclusive one among his devotees, is evident from the Jeho-

---

* Say rather, " for a god."

vistic narrative itself, which has not wholly succeeded in blotting out all traces of earlier religion. Samuel judged Israel every year at Bethel, the place of Jacob's sacred pillar: at Gilgal, the place where Joshua's twelve stones were set up; and at Mizpeh, where stood the cairn surmounted by the pillar of Laban's covenant. In other words, these were the sanctuaries of the chief ancient gods of Israel. Samuel himself "took a stone and set it between Mizpeh and Shem"; and its very name, Eben-ezer, "the stone of help," shows that it was originally worshipped before proceeding on warlike expeditions, though the Jehovistic gloss, "saying, Hitherto the Lord hath helped us," does its best, of course, to obscure the real meaning. So at Peran, in New Guinea, Mr. Chalmers saw "a large peculiarly-shaped stone," by name Ravai, considered very sacred. Sacrifices are made to it, and it is more particularly addressed in times of fighting. "Before setting forth, offerings are presented, with food," and the stone is entreated to precede the warriors into battle. Wherever a stone has a name, it is almost certainly of mortuary origin. It was to the stone-circle of Gilgal, once more, that Samuel directed Saul to go, saying, "I will come down unto thee, to offer burnt-offerings, and to sacrifice sacrifices of peace-offerings." It was at the cairn of Mizpeh that Saul was chosen king; and after the victory over the Ammonites, Saul went once more to the great Stonehenge at Gilgal to "renew the kingdom," and "there they made Saul king before Jahweh in Gilgal; and there they sacrificed sacrifices of peace-offerings before Jahweh." This passage is a very instructive and important one, because here we see that in the opinion of the writer at least Jahweh was then domiciled at Gilgal, amid the other sacred stones of that holy circle.

Observe, however, that when Saul was directed to go to find his father's asses, he was sent first to Rachel's pillar at Telzah, and then to the plain of Tabor, where he was to meet "three men going up to God [not to Jahweh] at

Bethel," evidently to sacrifice, "one carrying three kids, and another carrying three loaves of bread, and another carrying a bottle of wine." These and many other like memorials of stone-worship lie thickly scattered through the early books of the Hebrew Scriptures, sometimes openly avowed, and sometimes cloaked under a thin veil of Jehovism.

On the other hand, at the present day, the Palestine exploration has shown that no rude stone monuments exist in Palestine proper, though east of the Jordan they are common in all parts of the country. How, then, are we to explain their disappearance? Major Conder thinks that when pure Jehovism finally triumphed under Hezekiah and Josiah, the Jehovists destroyed all these "idolatrous" stones throughout the Jewish dominions, in accordance with the injunctions in the Book of Deuteronomy to demolish the religious emblems of the Canaanites. Jahweh, the god of the Hebrews, was a jealous God, and he would tolerate no alien sacred stones within his own jurisdiction.

And who or what was this Jahweh himself, this local and ethnic god of the Israelites, who would suffer no other god or sacred monolith to live near him?

I will not lay stress upon the point that when Joshua was dying, according to the legend, he "took a great stone" and set it up by an oak that was by the sanctuary of Jahweh, saying that it had heard all the words of Jahweh. That document is too doubtful in terms to afford us much authority. But I will merely point out that at the time when we first seem to catch clear historic glimpses of true Jahweh worship, we find Jahweh, whoever or whatever that mystic object might have been, located with his ark at the Twelve Stones at Gilgal. It is quite clear that in "the camp at Gilgal," as the later compilers believed, Jahweh, god of Israel, who had brought his people up out of Egypt, remained till the conquest of the land was completed. But after the end of the conquest, the tent in which he dwelt was removed to Shiloh; and that Jahweh went with it is clear from the fact that Joshua cast lots for the land there "before Jahweh, our God." He was there still when Hannah and her husband went up to Shiloh to sacrifice unto Jahweh; and when Samuel ministered unto Jahweh before Eli the priest. That Jahweh made a long stay at Shiloh is, therefore, it would seem, a true old tradition—a tradition of the age just before the historical beginnings of the Hebrew annals.

But Jahweh was an object of portable size, for, omitting for the present the descriptions in the Pentateuch, which seem likely to be of late date, and not too trustworthy, through their strenuous Jehovistic editing, he was carried from Shiloh in his ark to the front during the great battle with the Philistines at Ebenezer; and the Philistines were afraid, for they said, "A god is come into the camp." But when the Philistines captured the ark, the rival god, Dagon, fell down and broke in pieces—so Hebrew legend declared—before the face of Jahweh. After the Philistines restored the sacred object, it rested for a time at Kirjath-jearim, till David, on the capture of Jerusalem from the Jebusites, went down to that place to bring up from thence the ark of the god; and as it went, on a new cart, they "played before Jahweh on all manner of instruments," and David himself "danced before Jahweh." Jahweh was then placed in the tent or tabernacle that David had prepared for him, till Solomon built the first temple, "the house of Jahweh," and Jahweh's ark was set up in it, "in the oracle of the house, the most holy place, even under the wings of the cherubim." Just so Mr. Chalmers tells us that when he was at Peran, in New Guinea, the peculiarly-shaped holy stone, Ravai, and the two wooden idols, Epe and Kivava, "made long ago and considered very sacred," were for the moment "located in an old house, until all the arrangements necessary for their removal to the splendid new dubu prepared for them are completed." And so, too, at the opposite end of the scale of civilisation, as

Mr. Lang puts it, "the fetish-stones of Greece were those which occupied the holy of holies of the most ancient temples, the mysterious fanes within dark cedar or cypress groves, to which men were hardly admitted."

That Jahweh himself, in the most ancient traditions of the race, was similarly concealed within his chest or ark in the holy of holies, is evident, I think, to any attentive reader. It is true, the later Jehovistic glosses of Exodus and Deuteronomy, composed after the Jehovistic worship had become purified and spiritualised, do their best to darken the comprehension of this matter by making the presence of Jahweh seem always incorporeal; and even in the earlier traditions, the phrase "the ark of the covenant of Jahweh" is often substituted for the simpler and older one, "the ark of Jahweh." But through all the disfigurements with which the priestly scribes of the age of Josiah and the sacerdotalists of the return from the captivity have overlaid the primitive story, we can still see clearly in many places that Jahweh himself was at first personally present in the ark that covered him. And though the scribes (evidently ashamed of the early worship they had outlived) protest somewhat vehemently more than once, "There was nothing in the ark save the two tables of stone which Moses put there at Horeb, when Jahweh made a covenant with the children of Israel, when they came out of the land of Egypt," yet this much at least even they admit—that the object or objects concealed in the ark consisted of a sculptured stone or stones; and that to dance or sing before this stone or these stones was equivalent to dancing or singing before the face of Jahweh.

The question whether the mysterious body concealed in the ark was or was not a lingam or other phallic object I purposely omit to discuss here, as not cognate to our present enquiry. It is sufficient to insist that from the evidence before us, first, it *was* Jahweh himself, and second, it was an object made of stone. Further than that 'twere curious to enquire, and I for one do not desire to pry into the mysteries.

Not to push the argument too far, then, we may say this much is fairly certain. The children of Israel in early times carried about with them a tribal god, Jahweh, whose presence in their midst was intimately connected with a certain ark or chest, containing a stone object or objects. This chest was readily portable, and could be carried to the front in case of warfare. They did not know the origin of the object in the ark with certainty, but they regarded it emphatically as "Jahweh their god, which led them out of the land of Egypt." Even after its true nature had been spiritualised away into a great national deity, the most unlimited and incorporeal the world has ever known (as we get him in the best and purest work of the prophets), the imagery of later times constantly returns to the old idea of a stone pillar or menhir. In the embellished account of the exodus from Egypt, Jahweh goes before the Israelites as a pillar or monolith of cloud by day and of fire by night. According to Levitical law his altar must be built of unhewn stone, "for if thou lift up thy tool upon it thou hast polluted it." It is as a Rock that the prophets often figuratively describe Jahweh, using the half-forgotten language of an earlier day to clothe their own sublimer and more purified conceptions. It is to the Rock of Israel—the sacred stone of the tribe— that they look for succour. Nay, even when Josiah accepted the forged roll of the law and promised to abide by it, "the king stood by a pillar (a menhir) and made a covenant before Jahweh." Even to the last we see in vague glimpses the real original nature of the worship of that jealous god who caused Dagon to break in pieces before him, and would allow no other sacred stones to remain undemolished within his tribal boundaries.

I do not see, therefore, how we can easily avoid the obvious inference that Jahweh, the god of the Hebrews, who later became sublimated and etherealised into the

God of Christianity, was in his origin nothing more nor less than the ancestral sacred stone of the people of Israel, however sculptured, and perhaps, in the very last resort of all, the unhewn monumental pillar of some early Semitic sheikh or chieftain.

CHAPTER VI.

SACRED STAKES.

MILTON speaks in a famous sonnet of the time "when all our fathers worshipped stocks and stones." That familiar and briefly contemptuous phrase of the Puritan poet does really cover the vast majority of objects of worship for the human race at all times and in all places. We have examined the stones; the stocks must now come in for their fair share of attention. They need not, however, delay us quite so long as their sister deities, both because they are on the whole less important in themselves, and because their development from grave-marks into gods and idols is almost absolutely parallel to that which we have already followed out in detail in the case of the standing stone or megalithic monument.

Stakes or wooden posts are often used all the world over as marks of an interment. Like other grave-marks, they also share naturally in the honours paid to the ghost or nascent god. But they are less important as elements in the growth of religion than standing stones for two distinct reasons. In the first place, a stake or post most often marks the interment of a person of little social consideration; chiefs and great men have usually stone monuments erected in their honour; the commonalty have to be satisfied with wooden marks, as one may observe to this day at Père Lachaise, or any other great Christian cemetery. In the second place, the stone monument is far more lasting and permanent than the wooden one. Each of these points counts for something. For it is chiefs and great men whose ghosts most often grow into gods ; and it is the oldest ghosts, the oldest gods, the oldest monuments that are always the most sacred. For both these reasons, then, the stake is less critical than the stone in the history of religion.

Nevertheless, it has its own special importance. As the sacred stone derives ultimately from the great boulder piled above the grave to keep down the corpse, so the stake, I believe, derives from the sharp-pointed stick driven through the body to pin it down as we saw in the third chapter, and still so employed in Christian England to prevent suicides from walking. Such a stake or pole is usually permitted to protrude from the ground, so as to warn living men of the neighbourhood of a spirit.

At a very early date, however, the stake, I fancy, became a mere grave-mark ; and though, owing to its comparative inconspicuousness, it obtains relatively little notice, it is now and always has been by far the most common mode of preserving the memory of the spot where a person lies buried. A good example, which will throw light upon many subsequent modifications, is given by Mr. Wyatt Gill from Port Moresby in New Guinea. "The body," he says, "was buried. At the side was set up a stake, to which were tied the spear, club, bow and arrow of the deceased, but broken, to prevent theft. A little beyond was the grave of a woman : her cooking utensils, grass petticoats, etc., hung up on the stake." Similar customs, he adds, are almost universal in Polynesia.

Though worship of stakes or wooden posts is common all over the world, I can give but few quite unequivocal instances of such worship being paid to a post actually known to surmount an undoubted grave. Almost the best direct evidence I can obtain is the case of the grave-pole in Buru, already quoted from Mr. H. O. Forbes. But the following account of a Samoyed place of sacrifice, extracted from Baron Nordenskiöld's *Voyage of the Vega*, is certainly suggestive. On a hillock on Vaygats

Island the Swedish explorer found a number of reindeer skulls, so arranged that they formed a close thicket of antlers. Around lay other bones, both of bears and reindeer; and in the midst of all "the mighty beings to whom all this splendour was offered. They consisted of hundreds of small wooden sticks, the upper portions of which were carved very clumsily in the form of the human countenance, most of them from fifteen to twenty, but some of them three hundred and seventy centimetres in length. They were all stuck in the ground on the southeast part of the eminence. Near the place of sacrifice there were to be seen pieces of driftwood and remains of the fireplace at which the sacrificial meal was prepared. Our guide told us that at these meals the mouths of the idols were besmeared with blood and wetted with brandy; and the former statement was confirmed by the large spots of blood which were found on most of the large idols below the holes intended to represent the mouth." At a far earlier date, Stephen Burrough in 1556 writes as follows to much the same effect in his interesting narrative printed in Hakluyt: "There I met againe with Loshak, and went on shore with him, and he brought me to a heap of Samoeds idols, which were in number about 300, the worst and the most unartificiall worke that ever I saw: the eyes and mouthes of sundrie of them were bloodie, they had the shape of men, women, and children, very grosly wrought, and that which they had made for other parts was also sprinkled with blood. Some of their idols were an olde sticke with two or three notches, made with a knife in it. There was one of their sleds broken and lay by the heape of idols, and there I saw a deers skinne which the foules had spoyled: and before certaine of their idols blocks were made as high as their mouthes; being all bloody, I thought that to be the table wheron they offered their sacrifice."

In neither of these accounts, it is true, is it distinctly mentioned that the place of sacrifice was a Samoyed cemetery: but I believe this to be the case, partly from analogy, and partly because Nordenskiöld mentions elsewhere that an upturned sled is a frequent sign of a Samoyed grave. Compare also the following account of a graveyard among nominally Christian Ostyak Siberians, also from Nordenskiöld : " The corpses were placed in large coffins above ground, at which almost always a cross was erected." [The accompanying woodcut shews that these crosses were rude wooden stakes with one or two cross-bars.] " In one of the crosses a sacred picture was inserted which must be considered a further proof that a Christian rested in the coffin. Notwithstanding this, we found some clothes, which had belonged to the departed, hanging on a bush beside the grave, together with a bundle containing food, principally dried fish. At the graves of the richer natives the survivors are even said to place along with food some rouble notes, in order that the departed may not be altogether without ready money on his entrance into the other world."

To complete the parallel, I ought to add that money was also deposited on the sacrificial place on Vaygats Island. Of another such sacrificial place on Yalmal, Nordenskiöld says, after describing a pile of bones, reindeer skulls, and walrus jaws : " In the middle of the heap of bones stood four erect pieces of wood. Two consisted of sticks a metre in length, with notches cut in them. . . . The two others, which clearly were the proper idols of this place of sacrifice, consisted of driftwood roots, on which some carvings had been made to distinguish the eyes, mouth, and nose. The parts of the pieces of wood, intended to represent the eyes and mouth, had recently been besmeared with blood, and there still lay at the heap of bones the entrails of a newly killed reindeer."

Indeed, I learn from another source that "the Samoyedes feed the wooden images of the dead " ; while an instance from Erman helps further to confirm the same conclusion. According to that acute writer, among the

Ostyaks of Eastern Siberia there is found a most interesting custom, in which, says Dr. Tylor, "we see the transition from the image of the dead man to the actual idol." When a man dies, they set up a rude wooden image of him in the yurt, which receives offerings at every meal and has honours paid to it, while the widow continually embraces and caresses it. As a general rule, these images are buried at the end of three years or so: but sometimes "the image of a shaman (native sorcerer)," says Tylor, "is set up permanently, and remains as a saint for ever." For "saint" I should say "god"; and we see the transformation at once completed. Indeed, Erman adds acutely about the greater gods of the Ostyaks: "That these latter also have a historical origin, that they were originally monuments of distinguished men, to which prescription and the interest of the Shamans gave by degrees an arbitrary meaning and importance, seems to me not liable to doubt."

With regard to the blood smeared upon such Siberian wooden idols, it must be remembered that bowls of blood are common offerings to the dead; and Dr. Robertson Smith himself, no friendly witness in this matter, has compared the blood-offerings to ghosts with those to deities. In the eleventh book of the Odyssey, for example, the ghosts drink greedily of the sacrificial blood; and libations of gore form a special feature in Greek offerings to heroes. That blood was offered to the sacred stones we have already seen; and we noticed that there as here it was specially smeared upon the parts representing the mouth. Offerings of blood to gods, or pouring of blood on altars, are too common to demand particular notice; and we shall also recur to that part of the subject when we come to consider the important questions of sacrifice and sacrament. I will only add here that according to Maimonides the Sabians looked on blood as the nourishment of the gods; while the Hebrew Jahweh asks indignantly in the fiftieth Psalm, "Will I eat the flesh of bulls, or drink the blood of goats?"

To pass on to more unequivocal cases of stake-worship, where we can hardly doubt that the stake represents a dead man, Captain Cook noticed that in the Society Islands "the carved wooden images at burial-places were not considered mere memorials, but abodes into which the souls of the departed retired." So Ellis observes of Polynesians generally that the sacred objects might be either mere stocks and stones, or carved wooden images, from six to eight feet long down to as many inches. Some of these were to represent "tii," divine manes or spirits of the dead; while others were to represent "tu," or deities of higher rank and power. To my mind, this is almost a distinction without a difference; the first being ghosts of recently deceased ancestors, the second ghosts of remoter progenitors. The ancient Araucanians again fixed over a tomb an upright log, "rudely carved to represent the human frame." After the death of New Zealand chiefs, wooden images, 20 to 40 feet high, were erected as monuments. I might easily multiply instances; but I refrain lest the list grow tedious.

Dr. Codrington notes that the large mouths and lolling tongues of many New Zealand and Polynesian gods are due to the habit of smearing the mouth with blood and other offerings.

Where men preserve the corpses of their dead, images are not so likely to grow up; but where fear of the dead has brought about the practice of burial or burning, it is reasonable that the feelings of affection which prompted gifts and endearments to the mummy in the first stage of thought should seek some similar material outlet under the altered circumstances. Among ourselves, a photograph, a portrait, the toys of a dead child, are preserved and cherished. Among savages, ruder representations become necessary. They bury the actual corpse safely out of sight, but make some rough wooden imitation to represent it. Thus it does not surprise us to find that while the Marianne Islanders keep the dried bodies of their dead ancestors in their huts as household gods, and expect them to give oracles out of their skulls, the New Zealanders, on the other hand, "set up memorial idols of deceased persons near the burial-place, talking affectionately to them as if still alive, and casting garments to them when they pass by," while they also "preserve in their houses small carved wooden images, each dedicated to the spirit of an ancestor." The Coast Negroes "place several earthen images on the graves." Some Papuans, "after a grave is filled up, collect round an idol, and offer provisions to it." The Javans dress up an image in the clothes of the deceased. So, too, of the Caribs of the West Indies, we learn that they "carved little images in the shape in which they believed spirits to have appeared to them; and some human figures bore the names of ancestors in memory of them." From such little images, obviously substituted for the dead body which used once to be preserved and affectionately tended, are derived, I believe, most of the household gods of the world—the Lares and Penates of the Romans, the huacas of the Peruvians, the teraphim of the Semites.

How absolutely image and ancestor are identified we can see among the Tenimber Islanders, with whom "the *matmate* are the spirits of their ancestors which are worshipped as guardian spirits or household gods. They are supposed to enter the house through an opening in the roof, and to take up their abode temporarily in the skulls, or in images of wood or ivory, in order to partake of the offerings."

A few more facts in the same direction may help to bring out in still stronger relief this close equivalence of the corpse and the image. A New Guinea mother keeps the mummied body of her child, and carries it about with her; whereas a West African mother, living in a tribe where terror of the dead has induced the practice of burial, makes a little image of her lost darling out of a gourd or calabash, wraps it in skins, and feeds it or puts it to sleep like a living baby. Bastian saw Indian women in Peru, who had lost an infant, carrying about on their backs a wooden doll to represent it. At a somewhat higher level, "the spiritual beings of the Algonquins," says Dr. Tylor, to whom I owe not a few of these instances, "were represented by, and in language completely identified with, the carved wooden heads" (note this point) "or more complete images, to which worship and sacrifice were offered." In all these instances we see clearly, I think, the course of the genesis of household deities. In Siam, the ashes of the dead are similarly moulded into Buddhist images, which are afterwards worshipped as household gods.

Mr. Herbert Spencer has collected several interesting examples some of which I will borrow, as showing incidentally how much the growth of the idol or image depends upon such abstraction of the real body for burial or its equivalent. While a deceased king of Congo is being embalmed, a figure is set up in the palace to represent him, and is daily furnished with meat and drink. When Charles VI. of France was buried, "over the coffin was an image of the late king, bearing a rich crown of gold and diamonds, and holding two shields. . . . This image was dressed with cloth of gold. . . . In this state was he solemnly carried to the church of Notre Dame." Madame de Motteville says of the father of the great Condé, "The effigy of this prince was waited upon for three days, as was customary"—forty days having been the original time during which food was supplied to such effigies at the usual hours. Monstrelet describes a like figure used at the burial of Henry V. of England: and the Westminster Abbey images already noticed belong to the same category.

As in the case of sacred stones, once more, I am quite ready to admit that when once the sanctity of certain stakes or wooden poles came to be generally recognised, it would be a simple transference of feeling to suppose that any stake, arbitrarily set up, might become the shrine or home of an indwelling spirit. Thus we are told that the Brazilian tribes "set up stakes in the ground, and make offerings before them to appease their deities or demons." So also we are assured that among the Dinkas of the White Nile, "the missionaries saw an old woman in her hut offering the first of her food before a short thick staff planted in the ground." But in neither of these cases is there necessarily anything to show that the spot where the staff was set up was not a place of burial; while in the second instance this is even probable, as hut interments are extremely common in Africa. I will quote one other instance only, for its illustrative value in a subsequent connexion. In the Society Islands, rude logs are clothed in native cloth (like Monigan's idol) and anointed with oil, receiving adoration and sacrifice as the dwelling-place of a deity. This custom is parallel to that of the Caribs, who took a bone of a dead friend from the grave, wrapped it up in cotton, and enquired of it for oracles.

Mr. Savage Landor, in his interesting work *The Hairy Ainu*, figures and describes some curious grave-stakes of those Japanese aborigines. The stakes on the men's graves are provided with a phallic protuberance; those on the women's with an equally phallic perforation. This fact helps to illustrate the phallicism of sacred stones in Syria and elsewhere.

Among the Semitic peoples, always specially interesting to us from their genetic connexion with Judaism and Christianity, the worship of stakes usually took the form of adoration paid to the curious log of wood described as an *ashera*. What kind of object an *ashera* was we learn from the injunction in Deuteronomy, "Thou shalt not plant an *ashera* of any kind of wood beside the altar of Jahweh." This prohibition is clearly parallel to that against any hewn stone or "graven image." But the Semites in general worshipped as a rule at a rude stone altar, beside which stood an *ashera*, under a green tree,—all three of the great sacred objects of humanity being thus present together. A similar combination is not uncommon in India, where sacred stone and wooden image stand often under the shade of the same holy peepul tree. "The *ashera*," says Professor Robertson Smith, "is a sacred symbol, the seat of the deity, and perhaps the name itself, as G. Hoffmann has suggested, means nothing more than the 'mark' of the divine presence." Those who have followed me so far in the present work, however, will be more likely to conclude that it meant originally the mark of a place where an ancestor lay buried. "Every altar," says Professor Smith, again, "had its *ashera*, even such altars as in the popular preprophetic forms of the Hebrew religion were dedicated to Jehovah."

The Semitic sacred pole was treated in most respects like the other grave-stakes and idols we have hitherto considered; for an Assyrian monument from Khorsabad, figured by Rawlinson, represents an ornamental pole, planted beside an altar; priests stand before it engaged in an act of worship, and touch the pole with their hands, "or perhaps," says Professor Smith, "anoint it with some liquid substance." That the *ashera* was also draped, like the logs of the Society Islanders, or Monigan's Irish idol, we learn from the famous passage in Second Kings (xxiii. 7) where it is said that the women "wove *hangings* for the *ashera*." Dr. Robertson Smith illustrates this passage by the parallel of the sacred *erica* at Byblus, which was "a mere dead stump, for it was cut down by Isis and presented to the Byblians wrapped in a linen cloth and anointed with myrrh like a corpse. It therefore represented the dead god" (Osiris, or rather in its origin Adonis). "But as a mere stump, it also resembles the Hebrew *ashera*." So near may a man come to the perception of a truth, and yet so utterly may he miss its actual import.

I will dwell no longer upon these more or less remote derivatives of the grave-stake. I will only say briefly that in my opinion all wooden idols or images are directly or indirectly descended from the wooden headpost or still more primitive sepulchral pole. Not of course that I suppose every wooden image to have been necessarily once itself a funereal monument. Donatello's Magdalen in San Giovanni at Florence, the blue-robed and star-spangled Madonna of the wayside shrine, have certainly no such immediate origin. But I do believe that the habit of making and worshipping wooden images arose in the way I have pointed out; and to those who would accuse me of "gross Euhemerism," I would once more remark that even in these highest Christian instances the objects of veneration are themselves in the last resort admitted to have been at one time Galilean women. Nay, is not even the wayside shrine itself in most Catholic countries more often than not the mortuary chapel erected where some wayfarer has died a violent death, by murder, lightning, accident, or avalanche?

CHAPTER VII.

SACRED TREES.

The sacred tree stands less obviously in the direct line of ancestry of gods and of God than the sacred stone and the sacred stake which we have just considered. I would willingly pass it over, therefore, in this long preliminary inquisition, could I safely do so, in order to progress at once to the specific consideration of the God of Israel and the rise of Monotheism. But the tree is nevertheless so closely linked with the two other main objects of human worship that I hardly see how I can avoid considering it here in the same connexion: especially as in the end it has important implications with regard to the tree of the cross, as well as to the True Vine, and many other elements of Christian faith and Christian symbolism. I shall therefore give it a short chapter as I pass, premising that I have already entered into the subject at greater length in my excursus On the Origin of Tree-Worship, appended to my verse translation of the *Attis* of Catullus.

The worship of sacred trees is almost as widely diffused over the whole world as the worship of dead bodies, mummies, relics, graves, sacred stones, sacred stakes, and stone or wooden idols. The great authorities on the subject of Tree-Worship are Mannhardt's *Baumkultus* and Mr. J. G. Frazer's *The Golden Bough*. Neither of those learned and acute writers, however, has fully seen the true origin of worship from funeral practices: and therefore it becomes necessary to go over the same ground again briefly here from the point of view afforded us by the corpse-theory and ghost-theory of the basis of religion. I shall hope to add something to their valuable results, and also incidentally to show that all the main objects of worship together leads us back unanimously to the Cult of the Dead as their common starting-point.

Let us begin in this instance (contrary to our previous practice) by examining and endeavouring to understand a few cases of the behaviour of tree-spirits in various mythologies. Virgil tells us in the Third Æneid how, on a certain occasion, Æneas was offering a sacrifice on a tumulus crowned with dogwood and myrtle bushes. He endeavoured to pluck up some of these by the roots, in order to cover the altar, as was customary, with leaf-clad branches. As he did so, the first bush which he tore up astonished him by exuding drops of liquid blood, which trickled and fell upon the soil beneath. He tried again, and again the tree bled human gore. On the third trial, a groan was heard proceeding from the tumulus, and a voice assured Æneas that the barrow on which he stood covered the murdered remains of his friend Polydorus.

Now, in this typical and highly illustrative myth—no doubt an ancient and well-known story incorporated by Virgil in his great poem—we see that the tree which grows upon a barrow is itself regarded as the representative and embodiment of the dead man's soul, just as elsewhere the snake which glides from the tomb of Anchises is regarded as the embodied spirit of the hero, and just as the owls and bats which haunt sepulchral caves are often identified in all parts of the world with the souls of the departed.

Similar stories of bleeding or speaking trees or bushes occur abundantly elsewhere. "When the oak is being felled," says Aubrey, in his *Remains of Gentilisme*, "it gives a kind of shriekes and groanes that may be heard a mile off, as if it were the genius of the oak lamenting. E. Wyld, Esq., hath heared it severall times." Certain Indians, says Bastian, dare not cut a particular plant, because there comes out of it a red juice which they take for its blood. I myself remember hearing as a boy in Canada that wherever *Sanguinaria Canadensis*, the common American bloodroot, grew in the woods, an Indian had once been buried, and that the red drops of juice which exuded from the stem when one picked the flowers were the dead man's blood. In Samoa, says Mr. Turner, the special abode of Tuifiti, King of Fiji, was a grove of large and durable afzelia trees. "No one dared cut that timber. A story is told of a party from Upolu who once attempted it, and the consequence was that blood flowed from the tree, and that the sacrilegious strangers all took ill and died." Till 1855, says Mannhardt, there was a sacred larch-tree at Nauders in the Tyrol, which was thought to bleed whenever it was cut. In some of these cases, it is true, we do not actually know that the trees grew on tumuli, but this point is specially noticed about Polydorus's dogwood, and is probably implied in the Samoan case, as I gather from the title given to the spirit as king of Fiji.

In other instances, however, such a doubt does not exist. We are expressly told that it is the souls of the dead which are believed to animate the speaking or bleeding trees. "The Dieyerie tribe of South Australia," says Mr. Frazer, "regard as very sacred certain trees which are supposed to be their fathers transformed; hence they will not cut the trees down, and protest against settlers doing so." Some of the Philippine Islanders believe that the souls of their forefathers inhabit certain trees, which they therefore spare. If obliged to fell one of these sacred trunks, they excuse themselves by saying that it was the priests who made them fell it.

Now, how did this connexion between the tree and the ghost or ancestor grow up? In much the same way, I imagine, as the connexion between the sacred stone or the sacred stake and the dead chief who lies buried beneath it. Whatever grows or stands upon the grave is sure to share the honours paid to the spirit that dwells within it. Thus a snake or other animal seen to glide out of a tomb is instantly taken by savages and even by half-civilised men as the genius or representative of the dead inhabitant. But do trees grow out of graves? Undoubtedly, yes. In the first place, they may grow by mere accident, as they might grow anywhere else; the more so as the soil in such a case has been turned and laboured. But beyond this, in the second place, it is common all over the world to plant trees or shrubs over the graves of relatives or tribesmen. Though direct evidence on this point is difficult to obtain, a little is forthcoming. In Algeria, I observed, the Arab women went on Fridays to plant flowers and shrubs on the graves of their immediate dead. I learned from Mr. R. L. Stevenson that similar plantings take place in Samoa and Fiji. The Tahitians put young casuarinas on graves. In Roman Catholic countries the planting of shrubs in cemeteries takes place usually on the *jour des morts*, a custom which would argue for it an immense antiquity; for though it is a point of honour among Catholics to explain this *fête* as of comparatively recent origin, definitely introduced by a particular saint at a particular period, its analogy to similar celebrations elsewhere shows us that it is really a surviving relic of a very ancient form of Manes-worship. In Græco-Roman antiquity it is certain that trees were frequently planted around the barrows of the dead; and that leafy branches formed part of the established ceremonial of funerals. I cannot do better than quote in this respect once more the case of Polydorus:

> Ergo instauramus Polydoro funus, et ingens
> Aggeritur tumulo tellus ; stant Manibus aræ,
> Cæruleis mœstæ vittis atraque cupresso.

Suetonius again tells us how the tumulus of the divine Augustus was carefully planted; and the manner in which he notes the fact seems to me to argue that some special importance was attached to the ceremony. The acacia is one of the most sacred trees of Egypt ; and Egyptian monuments, with their usual frankness, show us a sarcophagus from which an acacia emerges, with the naïve motto, " Osiris springs forth."

An incident which occurred during the recent Sino-Japanese war shows how easily points of this sort may be overlooked by hasty writers in formal descriptions. One of the London illustrated papers printed an account of the burial of the Japanese dead at Port Arthur, and after mentioning the simple headstone erected at each grave volunteered the further statement that nothing else marked the place of interment. But the engraving which accompanied it, taken from a photograph, showed on the contrary that a little tree had also been planted on each tiny tumulus.

I learn from Mr. William Simpson that the Tombs of the Kings near Pekin are conspicuous from afar by their lofty groves of pine trees.

Evergreens, I believe, are specially planted upon graves or tumuli because they retain their greenness throughout the entire winter, and thus as it were give continuous evidence of the vitality and activity of the indwelling spirit. Mr. Frazer has shown in *The Golden Bough* that mistletoe similarly owes its special sanctity to the fact that it visibly holds the soul of the tree uninjured in itself, while all the surrounding branches stand bare and lifeless. Accordingly, tumuli are very frequently crowned by evergreens. Almost all the round barrows in southern England, for example, are topped by very ancient Scotch firs; and as the Scotch fir is not an indigenous tree south of the Tweed, it is practically certain that these old pines are the descendants of ancestors put in by human hands when the barrows were first raised over the cremated and buried bodies of prehistoric chieftains. In short, the Scotch fir is in England the sacred tree of the barrows. As a rule, however, in Northern Europe, the yew is the species specially planted in graveyards, and several such yews in various parts of England and Germany are held to possess a peculiar sanctity. The great clump of very ancient yews in Norbury Park near Dorking, known as the Druids' Grove, has long been considered a holy wood of remote antiquity. In southern Europe, the cypress replaces the yew as the evergreen most closely connected with tombs and cemeteries. In Provence and Italy, however, the evergreen holme-oak is almost equally a conventional denizen of places of interment. M. Lajard in his able essay *Sur le Culte du Cyprès* has brought together much evidence of this worship of evergreens, among the Greeks, Etruscans, Romans, Phœnicians, Arabs, Persians, Hindus, Chinese, and American nations.

Sacred trees, especially when standing alone, are treated in many respects with the same ceremonial as is employed towards dead bodies, mummies, graves, sacred stones, sacred stakes, and carved idols or statues. In other words, the offerings to the ghost or god may be made to the tree that grows on the grave just as well as to any other of the recognised embodiments of the indwelling spirit. Darwin in the *Voyage of the Beagle* describes how the Indians of South America would greet with loud shouts some sacred tree, standing solitary on some high part of the Pampas; libations of brandy and *maté* were poured into a hole at its base to gratify the soul of the deity who dwelt there. One of these tree-gods had a name, Walleechu. The Congo people, again, put calabashes of palm-wine at the foot of "trees treated as idols." In other cases, blood is smeared on the tree; or oil is offered to it. Mr. Duff Macdonald's Central Africans kill chickens at the foot of the "prayer tree," and let its blood trickle down to the roots. Oldfield saw at Addacoodah fowls and many other articles of food suspended as offerings to a gigantic tree. Sir William Hunter mentions that once a year at Beerbhoom the Santals "make simple offerings to a ghost who dwells in a Bela tree." In Tonga, the natives lay presents of food at the foot of particular trees which they believe to be inhabited by spirits. I need not multiply instances; they may be found by the hundred in Dr. Tylor and other great anthropological collections.

Furthermore, the sacred tree is found in the closest possible connection with the other indubitably ancestral monuments, the sacred stone and the idol. "A Bengal village," says Sir William Hunter, "has usually its local god, which it adores either in the form of a rude unhewn stone, or a stump, or a tree marked with red lead"; the last being probably a substitute for the blood of human or animal victims with which it was once watered. "Sometimes a lump of clay placed under a tree does duty for a deity; and the attendant priest, when there is one, generally belongs to one of the half-Hinduised low castes. The rude stone represents the non-Aryan fetish; and the tree seems to owe its sanctity to the non-Aryan belief that it forms the abode of the ghosts or gods of the village." That is to say, we have here ancestor-worship in its undisguised early native development.

I may mention here in brief that, as we shall hereafter see, this triple combination of stone, log, and tree forms almost the normal or invariable composition of the primitive shrine the whole world over.

The association of the sacred tree with actual idols or images of deceased ancestors is well seen in the following passage which I quote from Dr. Tylor: "A clump of larches on a Siberian steppe, a grove in the recesses of a forest, is the sanctuary of a Turanian tribe. Gaily-decked idols in their warm fur coats, each set up beneath its great tree swathed with cloth or tinplate, endless reindeer-hides and peltry hanging to the trees around, kettles and spoons and snuff-horns and household valuables strewn as offerings before the gods—such is the description of a Siberian holy grove, at the stage when the contact of foreign civilisation has begun by ornamenting the rude old ceremonial it must end by abolishing. A race ethnologically allied to these tribes, though risen to higher culture, kept up remarkable relics of tree-worship in Northern Europe.

THE TREE AND THE STONE. 145

In Esthonian districts, within the present century, the traveller might often see the sacred tree, generally an ancient lime, oak, or ash, standing inviolate in a sheltered spot near the dwelling-house ; and the old memories are handed down of the time when the first blood of a slaughtered beast was sprinkled on its roots, that the cattle might prosper, or when an offering was laid beneath the holy linden, on the stone where the worshipper knelt on his bare knees, moving from east to west and back, which stone he kissed when he had said, 'Receive the food as an offering.'" After the evidence already given, I do not think there can be a reasonable doubt, in such a combination of tree and stone, that we have here a sacrifice to an ancestral spirit.

Similarly, in the courtyard of a Bodo house is planted the sacred euphorbia of Batho, the national god, to which a priest offers prayer and kills a pig. In the island of Tjumba, in the East Indies, a festival is held after harvest, and vessels are filled with rice as a thank-offering to the gods. Then the sacred stone at the foot of a palm tree is sprinkled with the blood of a sacrificed animal, and rice is laid on the stone for the gods. When the Khonds settle a new village, a sacred cotton tree must be planted with solemn rites, and beneath it is placed the sacrificial stone which embodies or represents the village deity. Among the Semites, says Professor Robertson Smith, " no Canaanite high place was complete without its sacred tree standing beside the altar." We shall only fully understand the importance of these facts, however, when we come later to consider the subject of the manufacture of gods by deliberate process, and the nature of the bloody ceremonial which always accompanies it.

In some of the above instances it is incidentally mentioned that the trunks of sacred trees are occasionally draped, as we saw to be also the case with sacred stones, sacred stakes, idols, and relics. Another example of this practice is given in the account of the holy oak of Romowe, venerated by the ancient Prussians, which was hung with drapery like the *ashera*, and decked with little hanging images of the gods. The holy trees of Ireland are still covered with rag offerings. Other cases will be noticed in other connexions hereafter.

Once more, just as stones come to be regarded as ancestors, so by a like process do sacred trees. Thus Galton says in South Africa, "We passed a magnificent tree. It was the parent of all the Damaras. . . . The savages danced round it in great delight." Several Indian tribes believe themselves to be the sons of trees. Many other cases are noted by Mr. Herbert Spencer and Dr. Tylor. I do not think it is necessary for our argument to repeat them here. Sometimes, however, especially in later rationalising times, the sacred tree is merely said to have been planted by the god or hero whom it commemorates. Thus the cypresses of Herakles at Daphne were believed to have been set on the spot by that deity, while the tamarisk at Beersheba was supposed to have been placed there by Abraham.

I hope it is clear from this rapid *résumé* that all the facts about the worship of sacred trees stand exactly parallel to those with regard to the worship of graves, mummies, idols, sacred stones, sacred stakes, and other signs of departed spirits. Indeed, we have sometimes direct evidence of such affiliation. Thus Mr. Turner says of a sacred tree on a certain spot in the island of Savaii, which enjoyed rights of sanctuary like the cities of refuge or a mediæval cathedral : "It is said that the king of a division of Upolu, called Atua, once lived at that spot. After he died, the house fell into decay ; but the tree was fixed on as representing the departed king, and out of respect for his memory it was made the substitute of a living and royal protector." By the light of this remark we may surely interpret in a similar sense such other statements of Mr. Turner's as that a sweet-scented tree in another place " was held to be the habitat of a household god, and anything aromatic which the family happened to get was presented to it as an offering;" or again, "a family god was supposed to live" in another tree; "and hence no one dared to pluck a leaf or break a branch." For family gods, as we saw in a previous chapter, are really family ghosts, promoted to be deities.

In modern accounts of sacred trees much stress is usually laid upon the fact that they are large and well-grown, often very conspicuous, and occupying a height, where they serve as landmarks. Hence it has frequently been taken for granted that they have been selected for worship on account of their size and commanding position. This, however, I think, is a case of putting the cart before the horse, as though one were to say that St. Peter's and Westminster Abbey, the Temple of Karnak or the Mosque of Omar, owed their sanctity to their imposing dimensions. There is every reason why a sacred tree should grow to be exceptionally large and conspicuous. Barrows are usually built on more or less commanding heights, where they may attract general attention. The ground is laboured, piled high, freed from weeds, and enriched by blood and other offerings. The tree, being sacred, is tended and cared for. It is never cut down, and so naturally on the average of instances grows to be a big and well-developed specimen. Hence I hold the tree is usually big because it is sacred, not sacred because it is big. On the other hand, where a tree already full-grown is chosen for a place of burial, it would no doubt be natural to choose a large and conspicuous one. Thus I read of the tree under which Dr. Livingstone's heart was buried by his native servant, "It is the largest in the neighbourhood."

Looking at the question broadly, the case stands thus. We know that in many instances savages inter their dead under the shade of big trees. We know that such trees are thereafter considered sacred, and worshipped with blood, clothes, drapery, offerings. We know that young shrubs or trees are frequently planted on graves in all countries. We know that whatever comes up on or out of a grave is counted as representative of the ghost within it. The presumption is therefore in favour of any particular sacred tree being of funereal origin; and the onus of proving the opposite lies with the person who asserts some more occult and less obvious explanation.

At the same time I am quite ready to allow here, as in previous instances, when once the idea of certain trees being sacred has grown common among men, many trees may come to possess by pure association a sanctity of their own. This is doubtless the case in India with the peepul, and in various other countries with various other trees. Exactly the same thing has happened to stones. And so, again, though I believe the temple to have been developed out of the tomb or its covering, I do not deny that churches are now built apart from tombs, though always dedicated to the worship of a God who is demonstrably a particular deified personage.

Another point on which I must touch briefly is that of the sacred grove or cluster of trees. These often represent, I take it, the trees planted in the *temenos* or sacred tabooed space which surrounds the primitive tomb or temple. The *koubbas* or little dome-shaped tombs of Mahommedan saints so common in North Africa are all surrounded by such a walled enclosure, within which ornamental or other trees are habitually planted. In many cases these are palms—the familiar sacred tree of Mesopotamia, about which more must be said hereafter in a later chapter. The well-known *bois sacré* at Blidah is a considerable grove, with a *koubba* in its midst. A similar *temenos* frequently surrounded the Egyptian and the Greek temple. I do not assert that these were always of necessity actual tombs; but they were at any rate cenotaphs. When once people had got accustomed to the idea that certain trees were sacred to the memory of their ancestors or their gods, it would be but a slight step to plant such trees round an empty temple. When Xenophon, for example, built a shrine to Artemis, and planted around it a grove of many kinds of fruit trees, and placed in it an altar and an image of the goddess, nobody would for a moment suppose he erected it over the body of an actual dead Artemis. But men would never have begun building temples and consecrating groves at all if they had not first built houses for the dead god-chief, and planted shrubs and trees upon his venerated tumulus. Nay, even the naïve inscription upon Xenophon's shrine—" He who lives here and enjoys the fruits of the ground must every year offer the tenth part of the produce to the goddess, and out of the residue keep the temple in repair"—does it not carry us back implicitly to the origin of priesthood, and of the desire for perpetuity in the due maintenance of the religious offices?

I shall say nothing here about the evolution of the great civilised tree-gods like Attis and Adonis, so common in the region of the eastern Mediterranean, partly because I have already treated them at some length in the essay on Tree-Worship to which I have alluded above, and partly because they would lead us too far afield from our present subject. But a few words must be devoted in passing to the prevalence of tree-worship among the Semitic peoples, intimately connected as it is with the rise of certain important elements in the Christian cult.

"In all parts of the Semitic area," says Professor Robertson Smith, "trees were adored as divine." Among the species thus honoured he enumerates especially the pines and cedars of Lebanon, the evergreen oaks of the Palestinian hills, the tamarisks of the Syrian jungles, and the acacias of the Arabian wadies. Most of these, it will be noted, are evergreens. In Arabia, the most striking case on record is that of the sacred date-palm at Nejran. This was adored at an annual feast, when it was " all hung with fine clothes and women's ornaments." A similar tree existed at Mecca, to which the people resorted annually, and hung upon it weapons, garments, ostrich eggs, and other offerings. In a sacred acacia at Nakla a goddess was supposed to live. The modern Arabs still hang pieces of flesh on such sacred trees, honour them with sacrifices, and present them with rags of calico and coloured beads.

As regards the Phœnicians and Canaanites, Philo Byblius says that plants were in ancient times revered as gods, and honoured with libations and sacrifices. Dr. Robertson Smith gives several instances. Christianity has not extinguished the veneration for sacred trees in Syria, where they are still prayed to in sickness and hung with rags. The Moslems of Palestine also venerate the sacred trees of immemorial antiquity.

In the Hebrew scriptures tree-worship constantly appears, and is frankly dwelt with by Professor Robertson Smith, who does not refuse to connect with this set of beliefs the legend of Jahweh in the burning bush. The local altars of early Hebrew cult were habitually set up "under green trees." On this subject I would refer the reader to Dr. Smith's own interesting disquisition on p. 193 of *The Religion of the Semites*.

With regard to the general sacredness of vegetation, and especially of food-plants, such as corn, the vine, and the date-palm, I postpone that important subject for the present, till we come to consider the gods of cultivation, and the curious set of ideas which gradually led up to sacramental god-eating. In a theme so vast and so involved as that of human religion, it becomes necessary to take one point at a time, and to deal with the various parts in analytic isolation.

We have now examined briefly almost all the principal sacred objects of the world, according to classes—the corpse, the mummy, the idol, the sacred stone, the sacred stake, the sacred tree or grove; there remains but one other group of holy things, very generally recognised, which I do not propose to examine separately, but to which a few words may yet be devoted at the end of a chapter. I mean, the sacred wells. It might seem at first sight as if these could have no possible connection with death or burial; but that expectation is, strange to say, delusive. There appears to be some reason for bringing wells, too, into the widening category of funereal objects. The oxen's well at Acre, for example, was visited by Christian, Jewish, and Moslem pilgrims; it was therefore an object of great ancient sanctity; but observe this point: there is a *mashhed* or sacred tomb beside it, " perhaps the modern representative of the ancient Memnonium." Every Egyptian temple had in like manner its sacred lake. In modern Syria, " cisterns are always found beside the grave of saints, and are believed to be inhabited by a sort of fairy. A pining child is thought to be a fairy changeling, and must be lowered into the cistern." The similarity of the belief about holy wells in England and Ireland, and their frequent association with the name of a saint, would seem to suggest for them a like origin. Sacred rivers usually rise from sacred springs, near which stands a temple. The river Adonis took its origin at the shrine of Aphaca: and the grave of Adonis, about whom much more must be said hereafter, stood near the mouth of the holy stream that was reddened by his blood. The sacred river Belus had also its peculiar Memnonium or Adonis tomb. But I must add that sacred rivers had likewise their annual god-victims, about whom we shall have a great deal to say at a later stage of our enquiry, and from whom in part they probably derived their sanctity. Still, that their holiness was also due in part, and originally, to tombs at their sources, I think admits of no reasonable doubt.

The equivalence of the holy well and the holy stone is shown by the fact that while a woman whose chastity was suspected had to drink water of a sacred spring to prove her innocence, at Mecca she had to swear seventy oaths by the Kaaba.

Again, sacred wells and fountains were and are worshipped with just the same acts of sacrifice as ghosts and images. At Aphaca, the pilgrims cast into the holy pool jewels of gold and silver, with webs of linen and other precious stuffs. A holy grove was an adjunct of the holy spring: in Greece, according to Bötticher, they were seldom separated. At the annual fair of the Sacred Terebinth, or tree and well of Abraham at Mamre, the heathen visitors offered sacrifices beside the tree, and cast into the well libations of wine, with cakes, coins, myrrh, and incense: all of which we may compare with the Ostyak offerings to ancestral grave-stakes. At the holy waters of Karwa, bread, fruit, and other foods were laid beside the fountain. At Mecca, and at the Stygian Waters in the Syrian desert, similar gifts were cast into the holy source. In one of these instances at least we know that the holy well was associated with an actual burial; for at Aphaca, the holiest shrine of Syria, the tomb of the local Baal or god was shown beside the sacred fountain. "A buried god," says Dr. Robertson Smith quaintly, in commenting on this fact, "is a god that dwells under ground." It would be far truer and more philosophical to say that a god who dwells underground is a buried man.

I need not recall the offerings to Cornish and Irish well-spirits, which have now degenerated for the most part into pins and needles.

On the whole, though it is impossible to understand the entire genesis of sacred founts and rivers without previous consideration of deliberate god-making, a subject which I reserve for a later portion of our exposition, I do not think we shall go far wrong in supposing that the sacred well most often occurs in company with the sacred tree, the sacred stone or altar, and the sacred tomb; and that it owes its sanctity in the last resort, originally at least, to a burial by its side; though I do not doubt that this sanctity was in many cases kept up by the annual immolation of a fresh victim-god, of a type whose genesis will hereafter detain us. Indeed, Dr. Robertson Smith says of the Semitic worship in general, "The usual natural symbols are a fountain or a tree, while the ordinary artificial symbol is a pillar or pile of stones : but very often all three are found together, and this was the rule in the more developed sanctuaries." I cannot agree with him on the point of "symbolism" : but the collocation of objects is at least significant.

Thus, in ultimate analysis, we see that all the sacred objects of the world are either dead men themselves, as corpse, mummy, ghost, or god ; or else the tomb where such men are buried ; or else the temple, shrine, or hut which covers the tomb ; or else the tombstone, altar, image, or statue, standing over it and representing the ghost ; or else the stake, idol, or household god which is fashioned as their deputy ; or else the tree which grows above the barrow ; or else the well, or tank, or spring, natural or artificial, by whose side the dead man has been laid to rest. In one form or another, from beginning to end, we find only, in Mr. William Simpson's graphic phrase, "the Worship of Death," as the basis and root of all human religion.

CHAPTER VIII.

THE GODS OF EGYPT.

We have now completed our preliminary survey of the nature and origin of Gods in general. We have seen how men first came to believe in the objective existence of these powerful and invisible beings, how they learnt to invest them with majestic attributes, and how they grew to worship them under the various forms of mummies or boulders, stone or wooden idols, trees or stumps, wells, rivers, and fountains. In short, we have briefly arrived at the origin of Polytheism. We have now to go on to our second question—How from the belief in many gods did men progress to the belief in one single God, the creator and upholder of all things? Our task is now to reconstruct the origin of Monotheism.

But Monotheism bases itself entirely upon the great God of the Hebrews. To him, therefore, we must next address ourselves. Is he too resoluble, as I hinted before, into a Sacred Stone, the monument and representative of some prehistoric chieftain? Can we trace the origin of the Deity of Christendom till we find him at last in a forgotten Semitic ghost of the earliest period?

The chief Hebrew god Jahweh, when we first catch a passing glimpse of his primitive worship by his own people, was but one among a number of competing deities, mostly, it would appear, embodied by their votaries in the visible form of stone or wooden pillars, and adored by a small group of loosely-connected tribes among the mountain region in the southwest of Syria. The confederacy among whom he dwelt knew themselves as the Sons of Israel; they regarded Jahweh as their principal god, much as the Greeks did Zeus, or the early Teutons their national hero Woden. But a universal tradition among them bore witness to the fact that they had once lived in a subject condition in Egypt, the house of bondage, and that their god Jahweh had been instrumental in leading them thence into the rugged land they inhabited throughout the whole historical period, between the valley of Jordan and the Mediterranean coast. So consistent and so definite was this traditional belief that we can hardly regard it otherwise than as enclosing a kernel of truth; and not only do Kuenen and other Semitic scholars of the present day admit it as genuine, but the Egyptologists also seem generally to allow its substantial accuracy and full accord with hieroglyphic literature. This sojourn in Egypt cannot have failed to influence to some extent the Semitic strangers: therefore I shall begin my quest of the Hebrew god among the Egyptian monuments. Admitting that he was essentially in all respects a deity of the true Semitic pattern, I think it will do us good to learn a little beforehand about the people among whom his votaries dwelt so long, especially as the history of the Egyptian cults affords us perhaps the best historical example of the growth and development of a great national religion.

A peculiar interest, indeed, attaches in the history of the human mind to the evolution of the gods of Egypt. Nowhere else in the world can we trace so well such a continuous development from the very simplest beginnings of religious ideas to the very highest planes of mysticism and philosophic theology. There are savage cults, it is true, which show us more clearly the earliest stages in the process whereby the simple ancestral ghost passes imperceptibly into the more powerful form of a supernatural deity: there are elevated civilised creeds which show us more grandly in its evolved shape the final conception of a single supreme Ruler of the Cosmos. But there is no other religious system known to us in which we can follow so readily, without a single break, the whole evolutionary movement whereby the earlier ideas get gradually expanded and etherealised into the later. The origin of the other great historical religions is lost from our eyes among dim mists of fable : in Egypt alone, of all civilised countries, does our record go back to the remote period when the religious conception was still at the common savage level, and follow it forward continuously to the advanced point where it had all but achieved, in its syncretic movement, the ultimate goal of pure monotheism.

I would wish, however, to begin my review of this singular history by saying, once for all, that while I make no pretensions to special Egyptological knowledge, I must nevertheless dissent on general anthropological grounds from the attitude taken up by Mr. Le Page Renouf in his *Lectures on the Religion of Ancient Egypt*. That learned writer's work, indeed, is, scientifically speaking, half a century behind its time. It is written as though the doctrine of evolution had never been promulgated ; and every page contains glaring contradictions of the most elementary principles of human development. Mr. Renouf still adheres to the discredited ideas that polytheism grew out of an antecedent monotheism ; that animal-worship and other low forms of adoration are " symbolical " in origin ; and that " the sublimer portions of the Egyptian religion are not the comparatively late result of a process of development or elimination from the grosser." Such theories would of themselves be extremely improbable, even on the fullest and best evidence ; but the evidence which Mr. Renouf brings forward to support them is of the flimsiest description. A plain survey of the Egyptian monuments in the Nile valley, and of the known facts about Egyptian religion, will lead any unbiassed mind, free from the warping influence of preconception, and accustomed to wide anthropological enquiry, to precisely opposite and more probable conclusions. For it must be carefully borne in mind that on these subjects the specialist is the last man whose opinions should be implicitly and unhesitatingly accepted. The religion of Egypt, like the religion of Judæa or the religion of Hawaii, must be judged, not in isolation, but by the analogies of other religions elsewhere; the attempt to explain it as an unrelated phenomenon, which has already been found so disastrous in the case of the Semitic and the Aryan cults, must be abandoned once for all by the comparative psychologist as a hopeless error. The key to the origin of the Egyptian faith is to be found, not in the late philosophising glosses quoted by M. de Rougé and his English disciple, but in the simple, unvarying, ancestral creeds of existing African savages.

Looked at from this point of view, then—the evolutionary point of view—nothing can be clearer than the fact that the early Egyptian religion bases itself entirely upon two main foundations, ancestor-worship and totemism.

I will begin with the first of these, which all analogy teaches us to consider by far the earliest, and infinitely the most important. And I may add that it is also, to judge by the Egyptian evidence alone, both the element which underlies the whole religious conceptions of the Nile valley, and likewise the element which directly accounts, as we shall see hereafter, for all the most important gods of the national pantheon, including Osiris, Ptah, Khem, and Amen, as well perhaps as many of their correlative goddesses. There is not, in fact, any great ethnical religion on earth, except possibly the Chinese, in which the basal importance of the Dead Man is so immediately apparent as in the ancient cult of Pharaohnic Egypt.

The Egyptian religion bases itself upon the tomb. It is impossible for a moment to doubt that fact as one stands under the scanty shade of the desert date-palms among the huge sun-smitten dust-heaps that represent the streets of Thebes and Memphis. The commonest object of worship on all the monuments of Nile is beyond doubt the Mummy: sometimes the private mummy of an ancestor or kinsman, sometimes the greater deified mummies of immemorial antiquity, blended in the later syncretic mysticism with the sun-god and other allegorical deities, but represented to the very last in all ages of art—on the shattered Rameseum at Thebes or the Ptolemaic pillars of still unshaken Denderah—as always unmistakable and obvious mummies. If ever there was a country where the Worship of the Dead was pushed to an extreme, that country was distinctly and decisively Egypt.

"The oldest sculptures show us no acts of adoration or of sacrifice," says Mr. Loftie, "except those of worship at the shrine of a deceased ancestor or relative." This is fully in keeping with what we know of the dawn of religion elsewhere, and with the immense importance always attached to the preservation of the mummy intact throughout the whole long course of Egyptian history. The Egyptian, in spite of his high civilisation, remained always at the first or corpse-preserving stage of custom as regards the dead. To him, therefore, the life after death was far more serious than the life on earth: he realised it so fully that he made endless preparations for it during his days above, and built himself a tomb as an eternal mansion. The grave was a place of abode, where the mummy was to pass the greater part of his existence; and even in the case of private persons (like that famous Tih whose painted sepulchre at Sakkarah every tourist to Cairo makes a point of visiting) it was sumptuously decorated with painting and sculpture. In the mortuary chambers or chapels attached to the tombs, the relations of the deceased and the priests of the cemetery celebrated on certain fixed dates various ceremonies in honour of the dead, and offered appropriate gifts to the mummy within. "The tables of offerings, which no doubt formed part of the furniture of the chambers, are depicted on the walls, covered with the gifts of meat, fruits, bread, and wine which had to be presented in kind." These *parentalia* undoubtedly formed the main feature of the practical religion of early Egypt, as exhibited to us on all the monuments except the late tomb-caves of royal personages, devoted to the worship of the equally mummified great gods.

The Egyptian tomb was usually a survival of the cave artificially imitated. The outer chamber, in which the ceremonies of the offertory took place, was the only part accessible, after the interment had been completed, to the feet of survivors. The mummy itself, concealed in its sarcophagus, lay at the bottom of a deep pit beyond, by the end of a corridor often containing statues or idols of the deceased. These idols, says M. Maspero, were indefinitely multiplied, in case the mummy itself should be accidentally destroyed, in order that the *Ka* (the ghost or double) might find a safe dwelling-place. Compare the numerous little images placed upon the grave by the Coast Negroes. It was the outer chamber, however, that sheltered the *stele* or pillar which bore the epitaph, as well as the altar or table for offerings, the smoke from which was conveyed to the statues in the corridor through a small aperture in the wall of partition. Down the well beyond, the mummy in person reposed, in its eternal dwelling-place, free from all chance of violation or outrage. "The greatest importance," says Mr. Renouf, "was attached to the permanence of the tomb, to the continuance of the religious ceremonies, and to the prayers of passers-by." Again, "there is a very common formula stating that the person who raised the tablet 'made it as a memorial to his fathers who are in the nether world, built up what he found was imperfect, and renewed what was found out of repair.'" In the inscription on one of the great tombs at Beni-Hàssan the founder says: "I made to flourish the name of my father, and I built chapels for his *ka* [or ghost]. I caused statues to be conveyed to the holy dwelling, and distributed to them their offerings in pure gifts. I instituted the officiating priest, to whom I gave donations in land and presents. I ordered funeral offerings for all the feasts of the nether world [which are then enumerated at considerable length]. If it happen that the priest or any other cease to do this, may he not exist, and may his son not sit in his seat." All this is highly instructive from the point of view of the origin of priesthood.

How long these early religious endowments continued to be respected is shown by Mr. Renouf himself in one instructive passage. The kings who built the Pyramids in the Early Empire endowed a priestly office for the purpose of celebrating the periodical rites of offering to their ghosts or mummies. Now, a tablet in the Louvre shows that a certain person who lived under the Twenty-sixth Dynasty was priest of Khufu, the builder of the Great Pyramid, who had endowed the office two thousand years before his time. We have actually the tombs of some of his predecessors who filled the same office immediately after Khufu's death. So that in this instance at least, the worship of the deceased monarch continued for a couple of thousand years without interruption. "If in the case of private interments," says M. Maspero, "we find no proof of so persistent a veneration. that is because in ordinary tombs the ceremonies were performed not by special priests, but by the children or descendants of the deceased person. Often, at the end of a few generations, either through negligence, removals, ruin. or extinction of the family, the cult was suspended, and the memory of the dead died out altogether."

For this reason, as everywhere else among ancestor-worshippers, immense importance was attached by the Egyptians to the begetting of a son who should perform the due family rites, or see that they were performed by others after him. The duty of undertaking these rites is thoroughly insisted upon in all the maxims or moral texts ; while on the other hand, the wish that a man may not have a son to perform them for him is the most terrible of all ancient Egyptian imprecations. "Many centuries after the construction of a tomb. Egyptian travellers have left a record upon its walls of the splendour of the sacred abode, of the abundance of the materials which they found provided for the fulfilment of the rites for the departed, and of their own repetition of the funeral formula." In fact, the whole practical religion of the ordinary Egyptians, as a plain observer sees it to-day in the vast mass of the existing monuments, consists almost exclusively in the worship of the *ka*—the *genii, manes,* or *lares* of the departed.

If even the common herd were thus carefully embalmed—if even the lesser functionaries of the court or temple lay in expensive tombs, daintily painted and exquisitely sculptured—it might readily be believed that the great kings of the mighty conquering dynasties themselves would raise for their mummies eternal habitations of special spendour and becoming magnificence. And so they did. In Lower Egypt, their tombs are barrows or pyramids : in Upper Egypt they are artificial caves. The dreary desert district west of the Nile and south of Cairo consists for many miles, all but uninterruptedly, of the cemetery of Memphis—a vast and mouldering city of the dead—whose chief memorials are the wonderful series of Pyramids, the desecrated tombs piled up for the kings of the Third, Fourth, Fifth, and Sixth Dynasties. There, under stone tumuli of enormous size,—barrows or cairns more carefully constructed,—the Pharaohs of the Old Empire reposed in peace in sepulchres unmarked by any emblems of the mystic gods or sacred beasts of later imagination. But still more significant and infinitely more beautiful are the rock-hewn Tombs of the Kings at Thebes, belonging to the great monarchs of the Eighteenth, Nineteenth and Twentieth Dynasties, when the religion had assumed its full mystical development. Those magnificent subterranean halls form in the truest and most literal sense a real necropolis, a town of mummies, where each king was to inhabit an eternal palace of regal splendour, decorated with a profusion of polychromatic art, and filled with many mansions for the officers of state, still destined to attend upon their sovereign in the nether world. Some of the mural paintings would even seem to suggest that slaves or captives were sacrificed at the tomb, to serve their lord in his eternal home, as his courtiers had served him in the temporal palaces of Medinet-Hábu or the corridors of Luxor.

M. Mariette has further shown that the huge Theban temples which skirt in long line the edge of the desert near the Valley of Tombs were really cenotaphs where the memory of the kings buried hard by was preserved and worshipped. Thus the Rameseum was the *mastabah* or mortuary chapel for the tomb and ghost of Rameses II.; the temple of Medinet-Hábu fulfilled the same purpose for Rameses III.; the temple of Kurneh for Rameses I.; and so forth throughout the whole long series of those gigantic ruins, with their correlated group of subterranean excavations.

At any rate, it is quite impossible for any impartial person to examine the existing monuments which line the grey desert hills of the Nile without seeing for himself that the mummy is everywhere the central object of worship—that the entire practical religion of the people was based upon this all-pervading sense of the continuity of life beyond the grave, and upon the necessity for paying due reverence and funereal offerings to the *manes* of ancestors. Everything in Egypt points to this one conclusion. Even the great sacred ritual is the Book of the Dead: and the very word by which the departed are oftenest described means itself "the living," from the firm belief of the people that they were really enjoying everlasting life. *Mors janua vitæ* is the short summing-up of Egyptian religious notions. Death was the great beginning for which they all prepared, and the dead were the real objects of their most assiduous public and private worship.

Moreover, in the tombs themselves we can trace a gradual development of the religious sentiment from

Corpse-Worship to God-Worship. Thus, in the tombs of Sakkarah, belonging to the Old Empire (Fifth Dynasty), all those symbolical representations of the life beyond the tomb which came in with the later mysticism are almost wholly wanting. The quotations from (or anticipations of) the Book of the Dead are few and short. The great gods are rarely alluded to. Again, in the grottos of Beni-Hassan (of the Twelfth Dynasty) the paintings mostly represent scenes from the life of the deceased, and the mystic signs and deities are still absent. The doctrine of rewards and punishments remains as yet comparatively in abeyance. It is only at the Tombs of the Kings at Thebes (of the Eighteenth Dynasty) that entire chapters of the Book of the Dead are transcribed at length, and the walls are covered with "a whole army of grotesque and fantastic divinities."

"But the Egyptians," it will be objected, "had also great gods, distinct from their ancestors—national, or local, or common gods—whose names and figures have come down to us inscribed upon all the monuments." Quite true: that is to say, there are gods who are not immediately or certainly resolvable into deified ancestors —gods whose power and might were at last widely extended, and who became transfigured by degrees beyond all recognition in the latest ages. But it is by no means certain, even so, that we cannot trace these greater gods themselves back in the last resort to deified ancestors of various ruling families or dominant cities; and in one or two of the most important cases the suggestions of such an origin are far from scanty.

I will take, to begin with, one typical example. There is no single god in the Egyptian pantheon more important or more universally diffused than Osiris. In later forms of the national religion, he is elevated into the judge of the departed and king of the nether world: to be "justified by Osiris," or, as later interpreters say, "a justified Osiris," is the prayer of every corpse as set forth in his funeral inscription; and identification with Osiris is looked upon as the reward of all the happy and faithful dead. Now Osiris, in every one of his representations and modes, is simply—a Mummy. His myth, to be sure, assumed at last immense proportions; and his relations with Isis and Horus form the centre of an endless series of irreconcilable tales, repeated over and over again in art and literature. If we took mythology as our guide, instead of the monuments, we should be tempted to give him far other origins. He is identified often with other gods, especially with Amen; and the disentanglement of his personality in the monuments of the newer empire, when Ra, the sun-god, got mixed up inextricably with so many other deities, is particularly difficult. But if we neglect these later complications of a very ancient cult, and go back to the simplest origin of Egyptian history and religion, we shall, I think, see that this mystic god, so often explained away by elemental symbolism into the sun or the home of the dead, was in his first beginnings nothing more or less than what all his pictures and statues show him to be—a revered and worshipped Mummy, a very ancient chief or king of the town or little district of This by Abydos.

I do not deny that in later ages Osiris became much more than this. Nor do I deny that his name was accepted as a symbol for all the happy and pious dead. Furthermore, we shall find at a later stage that he was identified in the end with an annual slain Corn-God. I will even allow that there may have been more than one original Osiris—that the word may even at first have been generic, not specific. But I still maintain that the evidence shows us the great and principal Osiris of all as a Dead Chief of Abydos.

We must remember that in Egypt alone history goes back to an immense antiquity and yet shows us already at its very beginning an advanced civilisation and a developed picture-writing. Therefore the very oldest known state of Egypt necessarily presupposes a vast anterior era of slow growth in concentration and culture. Before ever Upper or Lower Egypt became united under a single crown, there must have been endless mud-built villages and petty palm-shadowed principalities along the bank of the Nile, each possessing its own local chief or king, and each worshipping its own local deceased potentates. The sheikh of the village, as we should call him nowadays, was then their nameless Pharaoh, and the mummies of his ancestors were their gods and goddesses. Each tribe had also its special totem, about which I shall have a little more to say hereafter; and these totems were locally worshipped almost as gods, and gave rise in all probability to the later Egyptian Zoolatry and the animal-headed deities. To the very last, Egyptian religion bore marked traces of this original tribal form; the great multiplicity of Egyptian gods seems to be due to the adoption of so many of them, after the unification of the country, into the national pantheon. The local gods and local totems, however, continued to be specially worshipped in their original sites. Thus the ithyphallic Amen-Khem was specially worshipped at Thebes, where his figure occurs with unpleasant frequency upon every temple; Apis was peculiarly sacred at Memphis; Pasht at Bubastis; Anubis at Sekhem; Neith at Sais; Ra at Heliopolis; and Osiris himself at Abydos, his ancient dwelling-place.

Even Egyptian tradition seems to preserve some dim memory of such a state of things, for it asserts that before the time of Menes, the first king of the First Dynasty, reputed the earliest monarch of a united Egypt, dynasties of the gods ruled in the country. In other words, it was recognised that the gods were originally kings of local lines which reigned in the various provinces of the Nile valley before the unification.

In the case of Osiris, the indications which lead us in this direction are almost irresistible. It is all but certain that Osiris was originally a local god of This or Thinis, a village near Abydos, wher a huge mound of rubbish still marks the site of the great deity's resting-place. The latter town is described in the Harris papyrus as Abud, the hand of Osiris ; and in the monuments which still remain at that site, Osiris is everywhere the chief deity represented, to whom kings and priests present appropriate offerings. But it is a significant fact that Menes, the founder of the united monarchy, was born at the same place ; and this suggests the probability that Osiris may have been the most sacred and most venerated of Menes's ancestors. The suggestion derives further weight from the fact that Osiris is invariably represented as a mummy, and that he wears a peculiar head-dress or cap of office, the same as that which was used in historical times as the crown of Upper Egypt. He also holds in his hands the crook and scourge which are the marks of kingly office— the crook to lead his own people like a shepherd, the scourge to punish evil-doers and to ward off enemies. His image is therefore nothing more nor less than the image of a Mummied King. Sometimes, too, he wears in addition the regal ostrich plumes. Surely, naught save the blind infatuation of mythologists could make them overlook the plain inference that Osiris was a mummified chief of Abydos in the days before the unification of Egypt under a single rule, and that he was worshipped by his successors in the petty principality exactly as we know other kingly mummies were worshipped by their family elsewhere—exactly, for example, as on the famous Tablet of Ancestors found at Abydos itself, Sethi I. and Rameses II. are seen offering homage to seventy-six historical kings, their predecessors on the throne of United Egypt.

Not only, however, is Osiris represented as a king and a mummy, but we are expressly told by Plutarch (or at least by the author of the tract *De Osiride* which bears his name) that the tomb of Osiris existed at Abydos, and that the richest and most powerful of the Egyptians were desirous of being buried in the adjacent cemetery, in order that they might lie, as it were, in the same grave with the great god of their country. All this is perfectly comprehensible and natural if we suppose that a Thinite dynasty first conquered the whole of Egypt ; that it extended the worship of its own local ancestor-god over the entire country ; and that in time, when this worship had assumed national importance, the local god became the chief figure in the common pantheon.

I had arrived at this opinion independently before I was aware that Mr. Loftie had anticipated me in it. But in his rare and interesting *Essay on Scarabs* I find he has reached the same conclusions.

"The divinity of Pharaoh," says Mr. Loftie, "was the first article in the creed of the pyramid period, the earliest of which we know anything. As time went on, though the king was still called divine, we see him engaged in the worship of other gods. At last he appears as a priest himself ; and when Herodotus and the later Greek historians visited Egypt, there was so little of this part of the old religion left that it is not even mentioned by them as a matter of importance." This is quite natural, I may remark parenthetically, for as the antiquity and grandeur of the great gods increased, the gulf between them and mere men, even though those men were kings, their offspring, must always have grown ever wider and wider. "I have myself no doubt whatever," Mr. Loftie goes on, "that the names of Osiris and of Horus are those of ancient rulers. I think that, long before authentic history begins, Asar and Aset his wife reigned in Egypt, probably in that wide valley of the Upper Nile which is now the site of Girgeh and Berbé" (exactly where I place the principality of Osiris). "Their son was Hor, or Horus, the first king of Upper and Lower Egypt; and the 'Hor seshoo,' the successors of Horus, are not obscurely mentioned by later chroniclers. I know that this view is not shared by all students of the subject, and much learning and ingenuity have been spent to prove that Asar, and Aset, and Hor, and Ptah, and Anep, are representations of the powers of nature ; that they do not point to ancient princes, but to ancient principles; and that Horus and his successors are gods and were never men. But in the oldest inscriptions we find none of that mysticism which is shown in the sculptures from the time of the eighteenth dynasty down to the Ptolemies and the Roman Emperors." In short, Mr. Loftie goes on to set forth a theory of the origin of the great gods essentially similar to the one I am here defending.

Though a little out of place, I cannot help noting here the curious confirmatory fact that a number of ibis mummies have been found at Abydos in close proximity to the mound where M. Mariette confidently expected to discover in the rock the actual tomb of Osiris himself. Hence we may conclude that the ibis was in all probability the totem of Abydos or This, as the bull was of Memphis, the crocodile of the Fayoum, the cat of Bubastis, and the baboon of Thebes. Now, the ibis-god of Abydos is Thoth; and it is noteworthy that Thoth, as recorder, always accompanies Osiris, in later legend, as judge of the dead: the local mummy-god, in other words, has as his assessor the local totem-god; and both are commonly to be seen on the monuments of Abydos, in company with Horus, Anubis, Isis, and other (probably) local divinities.

It is quite easy to see how, with this origin, Osiris would almost inevitably grow with time to be the King of the Dead, and supreme judge of the nether regions. For, as the most sacred of the ancestors of the regal line, he would naturally be the one whom the kings, in their turn, would most seek to propitiate, and whom they would look forward to joining in their eternal home. As the myth extended, and as mystical interpretations began to creep in, identifications being made of the gods with the sun or other natural energies, the original meaning of Osiris-worship would grow gradually obscured. But to the last, Osiris himself, in spite of all corruptions, is represented as a mummy: and even when identified with Amen, the later intrusive god, he still wears his mummy-bandages, and still bears the crook and scourge and sceptre of his primitive kingship.

It may be objected, however, that there were many forms of Orisis, and many local gods who bore the same name. He was buried at Abydos, but was also equally buried at Memphis, and at Philæ as well. The pretty little "Temple on the Roof" at Denderah is an exquisitely elaborate chapel to the local Osiris of that town, with chambers dedicated to the various other Osiris-gods of the forty-two nomes of ancient Egypt. Well, that fact runs exactly parallel with the local Madonnas and the local Apollos of other religions : and nobody has suggested doubts as to the human reality of the Blessed Virgin Mary because so many different Maries exist in different sacred sites or in different cathedrals. Our Lady of Loretto is the same as Our Lady of Lourdes. Jesus of Nazareth was nevertheless born at Bethlehem: he was the son of Joseph, but he was also the son of David, and the son of God. Perhaps Osiris was a common noun : perhaps a slightly different Osiris was worshipped in various towns of later Egypt; perhaps a local mummy-god, the ancestor of some extinct native line, often wrongly usurped the name and prerogatives of the great mummy-god of Abydos, especially under the influence of late priestly mysticism. Moreover, when we come to consider the subject of the manufacture of gods, we shall see that the body of an annual incarnation of Osiris may have been divided and distributed among all the nomes of Egypt. It is enough for my present purpose if I point out in brief that ancestor-worship amply explains the rise and prevalence of the cult of Osiris, the kingly mummy, with the associated cults of Horus, Isis, Thoth, and the other deities of the Osirian cycle.

I may add that a gradual growth of Osiris-worship is clearly marked on the monuments themselves. The simpler stelæ and memorials of the earliest age seldom contain the names of any god, but display votaries making offerings at the shrine of ancestors. Similarly, the scenes represented on the walls of tombs of early date bear no reference to the great gods of later ages, but are merely domestic and agricultural in character, as may be observed at Sakkarah and even to some extent also at Beni-Hassan. Under the Sixth Dynasty, the monuments begin to make more and more frequent mention of Osiris, who now comes to be regarded as Judge of the Dead and Lord of the Lower World ; and on a tablet of this age in the Boulak Museum occurs for the first time the expression afterwards so common, "justified by Osiris." Under the Twelfth Dynasty, legend becomes more prominent ; a solar and lunar character seems to be given by reflex to Osiris and Isis: and the name of Ra, the sun, is added to that of many previously distinct and independent deities. Khem, the ithyphallic god of the Thebaid, now also assumes greater importance, as is quite natural under a line of Theban princes: and Khem, a local mummy-god, is always represented in his swathing-clothes, and afterwards confounded, certainly with Amen, and probably also with the mummy-god of Abydos. But Osiris from this time forward rises distinctly into the front rank as a deity. "To him, rather than to the dead, the friends and family offer their sacrifices. A court is formed for him. Thoth, the recorder [totem-god of Abydos], Anubis the watcher, Ra the impersonation of truth, and others, assist in judgment on the soul." The name of the deceased is henceforth constantly accompanied by the formula "justified by Osiris." About the same time the Book of the Dead in its full form came into existence, with its developed conception of the lower world, and its complicated arrangement of planes of purgatorial progress.

Under the Eighteenth Dynasty, the legend thickens ; the identifications of the gods become more and more intricate ; Amen and Ra are sought and found under innumerable forms of other deities; and a foundation is laid for the esoteric Monotheism or pantheistic nature-worship of the later philosophising priesthood. It was under the Nineteenth Dynasty that the cult of local Triads or Trinities took fullest shape, and that the mystical interpretation of the religion of Egypt came well into the foreground. The great Osirian myth was then more and more minutely and mystically elaborated; and even the bull Apis, the totem-god of Memphis, was recognised as a special incarnation of Osiris, who thus becomes, with Amen, the mysterious summing-up of almost all the national pantheon. At last we find the myth going off into pure mysticism, Osiris being at once the father, brother, husband, and son of Isis, and also the son of his own child Horus.* Sentences with an almost Athanasian mixture of vagueness and definiteness inform us how "the son proceeds from the father, and the father proceeds from his son"; how "Ra is the soul of Osiris, and Osiris the soul of Ra"; and how Horus his child, awakened by magical rites from his dead body, is victorious over Set, the prince of darkness, and sits as Osiris upon the throne of the father whom he has revived and avenged. Here as elsewhere the myth, instead of being the explanation of the god, does nothing more than darken counsel.

In like manner, I believe, Ptah was originally a local mummy-god of Memphis, and Khem of Ap, afterwards known as Chemmis.

This gradual growth of a dead and mummified village chief, however, into a pantheistic god, strange as it may seem, is not in any way more remarkable than the gradual

---

* "Stories like the Osiris myth," says Mr. Lang, "spring from no pure religious source, but embody the delusions and fantastic dreams of the lowest and least developed human fancy and human speculation." This sentence enforces precisely the same idea that I have previously expressed in chapter ii. as to the real relations of religion and mythology. The myth nowhere explains the cult; it casts no light upon its origin or history; on the contrary, it only obscures and overshadows the underlying kernel of genuine fact.

growth of a Galilean peasant into the second person of an eternal and omnipotent Godhead. Nor does the myth of the death and resurrection of Osiris (to be considered hereafter in a later chapter) militate against the reality of his human existence any more than the history of the death and resurrection of Jesus Christ militates against the human existence of Jesus of Nazareth. "Gross and crude euhemerism" may be bad; but airy and fantastic Maxmüllerism appears to me just as unphilosophical.

The difficulty of the evolution, indeed, is not at all great, if we consider the further fact that even after the concept of godship had been fully developed, the king still remained of like nature with the gods, their son and descendant, a divine personage himself, differing from them only in not having yet received eternal life, the symbol of which they are often shown in sculpture as presenting with gracious expressions to their favoured scion. "The ruling sovereign of Egypt," says Mr. Le Page Renouf, "was the living image of and vicegerent of the sun-god. He was invested with the attributes of divinity, and that in the earliest times of which we possess monumental evidence." And quite naturally, for in antique times gods had ruled in Egypt, whose successor the king was: and the kings before Menes were significantly known as "the successors of Horus." As late as the times of the Ptolemies, we saw, there were priests of Menes and other Pharaohs of the most ancient dynasties. The pyramid kings took the title of the Golden Horus, afterwards copied by their descendants; and from Chafra onward the reigning monarch was known as the Son of Ra and the Great God. Amenophis II., during his own lifetime, is "a god good like Ra, the sacred seed of Amen, the son whom he begot." And on all the monuments the king is represented of the same superhuman stature as the gods themselves: he converses with them on equal terms; they lead him by the hand into their inmost sanctuaries, or present him with the symbols of royal rule and of eternal life, like friends of the family.

The former guerdon bestows upon him the same rank they themselves had held on earth; the latter advances him to share with them the glories of the other existence. In the temple of Kurneh, Rameses I. (then dead) receives the offerings and liturgies of his royal grandson. Hard by, Rameses II. offers to Amen-ra, Khonso, and Rameses I., without distinction of divinity. On the side wall, Sethi I. receives similar divine honours from the royal hands: while in the centre chamber Sethi himself officiates before the statue of his father placed in a shrine. The King is thus but the Living God : the God is thus but the Dead King.

I conclude, therefore, that a large part of the greater Egyptian gods—the national or local gods, as opposed to those worshipped by each family in its own necropolis— were early kings, whose myths were later expanded into legends, rationalised into nature-worship, and adorned by priestly care with endless symbolical or esoteric fancies. But down to the very latest age of independence, inscriptions of the god Euergetes, and the goddess Berenice, or representations like that at Philæ, of the god Philadelphus suckled by Isis, show that to the Egyptian mind the gulf between humanity and divinity was very narrow, and that the original manhood of all the deities was an idea quite familiar to priests and people.

There was, however, another class of gods about which we can be somewhat less certain ; these are the animal-gods and animal-headed gods which developed out of the totems of the various villages. Such bestial types, Professor Sayce remarks, "take us back to a remote prehistoric age, when the religious creed of Egypt," say rather, the custom of Egypt, "was still totemism." But in what precise relation totemism stood to the main line of the evolution of gods I do not feel quite so sure in my own mind as does Mr. Herbert Spencer. It seems to me possible that the totem may in its origin have been merely the lucky-beast or badge of a particular tribe (like the regimental goat or deer); and that from being at first petted, domesticated, and to some extent respected on this account, it may have grown at last, through a confusion of ideas, to share the same sort of divine honours which were paid to the ghosts of ancestors and the gods evolved from them. But Mr. Frazer has suggested a better origin of totemism from the doctrine of the Separable Soul, which is, up to date, the best explanation yet offered of this obscure subject. Be that as it may, if the totems were only gradually elevated into divinities, we can easily understand Mr. Renouf's remark that the long series of tombs of the Apis bulls at Sakkarah shows " how immeasurably greater the devotion to the sacred animals was in the later times than in the former."

May I add that the *worship* of totems, as distinct from the mere *care* implied by Mr. Frazer's suggestion, very probably arose from the custom of carving the totem-animal of the deceased on the grave-stake or grave-board? This custom is still universal among the Indian tribes of Northwestern America.

Nevertheless, whatever be the true origin of the totem-gods, I do not think totemism militates in any way against the general principle of the evolution of the idea of a god from the ghost, the Dead Man, or the deified ancestor. For only after the concept of a god had been formed from ancestor-cult, and only after worship had been evolved from the customary offerings to the mummy or spirit at the tomb, could any other object by any possibility be elevated to the godhead. Nor, on the other hand, as I have before remarked, do I feel inclined wholly to agree with Mr. Spencer that every individual god was necessarily once a particular Dead Man. It seems to me indubitable that after the idea of godhead had become fully fixed in the human mind, some gods at least began to be recognised who were directly framed either from abstract conceptions, from natural objects, or from pure outbursts of the mythopœic faculty. I do not think, therefore, that

EGYPTIAN TOTEM-GODS. 175

the existence of a certain (relatively unimportant) class of totem-gods in Egypt or elsewhere is necessarily inconsistent in any way with our main theory of the origin of godhead.

Be this as it may, it is at any rate clear that totemism itself was a very ancient and widespread institution in early Egypt. Totems are defined by Mr. Frazer as "a class of material objects which a savage regards with superstitious respect, believing that there exists between him and every member of the class an intimate and altogether special relation." "Observation of existing totem tribes in Africa, Australia, and elsewhere," says Sir Martin Conway, "shows us that one or more representatives of the totem are often fed or even kept alive in captivity by the tribe." Mr. Frazer tells us that "amongst the Narrinyeri in South Australia, men of the snake clan sometimes catch snakes, pull out their teeth, or sew up their mouths, and keep them as pets. In a pigeon clan of Samoa a pigeon was carefully kept and fed. Amongst the Kalong in Java, whose totem is a red dog, each family as a rule keeps one of these animals, which they will on no account allow to be struck or ill-used by any one." In the same way, no doubt, certain Egyptian clans kept sacred bulls, cats, crocodiles, hawks, jackals, cobras, lizards, ibises, asps, and beetles. Mummies of most of these sacred animals, and little images of others, are common in the neighbourhood of certain places where they were specially worshipped.

Whether the animal-headed gods represent a later stage of the same totem-worship, or whether they stand merely for real ancestor-gods belonging to a particular totem-clan, and therefore represented by its totem, is not a question easily settled. But at any rate it is clear that many gods are the equivalents of such totem-animals, as is the case with the hawk-headed Horus, the jackal-headed Anubis, the cow-headed Athor, the ram-headed Knum, the cat-headed Pasht, the lion-headed Sekhet, the ibis-headed Thoth, and the kestrel-headed Khons. These gods appear on the earlier monuments as beasts alone, not as human forms with bestial heads. Till the Twelfth Dynasty, when a totem-god is mentioned (which is not often), "he is represented," says Mr. Flinders Petrie, "by his animal." Anubis, for example, at this stage, is merely a jackal; and as M. Maspero puts it, "Whatever may have been the object of worship in Thoth-Ibis, it was a bird, not a hieroglyph, that the earliest ibis-worshippers adored." There were other totems, however, which were less fruitful in deities, but which entered largely in artistic forms into the later religious symbolism. Such were especially the asp and the sacred scarabæus, which almost rival the sun-disk in the large part they play in the developed religious art-language of the great temple-building dynasties. I may add that among the other symbols of this curious emblematical picture-writing are the Tau or *crux ansata*, by origin apparently a combined *linga* and *yoni*; the lotus, the sceptre, the leek, and the crescent.

There is, however, yet a third class of divine or quasi-divine beings in the newer Egyptian Pantheon to which Mr. Andrew Lang, in his able introduction to the *Euterpe* of Herodotus, still allows that great importance may be attached. These are the elemental or seemingly elemental deities, the Nature-Gods who play so large a part in all rationalistic or mystical mythologies. Such are no doubt Nut and Seb, the personal heaven and earth, named as early as the inscription on the coffin of Menkaoura of the Fourth Dynasty in the British Museum: such perhaps (though far less certainly) are Khons, identified with the rising sun, and Tum, regarded as the impersonation of his nightly setting. But none of the quite obviously elemental gods, except Ra, play any large part in the actual and practical worship of the people: to adopt the broad distinction I have ventured to draw in our second chapter, they are gods to talk about, not gods to adore—mythological conceptions rather than religious beings. Their names occur much in the sacred texts, but their images are rare and their temples unknown. It is not Nut or Seb whose figures we see carved abundantly in relief on the grey sandstone pillars of Karnak and Luxor, painted in endless file on the gesso-covered walls of the Tombs of the Kings, or represented by dozens in the great collection of little bronze idols that fill so many cabinets at the Boulak Museum. The actual objects of the highest worship are far other than these abstract elemental conceptions : they are Osiris, Isis, Horus, Anubis, Khem, Pasht, and Athor. The quaint or grotesque incised figures of Nut, represented as a female form with arms and legs extended like a living canopy over the earth, as at Denderah, belong, I believe, almost if not quite exclusively to the Ptolemaic period, when zodiacal and astrological conceptions had been freely borrowed by the Egyptians from Greece and Asia. Nut and Seb, as gods, not myths, are in short quite recent ideas in Egypt. Even sun-disk Ra, himself, important as he becomes in the later developed creed, is hardly so much in his origin a separate god as an adjunct or symbol of divinity united syncretically with the various other deities. To call a king the sun is a common piece of courtier flattery. It is as Amen-Ra or as Osiris that the sun receives most actual worship. His name is joined to the names of gods as to the names of kings : he is almost as much a symbol as the Tau or the Asp ; he obtains little if any adoration in his simple form, but plenty when conjoined in a compound conception with some more practical deity of strictly human origin. Even at the great " Temple of the Sun " at Heliopolis, it was as the bull Men or Mnevis that the luminary was adored : and that cult, according to Manetho, went back as far as the totemistic times of the Second Dynasty.

To put it briefly, then, I hold that the element of nature-worship is a late gloss or superadded factor in the Egyptian religion; that it is always rather mythological or explanatory than religious in the strict sense ; and that it does not in the least interfere with our general inference that the real Egyptian gods as a whole were either ancestral or totemistic in origin.

From the evidence before us, broadly considered, we may fairly conclude, then, that the earliest cult of Egypt consisted of pure ancestor-worship, complicated by a doubtfully religious element of totemism, which afterwards by one means or another interwove itself closely with the whole ghostly worship of the country. The later gods were probably deified ancestors of the early tribal kings, sometimes directly worshipped as mummies, and sometimes perhaps represented by their totem-animals or later still by human figures with animal heads. Almost every one of these great gods is localised to a particular place— "Lord of Abydos," "Mistress of Senem," "President of Thebes," "Dweller at Hermopolis," as would naturally be the case if they were locally-deified princes, admitted at last into a national pantheon. In the earliest period of which any monuments remain to us, the ancestor-worship was purer, simpler, and freer from symbolism or from the cult of the great gods than at any later time. With the gradual evolution of the creed and the pantheon, however, legends and myths increased, the syncretic tendency manifested itself everywhere, identifications multiplied, mysticism grew rife, and an esoteric faith, with leanings towards a vague pantheistic monotheism, endeavoured to rationalise and to explain away the more gross and foolish portions of the original belief. It is the refinements and glosses of this final philosophical stage that pass current for the most part in systematic works as the true doctrines of Egyptian religion, and that so many modern enquirers have erroneously treated as equivalent to the earliest product of native thought. The ideas as to the unity of God, and the sun-myths of Horus, Isis, and Osiris, are clearly late developments or excrescences on the original creed, and betray throughout the esoteric spirit of priestly interpretation. To the very last, the Worship of the Dead, and the crude polytheism based upon it, were the true religion of the ancient Egyptians, as we see it expressed in all the monuments.

Such was the religious world into which, if we may believe the oldest Semitic traditions, the Sons of Israel brought their God Jahweh and their other deities from beyond the Euphrates at a very remote period of their national history. And such, in its fuller and more mystical form, was the religion practised and taught in Ptolemaic and Roman Egypt, at the moment when the Christian faith was just beginning to evolve itself round the historical nucleus of the man Christ Jesus, and him crucified.

CHAPTER IX.

THE GODS OF ISRAEL.

THE only people who ever invented or evolved a pure monotheism at first hand were the Jews. Individual thinkers elsewhere approached or aimed at that ideal goal, like the Egyptian priests and the Greek philosophers: entire races elsewhere borrowed monotheism from the Hebrews, like the Arabs under Mohammad, or, to a less extent, the Romans and the modern European nations, when they adopted Christianity in its trinitarian form: but no other race ever succeeded as a whole in attaining by their own exertions the pure monotheistic platform, however near certain persons among them might have arrived to such attainment in esoteric or mystical philosophising. It is the peculiar glory of Israel to have *evolved* God. And the evolution of God from the diffuse gods of the earlier Semitic religion is Israel's great contribution to the world's thought.

The sacred books of the Jews, as we possess them in garbled forms to-day, assign this peculiar belief to the very earliest ages of their race: they assume that Abraham, the mythical common father of all the Semitic tribes, was already a monotheist; and they even treat monotheism as at a still remoter date the universal religion of the entire world, from which all polytheistic cults were but a corruption and a falling away. Such a belief is nowadays, of course, wholly untenable. So also is the crude notion that monotheism was smitten out at a single blow by the genius of one individual man, Moses, at the moment of the Hebrew exodus from Egypt. The bare idea that one particular thinker, just escaped from the midst of ardent polytheists, whose religion embraced an endless pantheon and a low form of animal-worship, could possibly have invented a pure monotheistic cult, is totally opposed to every known psychological law of human nature. The real stages by which monotheism was evolved out of a preceding polytheism in a single small group of Semitic tribes have already been well investigated by Dutch and German scholars : all that I propose to do in the present volume is to reconsider the subject from our broader anthropological standpoint, and show how in the great Jewish god himself we may still discern, as in a glass, darkly, the vague but constant lineaments of an ancestral ghost-deity.

Down to a comparatively late period of Jewish history, as we now know, Jahweh was but one and the highest among a considerable group of Israelitish divinities ; the first among his peers, like Zeus among the gods of Hellas, Osiris or Amen among the gods of Egypt, and Woden or Thunor among the gods of the old Teutonic pantheon. As late as the century of Hezekiah, the religion of the great mass of the Israelites and Jews was still a broad though vague polytheism. The gods seem to have been as numerous and as localised as in Egypt: "According to the number of thy cities are thy gods, O Judah," says the prophet Jeremiah in the sixth century. It was only by a slow process of syncretism, by the absorption into Jahweh-worship of all other conflicting creeds, that Israel at last attained its full ideal of pure monotheism. That ideal was never finally reached by the people at large till the return from the captivity : it had only even been aimed at by a few ardent and exclusive Jahweh-worshippers in the last dangerous and doubtful years of national independence which immediately preceded the Babylonish exile.

In order to understand the inner nature of this curious gradual revolution we must look briefly, first, at the general character of the old Hebrew polytheism; and secondly, at the original cult of the great ethnical god Jahweh himself.

In spite of their long sojourn in Egypt, the national religion of the Hebrews, when we first begin dimly to descry its features through the veil of later glosses, is regarded by almost all modern investigators as truly Semitic and local in origin. It is usually described as embracing three principal forms of cult: the worship of the *teraphim* or family gods; the worship of sacred stones; and the worship of certain great gods, partly native, partly perhaps borrowed; some of them adored in the form of animals, and some apparently elemental or solar in their acquired attributes. Although for us these three are one, I shall examine them here in that wonted order.

The cult of the *teraphim*, I think, we cannot consider, on a broad anthropological view, otherwise than as the equivalent of all the other family cults known to us; that is to say, in other words, as pure unadulterated domestic ancestor-worship. "By that name," says Kuenen, "were indicated larger or smaller images, which were worshipped as household gods, and upon which the happiness of the family was supposed to depend." In the legend of Jacob's flight from Laban, we are told how Rachel stole her father's teraphim: and when the angry chieftain overtakes the fugitives, he enquires of them why they have robbed him of his domestic gods. Of Micah, we learn that he made images of his teraphim, and consecrated one of his own sons to be his family priest: such a domestic and private priesthood being exactly what we are accustomed to find in the worship of ancestral *manes* everywhere. Even through the mist of the later Jehovistic recension we catch, in passing, frequent glimpses of the early worship of these family gods, one of which is described as belonging to Michal, the daughter of Saul and wife of David; while Hosea alludes to them as stocks of wood, and Zechariah as idols that speak lies to the people. It is clear that the teraphim were preserved in each household with reverential care, that they were sacrificed to by the family at stated intervals, and that they were consulted on all occasions of doubt or difficulty by a domestic priest clad in an ephod. I think, then, if we put these indications side by side with those of family cults elsewhere, we may conclude that the Jewish religion, like all others, was based upon an ultimate foundation of general ancestor-worship.

It has been denied, indeed, that ancestor-worship pure and simple ever existed among the Semitic races. A clear contradiction of this denial is furnished by M. Lenormant, who comments thus on sepulchral monuments from Yemen: "Here, then, we have twice repeated a whole series of human persons, decidedly deceased ancestors or relations of the authors of the dedications. Their names are accompanied with the titles they bore during life. They are invoked by their descendants in the same way as the gods. They are incontestably deified persons, objects of a family worship, and gods or genii in the belief of the people of their race." After this, we need not doubt that the teraphim were the images of such family gods or ancestral spirits.

It is not surprising, however, that these domestic gods play but a small part in the history of the people as it has come down to us in the late Jehovistic version of the Hebrew traditions. Nowhere in literature, even under the most favourable circumstances, do we hear much of the *manes* and *lares*, compared with the great gods of national worship. Nor were such minor divinities likely to provoke the wrath even of that "jealous god" who later usurped all the adoration of Israel: so that denunciations of their votaries are comparatively rare in the rhapsodies of the prophets. "Their use," says Kuenen, speaking of the teraphim, "was very general, and was by no means considered incompatible with the worship of Jahweh." They were regarded merely as family affairs, poor foemen for the great and awsome tribal god who bore no rival near his throne, and would not suffer the pretensions of Molech or of the Baalim. To use a modern analogy, their cult was as little inconsistent with Jahweh-worship as a belief in fairies, banshees, or family ghosts was formerly inconsistent with a belief in Christianity.

This conclusion will doubtless strike the reader at once as directly opposed to the oft-repeated assertion that the early Hebrews had little or no conception of the life beyond the grave and of the doctrine of future rewards and punishments. I am afraid it cannot be denied that such is the case. Hard as it is to run counter to so much specialist opinion, I can scarcely see how any broad anthropological enquirer may deny to the Semites of the tenth and twelfth centuries before Christ participation in an almost (or quite) universal human belief, common to the lowest savages and the highest civilisations, and particularly well developed in that Egyptian society with which the ancestors of the Hebrews had so long rubbed shoulders. The subject, however, is far too large a one for full debate here. I must content myself with pointing out that, apart from the *a priori* improbability of such a conclusion, the Hebrew documents themselves contain numerous allusions, even in their earliest traditional fragments, to the belief in ghosts and in the world of shades, as well as to the probability of future resurrection. The habit of cave-burial and of excavated grotto-burial; the importance attached to the story of the purchase of Machpelah; the common phrase that such-and-such a patriarch "was gathered to his people," or "slept with his fathers"; the embalming of Joseph, and the carrying up of his bones from Egypt to Palestine; the episode of Saul and the ghost of Samuel; and indeed the entire conception of Sheol, the place of the departed—all alike show that the Hebrew belief in this respect did not largely differ in essentials from the general belief of surrounding peoples. The very frequency of allusions to witchcraft and necromancy point in the same direction; while the common habit of assuming a priestly or sacrificial garment, the *ephod,* and then consulting the family teraphim as a domestic oracle, is strictly in accordance with all that we know of the minor ancestor-worship as it occurs elsewhere.

Closely connected with the teraphim is the specific worship at tombs or graves. "The whole north Semitic area," says Professor Robertson Smith, "was dotted over with sacred tombs, Memnonia, Semiramis mounds, and the like; and at every such spot a god or demigod had his subterranean abode." This, of course, is pure ancestor-worship. Traces of still older cave-burial are also common in the Hebrew Scriptures. "At the present day," says Professor Smith, "almost every sacred site in Palestine has its grotto, and that this is no new thing is plain from the numerous symbols of Astarte-worship found on the walls of caves in Phœnicia. There can be little doubt that the oldest Phœnician temples were natural or artificial grottoes."

We are fairly entitled to conclude, then, I believe, that a domestic cult of the *manes* or *lares,* the family dead, formed the general substratum of early Hebrew religion, though as in all other cases, owing to its purely personal nature, this universal cult makes but a small figure in the literature of the race, compared with the worship of the greater national gods and goddesses.

Second in the list of worshipful objects in early Israel come the sacred stones, about which I have already said a good deal in the chapter devoted to that interesting subject, but concerning whose special nature in the Semitic field a few more words may here be fitly added.

It is now very generally admitted that stone-worship played an exceedingly large and important part in the primitive Semitic religion. How important a part we may readily gather from many evidences, but from none more than from the fact that even Mohammad himself was unable to exclude from Islam, the most monotheistic of all known religious systems, the holy black stone of the Kaaba at Mecca. In Arabia, says Professor Robertson Smith, the altar or hewn stone is unknown, and in its place we find the rude pillar or the cairn, beside which the sacrificial victim is slain, the blood being poured out over the stone or at its base. But in Israel, the shaped stone seems the more usual mark of the ghost or god. Such a sacred stone, we have already seen, was known to the early Hebrews as a Beth-el, that is to say an "abode of deity," from the common belief that it was inhabited by a god, ghost, or spirit. The great prevalence of the cult of stones among the Semites, however, is further indicated by the curious circumstance that this word was borrowed by the Greeks and Romans (in a slightly altered form) to denote the stones so supposed to be inhabited by deities. References to such gods abound throughout the Hebrew books, though they are sometimes denounced as idolatrous images, and sometimes covered with a thin veneer of Jehovism by being connected with the national heroes and with the later Jahweh-worship.

In the legend of Jacob's dream we get a case where the sacred stone is anointed and a promise is made to it of a tenth of the speaker's substance as an offering. And again, on a later occasion, we learn that Jacob "set up a pillar of stone, and he poured a drink-offering thereon, and he poured oil thereon;" just as, in the great phallic worship of the linga in India (commonly called the *linga puja*), a cylindrical pillar, rounded at the top, and universally considered as a phallus in its nature, is worshipped by pouring upon it one of five sacred anointing liquids, water, milk, ghee, oil, and wine. Similar rites are offered in many other places to other sacred stones; and in many cases the phallic value assigned to them is clearly shown by the fact that it is usual for sterile women to pray to them for the blessing of children, as Hindu wives pray to Mahadeo, and as so many Hebrew women (to be noted hereafter) are mentioned in our texts as praying to Jahweh.

A brief catalogue of the chief stone-deities alluded to in Hebrew literature may help to enforce the importance of the subject: and it may be noted in passing that the stones are often mentioned in connexion with sacred trees —an association with which we are already familiar. In the neighbourhood of Sichem was an oak—the "oak of the prophets" or "oak of the soothsayers"—by which lay a stone, whose holiness is variously accounted for by describing it as, in one place, an altar of Abraham, in another an altar of Jacob, and in a third a memorial of Joshua. But the fact shows that it was resorted to for sacrifice, and that oracles or responses were sought from it by its votaries. That is to say, it was a sepulchral monument. Near Hebron stood "the oak of Mamre," and under it a sacred stone, accounted for as an altar of Abraham, to which in David's time sacrifices were offered. Near Beersheba we find yet a third tree, the tamarisk, said to have been planted by Abraham, and an altar or stone pillar ascribed to Isaac. In the camp at Gilgal were "the twelve stones," sometimes, apparently, spoken of as "the graven images," but sometimes explained away as memorials of Jahweh's help at the passing of the Jordan. Other examples are Ebenezer, "the helpful stone," and Tobeleth, the "serpent-stone," as well as the "great stone" to which sacrifices were offered at Bethshemesh, and the other great stone at Gibeon, which was also, no doubt, an early Hebrew deity.

So often is the name of Abraham connected with these stones, indeed, that, as some German scholars have suggested, Abraham himself may perhaps be regarded as a sacred boulder, the rock from which Israel originally sprang.

In any case, I need hardly say, we must look upon such sacred stones as themselves a further evidence of ancestor-worship in Palestine, on the analogy of all similar stones elsewhere. We may conclude that, as in previously noted instances, they were erected on the graves of deceased chieftains.

And now we come to the third and most difficult division of early Hebrew religion, the cult of the great gods whom the jealous Jahweh himself finally superseded. The personality of these gods is very obscure, partly because of the nature of our materials, which, being derived entirely from Jehovistic sources, have done their best to overshadow the "false gods"; but partly also, I believe, because, in the process of evolving monotheism, a syncretic movement merged almost all their united attributes into Jahweh himself, who thus becomes at last the all-absorbing synthesis of an entire pantheon. Nevertheless, we can point out one or two shadowy references to such greater gods, either by name alone, or by the form under which they were usually worshipped.

The scholarship of the elder generation would no doubt have enumerated first among these gods the familiar names of Baal and Molech. At present, such an enumeration is scarcely possible. We can no longer see in the Baal of the existing Hebrew scriptures a single great god. We must regard the word rather as a common substantive, —"the lord" or "the master,"—descriptive of the relation of each distinct god to the place he inhabited. The Baalim, in other words, seem to have been the local deities or deified chiefs of the Semitic region; doubtless the dead kings or founders of families, as opposed to the lesser gods of each particular household. It is not improbable, therefore, that they were really identified with the sacred stones we have just been considering, and with the wooden *ashera*. The Baal is usually spoken of indefinitely, without a proper name, much as at Delos men spoke of "the God," at Athens of "the Goddess," and now at Padua of "il Santo,"—meaning respectively Apollo, Athene, St. Antony. Melcarth is thus the Baal of Tyre, Astarte the Baalath of Byblos; there was a Baal of Lebanon, of

Mount Hermon, of Mount Peor, and so forth. A few specific Baalim have their names preserved for us in the nomenclature of towns ; such are Baal-tamar, the lord of the palm-tree ; with Baal-gad, Baal-Berith, Baal-meon, and Baal-zephon. But in the Hebrew scriptures, as a rule, every effort has been made to blot out the very memory of these " false gods," and to represent Jahweh alone as from the earliest period the one true prince and ruler in Israel.

As for Molech, that title merely means " the king "; and it may have been applied to more than one distinct deity. Dr. Robertson Smith does not hesitate to hold that the particular Molech to whom human sacrifices of children were offered by the Jews before the captivity was Jahweh himself ; it was to the national god, he believes, that these fiery rites were performed at the Tophet or pyre in the ravine just below the temple.

We are thus reduced to the most nebulous details about these great gods of the Hebrews, other than Jahweh, in the period preceding the Babylonian captivity. All that is certain appears to be that a considerable number of local gods were worshipped here and there at special sanctuaries, each of which seems to have consisted of an altar or stone image, standing under a sacred tree or sacred grove, and combined with an *ashera*. While the names of Chemosh, the god of Moab, and of Dagon, the god of the Philistines, have come down to us with perfect frankness and clearness, no local Hebrew god save Jahweh has left a name that can now be discerned with any approach to certainty. It should be added that the worship of many of the gods of surrounding Semitic tribes undoubtedly extended from the earliest times into Israel also.

I must likewise premise that the worship of the Baalim, within and without Israel, was specially directed to upright conical stones, the most sacred objects at all the sanctuaries ; and that these stones are generally admitted to have possessed for their worshippers a phallic significance.

Certain writers have further endeavoured to show that a few animal-gods entered into the early worship of the Hebrews. I do not feel sure that their arguments are convincing; but for the sake of completeness I include the two most probable cases in this brief review of the vague and elusive deities of early Israel.

One of these is the god in the form of a young bull, specially worshipped at Dan and Bethel, as the bull Apis was worshipped at Memphis, and the bull Mnevis at On or Heliopolis. This cult of the bull is pushed back in the later traditions to the period of the exodus, when the Israelites made themselves a "golden calf" in the wilderness. Kuenen, indeed, lays stress upon the point that this Semitic bull-worship differed essentially from the cult of Apis in the fact that it was directed to an image or idol, not to a living animal. This is true, and I certainly do not wish to press any particular connexion between Egypt and the golden bulls of Jeroboam in the cities of Ephraim: though I think too much may perhaps be made of superficial differences and too little of deep-seated resemblances in these matters, seeing that bull-worship is a common accompaniment of a phallic cult in the whole wide district between Egypt and India. It is the tendency of the scholastic mind, indeed, to over-elaborate trifles, and to multiply to excess minute distinctions. But in any case, we are on comparatively safe ground in saying that a bull-god was an object of worship in Israel down to a very late period; that his cult descended from an early age of the national existence; and that the chief seats of his images were at Dan and Bethel in Ephraim, and at Beersheba in Judah.

Was this bull-shaped deity Jahweh himself, or one of the polymorphic forms of Jahweh? Such is the opinion of Kuenen, who says explicitly, "Jahweh was worshipped in the shape of a young bull. It cannot be doubted that the cult of the bull-calf was really the cult of Jahweh in person." And certainly in the prophetic writings of the eighth century, we can clearly descry that the worshippers of the bull regarded themselves as worshipping the god Jahweh, who brought up his people from the land of Egypt. Nevertheless, dangerous as it may seem for an outsider to differ on such a subject from great Semitic scholars, I venture to think we may see reason hereafter to conclude that this was not originally the case: that the god worshipped under the form of the bull-calf was some other deity, like the Molech whom we know to have been represented with a bull's head; and that only by the later syncretic process did this bull-god come to be identified in the end with Jahweh, a deity (as seems likely) of quite different origin, much as Mnevis came to be regarded at Heliopolis as an incarnation of Ra, and as Apis came to be regarded at Memphis as an avatar of Ptah and still later of Osiris. On the other hand, we must remember that, as Mr. Frazer has shown, a sacred animal is often held to be the representative and embodiment of the very god to whom it is habitually sacrificed. Here again we trench on ground which can only satisfactorily be occupied at a later stage of our polymorphic argument.

A second animal-god, apparently, also adored in the form of a metal image, was the asp or snake, known in our version as "the brazen serpent," and connected by the Jehovistic editors of the earlier traditions with Moses in the wilderness. The name of this deity is given us in the Book of Kings as Nehushtan, "the brass god"; but whether this was really its proper designation or a mere contemptuous descriptive title we can hardly be certain. The worship of the serpent is said to have gone on uninterruptedly till the days of Hezekiah, when, under the influence of the exclusive devotion to Jahweh which was then becoming popular, the image was broken in pieces as an idolatrous object. It is scarcely necessary to point out in passing that the asp was one of the most sacred animals in Egypt : but, as in the case of the bull, the snake was also a widespread object of worship throughout all the surrounding countries ; and it is therefore probable that the Hebrew snake-worship may have been parallel to, rather than derived from, Egyptian ophiolatry.

Such, then, seen through the dim veil of Jehovism, are the misty features of that uncertain pantheon in which, about the eighth century at least, Jahweh found himself the most important deity. The most important, I say, because it is clear from our records that for many ages the worship of Jahweh and the worship of the Baalim went on side by side without conscious rivalry.

And what sort of god was this holy Jahweh himself, whom the Hebrews recognised from a very early time as emphatically and above all others " the God of Israel " ?

If ever he was envisaged as a golden bull, if ever he was regarded as the god of light, fire, or the sun, those concepts, I believe, must have been the result of a late transference of attributes and confusion of persons, such as we may see so rife in the more recent mystical religion of Egypt. What in his own nature Jahweh must have been in the earliest days of his nascent godhead I believe we can best judge by putting together some of the passages in old traditionary legend which bear most plainly upon his character and functions.

In the legendary account of the earliest dealings of Jahweh with the Hebrew race, we are told that the ethnical god appeared to Abraham in Haran, and promised to make of him " a great nation." Later on, Abraham complains of the want of an heir, saying to Jahweh, " Thou hast given me no seed." Then Jahweh "brought him forth abroad, and said, Look now toward heaven and tell the stars : so shall thy seed be." Over and over again we get similar promises of fruitfulness made to Abraham : " I will multiply thee exceedingly "; " thou shalt be a father of many nations "; " I will make thee exceeding fruitful ";' " kings shall come out of thee "; " for a father of many nations have I made thee." So, too, of Sarah: "she shall be a mother of nations; kings of people shall be of her." And of Ishmael: "I have blessed him and will make him fruitful, and will multiply him exceedingly: twelve princes shall he beget, and I will make him a great nation." Time after time these blessings recur for Abraham, Isaac, and all his family: "I will multiply thy seed as the stars of the heaven, and as the sand which is upon the seashore, and thy seed shall possess the gate of his enemies."

In every one of these passages, and in many more which need not be quoted, but which will readily occur to every reader, Jahweh is represented especially as a god of increase, of generation, of populousness, of fertility.

As such, too, we find him frequently and markedly worshipped on special occasions. He was the god to whom sterile women prayed, and from whom they expected the special blessing of a son, to keep up the cult of the family ancestors. This trait survived even into the poetry of the latest period. "He maketh the barrren woman to keep house," says a psalmist about Jahweh, "and to be a joyful mother of children." And from the beginning to the end of Hebrew legend we find a similar characteristic of the ethnical god amply vindicated. When Sarah is old and well stricken in years, Jahweh visits her and she conceives Isaac. Then Isaac in turn "intreated Jahweh for his wife, because she was barren; and Jahweh was intreated of him, and Rebekah his wife conceived." Again, "when Jahweh saw that Leah was hated, he opened her womb; but Rachel was barren." Once more, of the birth of Samson we are told that Manoah's wife "was barren and bare not": but "the angel of Jahweh appeared unto the woman and said unto her, Behold, now thou art barren and bearest not; but thou shalt conceive and bear a son." And of Hannah we are told, even more significantly, that Jahweh had "shut up her womb." At the shrine of Jahweh at Shiloh, therefore, she prayed to Jahweh that this disgrace might be removed from her and that a child might be born to her. If she bore "a man child," she would offer him up all his life long as an anchorite to Jahweh, to be a Nazarite of the Lord, an ascetic and a fanatic. "Jahweh remembered her," and she bore Samuel. And after that again, "Jahweh visited Hannah, so that she conceived and bare three sons and two daughters." In many other passages we get the self-same trait: Jahweh is regarded above everything as a god of increase and a giver of offspring. "Children are a heritage from Jahweh," says the much later author of a familiar ode: "the fruit of the womb are a reward from him."

It is clear, too, that this desire for children, for a powerful clan, for the increase of the people, was a dominant one everywhere in Ephraim and in Judah. "Thy wife shall be as a fruitful vine," says Jahweh to his votary by the mouth of the poet; "thy children like olive plants round about thy table." "Happy is the man that hath his quiver full of them," says another psalmist; "they shall speak with the enemies in the gate." Again and again the promise is repeated that the seed of Abraham or of Joseph or of Ishmael shall be numerous as the stars of heaven or the sands of the sea: Jahweh's chief prerogative is evidently the gift of increase, extended often to cattle and asses, but always including at least sons and daughters. If Israel obeys Jahweh, says the Deuteronomist, "Jahweh will make thee plenteous for good in the fruit of thy belly, and in the fruit of thy cattle, and in the fruit of thy ground": but if otherwise, then "cursed shall be the fruit of thy body, and the fruit of thy land, the increase of thy kine, and the flocks of thy sheep."

Now, elsewhere throughout the world we find in like manner a certain class of phallic gods who are specially conceived as givers of fertility, and to whom prayers and offerings are made by barren women who desire children. And the point to observe is that these gods are usually (perhaps one might even say always) embodied in stone pillars or upright monoliths. The practical great god of India—the god whom the people really worship—is Mahadeo; and Mahadeo is, as we know, a cylinder of stone, to whom the *linga puja* is performed, and to whom barren women pray for offspring. There are sacred stones in western Europe, now crowned by a cross, at which barren women still pray to God and the Madonna, or to some local saint, for the blessing of children. It is allowed that while the obelisk is from one point of view (in later theory) a ray of the sun, it is from another point of view (in earlier origin) a "symbol of the generative power of nature," —which is only another way of saying that it is an ancestral stone of phallic virtue. In short, without laying too much stress upon the connexion, we may conclude generally that the upright pillar came early to be regarded, not merely as a memento of the dead and an abode of the ghost or indwelling god, but also in some mysterious and esoteric way as a representative of the male and generative principle.

If we recollect that the stone pillar was often identified with the ancestor or father, the reason for this idea will not perhaps be quite so hard to understand. "From these stones we are all descended," thinks the primitive worshipper: "these are our fathers; therefore, they are the givers of children, the producers and begetters of all our generations, the principle of fertility, the proper gods to whom to pray for offspring." Add that many of them, being represented as human, or human in their upper part at least, grow in time to be ithyphallic, like Priapus, party by mere grotesque barbarism, but partly also as a sign of the sex of the deceased: and we can see the naturalness of this easy transition. From the Hermæ of the Greeks to the rude phallic deities of so many existing savage races, we get everywhere signs of this constant connexion between the sacred stone and the idea of paternity. Where the stone represents the grave of a woman, the deity of course is conceived as a goddess, but with the same implications. Herodotus saw in Syria stelæ engraved with the female pudenda. The upright stone god is thus everywhere and always liable to be regarded as a god of fruitfulness.

But did this idea of the stone pillar extend to Palestine and to the Semitic nations? There is evidence that it did, besides that of Herodotus. Major Conder, whose opinion on all questions of pure archæology (as opposed to philology) deserves the highest respect, says of Canaanitish times, " The menhir, or conical stone, was the emblem throughout Syria of the gods presiding over fertility, and the cup hollows which have been formed in menhirs and dolmens are the indications of libations, often of human blood, once poured on these stones by early worshippers." He connects these monuments with the linga cult of India, and adds that Dr. Chaplin has found such a cult still surviving near the Sea of Galilee. Lucian speaks of the two great pillars at the temple of Hierapolis as *phalli*. Of the Phœnicians Major Conder writes: " The chief emblem worshipped in the temples was a pillar or cone, derived no doubt from the rude menhirs which were worshipped by early savage tribes, such as Dravidians, Arabs, Celts, and Hottentots." That they were originally sepulchral in character we can gather from the fact that " they often stood beneath trilithons or dolmens, or were placed before an altar made by a stone laid flat on an upright base." " The representations on early Babylonian cylinders of tables whereon a small fire might be kindled, or an offering of some small object laid, seem to indicate a derivation from similar structures. The original temple in which the cone and its shrine, or its altar, were placed, was but a cromlech or enclosure, square or round, made by setting up stones." Remains of such enclosures, with dolmens on one side, are found at various spots in Moab and Phœnicia. Nothing could be more obviously sepulchral in character than these rude shrines or Gilgals, with the pillar or gravestone, from which, as Major Conder suggests, the hypæthral temples of Byblos and Baalbek are finally developed.

That Jahweh himself in his earliest form was such a stone god, the evidence, I think, though not perhaps exactly conclusive, is to say the least extremely suggestive. I have already called attention to it in a previous chapter, and need not here recapitulate it in full; but a few stray additions may not be without value. Besides the general probability, among a race whose gods were so almost universally represented by sacred stones, that any particular god, unless the contrary be proved, was so represented, there is the evidence of all the later language, and of the poems written after the actual stone god himself had perished, that Jahweh was still popularly regarded as, at least in a metaphorical sense, a stone or rock. " He is the Rock," says the Deuteronomist, in the song put into the mouth of Moses; " I will publish the name of Jahweh; ascribe greatness unto our god." " Jahweh liveth, and blessed be my rock," says the hymn which a later writer composes for David in the Second Book of Samuel: " exalted be the god of the rock of my salvation." And in the psalms the image recurs again and again: " Jahweh is my rock and my fortress"; "Who is a god save Jahweh, and who is a rock save our god?"; " He set my feet upon a rock, and established my goings"; " Lead me to the rock that is greater than I"; " Jahweh is my defence, and my god is the rock of my refuge"; " O come, let us sing to Jahweh; let us make a joyful noise to the rock of our salvation." And that the shape of this stone was probably that of a rounded pillar, bevelled at the top, we see in the fact that later ages pictured to themselves their transfigured Jahweh as leading the Sons of Israel in the wilderness as a pillar of fire by night and a pillar of cloud by daytime.

The earlier Israelites, however, had no such poetical illusions. To them, their god Jahweh was simply the object—stone pillar or otherwise—preserved in the ark or chest which long rested at Shiloh, and which was afterwards enshrined, "between the thighs of the building" (as a later gloss has it), in the Temple at Jerusalem. The whole of the early traditions embedded in the books of Judges, Samuel, and Kings show us quite clearly that Jahweh himself was then regarded as inhabiting the ark, and as carried about with it from place to place in all its wanderings. The story of the battle with the Philistines at Eben-ezer, the fall of Dagon before the rival god, the fortunes of the ark after its return to the Israelitish people, the removal to Jerusalem by David, the final enthronement by Solomon, all distinctly show that Jahweh in person dwelt within the ark, between the guardian cherubim. "Who is able to stand before the face of Jahweh, this very sacred god?" ask the men of Bethshemesh, when they ventured to look inside that hallowed abode, and were smitten down by the "jealous god" who loved to live in the darkness of the inmost sanctuary.*

It may be well to note in this connexion two significant facts: Just such an ark was used in Egypt to contain the sacred objects or images of the gods. And further, at the period when the Sons of Israel were tributaries in Egypt, a Theban dynasty ruled the country, and the worship of the great Theban phallic deity, Khem, was widely spread throughout every part of the Egyptian dominions.

Is there, however, any evidence of a linga or other stone pillar being ever thus enshrined and entempled as the great god of a sanctuary? Clearly, Major Conder has already supplied some, and more is forthcoming from various other sources. The cone which represented Aphrodite in Cyprus was similarly enshrined as the chief object of a temple, as were the stelæ of all Egyptian mummies. "The trilithon," says Major Conder, "becomes later a shrine, in which the cone or a statue stands." The signi-

---

* Mr. William Simpson has some excellent remarks on the analogies of the Egyptian and Hebrew arks and sanctuaries in his pamphlet on *The Worship of Death*.

ficance of this correlation will at once be seen if the reader remembers how, in the chapter on Sacred Stones, I showed the origin of the idol from the primitive menhir or upright pillar. "The Khonds and other non-Aryan tribes in India," says Conder once more, "build such temples of rude stones, daubed with red,—a survival of the old practice of anointing the menhirs and the sacred cone or pillar with blood of victims, sometimes apparently human. Among the Indians, the pillar is a lingam, and such apparently was its meaning among the Phœnicians." And in the Greek cities we know from Pausanias that an unhewn stone was similarly enshrined in the most magnificent adytum of the noblest Hellenic temples. In fact, it was rather the rule than otherwise that a stone was the chief object of worship in the noblest fanes.

One more curious trait must be noted in the worship of Jahweh. Not only did he rejoice in human sacrifices, but he also demanded especially an offering of the firstborn, and he required a singular and significant ransom from every man-child whom he permitted to live among his peculiar votaries. On the fact of human sacrifices I need hardly insist : they were an integral part of all Semitic worship, and their occurrence in the cult of Jahweh has been universally allowed by all unprejudiced scholars. The cases of Agag, whom Samuel hewed to pieces before the face of Jahweh, and of Jephthah's daughter, whom her father offered up as a thank-offering for his victory, though not of course strictly historical from a critical point of view, are quite sufficient evidence to show the temper and the habit of the Jahweh-worshippers who described them. So with the legend of the offering of Isaac, who is merely rescued at the last moment in order that the god of generation may make him the father of many thousands. Again, David seeks to pacify the anger of Jahweh by a sacrifice of seven of the sons of Saul. And the prophet Micah asks, " Shall I give my first-born for my transgression, the fruit of my body for the sin of my soul ?"—a passage which undoubtedly implies that in Micah's time such a sacrifice of the eldest child was a common incident of current Jahweh-worship.

From human sacrifice to circumcision the transition is less violent than would at first sight appear. An intermediate type is found in the dedication of the first-born, where Jahweh seems to claim for himself, not as a victim, but as a slave and devotee, the first fruits of that increase which it is his peculiar function to ensure. In various laws, Jahweh lays claim to the first-born of man and beast, —sometimes to all, sometimes only to the male first-born. The animals were sacrificed; the sons, in later ages at least, were either made over as Nazarites or redeemed with an offering or a money-ransom. But we cannot doubt that in the earliest times the first-born child was slain before Jahweh. In the curious legend of Moses and Zipporah we get a strange folk-tale connecting this custom indirectly with the practice of circumcision. Jahweh seeks to kill Moses, apparently because he has not offered up his child: but Zipporah his wife takes a stone knife, circumcises her son, and flings the bloody offering at Jahweh's feet, who thereupon lets her husband go. This, rather than the later account of its institution by Abraham, seems the true old explanatory legend of the origin of circumcision—a legend analogous to those which we find in Roman and other early history as embodying or explaining certain ancient customs or legal formulæ. Circumcision, in fact, appears to be a bloody sacrifice to Jahweh, as the god of generation: a sacrifice essentially of the nature of a ransom, and therefore comparable to all those other bodily mutilations whose origin Mr. Herbert Spencer has so well shown in the *Ceremonial Institutions*.

At the same time, the nature of the offering helps to cast light upon the character of Jahweh as a god of increase; exactly as the "emerods" with which the Philistines were afflicted for the capture of Jahweh and his ark show the nature of the vengeance which might naturally be expected from a deity of generation.

Last of all, how is it that later Hebrew writers believed the object concealed in the ark to have been, not a phallic stone, but a copy of the "Ten Words" which Jahweh was fabled to have delivered to Moses? That would be difficult to decide: but here at least is an aperçu upon the subject which I throw out for what it may be worth. The later Hebrews, when their views of Jahweh had grown expanded and etherealised, were obviously ashamed of their old stone-worship, if indeed they were archæologists enough after the captivity to know that it had ever really existed. What more natural, then, than for them to suppose that the stone which they heard of as having been enclosed in the ark was a copy of the "Ten Words,"—the covenant of Jahweh? Hence, perhaps, the later substitution of the term, "Ark of the Covenant," for the older and correcter phrase, "Ark of Jehweh." One more suggestion, still more purely hypothetical. Cones with pyramidal heads, bearing inscriptions to the deceased, were used by the Phœnicians for interments. It is just possible that the original Jahweh may have been such an ancient pillar, covered with writings of some earlier character, which were interpreted later as the equivalents or symbols of the "Ten Words."

Putting all the evidence together, then, as far as we can now recover it, and interpreting it on broad anthropological lines by analogy from elsewhere, I should say the following propositions seem fairly probable:

The original religion of Israel was a mixed polytheism, containing many various types of gods, and based like all other religions upon domestic and tribal ancestor-worship. Some of the gods were of animal shapes: others were more or less vaguely anthropomorphic. But the majority were worshipped under the form of sacred stones, trees, or wooden cones. The greater part of these gods were Semitic in type, and common to the Sons of Israel with their neighbours and kinsmen. The character of the Hebrew worship, however, apparently underwent some slight modification in Egypt; or at any rate, Egyptian influences led to the preference of certain gods over others at the period of the Exodus. One god, in particular, Jahweh by name, seems to have been almost peculiar to the Sons of Israel,—their ethnical deity, and therefore in all probability an early tribal ancestor or the stone representative of such an ancestor. The legends are probably right in their implication that this god was already worshipped (not of course exclusively) by the Sons of Israel before their stay in Egypt; they are almost certainly correct in ascribing the great growth and extension of his cult to the period of the Exodus. The Sons of Israel, at least from the date of the Exodus onward, carried this god or his rude image with them in an ark or box through all their wanderings. The object so carried was probably a conical stone pillar, which we may conjecture to have been the grave-stone of some deified ancestor: and of this ancestor "Jahweh" was perhaps either the proper name or a descriptive epithet. Even if, as Colenso suggests, the name itself was Canaanitish, and belonged already to a local god, its application to the sacred stone of the ark would be merely another instance of the common tendency to identify the gods of one race or country with those of another. The stone itself was always enshrouded in Egyptian mystery, and no private person was permitted to behold it. Sacrifices, both human and otherwise, were offered up to it, as to the other gods, its fellows and afterwards its hated rivals. The stone, like other sacred stones of pillar shape, was regarded as emblematic of the generative power. Circumcision was a mark of devotion to Jahweh, at first, no doubt, either voluntary, or performed by way of a ransom, but becoming with the growth and exclusiveness of Jahweh-worship a distinctive rite of Jahweh's chosen people. (But other Semites also circumcised themselves as a blood-offering to their own more or less phallic deities.)

More briefly still, among many Hebrew gods, Jahweh was originally but a single one, a tribal ancestor-god, worshipped in the form of a cylindrical stone, perhaps at first a grave-stone, and regarded as essentially a god of increase, a special object of veneration by childless women.

From this rude ethnical divinity, the mere sacred pillar of a barbarous tribe, was gradually developed the Lord God of later Judaism and of Christianity—a power, eternal, omniscient, almighty, holy; the most ethereal, the most sublime, the most superhuman deity that the brain of man has ever conceived. By what slow evolutionary process of syncretism and elimination, of spiritual mysticism and national enthusiasm, of ethical effort and imaginative impulse that mighty God was at last projected out of so unpromising an original it will be the task of our succeeding chapters to investigate and to describe.

CHAPTER X.

THE RISE OF MONOTHEISM.

WE have seen that the Hebrews were originally polytheists, and that their ethnical god Jahweh seems to have been worshipped by them in early times under the material form of a cylindrical stone pillar. Or rather, to speak more naturally, the object they so worshipped they regarded as a god, and called Jahweh. The question next confronts us, how from this humble beginning did Israel attain to the pure monotheism of its later age? What was there in the position or conditions of the Hebrew race which made the later Jews reject all their other gods, and fabricate out of their early national Sacred Stone the most sublime, austere, and omnipotent deity that humanity has known?

The answer, I believe, to this pregnant question is partly to be found in a certain general tendency of the Semitic mind; partly in the peculiar political and social state of the Israelitish tribes during the ninth, eighth, seventh, sixth, and fifth centuries before the Christian era. Or, to put the proposed solution of the problem, beforehand, in a still simpler form, Hebrew monotheism was to some extent the result of a syncretic treatment of all the gods, in the course of which the attributes and characters of each became merged in the other, only the names (if anything) remaining distinct; and to some extent the result of the intense national patriotism, of which the ethnical god Jahweh was at once the outcome, the expression, and the fondest hope. The belief that Jahweh fought for

Israel, and that by trust in Jahweh alone could Israel hold her own against Egypt and Assyria, wildly fanatical as it appears to us to-day, and utterly disproved by all the facts of the case as it ultimately was, nevertheless formed a central idea of the Hebrew patriots, and resulted by slow degrees in the firm establishment first of an exclusive, and afterwards of a truly monotheistic Jahweh-cult.

It is one of Ernest Renan's brilliant paradoxes that the Semitic mind is naturally monotheistic. As a matter of fact, the Semitic mind has shown this native tendency in its first stages by everywhere evolving pretty much the same polytheistic pantheon as that evolved by every other group of human beings everywhere. Nevertheless, there is perhaps this kernel of truth in Renan's paradoxical contention ; the Semites, more readily than most other people, merge the features of their deities one in the other. That is not, indeed, by any means an exclusive Semitic trait. We saw already, in dealing with the Egyptian religion, how all the forms and functions of the gods faded at last into an inextricable mixture, an olla podrida of divinity, from which it was practically impossible to disentangle with certainty the original personalities of Ra and Tum, of Amen and Osiris, of Neith and Isis, of Ptah and Apis. Even in the relatively fixed and individualised pantheon of Hellas, it occurs often enough that confusions both of person and prerogative obscure the distinctness of the various gods. Aphrodite and Herakles are polymorphic in their embodiments. But in the Semitic religions, at least in that later stage where we first come across them, the lineaments of the different deities are so blurred and indefinite that hardly anything more than mere names can with certainty be recognised. No other gods are so shadowy and so vague. The type of this pantheon is that dim figure of El-Shaddai, the early and terrible object of Hebrew worship, of whose attributes and nature we know positively nothing, but who stands in the background of all Hebrew thought as the embodiment of the nameless and trembling dread begotten on man's soul by the irresistible and ruthless forces of nature.

This vagueness and shadowiness of the Semitic religious conceptions seems to depend to some extent upon the inartistic nature of the Semitic culture. The Semite seldom carved the image of his god. Roman observers noted with surprise that the shrine of Carmel contained no idol. But it depended also upon deep-seated characteristics of the Semitic race. Melancholy, contemplative, proud, reserved, but strangely fanciful, the Arab of to-day perhaps gives us the clue to the indefinite nature of early Semitic religious thinking. There never was a netherworld more ghostly than Sheol; there never were gods more dimly awful than the Elohim who float through the early stories of the Hebrew mystical cycle. Their very names are hardly known to us: they come to us through the veil of later Jehovistic editing with such merely descriptive titles as the God of Abraham, the Terror of Isaac, the Mighty Power, the Most High Deity. Indeed, the true Hebrew, like many other barbarians, seems to have shrunk either from looking upon the actual form of his god itself, or from pronouncing aloud his proper name. His deity was shrouded in the darkness of an ark or the deep gloom of an inner tent or sanctuary; the syllables that designated the object of his worship were never uttered in full, save on the most solemn occasions, but were shirked or slurred over by some descriptive epithet. Even the unpronounceable title of Jahweh itself appears from our documents to have been a later name bestowed during the Exodus on an antique god: while the rival titles of the Baal and the Molech mean nothing more than the Lord and the King respectively. An excessive reverence forbade the Semite to know anything of his god's personal appearance or true name, and so left the features of almost all the gods equally uncertain and equally formless.

But besides the difficulty of accurately distinguishing between the forms and functions of the different Semitic deities which even their votaries must have felt from the beginning, there was a superadded difficulty in the developed creed, due to the superposition of elemental mysticism and nature-worship upon the primitive cult of ancestral ghosts as gods and goddesses. Just as Ra, the sun, was identified in the latest ages with almost every Egyptian god, so solar ideas and solar myths affected at last the distinct personality of almost every Semitic deity. The consequence is that all the gods become in the end practically indistinguishable : one is so like the other that different interpreters make the most diverse identifications, and are apparently justified in so doing (from the mythological standpoint) by the strong solar or elemental family likeness which runs through the whole pantheon in its later stages. It has even been doubted by scholars of the older school whether Jahweh is not himself a form of his great rival Baal : whether both were not at bottom identical—mere divergent shapes of one polyonymous sun-god. To us, who recognise in every Baal the separate ghost-god of a distinct tomb, such identification is clearly impossible.

To the worshippers of the Baalim or of Jahweh themselves, however, these abstruser mythological problems never presented themselves. The difference of name and of holy place was quite enough for them, in spite of essential identity of attribute or nature. They would kill one another for the sake of a descriptive epithet, or risk death itself rather than offer up sacrifices at a hostile altar.

Nevertheless, various influences conspired, here as elsewhere, to bring about a gradual movement of syncretism —that is to say, of the absorption of many distinct gods into one ; the final identification of several deities originally separate. What those influences were we must now briefly consider.

In the first place, we must recollect that while in Egypt, with its dry and peculiarly preservative climate, mummies, idols, tombs, and temples might be kept unchanged and undestroyed for ages, in almost all other countries rain, wind, and time are mighty levellers of human handicraft. Thus, while in Egypt the cult of the Dead Ancestor survives as such quite confessedly and openly for many centuries, in most other countries the tendency is for the actual personal objects of worship to be more and more forgotten; vague gods and spirits usurp by degrees the place of the historic man; rites at last cling rather to sites than to particular persons. The tomb may disappear; and yet the sacred stone may be reverenced still with the accustomed veneration. The sacred stone may go; and yet the sacred tree may be watered yearly with the blood of victims. The tree itself may die; and yet the stump may continue to be draped on its anniversary with festal apparel. The very stump may decay; and yet gifts of food or offerings of rags may be cast as of old into the sacred spring that once welled beside it. The locality thus grows to be holy in itself, and gives us one clear and obvious source of later nature-worship.

The gods or spirits who haunt such shrines come naturally to be thought of with the lapse of ages as much like one another. Godship is all that can long remain of their individual attributes. Their very names are often unknown; they are remembered merely as the lord of Lebanon, the Baal of Mount Peor. No wonder that after a time they get to be practically identified with one another, while similar myths are often fastened by posterity to many of them together. Indeed, we know that new names, and even foreign intrusive names, frequently take the place of the original titles, while the god himself still continues to be worshipped as the same shapeless stone, with the same prescribed rites, in the same squalid or splendid temples. Thus, Melcarth, the Baal of Tyre, was adored in later days under the Greek name of Herakles; and thus at Bablos two local deities, after being identified first with the Syrian divinities, Adonis and Astarte, were identified later with the Egyptian divinities, Osiris and

Isis. Yet the myths of the place show us that through all that time the true worship was paid to the dead stump of a sacred tree, which was said to have grown from the grave of a god—in other words, from the tumulus of an ancient chieftain. No matter how greatly mythologies change, these local cults remain ever constant; the sacred stones are here described as haunted by *djinns*, and there as memorials of Christian martyrs; the holy wells are dedicated here to nymph or hero, and receive offerings there to saint or fairy. So the holy oaks of immemorial worship in England become "Thor's oaks" under Saxon heathendom, and "Gospel oaks" under mediæval Christianity.

Finally, in the latest stages of worship, an attempt is always made to work in the heavenly bodies and the great energies of nature into the mythological groundwork or theory of religion. Every king is the descendant of the sun, and every great god is therefore necessarily the sun in person. Endless myths arise from these phrases, which are mistaken by mythologists for the central facts and sources of religion. But they are nothing of the kind. Mysticism and symbolism can never be primitive; they are well-meant attempts by cultivated religious thinkers of later days to read deep-seated meaning into the crude ideas and still cruder practices of traditional religion. I may add that Dr. Robertson Smith's learned and able works are constantly spoiled in this way by his dogged determination to see nature-worship as primitive, where it is really derivative, as the earliest starting-point, where it is really the highest and latest development.

Clearly, when all gods have come to be more or less solar in their external and acquired features, the process of identification and internationalisation is proportionately easy.

The syncretism thus brought about in the Hebrew religion by the superposition of nature-worship on the primitive cult must have paved the way for the later recognition of monotheism, exactly as we know it did in the esoteric creed of Egypt, by making all the gods so much alike that worshippers had only to change the name of their deity, not the attributes of the essential conception. Let us look first how far this syncretism affected the later idea of Jahweh, the phallic stone-god preserved in the ark; and then let us enquire afterward how the patriotic reaction against Assyrian aggression put the final coping-stone on the rising fabric of monotheistic Jahweh-worship.

It is often asserted that Jahweh was worshipped in many places in Israel under the form of a golden calf. That is to say, Hebrews who set up images of a metal bull believed themselves nevertheless to be worshipping Jahweh. Even the prophets of the eighth century regard the cult of the bull as a form of Jahweh-worship, though not a form to which they can personally give their approbation. But the bull is probably in its origin a distinct god from the stone in the ark; and if its worship was identified with that of the Rock of Israel, it could be only by a late piece of syncretic mysticism. Perhaps the link here, as in the case of Apis, was a priestly recognition of the bull as symbolising the generative power of nature; an idea which would be peculiarly appropriate to the god whose great function it was to encourage fruitfulness. But in any case, we cannot but see in this later calf-worship a superadded element wholly distinct from the older cult of the sacred stone, just as the worship of Ra was wholly distinct in origin from the totem-cult of Mnevis, or as the worship of Amen was wholly distinct from that of Khem and Osiris. The stone-god and the bull-god merge at last into one, much as at a far later date the man Jesus merges into the Hebrew god, and receives more reverence in modern faiths than the older deity whom he practically replaces.

Even in the Temple at Jerusalem itself, symbols of bull-worship were apparently admitted. The altar upon which the daily sacrifice was burnt had four horns; and the laver in the court, the "brazen sea," was supported upon the figures of twelve oxen. When we remember that the Molech had the head of a bull, we can hardly fail to see in these symbols a token of that gradual syncretism which invariably affects all developed pantheons in all civilised countries.

Much more important are the supposed signs of the later identification of Jahweh with the sun, and his emergence as a modified and transfigured sun-god. It may seem odd at first that such a character could ever be acquired by a sacred stone, did we not recollect the exactly similar history of the Egyptian obelisk, which in like manner represents, first and foremost, the upright pillar or monolith—that is to say, the primitive gravestone —but secondarily and derivatively, at once the generative principle and a ray of the sun. With this luminous analogy to guide us in our search, we shall have little difficulty in recognising how a solar character may have been given to the later attributes and descriptions of Jahweh.

I do not myself attach undue importance to these solar characteristics of the fully evolved Jahweh; but so much has been made of them by a certain school of modern thinkers that I must not pass them over in complete silence.

To his early worshippers, then, as we saw, Jahweh was merely the stone in the ark. He dwelt there visibly, and where the ark went, there Jahweh went with it. But the later Hebrews—say in the eighth century—had acquired a very different idea of Jahweh's dwelling-place. Astrological and solar ideas (doubtless Akkadian in origin) had profoundly modified their rude primitive conceptions. To Amos and to the true Isaiah, Jahweh dwells in the open sky above and is "Jahweh of hosts," the leader among the shining army of heaven, the king of the star-world. "Over those celestial bodies and celestial inhabitants Jahweh rules"; they surround him and execute his commands: the host of heaven are his messengers—in the more familiar language of our modern religion, "the angels of the Lord," the servants of Jahweh. To Micah, heaven is "the temple of Jahweh's holiness": "God on high," is the descriptive phrase by which the prophet alludes to him. In all this we have reached a very different conception indeed from that of the early and simple-minded Israelites who carried their god with them on an ox-cart from station to station.

Furthermore, light and fire are constantly regarded by these later thinkers as manifestations of Jahweh; and even in editing the earlier legends they introduce such newer ideas, making "the glory of Jahweh" light up the ark, or appear in the burning bush, or combining both views, the elder and the younger, in the pillar of fire that preceded the nomad horde of Israel in the wilderness. Jahweh is said to "send" or to "cast fire" from heaven, in which expressions we see once more the advanced concept of an elemental god, whose voice is the thunder, and whose weapon the lightning. All these are familiar developments of the chief god in a pantheon. Says Zechariah in his poem, "Ask ye of Jahweh rain in the time of the latter showers: Jahweh will make the lightnings." Says Isaiah, "The light of Israel shall be for a fire, And his holy one for a flame"; "Behold, the name of Jahweh cometh from afar, His anger burneth, and violently the smoke riseth on high: His lips are full of indignation, And his tongue is as a devouring fire." In these and a hundred other passages that might be quoted, we seem to see Jahweh envisaged to a great extent as a sun-god, and clothed in almost all the attributes of a fiery Molech.

Sometimes these Molech-traits come very close indeed to those of the more generally acknowledged fire-gods. "Thus we read," says Kuenen, "that 'the glory of Jahweh was like devouring fire on the top of Mount Sinai'; and that 'his angel appeared in a flame of fire out of the midst of a bush: the bush burned with fire but was not consumed '" So Jahweh himself is called " a consuming fire, a jealous god " : and a poet thus describes his appearance, " Smoke goeth up out of his nostrils, And fire out of his mouth devoureth ; coals of fire are kindled by him." These are obviously very derivative and borrowed prerogatives with which to deck out the primitive stone pillar that led the people of Israel up out of Egypt. Yet we know that precisely analogous evolutions have been undergone by other stone-gods elsewhere.

Once more, though this is to anticipate a little, the later Jahweh-worship seems to have absorbed into itself certain astrological elements which were originally quite alien to it, belonging to the cult of other gods. Such for example is the institution of the Sabbath, the unlucky day of the malign god Kewán or Saturn, on which it was undesirable to do any kind of work, and on which accordingly the superstitious Semite rested altogether from his weekly labours. The division of the lunar month (the sacred period of Astarte, the queen of heaven) into four weeks of seven days each, dedicated in turn to the gods of the seven planets, belongs obviously to the same late cult of the elemental and astrological gods, or, rather, of the gods with whom these heavenly bodies were at last identified under Akkadian influence. The earlier prophets of the exclusive Jahweh-worship denounce as idolatrous such observation of the Sabbath and the astrological feasts— " Your Sabbaths and your new moons are an abomination to me "; and according to Amos, Kewán himself had been the chief idolatrous object of worship by his countrymen in the wilderness. Later on, however, the Jehovistic party found itself powerless to break the current of superstition on the Sabbath question, and a new *modus vivendi* was therefore necessary. They arranged a prudent compromise. The Sabbath was adopted bodily into the monotheistic Jahweh-worship, and a mythical reason was given for its institution and its sacred character which nominally linked it on to the cult of the ethnical god. On that day, said the priestly cosmogonists, Jahweh rested from his labour of creation. In the same way, many other fragments of external cults were loosely attached to the worship of Jahweh by a verbal connection with some part of the revised Jehovistic legend, or else were accredited to national Jehovistic or Jehovised heroes.

Having thus briefly sketched out the gradual changes which the conception of Jahweh himself underwent during the ages when his supremacy was being slowly established in the confederacy of Israel, let us now hark back once more and attack the final problem, Why did the particular cult of Jahweh become at last exclusive and monotheistic?

To begin with, we must remember that from the very outset of the national existence, Jahweh was clearly regarded on all hands as the *ethnical* god, the special god of Israel. The relation of such ethnical gods to their people has been admirably worked out by Dr. Robertson Smith in *The Religion of the Semites*. Even though we cannot, however, accept as historical the view given us of the exodus in the Pentateuch, nor admit that Jahweh played anything like so large a part in the great national migration as is there indicated, it is yet obvious that from the moment when Israel felt itself a nation at all, Jahweh was recognised as its chief deity. He was the "god of Israel," just as Milcom was the god of the Ammonites, Chemosh the god of Moab, and Ashtaroth the goddess of Sidon. As distinctly as every Athenian, while worshipping Zeus and Hera and Apollo, held Athene to be the special patron of Athens, so did every Israelite, while worshipping the Baalim and the Molech and the local deities generally, hold Jahweh to be the special patron of Israel.

Moreover, from the very beginning, there is reason to suppose that the Israelites regarded Jahweh as their supreme god. Most pantheons finally settle down into a recognised hierarchy, in which one deity or another gradually assumes the first place. So, in Hellas, the supremacy of Zeus was undoubted; so, in Rome, was the supremacy of Jupiter. Sometimes, to be sure, as among our Teutonic ancestors, we see room for doubt between two rival gods : it would be difficult to assign the exact priority to either of the two leading deities : among the English, Woden rather bore it over Thunor ; among the Scandinavians, Thor rather bore it over Odin. In Israel, in like manner, there was apparently a time when the Presidency of the Immortals hovered between Jahweh and one or other of the local Baalim. But in the end, and perhaps even from the very beginning, the suffrages of the people were mainly with the sacred stone of the ark. He was the God of Israel, and they were the chosen people of Jahweh.

The custom of circumcision must have proved at once the symbol and in part the cause, in part the effect, of this general devotion of the people to a single supreme god. At first, no doubt, only the first-born or other persons specially dedicated to Jahweh, would undergo the rite which marked them out so clearly as the devotees of the god of fertility. But as time went on, long before the triumph of the exclusive Jahweh-worship, it would seem that the practice of offering up every male child to the national god had become universal. As early as the shadowy reign of David, the Philistines are reproachfully alluded to in our legends as " the uncircumcised " ; whence we may perhaps conclude (though the authority is doubtful) that even then circumcision had become coextensive with Israelitish citizenship. Such universal dedication of the whole males of the race to the national god must have done much to ensure his ultimate triumph.

If we look at the circumstances of the Israelites in Palestine, we shall easily see how both religious unity and intense national patriotism were fostered by the very nature of their tenure of the soil ; and also why a deity mainly envisaged as a god of generation should have become the most important member of their national pantheon. Their position during the first few centuries of their life in Lower Syria may be compared to that of the Dorians in Peloponnesus : they were but a little garrison in a hostile land fighting incessantly with half-conquered tributaries and encircling foes ; now hard-pressed by rebellions of their internal enemies ; and now again rendered subject themselves to the hostile Philistines on their maritime border. The handful of rude warriors who burst upon the land under such bloodthirsty leaders as the mystical Joshua could only hope for success by rapid and constant increase of their numbers, and by avoiding as far as possible those internal quarrels which were always the prelude to national disgrace. To be " a mother in Israel " is the highest hope of every Hebrew woman. Hence it was natural that a god of generation should become the chief among the local deities, and that the promise held out by his priests of indefinite multiplication should make him the most popular and powerful member of the Israelitish pantheon. And though all the stone gods were probably phallic, yet Jahweh, as the ethnical patron, seems most of all to have been regarded as the giver of increase to Israel.

It seems clear, too, that the common worship of Jahweh was at first the only solid bond of union between the scattered and discordant tribes who were afterwards to grow into the Israelitish people. This solidarity of god and tribe has well been insisted on by Professor Robertson Smith as a common feature of all Semitic worship. The ark of Jahweh in its house at Shiloh appears to have formed the general meeting-place for Hebrew patriotism, as the sanctuary of Olympia formed a focus later for the dawning sense of Hellenic unity. The ark was taken out to carry before the Hebrew army, that the god of Israel might fight for his worshippers. Evidently, therefore, from a very early date, Jahweh was regarded in a literal sense as the god of battles, the power upon whom Israel might specially rely to guard it against its enemies. When, as the legends tell us, the national unity was realised under David ; when the subject peoples were finally merged into a homogeneous whole ; when the last relics of Canaanitish nationality were stamped out by the final conquest of the Jebusites ; and when Jerusalem was made the capital of a united Israel, this feeling must have increased both in extent and intensity. The bringing of Jahweh to Jerusalem by David, and the building of his temple by Solomon (if these facts be historical), must have helped to stamp him as the great god of the race : and though Solomon also erected temples to other Hebrew gods, which remained in existence for some centuries, we may be sure that from the date of the opening of the great central shrine, Jahweh remained the principal deity of the southern kingdom at least, after the separation.

There was one characteristic of Jahweh-worship, however, which especially helped to make it at last an *exclusive* cult, and thus paved the way for its final development into a pure monotheism. Jahweh was specially known to be a "jealous god": this is a trait in his temperament early and often insisted on. We do not know when or where the famous "Ten Words" were first promulgated ; but we have every reason to believe that in essence at least they date from a very antique period. Now, at the head of these immemorial precepts of Jahweh stands the prohibition of placing any other gods before his face. Originally, no doubt, the prohibition meant exactly what it states ; that Jahweh would endure no companion gods to share his temple ; that wherever he dwelt, he would dwell alone without what the Greeks would have called fellow shrine-sharers. Thus we know that no ashera was to be driven into the ground near Jahweh's ark ; and that when Dagon found himself face to face with the Rock of Israel, he broke in pieces, and could not stand before the awful presence of the great Hebrew Pillar. No more than this, then, was at first demanded by "the jealous god" : he asked of his worshippers that they should keep him apart from the society of all inferior gods, should allow no minor or rival deity to enter his precincts.

Gradually, however, as Jahweh-worship grew deeper, and the conception of godhead became wider and more sublime, the Jahweh-worshipper began to put a stricter interpretation upon the antique command of the jealous god. It was supposed that every circumcised person, every man visibly devoted to Jahweh, owed to Jahweh alone his whole religious service. Nobody doubted as yet, indeed, that other gods existed: but the extreme Jehovists in the later days of national independence held as an article of faith that no true Israelite ought in any way to honour them. An internal religious conflict thus arose between the worshippers of Jahweh and the worshippers of the Baalim, in which, as might be expected, the devotees of the national god had very much the best of it. Exclusive Jahweh-worship became thenceforth the ideal of the extreme Jehovists: they began to regard all other gods as "idols," to be identified with their images; they began to look upon Jahweh alone as a living god, at least within the bounds of the Israelitish nation.

To this result, another ancient prohibition of the priests of Jahweh no doubt largely contributed. The priesthood held it unlawful to make or multiply images of Jahweh. The one sacred stone enclosed in the ark was alone to be worshipped: and by thus concentrating on Shiloh, or afterwards on Jerusalem, the whole religious spirit of the ethnical cult, they must largely have succeeded in cementing the national unity. Strict Jehovists looked with dislike upon the adoration paid to the bull-images in the northern kingdom, though those, too, were regarded (at least in later days) as representatives of Jahweh. They held that the true god of Abraham was to be found only in the ark at Jerusalem, and that to give to the Rock of Israel human form or bestial figure was in itself a high crime against the majesty of their deity. Hence arose the peculiar Hebrew dislike to "idolatry"; a dislike never equally shared by any but Semitic peoples, and having deep roots, apparently, at once in the inartistic genius of the people and in the profound metaphysical and dreamy character of Semitic thinking. The comparative emptiness of Semitic shrines, indeed, was always a stumbling-block to the Greek, with his numerous and exquisite images of anthropomorphic deities.

All that was now wanted to drive the increasingly exclusive and immaterial Jahweh-worship into pure monotheism for the whole people was the spur of a great national enthusiam, in answer to some dangerous external attack upon the existence of Israel and of Israel's god. This final touch was given by the aggression of Assyria, and later of Babylon. For years the two tiny Israelitish kingdoms had maintained a precarious independence between the mighty empires of Egypt and Mesopotamia. In the eighth century, it became certain that they could no longer play their accustomed game of clever diplomacy and polite subjection. The very existence of Israel was at stake ; and the fanatical worshippers of Jahweh, now pushed to an extreme of frenzy by the desperate straits to which they were reduced, broke out in that memorable ecstasy of enthusiasm which we may fairly call the Age of the Prophets, and which produced the earliest masterpieces of Hebrew literature in the wild effort to oppose to the arms of the invaders the passive resistance of a supreme Jahweh. In times of old, the prophets say, when Jahweh led the forces of Israel, the horses and the chariots of their enemies counted for naught : if in this crisis Israel would cease to think of aid from Egypt or alliance with Assyria—if Israel would get rid of all her other gods and trust only to Jahweh,—then Jahweh would break asunder the strength of Assyria and would reduce Babylon to nothing before his chosen people.

Such is the language that Isaiah ventured to use in the very crisis of a grave national danger.

Now, strange as it seems to us that any people should

have thrown themselves into such a general state of fanatical folly, it is nevertheless true that these extraordinary counsels prevailed in both the Israelitish kingdoms, and that the very moment when the national existence was most seriously imperilled was the moment chosen by the Jehovistic party for vigorously attempting a religious reformation. The downfall of Ephraim only quickened the bigoted belief of the fanatics in Judah that pure Jahweh-worship was the one possible panacea for the difficulties of Israel. Taking advantage of a minority and of a plastic young king, they succeeded in imposing exclusive Jehovism upon the half-unwilling people. The timely forgery of the Book of Deuteromony—the first germ of the Pentateuch—by the priests of the temple at Jerusalem was quickly followed by the momentary triumph of pure Jahweh-worship. In this memorable document, the exclusive cult of Jahweh was falsely said to have descended from the earliest periods of the national existence. Josiah, we are told, alarmed at the denunciations in the forged roll of the law, set himself to work at once to root out by violent means every form of "idolatry." He brought forth from the house of Jahweh "the vessels that were made for the Baal, and for the Ashera, and for all the Host of Heaven, and he burned them without Jerusalem in the fields of Kidron." He abolished all the shrines and priesthoods of other gods in the cities of Judah, and put down "them that burned incense to the Baal, to the sun, and to the moon, and to the planets, and all the Host of Heaven." He also brought out the Ashera from the temple of Jahweh, and burnt it to ashes; and "took away the horses that the kings of Judah had given to the sun, and burned the chariots of the sun with fire." And by destroying the temples said to have been built by Solomon for Chemosh, Milcom, and Ashtoreth, he left exclusive and triumphant Jahweh-worship the sole accredited religion of Israel.

All, however, was of no avail. Religious fanaticism

could not save the little principality from the aggressive arms of its powerful neighbours. Within twenty or thirty years of Josiah's reformation, the Babylonians ceased to toy with their petty tributaries, and thrice captured and sacked Jerusalem. The temple of Jahweh was burnt, the chief ornaments were removed, and the desolate site itself lay empty and deserted. The principal inhabitants were transported to Babylonia, and the kingdom of Judah ceased for a time to have any independent existence of any sort.

But what, in this disaster, became of Jahweh himself? How fared or fell the Sacred Stone in the ark, the Rock of Israel, in this general destruction of all his holiest belongings? Strange to say, the Hebrew annalist never stops to tell us. In the plaintive catalogue of the wrongs wrought by the Babylonians at Jerusalem, every pot and shovel and vessel is enumerated, but "the ark of God" is not so much as once mentioned. Perhaps the historian shrank from relating that final disgrace of his country's deity; perhaps a sense of reverence prevented him from chronicling it; perhaps he knew nothing of what had finally been done with the cherished and time-honoured stone pillar of his ancestors. It is possible, too, that with his later and more etherealised conceptions of the cult of his god, he had ceased to regard the ark itself as the abode of Jahweh, and was unaware that his tribal deity had been represented in the innermost shrine of the temple by a rough-hewn pillar. Be that as it may, the actual fate of Jahweh himself is involved for us now in impenetrable obscurity. Probably the invaders who took away "the treasures of the house of Jahweh, and cut in pieces all the vessels of gold which Solomon, King of Israel, had made," would care but little for the rude sacred stone of a conquered people. We may conjecture that they broke Jahweh into a thousand fragments and ground him to powder, as Josiah had done with the Baalim and the Ashera, so that his very relics could no longer be recognised or worshipped by his followers. At any rate, we hear no more, from that time forth, of Jahweh himself, as a material existence, or of the ark he dwelt in. His spirit alone survived unseen, to guard and protect his chosen people.

Yet, strange to say, this final disappearance of Jahweh himself, as a visible and tangible god, from the page of history, instead of proving the signal for the utter downfall of his cult and his sanctity, was the very making of Jahweh-worship as a spiritual, a monotheistic, and a cosmopolitan religion. At the exact moment when Jahweh ceased to exist, the religion of Jahweh began to reach its highest and fullest development. Even before the captivity, as we have seen, the prophets and their party had begun to form a most exalted and spiritualised conception of Jahweh's greatness, Jahweh's holiness, Jahweh's unapproachable nature, Jahweh's superhuman sublimity and omnipotence. But now that the material Jahweh itself, which clogged and cramped their ideas, had disappeared for ever, this spiritual conception of a great Unseen God widened and deepened amazingly. Forbidden by their creed and by Jahweh's own express command to make any image of their chosen deity, the Hebrews in Babylonia gradually evolved for themselves the notion of a Supreme Ruler wholly freed from material bonds, to be worshipped without image, representative, or symbol ; a dweller in the heavens, invisible to men, too high and pure for human eyes to look upon. The conical stone in the ark gave place almost at once to an incorporeal, inscrutable, and almighty Being.

It was during the captivity, too, that pure monotheism became for the first time the faith of Israel. Convinced that desertion of Jahweh was the cause of all their previous misfortunes, the Jews during their exile grew more deeply attached than ever to the deity who represented their national unity and their national existence. They made their way back in time to Judæa, after two generations had passed away, with a firm conviction that all their happiness depended on restoring in ideal purity a cult that had never been the cult of their fathers. A new form of Jahweh-worship had become a passion among those who sat disconsolate by the waters of Babylon. Few if any of the zealots who returned at last to Jerusalem had ever themselves known the stone god who lay shrouded in the ark : it was the etherealised Jahweh who ruled in heaven above among the starry hosts to whom they offered up aspirations in a strange land for the restoration of Israel. In the temple that they built on the sacred site to the new figment of their imaginations, Jahweh was no longer personally present: it was not so much his "house," like the old one demolished by the Babylonian invaders, as the place where sacrifice was offered and worship paid to the great god in heaven. The new religion was purely spiritual ; Jahweh had triumphed, but only by losing his distinctive personal characteristics, and coming out of the crisis, as it were, the blank form or generic conception of pure deity in general.

It is this that gives monotheism its peculiar power, and enables it so readily to make its way everywhere. For monotheism is religion reduced to its single central element ; it contains nothing save what every votary of all gods already implicitly believes, with every unnecessary complexity or individuality smoothed away and simplified. Its simplicity recommends it to all intelligent minds ; its uniformity renders it the easiest and most economical form of pantheon that man can frame for himself.

Under the influence of these new ideas, before long, the whole annals of Israel were edited and written down in Jehovistic form ; the Pentateuch and the older historical books assumed the dress in which we now know them. From the moment of the return from the captivity, too, the monotheistic conception kept ever widening. At first, no doubt, even with the Jews of the Sixth Century, Jahweh was commonly looked upon merely as the ethnical god of Israel. But, in time, the sublimer and broader conception of some few among the earlier poetical prophets began to gain general acceptance, and Jahweh was regarded as in very deed the one true God of all the world—somewhat such a God as Islam and Christendom to-day acknowledge. Still, even so, he was as yet most closely connected with the Jewish people, through whom alone the gentiles were expected in the fulness of time to learn his greatness. It was reserved for a Græco-Jewish Cilician, five centuries later, to fulfil the final ideal of pure cosmopolitan monotheism, and to proclaim abroad the unity of god to all nations, with the Catholic Church as its earthly witness before the eyes of universal humanity. To Paul of Tarsus we owe above all men that great and on the whole cosmopolitanising conception.

CHAPTER XI.

HUMAN GODS.

WE have now in a certain sense accomplished our intention of tracing the evolution of gods and of God. We have shown how polytheism came to be, and how from it a certain particular group of men, the early Israelites, rose by slow degrees, through natural stages, to the monotheistic conception. It might seem, therefore, as though the task we set before ourselves was now quite completed. Nevertheless, many abstruse and difficult questions still lie before us. Our problem as yet is hardly half solved. We have still to ask, I think, How did this purely local and national Hebrew deity advance to the conquest of the civilised world? How from an obscure corner of Lower Syria did the god of a small tribe of despised and barbaric tributaries slowly live down the great conquering deities of Babylon and Susa, of Hellas and Italy? And again, we have further to enquire, Why do most of the modern nations which have nominally adopted monotheism yet conceive of their god as compounded in some mystically incomprehensible fashion of Three Persons, the Father, the Son, and the Holy Ghost? In short, I am not satisfied with tracing the idea of a god from the primitive mummy or the secondary ghost to the one supreme God of the ancient Hebrews; I desire also to follow on that developed concept till it merges at last in the triune God of modern Christendom. For, naturally, it is the god in whom men believe here and now that most of all concerns and interests us.

I may also add that, incidentally to this supplementary enquiry, we shall come upon several additional traits in the idea of deity and several important sources of earlier godhead, the consideration of which we had to postpone before till a more convenient season. We shall find that the process of tracking down Christianity to its hidden springs suggests to us many aspects of primitive religion which we were compelled to neglect in our first hasty synthesis.

The reader must remember that in dealing with so complex a subject as that of human beliefs and human cults, it is impossible ever to condense the whole of the facts at once into a single conspectus. We cannot grasp at a time the entire mass of evidence. While we are following out one clue, we must neglect another. It is only by examining each main set of components in analytical distinctness that we can proceed by degrees to a full and complete synthetic reconstruction of the whole vast fabric. We must therefore correct and supplement in the sequel much that may have seemed vague, inaccurate, or insufficient in our preliminary survey.

The Christian religion with which we have next to deal bases itself fundamentally upon the personality of a man, by name Jesus, commonly described as the Christ, that is to say "the anointed." Of this most sacred and deified person it is affirmed by modern Christianity, and has been affirmed by orthodox Christians from a very early period, that he was not originally a mere man, afterwards taken into the godhead, but that he was born from the first the son of God, that is to say, of the Hebrew Jahweh; that he existed previously from all time; that he was miraculously conceived of a virgin mother; that he was crucified and buried; that on the third day he arose from the dead; and that he is now a living and distinct person in a divine and mystically-united Trinity. I propose to show in the subsequent chapters how far all these conceptions were already familiar throughout the world in which Christianity was promulgated, and to how large an extent the new religion owed its rapid success to the fact that it was but a *résumé* or idealised embodiment of all the chief conceptions already common to the main cults of Mediterranean civilisation. At the moment when the empire was cosmopolitanising the world, Christianity began to cosmopolitanise religion, by taking into itself whatever was central, common, and universal in the worship of the peoples among whom it originated.

We will begin with the question of the incarnation, which lies at the very root of the Christian concept.

I have said already that in ancient Egypt and elsewhere, " The God was the Dead King, the King was the Living God." This is true, literally and absolutely. Since the early kings are gods, the present kings, their descendants, are naturally also gods by descent ; their blood is divine ; they differ in nature as well as in position from mere common mortals. While they live, they are gods on earth ; when they die, they pass over to the community of the gods their ancestors, and share with them a happy and regal immortality. We have seen how this essential divinity of the Pharaoh is a prime article in the religious faith of the Egyptian Pyramid-builders. And though in later days, when a Greek dynasty, not of the old divine native blood, bore sway in Egypt, this belief in the divinity of the king grew fainter, yet to the very last the Ptolemies and the Cleopatras bear the title of god or goddess, and carry in their hands the sacred *tau* or *crux ansata*, the symbol and mark of essential divinity.

The inference made in Egypt that the children of gods must be themselves divine was also made in most other countries, especially in those where similar great despotisms established themselves at an early grade of culture. Thus in Peru, the Incas were gods. They were the children of the Sun ; and when they died, it was said that their father, the Sun, had sent to fetch them. The Mexican kings were likewise gods, with full control of the course of nature; they swore at their accession to make the sun shine, the rain fall, the rivers flow, and the earth bring forth her fruit in due season. How they could promise all this seems at first a little difficult for us to conceive; but it will become more comprehensible at a later stage of our investigation, when we come to consider the gods of cultivation: even at present, if we remember that kings are children of the Sun, and that sacred trees, sacred groves, and sacred wells are closely connected with the tombs of their ancestors, we can guess at the beginning of such a mental connexion. Thus the Chinese emperor is the Son of Heaven; he is held responsible to his people for the occurrence of drought or other serious derangements of nature. The Parthian kings of the Arsacid house, says Mr. Frazer, to whom I am greatly indebted for most of the succeeding facts, styled themselves brothers of the sun and moon, and were worshipped as deities. Numberless other cases are cited by Mr. Frazer, who was the first to point out the full importance of this widespread belief in man-gods. I shall follow him largely in the subsequent discussion of this cardinal subject, though I shall often give to the facts an interpretation slightly different from that which he would allow to be the correct one. For to me, godhead springs always from the primitive Dead Man, while to Mr. Frazer it is spiritual or animistic in origin.

Besides these human gods who are gods by descent from deified ancestors, there is another class of gods who are gods by inspiration or indwelling of the divine spirit, that is to say of some ghost or god who temporarily or permanently inhabits the body of a living man. The germ-idea of such divine possession we may see in the facts of epilepsy, catalepsy, dream, and madness. In all such cases of abnormal nervous condition it seems to primitive man, as it still seemed to the Jews of the age of the Gospels, that the sufferer is entered or seized upon by some spirit, who bodily inhabits him. The spirit may throw the man down, or may speak through his mouth in strange unknown tongues ; it may exalt him so that he can perform strange feats of marvellous strength, or may debase him to a position of grovelling abjectness. By fasting and religious asceticism men and women can even artificially attain this state, when the god speaks through them, as he spoke through the mouth of the Pythia at Delphi. And fasting is always one of the religious exercises of god-possessed men, priests, monks, anchorites, and ascetics in general. Where races have learnt how to manufacture intoxicating drinks, or to express narcotic juices from plants, they also universally attribute the effects of such plants to the personal action of an inspiring spirit—an idea so persistent even into civilised ages that we habitually speak of alcoholic liquors as spirits. Both these ways of attaining the presence of an indwelling god are commonly practised among savages and half-civilised people.

When we recollect how we saw already that ancestral spirits may descend from time to time into the skulls that once were theirs, or into the clay or wooden images that represent them, and there give oracles, we shall not be surprised to find that they can thus enter at times into a human body, and speak through its lips, for good or for evil. Indeed, I have dwelt but little in this book on this migratory power and this ubiquitousness of the spirits, because I have desired to fix attention chiefly on that primary aspect of religion which is immediately and directly concerned with Worship ; but readers familiar with such works as Dr. Tylor's and Mr. Frazer's will be well aware of the common power which spirits possess of projecting themselves readily into every part of nature. The faculty of possession or of divination is but one particular example of this well-known attribute. The mysteries and oracles of all creeds are full of such phenomena.

Certain persons, again, are born from the womb as incarnations of a god or an ancestral spirit. " Incarnate gods," says Mr. Frazer, "are common in rude society. The incarnation may be temporary or permanent. . . . When the divine spirit has taken up its abode in a human body, the god-man is usually expected to vindicate his character by working miracles." Mr. Frazer gives several excellent examples of both these classes. I extract a few almost verbatim.

Certain persons are possessed from time to time by a spirit or deity ; while possession lasts, their own personality lies in abeyance, and the presence of the spirit is revealed by convulsive shakings and quiverings of the body. In this abnormal state, the man's utterances are accepted as the voice of the god or spirit dwelling in him and speaking through him. In Mangaia, for instance, the priests in whom the gods took up their abode were called god-boxes or gods. Before giving oracles, they drank an intoxicating liquor, and the words they spoke in their frenzy were then regarded as divine. In other cases, the inspired person produces the desired condition of intoxication by drinking the fresh blood of a victim, human or animal, which, as we shall see hereafter, is probably itself an avatar of the inspiring god. In the temple of Apollo Diradiotes at Argos, a lamb was sacrificed by night once a month ; a woman, who had to observe the rule of chastity, tasted its blood, and then gave oracles. At Ægira in Achæa the priestess of the Earth drank the fresh blood of a bull before she descended into her cave to prophesy. (Note in passing that caves, the places of antique burial, are also the usual places for prophetic inspiration.) In southern India, the so-called devil-dancer drinks the blood of a goat, and then becomes seized with the divine afflatus. He is worshipped as a deity, and bystanders ask him questions requiring superhuman knowledge to answer. Mr. Frazer extends this list of oracular practices by many other striking instances, for which I would refer the reader to the original volume.

Of permanent living human gods, inspired by the constant indwelling of a deity, Mr. Frazer also gives several apt examples. In the Marquesas Islands there was a class of men who were deified in their lifetime. They were supposed to wield supernatural control over the elements. They could give or withhold rain and good harvests. Human sacrifices were offered them to appease their wrath. "A missionary has described one of these human gods from personal observation. The god was a very old man who lived in a large house within an enclosure." (A temple in its *temenos*.) "In the house was a kind of altar, and on the beams of the house and on the trees around it were hung human skeletons, head down. No one entered the enclosure, except the persons dedicated to the service of the god ; only on days when human victims were sacrificed might ordinary people penetrate into the precinct. This human god received more sacrifices than all the other gods ; often he would sit on a sort of scaffold in front of his house and call for two or three human victims at a time. They were always brought, for the terror he inspired was extreme. He was invoked all over the island, and offerings were sent to him from every side." Indeed, throughout the South Sea Islands, each island had usually a man who embodied its deity. Such men were called gods, and were regarded as of divine substance. The man-god was sometimes a king ; oftener he was a priest or a subordinate chief. The gods of Samoa were sometimes permanently incarnate in men, who gave oracles, received offerings (occasionally of human flesh), healed the sick, answered prayer, and generally performed all divine functions. Of the Fijians it is said : "There appears to be no certain line of demarcation between departed spirits and gods, nor between gods and living men, for many of the priests and old chiefs are considered as sacred persons, and not a few of them will also claim to themselves the right of divinity. 'I am a god,' Tuikilakila would say ; and he believed it too." There is said to be a sect in Orissa who worship the Queen of England as their chief divinity; and another sect in the Punjab worshipped during his lifetime the great General Nicholson.

Sometimes, I believe, kings are divine by birth, as descendants of gods; but sometimes divinity is conferred upon them with the kingship, as indeed was the case even in the typical instance of Egypt. Tanatoa, king of Raiatea, was deified by a certain ceremony performed at the chief temple. He was made a god before the gods his ancestors, as Celtic chiefs received the chieftainship standing on the sacred stone of their fathers. As one of the deities of his subjects, therefore, the king was worshipped, consulted as an oracle, and honoured with sacrifices. The king of Tahiti at his inauguration received a sacred girdle of red and yellow feathers, which not only raised him to the highest earthly station, but also identified him with the heavenly gods. Compare the way in which the gods of Egypt make the king one of themselves, as represented in the bas-reliefs, by the presentation of the divine *tau*. In the Pelew Islands, a god may incarnate himself in a common person; this lucky man is thereupon raised to sovereign rank, and rules as god and king over the community. Not unsimilar is the mode of selection of a Grand Lama. In later stages, the king ceases to be quite a god, but retains the anointment, the consecration on a holy stone, and the claim to "divine right"; he also shows some last traces of deity in his divine power to heal diseases, which fades away at last into the practice of "touching for king's evil." On all these questions, again, Mr. Frazer's great work is a perfect thesaurus of apposite instances. I abstain from quoting his whole two volumes.

But did ideas of this character still survive in the Mediterranean world of the first and second centuries, where Christianity was evolved? Most undoubtedly they did. In Egypt, the divine line of the Ptolemies had only just become extinct. In Rome itself, the divine Cæsar had recently undergone official apotheosis; the divine Augustus had ruled over the empire as the adopted son of the new-made god; and altars rose in provincial cities to the divine spirit of the reigning Trajan or Hadrian. Indeed, both forms of divinity were claimed indirectly for the god Julius; he was divine by apotheosis, but he was also descended from the goddess Venus. So the double claim was made for the central personage of the Christian faith: he was the son of God—that is to say of Jahweh; but he was also of kingly Jewish origin, a descendant of David, and in the genealogies fabricated for him in the Gospels extreme importance is attached to this pretended royal ancestry. Furthermore, how readily men of the Mediterranean civilisation could then identify living persons with gods we see in the familiar episode of Paul and Barnabas at Lystra. Incarnation, in short, was a perfectly ordinary feature of religion and daily life as then understood. And to oriental ideas in particular, the conception was certainly no novelty. "Even an infant king," say the laws of Manu, which go to the root of so much eastern thinking, "must not be despised from an idea that he is a mere mortal: for he is a great deity in human form."

To most modern thinkers, however, it would seem at first sight like a grave difficulty in the way of accepting the deity of an ordinary man that he should have suffered a violent death at the hands of his enemies. Yet this fact, instead of standing in the way of acceptance of Christ's divinity, is really almost a guarantee and proof of it. For, strange as it sounds to us, the human gods were frequently or almost habitually put to death by their votaries. The secret of this curious ritual and persistent custom has been ingeniously deciphered for us by Mr. Frazer, whose book is almost entirely devoted to these two main questions, "Why do men kill their gods?" and "Why do they eat and drink their flesh and blood under the form of bread and wine?" We must go over some of the same ground here in rapid summary, with additional corollaries; and we must also bring Mr. Frazer's curious facts into line with our general principles of the origin of godhead.

Meanwhile, it may be well to add here two similar instances of almost contemporary apotheoses. The dictator Julius was killed by a band of reactionary conspirators, and yet was immediately raised to divine honours. A little later, Antinous, the favourite of the emperor Hadrian, devoted himself to death in order to avert misfortune from his master; he was at once honoured with temples and worship. The belief that it is expedient that "one man should die for the people," and that the person who so dies is a god in human shape, formed, as we shall see, a common component of many faiths, and especially of the faiths of the eastern Mediterranean. Indeed, a little later, each Christian martyrdom is followed as a matter of course by canonisation—that is to say, by minor apotheosis. Mr. Frazer has traced the genesis of this group of allied beliefs in the slaughter of the man-god in the most masterly manner. They spring from a large number of converging ideas, some of which can only come out in full as we proceed in later chapters to other branches of our subject.

In all parts of the world, one of the commonest prerogatives and functions of the human god is the care of the weather. As representative of heaven, it is his business to see that rain falls in proper quantities, and that the earth brings forth her increase in due season. But, god though he is, he must needs be coerced if he does not attend to this business properly. Thus, in West Africa, when prayers and offerings presented to the king have failed to procure rain, his subjects bind him with ropes, and take him to the grave of his deified forefathers, that he may obtain from them the needful change in the weather. Here we see in the fullest form the nature of the relation between dead gods and living ones. The Son is the natural mediator between men and the Father. Among the Antaymours of Madagascar, the king is responsible for bad crops and all other misfortunes. The ancient Scythians, when food was scarce, put their kings in bonds. The Banjars in West Africa ascribe to their king the power of causing rain or fine weather. As long as the climate is satisfactory, they load him with presents of grain and cattle. But if long drought or rain does serious harm, they insult and beat him till the weather changes. The Burgundians deposed their king if he failed to make their crops grow to their satisfaction.

Further than that, certain tribes have even killed their kings in times of scarcity. In the days of the Swedish king Domalde, a mighty famine broke out, which lasted several years, and could not be stayed by human or animal sacrifices. So, in a great popular assembly held at Upsala, the chiefs decided that King Domalde himself was the cause of the scarcity, and must be sacrificed for good seasons. Then they slew him, and smeared with his blood the altars of the gods. Here we must recollect that the divine king is himself a god, the descendant of gods, and he is sacrificed to the offended spirits of his own forefathers. We shall see hereafter how often similar episodes occur—how the god is sacrificed, himself to himself ; how the Son is sacrificed to the Father, both being gods ; and how the Father sacrifices his Son, to make a god of him. To take another Scandinavian example from Mr. Frazer's collection : in the reign of King Olaf, there came a great dearth, and the people thought that the fault was the king's, because he was sparing in sacrifices. So they mustered an army and marched against him ; then they surrounded his palace and burnt it, with him within it, "giving him to Odin as a sacrifice for good crops." Many points must here be noted. Olaf himself was of divine stock, a descendant of Odin. He is burnt as an offering to his father, much as the Carthaginians burnt their sons, or the king of Moab his first-born, as sacrifices to Melcarth and to Chemosh. The royal and divine person is here offered up to his own fathers, just as on the cross of the founder of Christendom the inscription ran, "Jesus of Nazareth, king of the Jews," and just as in

Christian theology God offers his Son as a sacrifice to his own offended justice.

Other instances elsewhere point to the same analogies. In 1814, a pestilence broke out among the reindeer of the Chukches (a Siberian tribe); and the shamans declared that the beloved chief Koch must be sacrificed to the angry gods (probably his ancestors); so the chief's own son stabbed him with a dagger. On the coral island of Niue in the South Pacific there once reigned a line of kings; but they were also "high-priests" (that is to say, divine representatives of divine ancestors); and they were supposed to make the crops grow, for a reason which will come out more fully in the sequel. In times of scarcity, the people "grew angry with them and killed them," or more probably, as I would interpret the facts, sacrificed them for crops to their own deified ancestors. So in time there were no kings left, and the monarchy ceased altogether on the island.

The divine kings being thus responsible for rain and wind, and for the growth of crops, whose close dependence upon them we shall further understand hereafter, it is clear that they are persons of the greatest importance and value to the community. Moreover, in the ideas of early men, their spirit is almost one with that of external nature, over which they exert such extraordinary powers. A subtle sympathy seems to exist between the king and the world outside. The sacred trees which embody his ancestors; the crops, which, as we shall see hereafter, equally embody them; the rain-clouds in which they dwell; the heaven they inhabit;—all these, as it were, are parts of the divine body, and therefore by implication part of the god-king's, who is but the avatar of his deified fathers. Hence, whatever affects the king, affects the sky, the crops, the rain, the people. There is even reason to believe that the man-god, representative of the ancestral spirit and tribal god, is therefore the representative and embodiment of the tribe itself—the soul of the nation.

L'état, c'est moi is no mere personal boast of Louis Quatorze; it is the belated survival of an old and once very powerful belief, shared in old times by kings and peoples. Whatever hurts the king, hurts the people, and hurts by implication external nature. Whatever preserves the king from danger, preserves and saves the world and the nation.

Mr. Frazer has shown many strange results of these early beliefs—which he traces, however, to the supposed primitive animism, and not (as I have done) to the influence of the ghost-theory. Whichever interpretation we accept, however, his facts at least are equally valuable. He calls attention to the number of kingly taboos which are all intended to prevent the human god from endangering or imperilling his divine life, or from doing anything which might react hurtfully upon nature and the welfare of his people. The man-god is guarded by the strictest rules, and surrounded by precautions of the utmost complexity. He may not set his sacred foot on the ground, because he is a son of heaven; he may not eat or drink with his sacred mouth certain dangerous, impure, or unholy foods; he may not have his sacred hair cut, or his sacred nails pared; he must preserve intact his divine body, and every part of it—the incarnation of the community,—lest evil come of his imprudence or his folly.

The Mikado, for example, was and still is regarded as an incarnation of the sun, the deity who rules the entire universe, gods and men included. The greatest care must therefore be taken both *by* him and *of* him. His whole life, down to its minutest details, must be so regulated that no act of his may upset the established order of nature. Lest he should touch the earth, he used to be carried wherever he went on men's shoulders. He could not expose his sacred person to the open air, nor eat out of any but a perfectly new vessel. In every way his sanctity and his health were jealously guarded, and he was treated like a person whose security was important to the whole course of nature.

Mr. Frazer quotes several similar examples, of which the most striking is that of the high pontiff of the Zapotecs, an ancient people of Southern Mexico. This spiritual lord, a true Pope or Lama, governed Yopaa, one of the chief cities of the kingdom, with absolute dominion. He was looked upon as a god "whom earth was not worthy to hold or the sun to shine upon." He profaned his sanctity if he touched the common ground with his holy foot. The officers who bore his palanquin on their shoulders were chosen from the members of the highest families; he hardly deigned to look on anything around him; those who met him prostrated themselves humbly on the ground, lest death should overtake them if they even saw his divine shadow. (Compare the apparition of Jahweh to Moses.) A rule of continence was ordinarily imposed upon him; but on certain days in the year which were high festivals, it was usual for him to get ceremonially and sacramentally drunk. On such days, we may be sure, the high gods peculiarly entered into him with the intoxicating pulque, and the ancestral spirits reinforced his godhead. While in this exalted state ("full of the god," as a Greek or Roman would have said) the divine pontiff received a visit from one of the most beautiful of the virgins consecrated to the service of the gods. If the child she bore him was a son, it succeeded in due time to the throne of the Zapotecs. We have here again an instructive mixture of the various ideas out of which such divine kingship and godship is constructed.

It might seem at first sight a paradoxical corollary that people who thus safeguard and protect their divine king, the embodiment of nature, should also habitually and ceremonially kill him. Yet the apparent paradox is, from the point of view of the early worshipper, both natural and reasonable. We read of the Congo negroes that they have a supreme pontiff whom they regard as a god upon earth, and all-powerful in heaven. But, "if he were to die a natural death, they thought the world would perish, and the earth, which he alone sustained by his power and merit, would immediately be annihilated." This idea of a god as the creator and supporter of all things, without whom nothing would be, is of course a familiar component element of the most advanced theology. But many nations which worship human gods carry out the notion to its logical conclusion in the most rigorous manner. Since the god is a man, it would obviously be quite wrong to let him grow old and weak; since thereby the whole course of nature might be permanently enfeebled; rain would but dribble; crops would grow thin; rivers would trickle away; and the race he ruled would dwindle to nothing. Hence senility must never overcome the sacred man-god; he must be killed in the fulness of his strength and health (say, about his thirtieth year), so that the indwelling spirit, yet young and fresh, may migrate unimpaired into the body of some newer and abler representative. Mr. Frazer was the first, I believe, to point out this curious result of primitive human reasoning, and to illustrate it by numerous and conclusive instances.

I cannot transcribe here in full Mr. Frazer's admirable argument, with the examples which enforce it; but I must at least give so much of it in brief as will suffice for comprehension of our succeeding exposition. "No amount of care and precaution," he says, "will prevent the man-god from growing old and feeble, and at last dying. His worshippers have to lay their account with this sad necessity and to meet it as best they can. The danger is a formidable one; for if the course of nature is dependent on the man-god's life, what catastrophes may not be expected from the gradual enfeeblement of his powers and their final extinction in death? There is only one way of averting these dangers. The man-god must be killed as soon as he shows symptoms that his powers are beginning to fail, and his soul must be transferred to a vigorous successor before it has been seriously impaired by the threatened decay. The advantages of thus putting the man-god to death instead of allowing him to die of old age and disease are, to the savage, obvious enough. For if the man-god dies what we call a natural death, it means, according to the savage, that his soul has either voluntarily departed from his body and refuses to return, or more commonly that it has been extracted or at least detained in its wanderings by a demon or sorcerer. In any of these cases the soul of the man-god is lost to his worshippers ; and with it their prosperity is gone and their very existence endangered. Even if they could arrange to catch the soul of the dying god as it left his lips or his nostrils and so transfer it to a successor, this would not effect their purpose ; for, thus dying of disease, his soul would necessarily leave his body in the last stage of weakness and exhaustion, and as such it would continue to drag out a feeble existence in the body to which it might be transferred. Whereas by killing him his worshippers could, in the first place, make sure of catching his soul as it escaped and transferring it to a suitable successor ; and, in the second place, by killing him before his natural force was abated, they would secure that the world should not fall into decay with the decay of the man-god. Every purpose, therefore, was answered, and all dangers averted by thus killing the man-god and transferring his soul, while yet at its prime, to a vigorous successor."

For this reason, when the pontiff of Congo grew old, and seemed likely to die, the man who was destined to succeed him in the pontificate entered his house with a rope or club, and strangled or felled him. The Ethiopian kings of Meroe were worshipped as gods ; but when the priests thought fit, they sent a messsenger to the king, ordering him to die, and alleging an oracle of the gods (or earlier kings) as the reason of their command. This command the kings always obeyed down to the reign of Ergamenes, a contemporary of Ptolemy II. of Egypt. So, when the king of Unyoro in Central Africa falls ill, or begins to show signs of approaching age, one of his own wives is compelled by custom to kill him. The kings of Sofala were regarded by their people as gods who could give rain or sunshine; but the slightest bodily blemish, such as the loss of a tooth, was considered a sufficient reason for putting one of these powerful man-gods to death; he must be whole and sound, lest all nature pay for it. Many kings, human gods, divine priests, or sultans are enumerated by Mr. Frazer, each of whom must be similarly perfect in every limb and member. The same perfect manhood is still exacted of the Christian Pope, who, however, is not put to death in case of extreme age or feebleness. But there is reason to believe that the Grand Lama, the divine Pope of the Tibetan Buddhists, is killed from time to time, so as to keep him " ever fresh and ever young," and to allow the inherent deity within him to escape full-blooded into another embodiment.

In all these cases the divine king or priest is suffered by his people to retain office, or rather to house the godhead, till by some outward defect, or some visible warning of age or illness, he shows them that he is no longer equal to the proper performance of his divine functions. Until such symptoms appear, he is not put to death. Some peoples, however, as Mr. Frazer shows, have not thought it safe to wait for even the slightest symptom of decay before killing the human god or king; they have destroyed him in the plenitude of his life and vigour. In such cases, the people fix a term beyond which the king may not reign, and at the close of which he must die, the term being short enough to prevent the probability of degeneration meanwhile. In some parts of Southern India, for example, the term was fixed at twelve years; at the expiration of that time, the king had to cut himself to pieces visibly, before the great local idol, of which he was in all probability the human equivalent. "Whoever desires to reign other twelve years," says an early observer, " and to undertake this martyrdom for the sake of the idol, has to be present looking on at this; and from that place they raise him up as king."

The king of Calicut, on the Malabar coast, had also to cut his throat in public after a twelve years' reign. But towards the end of the seventeenth century, the rule was so far relaxed that the king was allowed to retain the throne, and probably the godship, if he could protect himself against all comers. As long as he was strong enough to guard his position, it was held that he was strong enough to retain the divine power unharmed. The King of the Wood at Aricia held his priesthood and ghostly kingship on the same condition; as long as he could hold his own against all comers, he might continue to be priest; but any runaway slave had the right of attacking the king; and if he could kill him, he became the King of the Wood till some other in turn slew him. This curious instance has been amply and learnedly discussed by Mr. Frazer, and forms the central subject of his admirable treatise.

More often still, however, the divine priesthood, kingship, or godhead was held for one year alone, for a reason which we shall more fully comprehend after we have considered the annual gods of cultivation. The most interesting example, and the most cognate to our present enquiry, is that of the Babylonian custom cited by Berosus. During the five days of the festival called the Sacæa, a prisoner condemned to death was dressed in the king's robes, seated on the king's throne, allowed to eat, drink, and order whatever he chose, and even permitted to sleep with the king's concubines. But at the end of five days, he was stripped of his royal insignia, scourged, and crucified. I need hardly point out the crucial importance of this singular instance, occurring in a country within the Semitic circle. Mr. Frazer rightly concludes that the condemned man was meant to die in the king's stead; was himself, in point of fact, a king substitute; and was therefore invested for the time being with the fullest prerogatives of royalty. Doubtless we have here to deal with a modification of an older and sterner rule, which compelled the king himself to be slain annually. "When the time drew near for the king to be put to death," says Mr. Frazer, "he abdicated for a few days, during which a temporary king reigned and suffered in his stead. At first the temporary king may have been an innocent person, possibly a member of the king's own family ; but with the growth of civilisation, the sacrifice of an innocent person would be revolting to the public sentiment, and accordingly a condemned criminal would be invested with the brief and fatal sovereignty. . . . We shall find other examples of a criminal representing a dying god. For we must not forget that the king is slain in his character of a god, his death and resurrection, as the only means of perpetuating the divine life unimpaired, being deemed necessary for the salvation of his people and the world." I need not point out the importance of such ideas as assisting in the formation of a groundwork for the doctrines of Christianity

Other evidence on this point, of a more indirect nature, has been collected by Mr. Frazer ; and still more will come out in subsequent chapters. For the present I will only add that the annual character of some such sacrifices seems to be derived from the analogy of the annually-slain gods of cultivation, whose origin and meaning we have yet to examine. These gods, being intimately connected with each year's crop, especially with crops of cereals, pulses, and other annual grains, were naturally put to death at the beginning of each agricultural year, and as a rule about the period of the spring equinox,—say, at Easter. Starting from that analogy, as I believe, many races thought it fit that the other divine person, the man-god king, should also be put to death annually, often about the same period. And I will even venture to suggest the possibility that the institution of annual consuls, archons, etc., may have something to do with such annual sacrifices. Certainly the legend of Codrus at Athens and of the Regifugium at Rome seem to point to an ancient king-slaying custom.

At any rate, it is now certain that the putting to death of a public man-god was a common incident of many religions. And it is also clear that in many cases travellers and other observers have made serious mistakes by not understanding the inner nature of such god-slaying practices. For instance it is now pretty certain that Captain Cook was killed by the people of Tahiti just *because* he was a god, perhaps in order to keep his spirit among them. It is likewise clear that many rites, commonly interpreted as human sacrifices to a god, are really god-slayings; often the god in one of his human avatars seems to be offered to himself, in his more permanent embodiment as an idol or stone image. This idea of sacrificing a god, himself to himself, is one which will frequently meet us hereafter; and I need hardly point out that, as "the sacrifice of the mass," it has even enshrined itself in the central sanctuary of the Christian religion.

Christianity apparently took its rise among a group of irregular northern Israelites, the Galilæans, separated from the mass of their coreligionists, the Jews, by the intervention of a heretical and doubtfully Israelitish wedge, the Samaritans. The earliest believers in Jesus were thus intermediate between Jews and Syrians. According to their own tradition, they were first described by the name of Christians at Antioch; and they appear on many grounds to have attracted attention first in Syria in general, and particularly at Damascus. We may be sure, therefore, that their tenets from the first would contain many elements more or less distinctly Syrian, and especially such elements as formed ideas held in common by almost all the surrounding peoples. As a matter of fact, Christianity, as we shall see hereafter, may be regarded historically as a magma of the most fundamental religious ideas of the Mediterranean basin, and especially of the

THE BLOOD OF THE GOD. 245

eastern Mediterranean, grafted on to the Jewish cult and
the Jewish scriptures, and clustering round the personality
of the man-god, Jesus. It is interesting therefore to note
that in Syria and the north Semitic area the principal cult
was the cult of just such a slain man-god, Adonis,—originally, as Mr. Frazer shows, an anually slain man-god,
afterwards put to death and bewailed in effigy, after a
fashion of which we shall see not a few examples in the
sequel, and of which the Mass itself is but an etherealised
survival. Similarly in Phrygia, where Christianity early
made a considerable impression, the most devoutly worshipped among the gods was Attis, who, as Professor
Ramsay suggests, was almost certainly embodied in early
times as an annually slain man-god, and whose cult was
always carried on by means of a divine king-priest, bearing
himself the name of Attis. Though in later days the
priest did not actually immolate himself every year, yet
on the yearly feast of the god, at the spring equinox (corresponding to the Christian Easter) he drew blood from
his own arms, as a substitute no doubt for the earlier
practice of self-slaughter. And I may add in this connexion (to anticipate once more) that in all such god-
slaughtering rites, immense importance was always attached to the blood of the man-god ; just as in Christianity "the blood of Christ" remains to the end of most
saving efficacy. Both Adonis and Attis were conceived
as young men in the prime of life, like the victims chosen
for other god-slaying rites.

I have dealt in this chapter only in very brief summary
with this vast and interesting question of human deities.
Mr. Frazer has devoted to it two large and fascinating
volumes. His work is filled with endless facts as to such
man-gods themselves, the mode of their vicarious or expiatory slaughter on behalf of the community, the gentler
substitution of condemned criminals for the divine kings
in more civilised countries, the occasional mitigation
whereby the divine king merely draws his own blood in-

stead of killing himself, or where an effigy is made to take the place of the actual victim, and so forth *ad infinitum*. All these valuable suggestions and ideas I could not reproduce here without transcribing in full many pages of *The Golden Bough*, where Mr. Frazer has marshalled the entire evidence on the point with surprising effectiveness. I will content myself therefore by merely referring readers to that most learned yet interesting and amusing book. I will only say in conclusion that what most concerns us here is Mr. Frazer's ample and convincing proof of the large part played by such slain (and risen) man-gods in the religion of those self-same east-Mediterranean countries where Christianity was first evolved as a natural product of the popular imagination. The death and resurrection of the humanly-embodied god form indeed the keynote of the greatest and most sacred religions of western Asia and northeastern Africa.

CHAPTER XII.

THE MANUFACTURE OF GODS.

NORMALLY and originally, I believe, all gods grow spontaneously. They evolve by degrees out of dead and deified ancestors or chieftains. The household gods are the dead of the family; the greater gods are the dead chiefs of the state or town or village. But upon this earlier and spontaneous crop of gods there supervenes later an artificial crop, deliberately manufactured. The importance of this later artificial class is so great, especially in connexion with the gods of agriculture, and with the habit of eating the god's body as corn and drinking his blood as wine, that it becomes necessary for us here to examine their nature in due order. We shall find that some knowledge of them is needed preliminary to the comprehension of the Christian system.

We saw that in West Africa the belief in another world is so matter-of-fact and material that a chief who wishes to communicate with his dead father kills a slave as a messenger, after first impressing upon him the nature of the message he will have to deliver. If he forgets anything, says Mr. Duff Macdonald, he kills a second and sends him after "as a postscript." A Khond desired to be avenged upon an enemy; so he cut off the head of his mother, who cheerfully suggested this domestic arrangement, in order that her ghost might haunt and terrify the offender. Similar plenitude of belief in the actuality and nearness of the Other World makes attendants, wives, and even friends of a dead man, in many countries, volunteer to kill themselves at his funeral, in order that they may accompany their lord and master to the nether realms. All these examples combine to show us two things : first, that the other life is very real and close to the people who behave so ; and second, that no great unwillingness habitually exists to migration from this life to the next, if occasion demands it.

Starting with such ideas, it is not surprising that many races should have deliberately made for themselves gods by killing a man, and especially a man of divine or kingly blood, the embodiment of a god, in order that his spirit might perform some specific divine function. Nor is it even remarkable that the victim selected for such a purpose should voluntarily submit to death, often preceded by violent torture, so as to attain in the end to a position of trust and importance as a tutelary deity. We have only to remember the ease with which Mahommedan fanatics will face death, expecting to enjoy the pleasures of Paradise, or the fervour with which Christian believers used to embrace the crown of martyrdom, in order to convince ourselves of the reality and profundity of such a sentiment. The further back we go in time or culture, the stronger does the sentiment in question become ; it is only the civilised and sceptical thinker who hesitates to exchange the solid comforts of this world for the shadowy and uncertain delights of the next.

The existence of such artificially-manufactured gods has been more or less recognised for some time past, and attention has been called to one or other class of them by Mr. Baring Gould and Mr. J. G. Frazer ; but I believe the present work will be the first in which their profound importance and their place in the genesis of the higher religions has been fully pointed out in systematic detail.

The best known instances of such deliberate godmaking are those which refer to the foundation of cities, city walls, and houses. In such cases, a human victim is often sacrificed in order that his blood may be used as cement, and his soul be built in to the very stones of the fabric. Thereafter he becomes the tutelary deity or "fortune" of the house or city. In many cases, the victim offers himself voluntarily for the purpose; frequently he is of kingly or divine ancestry. As a sheep before her shearers is dumb, so he opens not his mouth. In Polynesia, where we usually stand nearest to the very core of religion, Ellis heard that the central pillar of the temple at Mæva was planted upon the body of a human victim. Among the Dyaks of Borneo, a slave girl was crushed to death under the first post of a house. In October 1881, the king of Ashanti put fifty girls to death that their blood might be mixed with the "swish" or mud used in the repair of the royal buildings. Even in Japan, a couple of centuries since, when a great wall was to be built, "some wretched slave would offer himself as a foundation." Observe in this instance the important fact that the immolation was purely voluntary. Mr. Tylor, it is true, treats most of these cases as though the victim were intended to appease the earth-demons, which is the natural interpretation for the elder school of thinkers to put upon such ceremonies; but those who have read Mr. Frazer and Mr. Baring Gould will know that the offering is really a piece of deliberate god-making. Many of the original witnesses, indeed, correctly report this intention on the part of the perpetrators; thus Mason was told by an eye-witness that at the building of the new city of Tavoy in Tennasserim "a criminal was put in each post-hole to become a protecting demon" or rather deity. So in Siam, when a new city gate was being erected, says Mr. Speth, officers seized the first four or eight people who passed, and buried them under it "as guardian angels." And in Roumania a *stahic* is defined as "the ghost of a person who has been immured in the walls of a building in order to make it more solid." The Irish Banshee is doubtless of similar origin.

Other curious examples are reported from Africa. In

Galam, a boy and girl used to be buried alive before the great gate of a city, to make it impregnable ; and I gather here that the sacrifice was periodically renewed, as we shall see it to have been in many other cases. In Great Bassam and Yarriba, similar sacrifices were usual at the foundation of a house or village. Clearly the idea in these cases was to supply the site with a tutelary deity, a god whose existence was bound up with the place thus consecrated to him. He and the town henceforth were one ; he was its soul, and it was his body. Human victims are said to have been buried "for spirit-watchers" under the gates of Mandelay. So too, according to legend, here a tolerably safe guide, a queen was drowned in a Burmese reservoir, to make the dyke safe; while the choice for such a purpose of a royal victim shows clearly the desirability of divine blood being present in the body of the future deity. When Rajah Sala Byne was building the fort of Sialkot in the Punjaub, the foundation gave way so often that he consulted a soothsayer. The soothsayer advised that the blood of an only son should be shed on the spot ; and the only son of a widow was accordingly killed there. I may add that the blood of "an only-begotten son" has always been held to possess peculiar efficacy.

In Europe itself, not a few traces survive of such foundation-gods, or spirits of towns, town-walls, and houses. The Picts are said to have bathed their foundation-stones in human blood, especially in building their forts and castles. St. Columba himself, though nominally a Christian, did not scruple thus to secure the safety of his monastery. "Columbkille said to his people, 'It would be well for us that our roots should pass into the earth here.' And he said to them, 'It is permitted to you that some one of you go under the earth to consecrate it.'" St. Oran volunteered to accept the task, and was ever after honoured as the patron saint of the monastery. Here again it may be noted that the offering was voluntary. As late as 1463, when the broken dam of the Nogat had to be repaired, the peasants, being advised to throw in a living man, are said to have made a beggar drunk (in which state he would of course be "full of the god") and utilised him for the purpose. In 1885, on the restoration of Holsworthy church in Devon, a skeleton with a mass of mortar plastered over the mouth was found embedded in an angle of the building. To make the castle of Liebenstein fast and impregnable, a child was bought for hard money of its mother, and walled into the building. Again, when the church at Blex in Oldenburg was being built, the authorities of the village crossed the Weser, "bought a child from a poor mother at Bremerleke, and built it alive into the foundations." We shall see hereafter that "to be brought with a price" is a variant, as it were, on the voluntary offering; great stress is often laid when a victim is offered on this particular fact, which is held to absolve the perpetrators from the crime of god-murder. So, we shall see in the sequel, the divine animal-victim, which is the god offered to himself, his animal embodiment to his image or altar, must always consent to its own sacrifice; if it refuse or show the slightest disinclination, it is no good victim. Legend says that the child in the case of the Liebenstein offering was beguiled with a cake, probably so as to make it a consenting party, and was slowly walled up before the eyes of the mother. All these details are full of incidental instructiveness and importance. As late as 1865, according to Mr. Speth, some Christian labourers, working at a block-house at Duga, near Scutari, found two young Christian children in the hands of Mahommedan Arnauts, who were trying to bury them alive under the block-house.

It is about city walls, however, that we oftenest read such legendary stories. Thus the wall of Copenhagen sank as fast as it was built; so they took an innocent little girl, and set her at a table with toys and eatables. Then, while she played and eat, twelve master masons closed a vault over her. With clanging music, to drown the child's cries, the wall was raised, and stood fast ever after. In Italy, once more, the bridge of Arta fell in, time after time, till they walled in the master builder's wife; the last point being a significant detail, whose meaning will come out still more clearly in the sequel. At Scutari in Servia, once more, the fortress could only be satisfactorily built after a human victim was walled into it; so the three brothers who wrought at it decided to offer up the first of their wives who came to the place to bring them food. (Compare the case of Jephtha's daughter, where the first living thing met by chance is to be sacrificed to Jahweh.) So, too, in Welsh legend, Vortigern could not finish his tower till the foundation-stone was wetted with "the blood of a child born of a mother without a father"—this episode of the virgin-born infant being a common element in the generation of man-gods, as Mr. Sidney Hartland has abundantly proved for us.

In one case cited above, we saw a mitigation of the primitive custom, in that a criminal was substituted for a person of royal blood or divine origin—a form of substitution of which Mr. Frazer has supplied abundant examples in other connexions. Still further mitigations are those of building-in a person who has committed sacrilege or broken some religious vow of chastity. In the museum at Algiers is a plaster cast of the mould left by the body of one Geronimo, a Moorish Christian (and therefore a recusant of Islam), who was built into a block of concrete in the angle of the fort in the sixteenth century. Faithless nuns were so immured in Europe during the middle ages; and Mr. Rider Haggard's statement that he saw in the museum at Mexico bodies similarly immured by the Inquisition has roused so much Catholic wrath and denial that one can hardly have any hesitation in accepting its substantial accuracy. But in other cases, the substitution has gone further still; instead of criminals, recusants, or heretics, we get an animal victim in place of the human one. Mr. St. John saw a chicken sacrificed for a slave girl at a building among the Dyaks of Borneo. A lamb was walled-in under the altar of a church in Denmark, to make it stand fast; or the churchyard was hanselled by burying first a live horse, an obvious parallel to the case of St Oran. When the parish church of Chumleigh in Devonshire was taken down a few years ago, in a wall of the fifteenth century was found a carved figure of Christ, crucified to a vine—a form of substitution to which we shall find several equivalents later. In modern Greece, says Dr. Tylor, to whom I owe many of these instances, a relic of the idea survives in the belief that the first passer-by after a foundation-stone is laid will die within the year; so the masons compromise the matter by killing a cock or a black lamb on the foundation-stone. This animal then becomes the spirit of the building.

We shall see reason to suspect, as we proceed, that every slaughtered victim in every rite was at first a divine-human being; and that animal victims are always substitutes, though supposed to be equally divine with the man-god they personate. I will ask the reader to look out for such cases as we proceed, and also to notice, even when I do not call attention to them, the destination of the oracular head, and the frequent accompaniment of "clanging music."

Elsewhere we find other customs which help to explain these curious survivals. The shadow is often identified with the soul; and in Roumania, when a new building is to be erected, the masons endeavour to catch the shadow of a passing stranger, and then lay the foundation-stone upon it. Or the stranger is enticed by stealth to the stone, when the mason secretly measures his body or his shadow, and buries the measure thus taken under the foundation. Here we have a survival of the idea that the victim must at least be not unwilling. It is believed that the person thus measured will languish and die within forty days; and we may be sure that originally the belief ran that his soul became the god or guardian spirit of the edifice. If the Bulgarians cannot get a human shadow to wall in, they content themselves with the shadow of the first animal that passes by. Here again we get that form of divine chance in the pointing out of a victim which is seen in the case of Jephtha's daughter. Still milder substitutions occur in the empty coffin walled into a church in Germany, or the rude images of babies in swaddling-clothes similarly immured in Holland. The last trace of the custom is found in England in the modern practice of putting coins and newspapers under the foundation-stone. Here it would seem as if the victim were regarded as a sacrifice to the Earth (a late and derivative idea), and the coins were a money payment in lieu of the human or animal offering. I owe many of the cases here instanced to the careful research of my friend Mr. Clodd. But since this chapter was written, all other treatises on the subject have been superseded by Mr. Speth's exhaustive and scholarly pamphlet on "Builder's Rites and Ceremonies," a few examples from which I have intercalated in my argument.

Other implications must be briefly treated. The best ghost or god for this purpose seems to be a divine or kingly person; and in stages when the meaning of the practice is still quite clear to the builders, the dearly-beloved son or wife of the king is often selected for the honour of tutelary godship. Later this notion passes into the sacrifice of the child or wife of the master mason; many legends or traditions contain this more recent element. In Vortigern's case, however, the child is clearly a divine being, as we shall see to be true a little later on in certain Semitic instances. To the last, the connexion of children with such sacrifices is most marked; thus when in 1813 the ice on the Elbe broke down one of the dams, an old peasant sneered at the efforts of the Government engineer, saying to him, "You will never get the dyke to hold unless you first sink an innocent child under the foundations." Here the very epithet "innocent" in itself reveals some last echo of godship. So too, in 1843, when a new bridge was to be built at Halle in Germany, the people told the architects that the pier would not stand unless a living child was immured under the foundations. Schrader says that when the great railway bridge over the Ganges was begun, every mother in Bengal trembled for her infant. The Slavonic chiefs who founded Detinez " sent out men to catch the first boy they met and bury him in the foundation." Here once more we have the sacred-chance victim. Briefly I would say there seems to be a preference in all such cases for children, and especially for girls ; of kingly stock, if possible, but at least a near relation of the master builder.

Mr. Speth points out that horses' heads were frequently fastened on churches or other buildings, and suggests that they belong to animal foundation-victims. This use of the skull is in strict accordance with its usual oracular destination.

Some notable historical or mythical tales of town and village gods, deliberately manufactured, may now be considered. We read in First Kings that when Hiel the Bethelite built Jericho, " he laid the foundation thereof in Abiram his first-born, and set up the gates thereof in his youngest Segub." Here we see evidently a princely master builder, sacrificing his own two sons as guardian gods of his new city. Abundant traces exist of such deliberate production of a Fortune for a town. And it is also probable that the original sacrifice was repeated annually, as if to keep up the constant stream of divine life, somewhat after the fashion of the human gods we had to consider in the last chapter. Dido appears to have been the Fortune or foundation-goddess of Carthage; she is represented in the legend as the foundress-queen, and is said to have lept into her divine pyre from the walls of her palace. But the annual human sacrifice appears to have been performed at the same place ; for " It can hardly be doubted," says Professor Robertson Smith, "that the spot at which legend placed the self-sacrifice of Dido to her husband Sicharbas was that at which the later Carthaginian human sacrifices were performed." At Laodicea, again, an annual sacrifice took place of a deer, in lieu of a maiden; and this sacrifice, we are expressly told, was offered to the goddess of the city. Legend said that the goddess was a maiden, who had been similarly sacrificed to consecrate the foundation of the town, and was thenceforth worshipped as its Fortune, like Dido at Carthage; "it was therefore the death of the goddess herself," says Professor Robertson Smith, "that was annually renewed in the piacular rite." (I do not admit the justice of the epithet "piacular.") Again, Malalas tells us that the 22d of May was kept at Antioch as the anniversary of a maiden sacrificed at the foundation of the city, and worshipped thereafter as the Tyche, or luck, of the town. At Durna in Arabia an annual victim was similarly buried under the stone which formed the altar.

In most of the legends, as they come down to us from civilised and lettered antiquity, the true nature of this sanguinary foundation-rite is overlaid and disguised by later rationalising guesses; and I may mention that Dr. Robertson Smith in particular habitually treats the rationalising guesses as primitive, and the real old tradition of the slaughtered virgin as a myth of explanation of "the later Euhemeristic Syrians." But after the examples we have already seen of foundation-gods, I think I can hardly be doubted that this is to reverse the true order; that a girl was really sacrificed for a tutelary deity when a town was founded, and that the substitution of an animal victim at the annual renewal was a later refinement. Mr. Speth quotes a case in point of a popular tradition that a young girl had been built into the castle of Nieder-Manderschied; and when the wall was opened in 1844, the Euhemeristic workmen found a cavity enclosing a human skeleton. I would suggest, again, that in the original legend of the foundation of Rome, Romulus was represented as having built-in his brother Remus as a Fortune, or god, of the city, and that to this identification of Remus with the city we ought to trace such phrases as *turba Remi* for the Roman people. The word *forum* in its primitive signification means the empty space left before a tomb—the *llan* or *temenos*. Hence I would suggest that the Roman Forum and other Latin *fora* were really the tomb-enclosures of the original foundation-victims.* So, too, the English village green and "play-field" are probably the space dedicated to the tribal or village god—a slain man-god; and they are usually connected with the sacred stone and sacred tree. I trust this point will become clearer as we proceed, and develop the whole theory of the foundation god or goddess, the allied sacred stone and the tree or trunk memorial.

For, if I am right, the entire primitive ritual of the foundation of a village consisted in killing or burying alive or building into the wall a human victim, as town or village god, and raising a stone and planting a tree close by to commemorate him. At these two monuments the village rites were thereafter performed. The stone and tree are thus found in their usual conjunction; both coexist in the Indian village to the present day, as in the Siberian woodland or the Slavonic forest. Thus, at Rome, we have not only the legend of the death of Remus, a prince of the blood-royal of Alba Longa, intimately connected with the building of the wall of Roma Quadrata, but we have also the sacred fig-tree of Romulus in the Forum, which was regarded as the embodiment of the city life of the combined Rome, so that when it showed signs of withering, consternation spread through the city; and hard by we have the sacred stone or Palladium, guarded by the sacred Vestal Virgins who kept the city hearth-fire, and still more closely bound up with the fortune of that secondary Rome which had its home in the Forum. Are not these three

* In the case of Rome, the Forum would represent the grave of the later foundation-god of the compound Latin and Sabine city.

the triple form of the foundation-god of that united Capitoline and Palatine Rome? And may not the sacred cornel on the Palatine, again, have been similarly the holy foundation-tree of that older Roma Quadrata which is more particularly associated with the name of Romulus? Of this tree Plutarch tells us that when it appeared to a passer-by to be drooping, he set up a hue and cry, which was soon responded to by people on all sides rushing up with buckets of water to pour upon it, as if they were hastening to put out a fire. Clearly, here again we have to deal with an embodied Fortune.

We do not often get all three of these Fortunes combined—the human victim, the stone, and the tree, with the annual offering which renews its sanctity. But we find traces so often of one or other of the trio that we are justified, I think, in connecting them together as parts of a whole, whereof here one element survives, and there another. "Among all primitive communities," says Mr. Gomme, "when a village was first established, a stone was set up. To this stone, the headman of the village made an offering once a year." To the present day, London preserves her foundation-god in the shape of London Stone, now enclosed in a railing or iron grill just opposite Cannon Street Station. Now, London Stone was for ages considered as the representative and embodiment of the entire community. Proclamations and other important state businesses were announced from its top; and the defendant in trials in the Lord Mayor's court was summoned to attend from London Stone, as though the stone itself spoke to the wrong-doer with the united voice of the assembled citizens. The first Lord Mayor, indeed, was Henry de Lundonstone, no doubt, as Mr. Loftie suggests, the hereditary keeper of this urban fetish,—in short, the representative of the village headman. I have written at greater length on the implications of this interesting relic in an article on London Stone in *Longman's Magazine*, to which I would refer the reader for further information. I will only add here the curious episode of Jack Cade, who, when he forced his way, under his assumed name of Mortimer, into the city in 1450, first of all proceeded to this sacred relic, the embodiment of palladium of ancient London, and having struck it with his sword exclaimed, " Now is Mortimer lord of this city."

A similar sacred stone exists to this day at Bovey Tracey in Devon, of which Ormerod tells us that the mayor of Bovey used to ride round it on the first day of his tenure of office, and strike it with a stick,—which further explains Jack Cade's proceeding. According to the *Totnes Times* of May 13, 1882, the young men of the town were compelled on the same day to kiss the magic stone and pledge allegiance in upholding the ancient rights and privileges of Bovey. (I owe these details to Mr. Lawrence Gomme's *Village Community*.) I do not think we can dissociate from these two cases the other sacred stones of Britain, such as the King's Stone at Kingston in Surrey, where several of the West Saxon kings were crowned ; nor the Scone Stone in the coronation-chair at Westminster Abbey ; nor the Stone of Clackmannan, and the sacred stones already mentioned in a previous chapter on which the heads of clans or of Irish septs succeeded to the chieftainship of their respective families. These may in part have been ancestral and sepulchral monuments : but it is probable that they also partook in part of this artificial and factitious sanctity. Certainly in some cases that sanctity was renewed by an animal sacrifice.

With these fairly obvious instances I would also connect certain other statements which seem to me to have been hitherto misinterpreted. Thus Mesha, king of Moab, when he is close beleaguered, burns his son as a holocaust on the wall of the city. Is not this an offering to protect the wall by the deliberate manufacture of an additional deity ? For straightway the besiegers seem to feel they are overpowered, and the siege is raised. Observe here once more that it is the king's own dearly-beloved son who is chosen as victim. Again, at Amathus, human sacrifices were offered to Jupiter Hospes "before the gates"; and this Jupiter Hospes, as Ovid calls him, is the Amathusian Herakles or Malika, whose name, preserved for us by Hesychius, identifies him at once as a local deity similar to the Tyrian Melcarth. Was not this again, therefore, the Fortune of the city? At Tyre itself, the sepulchre of Herakles Melcarth was shown, where he was said to have been cremated. For among cremating peoples it was natural to burn, not slaughter, the yearly god-victim. At Tarsus, once more, there was an annual feast, at which a very fair pyre was erected, and the local Herakles or Baal was burned on it in effigy. We cannot doubt, I think, that this was a mitigation of an earlier human holocaust. Indeed, Dr. Robertson Smith says of this instance: "This annual commemoration of the death of the god in fire must have its origin in an older rite, in which the victim was not a mere effigy, but a theanthropic sacrifice, i.e., an actual man or sacred animal, whose life, according to the antique conception now familiar to us, was an embodiment of the divine-human life." This is very near my own view on the subject.

From these instances we may proceed, I think, to a more curious set, whose implications seem to me to have been even more grievously mistaken by later interpreters. I mean the case of children of kings or of ruling families, sacrificed in time of war or peril as additional or auxiliary deities. Thus Philo of Byblos says: "It was an ancient custom in a crisis of great danger that the ruler of a city or nation should give his beloved son to die for the whole people, as a ransom offered to the avenging demons; and the children thus offered were slain with mystic rites. So Cronus, whom the Phœnicians call Israel, being king of the land, and having an only-begotten son called Jeoud (for in the Phœnicians tongue Jeoud signifies only-begotten), dressed him in royal robes and sacrificed him upon an altar in a time of war, when the country was in great danger from the enemy." I do not think Philo is right in his gloss or guess about "the avenging demons"; but otherwise his story is interesting evidence. It helps us more or less directly to connect the common Phœnician and Hebrew child-sacrifices with this deliberate manufacture of artificial gods. I do not doubt, indeed, that the children were partly sacrificed to pre-existent and well-defined great gods; but I believe also that the practice first arose as one of deliberate manufacture of gods, and retained to the end many traces of its origin.

We know that in times of national calamity the Phœnicians used thus to sacrifice their dearest to Baal. Phœnician history, we know from Porphyry, is full of such sacrifices. When the Carthaginians were defeated and besieged by Agathocles, they ascribed their disasters to the anger of the god; for whereas in former times they used to sacrifice to him their own children, they had latterly fallen (as we shall see hereafter the Khonds did) into the habit of buying children and rearing them as victims. So two hundred young people of the noblest families were picked out for sacrifice; and these were accompanied by no less than three hundred more, who volunteered to die for the fatherland. They were sacrificed by being placed, one by one, on the sloping hands of the brazen image, from which they rolled into a pit of fire. So too at Jerusalem, in moments of great danger, children were sacrificed to some Molech, whether Jahweh or another, by being placed in the fiery arms of the image at the Tophet. I will admit that in these last cases we approach very near to the mere piacular human sacrifice; but we shall see, when we come to deal with gods of cultivation, and the doctrine of the atonement, that it is difficult to draw a line between the two; while the fact that a dearly-beloved or only-begotten son is the victim—especially the son of a king of divine blood—links such cases on directly to the more obvious instances of deliberate god-making. Some such voluntary sacrifice seems to me to be commemorated in the beautiful imagery of the 53d of Isaiah. But there the language is distinctly piacular.

That annual human sacrifices originated in deliberate god-making of this sort is an inference which has already been almost arrived at by more orthodox thinkers. "Among the Semites," says Dr. Robertson Smith, "the most current view of annual piacula seems to have been that they commemorate a divine tragedy—the death of some god or goddess. The origin of such myths is easily explained from the nature of the ritual. Originally, the death of the god was nothing else than the death of the theanthropic victim; but when this ceased to be understood, it was thought that the piacular sacrifice represented an historical tragedy in which the god was killed." But we shall see hereafter that the idea of expiation in sacrifice is quite a late and derivative one; it seems more probable that the victim was at first a human god, for whom later an animal victim was substituted. In the Athenian Thargelia, the victims were human to the very end, though undoubtedly they were thought of as bearing vicariously the sins of the people. We shall come across similar intrusions of the idea of expiation in later chapters; that idea belongs to a stage of thought when men considered it necessary to explain away by some ethical reference the sanguinary element of primitive ritual. Thus in two Greek towns, as we learn from Pausanias—at Potniæ and Patræ,—an annual sacrifice existed which had once been the sacrifice of a human victim; but this was later explained as an expiation of an ancient crime for which satisfaction had to be made from generation to generation. Indeed, as a rule, later ages looked upon the murder of a god as obviously criminal, and therefore regarded the slaughter of the victim, who replaced the god, as being an atonement for his death, instead of regarding it as a deliberate release of his divine spirit.

I have dwelt here mainly on that particular form of

artificial god-making which is concerned with the foundation of houses, villages, cities, walls, and fortresses, because this is the commonest and most striking case, outside agriculture, and because it is specially connected with the world-wide institution of the village or city god. But other types occur in abundance; and to them a few lines must now be devoted.

When a ship was launched, it was a common practice to provide her with a guardian spirit or god by making her roll over the body of a human victim. The Norwegian vikings used to "redden their rollers" with human blood. That is to say, when a warship was launched, human victims were lashed to the round logs over which the galley was run down to the sea, so that the stem was sprinkled with their spurting blood. Thus the victim was incorporated, as it were, in the very planks of the vessel. Captain Cook found the South Sea Islanders similarly christening their war-canoes with blood. In 1784, says Mr. William Simpson, at the launching of one of the Bey of Tripoli's cruisers, "a black slave was led forward and fastened at the prow of the vessel to influence a happy reception in the ocean." And Mr. Speth quotes a newspaper account of the sacrifice of a sheep when the first caique for "Constantinople at Olympia" was launched in the Bosphorus. In many other cases, it is noted that a victim, human or animal, is slaughtered at the launching of a ship. Our own ceremony of breaking a bottle of wine over the bows is the last relic of this barbarous practice. Here as elsewhere red wine does duty for blood, in virtue of its colour. I do not doubt that the images of gods in the bow of a ship were originally idols in which the spirits thus liberated might dwell, and that it was to them the sailors prayed for assistance in storm or peril. The god was bound up in the very fabric of the vessel. The modern figure-head still represents these gods; figure-heads essentially similar to the domestic idols occur on New Zealand and Polynesian war-canoes.

The canoes of the Solomon Islanders, for example, "often have as figure-head a carved representation of the upper half of a man, who holds in his hands a human head." This head, known as the "canoe-god" or "charm," "represents the life taken when the canoe was first used." A canoe of importance "required a life for its inauguration," says Dr. Codrington.

Another curious instance is to be found in the customs and beliefs regarding river gods. Rivers, I have suggested, are often divine because they spring near or are connected with the grave of a hero. But often their divinity has been deliberately given them, and is annually renewed by a god-making sacrifice: just as at the Jewish Passover an annual animal-victim was slain, and his blood smeared on the lintels, as a renewal of the foundation sacrifice. The best instance I have found of this curious custom is one cited by Mr. Gomme from Major Ellis. Along the banks of the Prah in West Africa there are many deities, all bearing the common name of Prah, and all regarded as spirits of the river. At each town or considerable village along the stream, a sacrifice is held on a day about the middle of October. The usual sacrifice was two human adults, one male and one female. The inhabitants of each village believe in a separate spirit of the Prah, who resides in some part of the river close to their own hamlet. Everywhere along the river the priests of these gods officiate in groups of three, two male and one female, an arrangement which is peculiar to the river gods. Here, unless I mistake, we have an obvious case of deliberate god-making.

This savage instance, and others like it, which space precludes me from detailing, suggest the conclusion that many river gods are of artificial origin. The Wohhanda in Esthonia received offerings of little children, whom we may fairly compare with the children immured in buildings or offered to the Molech. Many other rivers spontancously take their victim annually ; thus the Devonshire rhyme goes —

> River of Dart, river of Dart,
> Every year thou claimest a heart.

The Spey also takes one life each year, and so do several British rivers elsewhere. Originally, no doubt, the victim was deliberately chosen and slain annually ; but later on, as a mitigation of the custom, the river itself seems to have selected its own spirit by divine chance, such as we have already seen in action more than once in the earlier cases. In other words, if a passer-by happened to be accidentally drowned, he was accepted in place of a deliberate victim.* Hence the danger of rescuing a man from drowning ; you interfere with the course of divine selection, and you will pay for it yourself by being the next victim. "When, in the Solomon Islands, a man accidentally falls into a river, and a shark attacks him, he is not allowed to escape. If he succeeds in eluding the shark, his fellow-tribesmen throw him back to his doom, believing him to be marked out for sacrifice to the god of the river." Similarly, in Britain itself, the Lancashire Ribble has a water-spirit called Peg o' Nell, represented by a stone image, now headless, which stands at the spring where the river rises in the grounds of Waddon. (Compare the Adonis tomb and grove by the spring at Aphaca.) This Peg o' Nell was originally, according to tradition, a girl of the neighbourhood ; but she was done to death by incantations, and now demands every seven years that a life should be quenched in the waters of the Ribble. When "Peg's night" came round at the close of the septennate, unless a bird, a cat, or a dog was drowned in the river, it was sure to claim its human victim. This name of Peg is evidently a corruption of some old local Celtic or pre-Celtic

---

* Here is an analogue in foundation sacrifices. A house was being built at Hind Head while this book was in progress. A workman fell from a beam and was killed. The other workmen declared this was *luck* for the house and would ensure its stability.

word for a nymph or water-spirit; for there is another Peg in the Tees, known as Peg Powler; and children used there to be warned against playing on the banks of the stream, for fear Peg should drag them into the water. Such traces of a child-sacrifice are extremely significant.

I cannot do more than suggest here in passing that we have in these stories and practices the most probable origin of the common myth which accounts for the existence of river gods or river nymphs by some episode of a youth or maiden drowned there. Arethusa is the example that occurs to everyone. Grossly Euhemeristic as it may sound to say so, I yet believe that such myths of metamorphosis have their origin in the deliberate manufacture of a water-deity by immolation in the stream; and that the annual renewal of such a sacrifice was due in part to the desire to keep alive the memory of the gods—to be sure they were there, to make them "fresh and fresh," if one may venture to say so—and in part to the analogy of those very important artificial gods of agriculture whose origin and meaning we have still to consider. I would add that the commonness of sea-horses and river-horses in the mythology of the world doubtless owes its origin partly to the natural idea of "white horses" on the waves, but partly also to the deliberate sacrifice of horses to the sea or rivers, which this notion suggested, and which tended to intensify it. It is as though the worshipper wished to keep up a continuous supply of such divine and ghostly steeds. At Rhodes, for example, four horses were annually cast into the sea; and I need hardly refer to the conventional horses of Poseidon and Neptune. The Ugly Burn in Ross-shire is the abode of a water-horse; in the remains of the Roman temple at Lydney, the god Nodens, who represents the Severn, is shown in the mosaic pavement as drawn in a chariot by four horses; and the Yore, near Middleham, is still infested by a water-horse who annually claims at least one human victim. Elsewhere other animals take the place of the horse. The

Ostyaks sacrifice to the river Ob by casting in a live reindeer when fish are scanty.

I do not deny that in many of these cases two distinct ideas—the earlier idea of the victim as future god, and the later idea of the victim as prey or sacrifice—have got inextricably mixed up; but I do think enough has been said to suggest the probability that many river-gods are artificially produced, and that this is in large part the origin of nymphs and kelpies. Legend, indeed, almost always represents them so; it is only our mythologists, with their blind hatred of Euhemerism, who fail to perceive the obvious implication. And that even the accidental victim was often envisaged as a river-god, after his death, we see clearly from the Bohemian custom of going to pray on the river bank where a man has been drowned, and casting into the river a loaf of new bread and a pair of wax candles, obvious offerings to his spirit.

Many other classes of manufactured gods seem to me to exist, whose existence I must here pass over almost in silence. Such are the gods produced at the beginning of a war, by human or other sacrifice; gods intended to aid the warriors in their coming enterprise by being set free from fleshly bonds for that very purpose. Thus, according to Phylarchus, a human sacrifice was at one time customary in Greece at the beginning of hostilities; and we know that as late as the age of Themistocles three captives were thus offered up before the battle of Salamis. The sacrifice of Iphigenia is a good legendary case in point, because it is one of a virgin, a princess, the daughter of the leader, and therefore a typical release of a divine or royal spirit. Here, as usual, later philosophising represents the act as an expiation for mortal guilt; but we may be sure the original story contained no such ethical or piacular element. Among the early Hebrews, the summons to a war seems similarly to have been made by sending round pieces of the human victim; in later Hebrew usage, this rite declines into the sacrifice of a burnt offering; though we get an intermediate stage when Saul sends round portions of a slaughtered ox, as the Levite in Judges had sent round the severed limbs of his concubine to rouse the Israelites. In Africa, a war is still opened with a solemn sacrifice, human or otherwise; and Mr. H. O. Forbes gives a graphic account of the similar ceremony which precedes an expedition in the island of Timor.

In conclusion, I will only say that a great many other obscure rites or doubtful legends seem to me explicable by similar deliberate exercises of god-making. How common such sacrifice was in agricultural relations we shall see in the sequel; but I believe that even in other fields of life future research will so explain many other customs. The self-immolation of Codrus, of Sardanapalus, of P. Decius Mus, as of so many other kings or heroes or gods or goddesses; the divine beings who fling themselves from cliffs into the sea; M. Curtius devoting himself in the gulf in the Forum; the tombs of the lovers whom Semiramis buried alive; all these, I take it, have more or less similar implications. Even such tales as that of T. Manlius Torquatus and his son must be assimilated, I think, to the story of the king of Moab killing his son on the wall, or to that of the Carthaginians offering up their children to the offended deity; only, in later times, the tale was misinterpreted and used to point the supposed moral of the stern and inflexible old Roman discipline.

Frequent reiteration of sacrifices seems necessary, also, in order to keep up the sanctity of images and sacred rites —to put, as it were, a new soul into them. Thus, rivers needed a fresh river-god every year; and recently in Ashantee it was discovered that a fetish would no longer "work" unless human victims were abundantly immolated for it.

This is also perhaps the proper place to observe that just as the great god Baal has been resolved by modern scholarship into many local Baalim, and just as the great god Adonis has been reduced by recent research in each case to some particular Adon or lord out of many, so each such separate deity, artificially manufactured, though called by the common name of the Prah or the Tiber, yet retains to the last some distinct identity. In fact, the great gods appear to be rather classes than individuals. That there were many Nymphs and many Fauni, many Silvani and many Martes, has long been known; it is beginning to be clear that there were also many Saturns, many Jupiters, many Junones, many Vestæ. Even in Greece it is more than probable that the generalised names of the great gods were given in later ages to various old sacred stones and holy sites of diverse origin: the real object of worship was in each case the spontaneous or artificial god; the name was but a general title applied in common, perhaps adjectivally, to several such separate deities. In the Roman pantheon, this principle is now quite well established; in the Semitic it is probable; in most others, the progress of modern research is gradually leading up to it. Even the elemental gods themselves do not seem in their first origin to be really singular; they grow, apparently, from generalised phrases, like our "Heaven" and "Providence," applied at first to the particular deity of whom at the moment the speaker is thinking. The Zeus or Jupiter varies with the locality. Thus, when the Latin prætor, at the outbreak of the Latin war, defied the Roman Jupiter, we may be sure it was the actual god there visible before him at whom he hurled his sacrilegious challenge, not the ideal deity in the sky above his head. Indeed, we now know that each village and each farm had a Jovis of its own, regarded as essentially a god of wine, and specially worshipped at the wine-feast in April, when the first cask was broached. This individuality of the gods is an important point to bear in mind; for the tendency of language is always to treat many similar deities as practically identical, especially in late and etherealised forms of religion. And mythologists have made the most of this syncretic tendency.

A single concrete instance will help to make this general principle yet clearer. Boundaries, I believe, were originally put under the charge of local and artificial deities, by slaughtering a human victim at each turning-point in the limits, and erecting a sacred stone on the spot where he died to preserve his memory. Often, too, in accordance with the common rule, a sacred tree seems to have been planted beside the sacred stone monument. Each such victim became forthwith a boundary god, a protecting and watching spirit, and was known thenceforth as a Hermes or a Terminus. But there were many Hermæ and many Termini, not in Greece and Italy alone, but throughout the world. Only much later did a generalised god, Hermes or Terminus, arise from the union into a single abstract concept of all these separate and individual deities. Once more, the boundary god was renewed each year by a fresh victim. Our own practice of "beating the bounds" appears to be the last expiring relic of such annual sacrifices. The bounds are beaten, apparently, in order to expel all foreign gods or hostile spirits; the boys who play a large part in the ceremony are the representatives of the human victims. They are whipped at each terminus stone, partly in order to make them shed tears as a rain-charm (after the fashion with which Mr. Frazer has made us familiar), but partly also because all artificially-made gods are scourged or tortured before being put to death, for some reason which I do not think we yet fully understand. The rationalising gloss that the boys are whipped "in order to make them remember the boundaries" is one of the usual shallow explanations so glibly offered by the eighteenth century. The fact that the ceremony takes place at sacred stones or "Gospel oaks" sufficiently proclaims its original meaning.

The idea underlying Christian martyrdom, where the

martyr voluntarily devotes himself or herself to death in order to gain the crown and palm in heaven, is essentially similar to the self-immolation of the artificial gods, and helps to explain the nature of such self-sacrifice. For Christianity is only nominally a monotheistic religion, and the saints and martyrs form in it practically a secondary or minor rank of deities.

On the other hand, the point of view of the god-slayers cannot be more graphically put than in the story which Mr. William Simpson relates of Sir Richard Burton. Burton, it seems, was exploring a remote Mahommedan region on the Indian frontier, and in order to do so with greater freedom and ease had disguised himself as a fakir of Islam. So great was his knowledge of Muslim devotions that the people soon began to entertain a great respect for him as a most holy person. He was congratulating himself upon the success of his disguise, and looking forward to a considerable stay in the valley, when one night one of the elders of the village came to him stealthily, and begged him, if he valued his own safety, to go away. Burton asked whether the people did not like him. The elder answered, yes ; that was the root of the trouble. They had conceived, in fact, the highest possible opinion of his exceptional sanctity, and they thought it would be an excellent thing for the village to possess the tomb of so holy a man. So they were casting about now how they could best kill him. Whether this particular story is true or not, it at least exhibits in very vivid colours the state of mind of the ordinary god-slayer.

Dr. Tylor, Mr. Speth, and other writers on foundation sacrifices treat them as springing from primitive animism. To me, they seem rather to imply the exact opposite. For if everything has already a soul by nature, why kill a man or criminal to supply it with one ?

CHAPTER XIII.

GODS OF CULTIVATION.

By far the most interesting in the curious group of artifically-made gods are those which are sacrificed in connexion with agriculture. These deities appeal to us from several points of view. In the first place, they form, among agricultural races as a whole, the most important and venerated objects of worship. In the second place, it is largely through their influence or on their analogy, as I believe, that so many other artificial gods came to be renewed or sacrificed annually. In the third place, it is the gods of agriculture who are most of all slain sacramentally, whose bodies are eaten by their votaries in the shape of cakes of bread or other foodstuffs, and whose blood is drunk in the form of wine. The immediate connexion of these sacramental ceremonies with the sacrifice of the mass, and the identification of the Christ with bread and wine, give to this branch of our enquiry a peculiar importance from the point of view of the evolution of Christianity. We must therefore enter at some little length into the genesis of these peculiar and departmental gods, who stand so directly in the main line of evolution of the central divine figure in the Christian religion.

All over the world, wherever cultivation exists, a special class of corn-gods or grain-gods is found, deities of the chief foodstuff,—be it maize, or dates, or plantain, or rice —and it is a common feature of all these gods that they are represented by human or quasi-human victims, who are annually slain at the time of sowing. These human gods are believed to reappear once more in the form of the crop that rises from their sacred bodies ; their death and resurrection are celebrated in festivals ; and they are eaten and drunk sacramentally by their votaries, in the shape of first-fruits, or of cakes and wine, or of some other embodiment of the divine being. We have therefore to enquire into the origin of this curious superstition, which involves, as it seems to me, the very origin of cultivation itself as a human custom. And I must accordingly bespeak my readers' indulgence if I diverge for a while into what may seem at first a purely botanical digression.

Most people must have been struck by the paradox of cultivation. A particular plant in a state of nature, let us say, grows and thrives only in water, or in some exceedingly moist and damp situation. You take up this waterside plant with a trowel one day, and transfer it incontinently to a dry bed in a sun-baked garden ; when lo ! the moisture-loving creature, instead of withering and dying, as one might naturally expect of it, begins to grow apace, and to thrive to all appearance even better and more lustily than in its native habitat. Or you remove some parched desert weed from its arid rock to a moist and rainy climate ; and instead of dwindling, as one imagines it ought to do under the altered conditions, it spreads abroad in the deep rich mould of a shrubbery bed, and attains a stature impossible to its kind in its original surroundings. Our gardens, in fact, show us side by side plants which, in the wild state, demand the most varied and dissimilar habitats. Siberian squills blossom amicably in the same bed with Italian tulips ; the alpine saxifrage spreads its purple rosettes in friendly rivalry with the bog-loving marsh-marigold or the dry Spanish iris. The question, therefore, sooner or later occurs to the enquiring mind : How can they all live together so well here in man's domain, when in the outside world each demands and exacts so extremely different and specialised a situation ?

Of course it is only an inexperienced biologist who could long be puzzled by this apparent paradox. He must soon see the true solution of the riddle, if he has read and digested the teachings of Darwin. For the real fact is, in a garden or out of it, most of these plants could get on very well in a great variety of climates or situations—if only they were protected against outside competition. There we have the actual crux of the problem. It is not that the moisture-loving plants cannot live in dry situations, but that the dry-loving plants, specialised and adapted for the post, can compete with them there at an immense advntage, and so, in a very short time, live them down altogether. Every species in a state of nature is continually exposed to the ceaseless competition of every other; and each on its own ground can beat its competitors. But in a garden, the very thing we aim at is just to restrict and prevent competition; to give each species a fair chance for life, even in conditions where other and better-adapted species can usually outlive it. This, in fact, is really at bottom all that we ever mean by a garden—a space of ground cleared, and kept clear, of its natural vegetation (commonly called in this connexion *weeds*), and deliberately stocked with other plants, most or all of which the weeds would live down if not artificially prevented.

We see the truth of this point of view the moment the garden is, as we say, abandoned—that is to say, left once more to the operation of unaided nature. The plants with which we have stocked it loiter on for a while in a feeble and uncertain fashion, but are ultimately choked out by the stronger and better-adapted weeds which compose the natural vegetation of the locality. The dock and nettle live down in time the larkspur and the peony. The essential thing in the garden is, in short, the clearing of the ground from the weeds—that is, in other words, from the native vegetation. A few minor things may or may not be added, such as manuring, turning the soil, protecting

ORIGIN OF CULTIVATION.

with shelter, and so forth; but the clearing is itself the one thing needful.

Slight as this point seems at first sight, I believe it includes the whole secret of the origin of tillage, and therefore, by implication, of the gods of agriculture. For, looked at in essence, cultivation is weeding, and weeding is cultivation. When we say that a certain race cultivates a certain plant-staple, we mean no more in the last resort than that it sows or sets it in soil artificially cleared of competing species. Sowing without clearing is absolutely useless. So the question of the origin of cultivation resolves itself at last simply into this—how did certain men come first to know that by clearing ground of weeds and keeping it clear of them they could promote the growth of certain desirable human foodstuffs?

To begin with, it may be as well to premise that the problem of the origin of cultivation is a far more complex one than appears at first sight. For we have not only to ask, as might seem to the enquirer unaccustomed to such investigations, "How did the early savage first find out that seeds would grow better when planted in open soil, already freed from weeds or natural competitors?" but also the other and far more difficult question, "How did the early savage ever find out that plants would grow from seeds at all?" That, I take it, is the real riddle of the situation, and it is one which, so far as I know, has hitherto escaped all enquirers into the history and origin of human progress.

Fully to grasp the profound nature of this difficulty we must throw ourselves back mentally into the condition and position of primitive man. We ourselves have known so long and so familiarly the fact that plants grow from seeds—that the seed is the essential reproductive part of the vegetable organism—that we find it hard to unthink that piece of commonplace knowledge, and to realise that what to us is an almost self-evident truth is to the primitive savage a long and difficult inference. Our own common and certain acquaintance with the fact, indeed, is entirely derived from the practice of agriculture. We have seen seeds sown from our earliest childhood. But before agriculture grew up, the connexion between seed and seedling could not possibly be known or even suspected by primitive man, who was by no means prone to make abstract investigations into the botanical nature or physiological object of the various organs in the herbs about him. That the seed is the reproductive part of the plant was a fact as little likely in itself to strike him as that the stamens were the male organs, or that the leaves were the assimilative and digestive surfaces. He could only have found out that plants grew from seeds by the experimental process of sowing and growing them. Such an experiment he was far from likely ever to try for its own sake. He must have been led to it by some other and accidental coincidence.

Now what was primitive man likely to know and observe about the plants around him? Primarily one thing only: that some of them were edible, and some were not. There you have a distinction of immediate interest to all humanity. And what parts of plants were most likely to be useful to him in this respect as foodstuffs? Those parts which the plant had specially filled up with rich material for its own use or the use of its offspring. The first are the roots, stocks, bulbs, corms, or tubers in which it lays by foodstuffs for its future growth; the second are the seeds which it produces and enriches in order to continue its kind to succeeding generations.

Primitive man, then, knows the fruits, seeds, and tubers, just as the squirrel, the monkey, and the parrot know them, as so much good foodstuff, suitable to his purpose. But why should he ever dream of saving or preserving some of these fruits or seeds, when he has found them, and of burying them in the soil, on the bare off-chance that by pure magic, as it were, they might give rise to others? No idea could be more foreign to the nature and habits of early man. In the first place, he is far from provident ; his way is to eat up at once what he has killed or picked ; and in the second place, how could he ever come to conceive that seeds buried in the ground could possibly produce more seeds in future ? Nay, even if he did know it—which is well-nigh impossible—would he be likely, feckless creature that he is, to save or spare a handful of seeds to-day in order that other seeds might spring from their burial-place in another twelvemonth ? The difficulty is so enormous when one fairly faces it that it positively staggers one ; we begin to wonder whether really, after all, the first steps in cultivation could ever have been taken.

The savage, when he has killed a deer or a game-bird, does not bury a part of it or an egg of it in the ground, in the expectation that it will grow into more deer or more bird hereafter. Why, then, should he, when he has picked a peck of fruits or wild cereals, bury some of them in the ground, and expect a harvest ? The savage is a simple and superstitious person ; but I do not think he is quite such a fool as this proceeding would make him out to be. He is not likely ever to have noticed that plants in the wild state grow from seeds—at least prior to the rise of agriculture, from which, as I believe, he first and slowly gained that useful knowledge. And he certainly is not likely ever to have tried deliberate experiments upon the properties of plants, as if he were a Fellow of the Royal Society. These two roads being thus effectually blocked to us, we have to enquire, "Was there ever any way in which primitive man could have blundered blindfold upon a knowledge of the truth, and could have discovered incidentally to some other function of his life the two essential facts that plants grow from seeds, and that the growth and supply of useful food-plants can be artificially increased by burying or sowing such seeds in ground cleared of weeds, that is to say of the natural competing vegetation ? "

I believe there *is* one way, and one way only, in which primitive man was at all likely to become familiar with these facts. I shall try to show that all the operations of primitive agriculture very forcibly point to this strange and almost magical origin of cultivation ; that all savage agriculture retains to the last many traces of its origin ; and that the sowing of the seed itself is hardly considered so important and essential a part of the complex process as certain purely superstitious and bloodthirsty practices that long accompany it. In one word, not to keep the reader in doubt any longer, I am inclined to believe that cultivation and the sowing of seeds for crops had their beginning as an adjunct of the primitive burial system.

Up to the present time, so far as I know, only one origin for cultivation has ever been even conjecturally suggested; and that is a hard one. It has been said that the first hint of cultivation may have come from the observation that seeds accidentally cast out on the kitchen-middens, or on the cleared space about huts, caves, or other human dwelling-places, germinated and produced more seeds in succeeding seasons. Very probably many savages have observed the fact that food-plants frequently grow on such heaps of refuse. But that observation alone does not bring us much nearer to the origin of cultivation. For why should early man connect such a fact with the seeds more than with the bones, the shells, or the mere accident of proximity ? We must rid our minds of all the preconceptions of inductive and experimental science, and throw ourselves mentally back into the position of the savage to whom nature is one vast field of unrelated events, without fixed sequence or physical causation. Moreover, a kitchen-midden is *not* a cleared space : on the contrary, it is a weed-bed of extraordinary luxuriance. It brings us no nearer the origin of clearing.

There is, however, one set of functions in which primitive men do actually perform all the essential acts of agriculture, without in the least intending it ; and that is the almost universal act of the burial of the dead. Burial is, so far as I can see, the only object for which early races, or, what comes to the same thing, very low savages, ever turn or dig the ground. We have seen already that the original idea of burial was to confine the ghost or corpse of the dead man by putting a weight of earth on top of him ; and lest this should be insufficient to keep him from troublesome reappearances, a big stone was frequently rolled above his mound or tumulus, which is the origin of all our monuments, now diverted to the honour and commemoration of the deceased. But the point to which I wish just now to direct attention is this—that in the act of burial, and in that act alone, we get a first beginning of turning the soil, exposing fresh earth, and so incidentally eradicating the weeds. We have here, in short, the first necessary prelude to the evolution of agriculture.

The next step, of course, must be the sowing of the seed. And here, I venture to think, funeral customs supply us with the only conceivable way in which such sowing could ever have begun. For early men would certainly not waste the precious seeds which it took them so much time and trouble to collect from the wild plants around them, in mere otiose scientific experiments on vegetable development. But we have seen that it is the custom of all savages to offer at the tombs of their ancestors food and drink of the same kind as they themselves are in the habit of using. Now, with people in the hunting stage, such offerings would no doubt most frequently consist of meat, the flesh of the hunted beasts or game-birds ; but they would also include fish, fruits, seeds, tubers, and berries, and in particular such rich grains as those of the native pulses and cereals. Evidence of such things being offered at the graves of the dead has been collected in such abundance by Dr. Tylor, Mr. Frazer, and Mr. Herbert Spencer, that I need not here adduce any further examples of so familiar a practice.

What must be the obvious result ? Here, and here

alone, the savage quite unconsciously sows seeds upon newly-turned ground, deprived of its weeds, and further manured by the blood and meat of the frequent sacrificial offerings. These seeds must often spring up and grow apace, with a rapidity and luxuriance which cannot fail to strike the imagination of the primitive hunter. Especially will this be the case with that class of plants which ultimately develop into the food-crops of civilised society. For the peculiarity of these plants is that they are one and all—maize, corn, or rice, pease, beans, or millet—annuals of rapid growth and portentous stature; plants which have thriven in the struggle for existence by laying up large stores of utilisable material in their seeds for the use of the seedling; and this peculiarity enables them to start in life in each generation exceptionally well endowed, and so to compete at an advantage with all their fellows. Seeds of such a sort would thrive exceedingly in the newly-turned and well-manured soil of a grave or barrow; and producing there a quantity of rich and edible grain, would certainly attract the attention of that practical and observant man, the savage. For though he is so incurious about what are non-essentials, your savage is a peculiarly long-headed person about all that concerns his own immediate advantage.

What conclusion would at once be forced upon him? That seeds planted in freshly-turned and richly-manured soil produce threefold and fourfold? Nothing of the sort. He knows naught of seeds and manures and soils; he would at once conclude, after his kind, that the dreaded and powerful ghost in the barrow, pleased with the gifts of meat and seeds offered to him, had repaid those gifts in kind by returning grain for grain a hundredfold out of his own body. This original connexion of ideas seems to me fully to explain that curious identification of the ghost or spirit with the corn or other foodstuff which Mr. Frazer has so wonderfully and conclusively elaborated in *The Golden Bough.*

FOOD PLANTS ON GRAVES.

Some little evidence is even forthcoming that vegetation actually *does* show exceptional luxuriance on graves and barrows. The Rev. Alexander Stewart of Ballachulish mentions that the milkmaids in Lochaber and elsewhere in the Scotch highlands used to pour a little milk daily from the pail on the "fairy knowes," or prehistoric barrows; and the consequence was that "these fairy knolls were clothed with a more beautiful verdure than any other spot in the country." In Fiji, Mr. Fison remarks that yam-plants spring luxuriantly from the heaps of yam presented to ancestral spirits in the sacred stone enclosure or *temenos;* and two or three recent correspondents (since this chapter was first printed in a monthly review) have obligingly communicated to me analogous facts from Madagascar, Central Africa, and the Malay Archipelago. It is clear from their accounts that graves do often give rise to crops of foodstuffs, accidentally springing from the food laid upon them.

Just at first, under such circumstances, the savage would no doubt be content merely to pick and eat the seeds that thus grew casually, as it were, on the graves or barrows of his kings and kinsfolk. But in process of time it would almost certainly come about that the area of cultivation would be widened somewhat. The first step toward such widening, I take it, would arise from the observation that cereals and other seeds only throve exceptionally upon newly-made graves, not on graves in general. For as soon as the natural vegetation reasserted itself, the quickening power of the ghost would seem to be used up. Thus it might be found well to keep fresh ghosts always going for agricultural purposes. Hence might gradually arise a habit of making a new grave annually, at the most favourable sowing-time, which last would come to be recognised by half-unconscious experiment and observation. And this new grave, as I shall show reason for believing a little later, would be the grave, not of a person who happened to die then and there accidentally, but of a deliberate victim, slain in order to provide a spirit of vegetation,—an artificial god,—and to make the corn grow with vigour and luxuriance. Step by step, I believe, it would at length be discovered that if only you dug wide enough, the corn would grow well *around* as well as *upon* the actual grave of the divine victim. Thus slowly there would develop the cultivated field, the wider clearing, dug up or laboured by hand, and finally the ploughed field, which yet remains a grave in theory and in all essentials.

I have ventured to give this long and apparently unessential preamble, because I wish to make it clear that the manufactured or artificial god of the corn-field or other cultivated plot really dates back to the very origin of cultivation. Without a god, there would be no corn-field at all; and the corn-field, I believe, is long conceived merely as the embodiment of his vegetative spirit. Nay, the tilled field is often at our own day, and even in our own country, a grave in theory.

It is a mere commonplace at the present time to say that among early men and savages every act of life has a sacred significance; and agriculture especially is everywhere and always invested with a special sanctity. To us, it would seem natural that the act of sowing seed should be regarded as purely practical and physiological; that the seed should be looked upon merely as the part of the plant intended for reproduction, and that its germination should be accepted as a natural and normal process. Savages and early men, however, have no such conceptions. To them the whole thing is a piece of natural magic; you sow seeds, or, to be more accurate, you bury certain grains of foodstuff in the freshly-turned soil, with certain magical rites and ceremonies; and then, after the lapse of a certain time, plants begin to grow upon this soil, from which you finally obtain a crop of maize or wheat or barley. The burial of the seeds or grains is only one part of the magical cycle, no more necessarily important for the realisation of the desired end than many others.

And what are the other magical acts necessary in order that grain-bearing plants may grow upon the soil prepared for their reception ? Mr. Frazer has collected abundant evidence for answering that question, a small part of which I shall recapitulate here for the benefit of those who have not read his remarkable work, referring students to *The Golden Bough* itself for fuller details and collateral developments. At the same time I should like to make it clearly understood that Mr. Frazer is personally in no way responsible for the use I here make of his admirable materials.

All the world over, savages and semi-civilised people are in the habit of sacrificing human victims, whose bodies are buried in the field with the seed of corn or other breadstuffs. Often enough the victim's blood is mixed with the grain in order to fertilise it. The most famous instance is that of the Khonds of Orissa, who chose special victims, known as Meriahs, and offered them up to ensure good harvests. The Meriah was often kept for years before being sacrificed. He was regarded as a consecrated being, and treated with extreme affection, mingled with deference. A Meriah youth, on reaching manhood, was given a wife who was herself a Meriah ; their offspring were all brought up as victims. "The periodical sacrifices," says Mr. Frazer, "were generally so arranged by tribes and divisions of tribes that each head of a family was enabled, at least once a year, to procure a shred of flesh for his fields, generally about the time when his chief crop was laid down." On the day of the sacrifice, which was horrible beyond description in its details, the body was cut to pieces, and the flesh hacked from it was instantly taken home by the persons whom each village had deputed to bring it. On arriving at its destination, it was divided by the priest into two portions, one of which he buried in a hole in the ground, with his back turned and without looking at it. Then each man in the village added a little earth to cover it, and the priest poured water over the mimic tumulus. The other portion of the flesh the priest divided into as many shares as there were heads of houses present. Each head of a house buried his shred in his own field, placing it in the earth behind his back without looking. The other remains of the human victim—the head, the bones, and the intestines—were burned on a funeral-pile, and the ashes were scattered over the fields, or mixed with the new corn to preserve it from injury. Every one of these details should be carefully noted.

Now, in this case, it is quite clear to me that every field is regarded as essentially a grave ; portions of the divine victim are buried in it ; his ashes are mixed with the seed ; and from the ground thus treated he springs again in the form of corn, or rice, or turmeric. These customs, as Mr. Frazer rightly notes, "imply that to the body of the Meriah there was ascribed a direct or intrinsic power of making the crops to grow. In other words, the flesh and ashes of the victim were believed to be endowed with a magical or physical power of fertilising the land." More than that, it seems to me that the seed itself is not regarded as sufficient to produce a crop : it is the seed buried in the sacred grave with the divine flesh which germinates at last into next year's foodstuffs.

A few other points must be noticed about this essential case, which is one of the most typical instances of manufactured godhead. The Meriah was only satisfactory if he had been purchased—"bought with a price," like the children who were built as foundation-gods into walls ; or else was the child of a previous Meriah—in other words, was of divine stock by descent and inheritance. Khonds in distress often sold their children as Meriahs, "considering the beatification" (apotheosis, I would rather say) "of their souls certain, and their death, for the benefit of mankind, the most honourable possible." This sense of the sacrifice as a case of "one man dying for the people" is most marked in our accounts, and is especially interesting from its analogy to Christian reasoning. A man of the Panua tribe was once known to upbraid a Khond because he had sold for a Meriah his daughter whom the Panuá wished to marry; the Khonds around at once comforted the insulted father, exclaiming, " Your child died that all the world may live." Here and elsewhere we have the additional idea of a piacular value attached to the sacrifice, about which more must be said in a subsequent chapter. The death of the Meriah was supposed to ensure not only good crops, but also " immunity from all disease and accident." The Khonds shouted in his dying ear, " We bought you with a price; no sin rests with us." It is also worthy of notice that the victim was anointed with oil, a point which recalls the very name of Christus. Once more, the victim might not be bound or make any show of resistance; but the bones of his arms and his legs were often broken to render struggling impossible. Sometimes, however, he was stupefied with opium, one of the ordinary features in the manufacture of gods, as we have already seen, being such preliminary stupefaction. Among the various ways in which the Meriah was slain I would particularly specify the mode of execution by squeezing him to death in the cleft of a tree. I mention these points here, though they somewhat interrupt the general course of our argument, because of their great importance as antecedents of the Christian theory. In fact, I believe the Christian legend to have been mainly constructed out of the details of such early god-making sacrifices; I hold that Christ is essentially one such artificial god; and I trust the reader will carefully observe for himself as we proceed how many small details (such as the breaking of the bones) recall in many ways the incidents of the passion and the crucifixion.

The Khonds, however, have somewhat etherealised the conception of artificial god-making by allowing one victim to do for many fields together. Other savages are more prodigal of divine crop-raisers. To draw once more from Mr. Frazer's storehouse—the Indians of Guayaquil, in South America, used to sacrifice human blood and the hearts of men when they sowed their fields. The ancient Mexicans, conceiving the maize as a personal being who went through the whole course of life between seed-time and harvest, sacrificed new-born babes when the maize was sown, older children when it had sprouted, and so on till it was fully ripe, when they sacrificed old men. May we not parallel with this instance the singular fact that the Romans had as their chief agricultural deity Saturnus, the god of sowing, but had also several other subsidiary crop-deities, such as Seia, who has to do with the corn when it sprouts, Segetia, with the corn when shot up, and Tutilina with the corn stored in the granary? (An obvious objection based on the numerous gods of childhood and practical arts at Rome will be answered in a later chapter.) The Pawnees, again, annually sacrificed a human victim in spring, when they sowed their fields. They thought that an omission of this sacrifice would be followed by the total failure of the crops of maize, beans, and pumpkins. In the account of one such sacrifice of a girl in 1837 or 1838, we are told: "While her flesh was still warm, it was cut in small pieces from the bones, put in little baskets, and taken to a neighbouring corn-field. Here the head chief took a piece of the flesh from a basket, and squeezed a drop of blood upon the newly-deposited grains of corn. His example was followed by the rest, till all the seed had been sprinkled with the blood; it was then covered up with earth." Many other cases might be quoted from America.

In West Africa, once more, a tribal queen used to sacrifice a man and woman in the month of March. They were killed with spades and hoes, and their bodies buried in the middle of a field which had just been tilled. At Lagos, in Guinea, it was the custom annually to impale a young girl alive soon after the spring equinox in order to secure good crops. A similar sacrifice is still annually offered at Benin. The Marimos, a Bechuana tribe, sacrifice a human being for the crops. The victim chosen is generally a short stout man. He is seized by violence or intoxicated (note that detail) and taken to the fields, where he is killed amongst the wheat " to serve as seed." After his blood has coagulated in the sun, it is burned, along with that peculiarly sacred part, the frontal bone, the flesh attached to it, and the brain ; the ashes are then scattered over the ground to fertilise it. Such scattering of the ashes occurs in many instances, and will meet us again in the case of Osiris.

In India, once more, the Gonds, like the Khonds, kidnapped Brahman boys, and kept them as victims to be sacrificed on various occasions. At sowing and reaping, after a triumphal procession, one of the lads was killed by being punctured with a poisoned arrow. His blood was then sprinkled over the ploughed field or the ripe crop, and his flesh was sacramentally devoured. The last point again will call at a later stage for further examination.

I will detail no more such instances (out of the thousands that exist) for fear of seeming tedious. But the interpretation I put upon the facts is this. Originally, men noticed that food-plants grew abundantly from the laboured and well-manured soil of graves. They observed that this richness sprang from a coincidence of three factors—digging, a sacred dead body, and seeds of foodstuffs. In time, they noted that if you dug wide enough and scattered seed far enough, a single corpse was capable of fertilising a considerable area. The grave grew into the field or garden. But they still thought it necessary to bury some one in the field ; and most of the evidence shows that they regarded this victim as a divine personage ; that they considered him the main source of growth or fertility ; and that they endeavoured to deserve his favour by treating him well during the greater part of his lifetime. For in many of the accounts it is expressly stated that the intended victim was treated as a god or as a divine king, and was supplied with every sort of luxury up to the moment of his immolation. In process of time, the conception of the field as differing from the grave grew more defined, and the large part borne by seed in the procedure was more fully recognised. Even so, however, nobody dreamed of sowing the seed alone without the body of a victim. Both grain and flesh or blood came to be regarded alike as "seed": that is to say, the concurrence of the two was considered necessary to produce the desired effect of germination and fertility. Till a very late period, either the actual sacrifice or some vague remnant of it remained as an essential part of cultivation. Mr. Frazer's pages teem with such survivals in modern folk-custom. From his work and from other sources, I will give a few instances of these last dying relics of the primitive superstition.

Mr. Gomme, in his *Ethnology in Folklore*, supplies an account of a singular village festival in Southern India. In this feast, a priest, known as the Pótraj, and specially armed with a divine whip, like the scourge of Osiris, sacrifices a sacred buffalo, which is turned loose when a calf, and allowed to feed and roam about the village. In that case, we have the common substitution of an animal for a human victim, which almost always accompanies advancing civilisation. At the high festival, the head of the buffalo was struck off at a single blow, and placed in front of the shrine of the village goddess. Around were placed vessels containing the different cereals, and hard by a heap of mixed grains with a drill-plough in the centre. The carcase was then cut up into small pieces, and each cultivator received a portion to bury in his field. The heap of grain was finally divided among all the cultivators, to be buried by each one in his field with the bit of flesh. At last, the head, that very sacred part, was buried before a little temple, sacred to the goddess of boundaries. The goddess is represented by a shapeless stone—no doubt a

Terminus, or rather the tombstone of an artificial goddess, a girl buried under an ancient boundary-mark. Here we have evidently a last stage of the same ritual which in the case of the Khonds was performed with a human victim. It is worth while noting that, as part of this ceremony, a struggle took place for portions of the victim.

A still more attenuated form of the same ceremony is mentioned by Captain Harkness and others, as occurring among the Badagas of the Nilgiri Hills. I condense their accounts, taking out of each such elements as are most cognate to our purpose. Among these barbarians, the first furrow is ploughed by a low-caste Kurrumbar, who gives his benediction to the field, without which there would be no harvest. Here, the member of the aboriginal race is clearly looked upon as a priest or kinsman of the local gods, whose cooperation must be obtained by later intrusive races. But the Kurrumbar does not merely bless the field; he also sets up a stone in its midst; and then, prostrating himself before the stone, he sacrifices a goat, the head of which he keeps as his perquisite. This peculiar value of the oracular head retained by the priest is also significant. When harvest-time comes, the same Kurrumbar is summoned once more, in order that he may reap the first handful of corn, an episode the full importance of which will only be apparent to those who have read Mr. Frazer's analysis of harvest customs. But in this case also, the appearance of the sacred stone is pregnant with meaning. We can hardly resist the inference that we have here to do with the animal substitute for a human sacrifice of the god-making order, in which the victim was slaughtered, a stone set up to mark the site of the sacrifice, and the head preserved as a god to give oracles, in the fashion with which we are already familiar. Comparing this instance with the previous one of the sacred buffalo and the still earlier cases of ancestral heads preserved as gods for oracular purposes, I think the affiliation is too clear to be disregarded.

Evidence of similar customs elsewhere exists in such abundance that I can only give a very small part of it at present, lest I should assign too much space to a subordinate question ; I hope to detail the whole of it hereafter in a subsequent volume. Here is a striking example from Mr. Gomme's *Ethnology in Folklore,* the analogy of which with preceding instances will at once be apparent.

"At the village of Holne, situated on one of the spurs of Dartmoor, is a field of about two acres, the property of the parish, and called the Ploy Field. In the centre of this field stands a granite pillar (Menhir) six or seven feet high. On May-morning, before daybreak, the young men of the village used to assemble there, and then proceed to the moor, where they selected a ram lamb, and, after running it down, brought it in triumph to the Ploy Field, fastened it to the pillar, cut its throat, and then roasted it whole, skin, wool, etc. At midday a struggle took place, at the risk of cut hands, for a slice, it being supposed to confer luck for the ensuing year on the fortunate devourer. As an act of gallantry the young men sometimes fought their way through the crowd to get a slice for the chosen amongst the young women, all of whom, in their best dresses, attended the Ram Feast, as it was called. Dancing, wrestling, and other games, assisted by copious libations of cider during the afternoon, prolonged the festivity till midnight."

Here again we get several interesting features of the primitive ritual preserved for us. The connexion with the stone which enshrines the original village deity is perfectly clear. This stone no doubt represents the place where the local foundation-god was slain in very remote ages ; and it is therefore the proper place for the annual renewal sacrifices to be offered. The selection of May-morning for the rite ; the slaughter at the stone pillar ; the roasting of the beast whole ; the struggle for the pieces ; and the idea that they would confer luck, all show survival of primitive feeling. So does the cider, sacramental intoxication being an integral part of all these proceedings. Every detail, indeed, has its meaning for those who look close ; for the struggle at midday is itself significant, as is also the prolongation of the feast till midnight. But we miss the burial of the pieces in the fields ; in so far, the primitive object of the rite seems to have been forgotten or overlooked in Devonshire.

A still more attenuated survival is quoted by Mr. Gomme from another English village. "A Whitsuntide custom in the parish of King's Teignton, Devonshire, is thus described : A lamb is drawn about the parish on Whitsun Monday in a cart covered with garlands of lilac, laburnum, and other flowers, when persons are requested to give something towards the animal and attendant expenses ; on Tuesday it is killed and roasted whole in the middle of the village. The lamb is then sold in slices to the poor at a cheap rate. The origin of the custom is forgotten, but a tradition, supposed to trace back to heathen days, is to this effect : The village suffered from a dearth of water, when the inhabitants were advised by their priests to pray to the gods for water ; whereupon the water sprang up spontaneously in a meadow about a third of a mile above the river, in an estate now called Rydon, amply sufficient to supply the wants of the place, and at present adequate, even in a dry summer, to work three mills. A lamb, it is said, has ever since that time been sacrificed as a votive thank-offering at Whitsuntide in the manner before mentioned. The said water appears like a large pond, from which in rainy weather may be seen jets springing up some inches above the surface in many parts. It has ever had the name of ' Fair Water.'"

I mention this curious instance here, because it well illustrates the elusive way in which such divine customs of various origins merge into one another ; and also the manner in which different ideas are attached in different places to very similar ceremonies. For Mr. Frazer has shown that the notion of a rain-charm is also closely bound up with the gods of agriculture; the Khond Meriah must weep, or there will be no rain that year; his red blood must flow, or the turmeric will not produce its proper red colour. (Compare the red blood that flowed from Polydorus's cornel, and the Indian's blood that drops from the Canadian bloodroot.) In this last instance of the King's Teignton ceremony, it is the rain-charm that has most clearly survived to our days: and there are obvious references to a human sacrifice offered up to make a river-god in times long gone, and now replaced by an animal victim. The garlands of lilac, laburnum, and other flowers are, however, common adornments of the artificial god of cultivation; they occurred in the Dionysiac rites and the Attis festival, and are still preserved in many European customs.

Very closely bound up with the artificial gods of cultivation are the terminal gods with whom I dealt in the last chapter; so closely that it is sometimes impossible to separate them. We have already seen some instances of this connexion; the procession of the sacred victim usually ends with a perlustration of the boundaries. This perlustration is often preceded by the head of the theanthropic victim. Such a ceremony extends all over India; in France and other European countries it survives in the shape of the rite known as Blessing the Fields, where the priest plays the same part as is played among the Nilgiri hillsmen by the low-caste Kurrumbar. In this rite, the Host is carried round the bounds of the parish, as the head of the sacred buffalo is carried round at the Indian festival. In some cases every field is separately visited. I was told as a boy in Normandy that a portion of the Host (stolen or concealed, I imagine) was sometimes buried in each field, but of this curious detail I can now obtain no confirmatory evidence, and I do not insist upon it. We must remember, however, that the Host is the body of Christ, and that its presence in such cases is the exact analogue of the carrying round the pieces of the Meriah.

In England, the ceremony merges into that of Beating the Bounds, already described ; though I believe the significance of the boy-victims, and the necessity for whipping them as a rain-charm, will now be more apparent than when we last met with it.

In many cases, all the world over, various animals come to replace the human victim-god. Thus we learn from Festus that the Romans sacrificed red-haired puppies in spring, in the belief that the crops would thus grow ripe and ruddy ; and there can be little doubt that these puppies, like the lamb sacrifice at Holne and King's Teignton, were a substitute for an original human victim. Even so, the Egyptians, as we shall see, sacrificed red-haired men as the representatives of Osiris, envisaged as a corn-god. In some cases, indeed, we have historical evidence of the human god being replaced at recent dates by a divine animal-victim ; for example, in Chinna Kimedy, after the British had suppressed human sacrifices, a goat took the place of the sacred Meriah.

Mannhardt has collected much evidence of the curious customs still (or lately) existing in modern Europe, which look like survivals in a very mitigated form of the same superstition. These are generally known by the name of " Carrying out Death," or " Burying the Carnival." They are practised in almost every country of Europe, and relics of them survive even in England. The essence of these ceremonies consists in an effigy being substituted for the human victim. This effigy is treated much as the victim used to be. Sometimes it is burned, sometimes thrown into a river, and sometimes buried piecemeal. In Austrian Silesia, for example, the effigy is burned, and while it is burning a general struggle takes place for the pieces, which are pulled out of the flames with bare hands. (Compare the struggle among the Khonds, and also at the Potraj festival and the Holne sacrifice.) Each person who secures a fragment of the figure ties it to a branch of the largest tree in his garden, or buries it in his field, in the belief that this causes the crops to grow better. Sometimes a sheaf of corn does duty for the victim, and portions of it are buried in each field as fertilisers. In the Hartz Mountains, at similar ceremonies, a living man is laid on a baking-trough and carried with dirges to a grave; but a glass of brandy is substituted for him at the last moment. Here the spirit is the equivalent of a god. In other cases the man is actually covered with straw, and so lightly buried. In Italy and Spain, a similar custom bore the name of "Sawing the Old Woman." In Palermo, a real old woman was drawn through the streets on a cart, and made to mount a scaffold, where two mock executioners proceeded to saw through a bladder of blood which had been fitted to her neck. The blood gushed out, and the old woman pretended to swoon and die. This is obviously a mitigation of a human sacrifice. At Florence, an effigy stuffed with walnuts and dried figs represented the Old Woman. At mid-Lent, this figure was sawn through the middle in the Mercato Nuovo, and when the dried fruits tumbled out they were scrambled for by the crowd, as savages scrambled for fragments of the human victim or his animal representative. Upon all this subject a mass of material has been collected by Mannhardt and Mr. Frazer. Perhaps the most interesting case of all is the Russian ceremony of the Funeral of Yarilo. In this instance, the people chose an old man and gave him a small coffin containing a figure representing Yarilo. This he carried out of the town, followed by women chanting dirges, as the Syrian women mourned for Adonis, and the Egyptians for Osiris. In the open fields a grave was dug, and into it the figure was lowered amid weeping and wailing.

Myth and folk-lore also retain many traces of the primitive connexion. Thus, in the genuine American legend of Hiawatha, the hero wrestles with and vanquishes Mondamin, and where he buries him springs up for the first time the maize, or Indian-corn plant. Similar episodes occur in the Finnish Kalevala and other barbaric epics. According to Mr. Chalmers, the Motu tribe in New Guinea say that yams sprang first from the bones of a murdered man, which were buried in a grave. After some time, the grave was opened, and the bones were found to be no longer bones, but large and small yams of different colours.

In order to complete our preliminary survey of these artificial gods of cultivation, before we proceed to the consideration of the great corn-gods and wine-gods, it may be well to premise that in theory at least the original victim seems to have been a king or chief, himself divine, or else at least a king's son or daughter, one of the divine stock, in whose veins flowed the blood of the earlier deities. Later on, it would seem, the temporary king was often allowed to do duty for the real king ; and for this purpose he seems frequently to have been clad in royal robes, and treated with divine and royal honours. Examples of this complication will crop up in the sequel. For the present I will only refer to the interesting set of survivals, collected by Mr. Gomme, where temporary kings or mayors in England are annually elected, apparently for the sake of being sacrificed only. In many of these cases we get mere fragmentary portions of the original rite ; but by piecing them all together, we obtain on the whole a tolerably complete picture of the original ceremonial observance. At St. Germans in Cornwall, the mock mayor was chosen under the large walnut-tree at the May-fair ; he was made drunk overnight, in order to fit him for office, and was in that state drawn round the nut-tree, much as we saw the mayor of Bovey rode round the Bovey stone on his accession to the mayoralty. The mayor of St. Germans also displayed his royal character by being mounted on the wain or cart of old Teutonic and Celtic sovereignty. At Lostwithiel, the mock mayor was dressed with a crown on his head, and a sceptre in his hand, and had a sword borne before him. At Penrhyn, the mayor was preceded by torch-bearers and town sergeants, and though he was not actually burnt, either in play or in effigy, bonfires were lighted, and fireworks discharged, which connect the ceremony with such pyre-sacrifices of cremationists as the festival of the Tyrian Melcarth and the Baal of Tarsus. On Halgaver Moor, near Bodmin, a stranger was arrested, solemnly tried in sport, and then trained in the mire or otherwise ill-treated. At Polperro, the mayor was generally " some half-witted or drunken fellow," in either case, according to early ideas, divine ; he was treated with ale, and, " having completed the perambulation of the town," was wheeled by his attendants into the sea. There, he was allowed to scramble out again, as the mock victim does in many European ceremonies ; but originally, I do not doubt, he was drowned as a rain-charm.

These ceremonies, at the time when our authorities learnt of them, had all degenerated to the level of mere childish pastimes ; but they contain in them, none the less, persistent elements of most tragic significance, and they point back to hideous and sanguinary god-making festivals. In most of them we see still preserved the choice of the willing or unconscious victim ; the preference for a stranger, a fool, or an idiot ; the habit of intoxicating the chosen person ; the treatment of the victim as king, mayor, or governor ; his scourging or mocking ; his final death ; and his burning on a pyre, or his drowning as a rain-charm. All these points are still more clearly noticeable in the other form of survival where the king or divine victim is represented, not by a mock or temporary king, but by an image or effigy. Such is the common case of King Carnival, who is at last burnt in all his regalia, or thrown into a river. Our own Guy Fawkes, though fastened upon the personality of a particular unpopular historical character, seems to be the last feeble English representative of such a human victim. I will not elaborate this point any further (considerations of space forbid), but will refer the reader for additional examples to Mr.

Gomme's *Village Community*, and Mr. Frazer's wonderful collection of examples in *The Golden Bough*.

The general conclusion I would incline to draw from all these instances is briefly this. Cultivation probably began with the accidental sowing of grains upon the tumuli of the dead. Gradually it was found that by extending the dug or tilled area and sowing it all over, a crop would grow upon it, provided always a corpse was buried in the centre. In process of time divine corpses were annually provided for the purpose, and buried with great ceremony in each field. By-and-bye it was found sufficient to offer up a single victim for a whole tribe or village, and to divide his body piecemeal among the fields of the community. But the crops that grew in such fields were still regarded as the direct gifts of the dead and deified victims, whose soul was supposed to animate and fertilize them. As cultivation spread, men became familiarised at last with the conception of the seed and the ploughing as the really essential elements in the process; but they still continued to attach to the victim a religious importance, and to believe in the necessity of his presence for good luck in the harvest. With the gradual mitigation of savagery an animal sacrifice was often substituted for a human one; but the fragments of the animal were still distributed through the fields with a mimic or symbolical burial, just as the fragments of the man-god had formerly been distributed. Finally, under the influence of Christianity and other civilised religions, an effigy was substituted for a human victim, though an animal sacrifice was often retained side by side with it, and a real human being was playfully killed in pantomime.

In early stages, however, I note that the field or garden sometimes retains the form of a tumulus. Thus Mr. Turner, the Samoan missionary, writes of the people of Tana, in the New Hebrides:

"They bestow a great deal of labour on their yam plantations, and keep them in fine order. You look over a reed fence, and there you see ten or twenty mounds of earth, some of them seven feet high and sixty in circumference. These are heaps of loose earth without a single stone, all thrown up by the hand. In the centre they plant one of the largest yams whole, and round the sides some smaller ones."

This looks very much like a tumulus in its *temenos*. I sould greatly like to know whether a victim is buried in it.

I may add that the idea of the crop being a gift from the deified ancestor or the divine-human victim is kept up in the common habit of offering the first-fruits to the dead, or to the gods, or to the living chief, their representative and descendant. Of the equivalence of these three ceremonies, I have given some evidence in my essay on Tree-Worship appended to my translation of the *Attis* of Catullus. For example, Mr. Turner says of these same Tanese in the New Hebrides:

"The spirits of their departed ancestors were among their gods. Chiefs who reached an advanced age were, after death, deified, addressed by name, and prayed to on various occasions. They were supposed especially to preside over the growth of the yams and the different fruit-trees. The first-fruits were presented to them, and in doing this they laid a little of the fruit on some stone or shelving branch of the tree, or some more temporary altar . . . in the form of a table. . . . All being quiet, the chief acted as high priest and prayed aloud thus: 'Compassionate father, here is some food for you; eat it; be kind to us on account of it.' And instead of an Amen, all united in a loud shout."

Similar evidence is abundant elsewhere. I summarise a little of it. Every year the Kochs of Assam, when they gather their first-fruits, offer some to their ancestors, calling them even by name, and clapping their hands to summon them. The people of Kobi and Sariputi, two villages in Ceram, "offer the first-fruits of the paddy in the form of cooked rice to their ancestors as a token of gratitude." The ceremony is called "Feeding the Dead." In the Tenimber and Timorlaut Islands, the first-fruits of the paddy are offered to the spirits of the ancestors, who are worshipped as guardian gods or household lares. The people of Luzon worship chiefly the souls of their ancestors, and offer to them the first-fruits of the harvest. In Fiji the earliest of the yams are presented to the ancestral ghosts in the sacred stone enclosure; and no man may taste of the new crop till after this presentation.

In other cases it is gods rather than ghosts to whom the offering is made, though among savages the distinction is for the most part an elusive one. But in not a few instances the first-fruits are offered, not to spirits or gods at all, but to the divine king himself, who is the living representative and earthly counterpart of his deified ancestors. Thus in Ashantee a harvest festival is held in September, when the yams are ripe. During the festival the king eats the new yams, but none of the people may eat them till the close of the festival, which lasts a fortnight. The Hovas, of Madagascar, present the first sheaves of the new grain to the sovereign. The sheaves are carried in procession to the palace from time to time as the grain ripens. So, in Burmah, when the *pangati* fruits ripen, some of them used to be taken to the king's palace that he might eat of them; no one might partake of them before the king. In short, what is offered in one place to the living chief is offered in another place to his dead predecessor, and is offered in a third place to the great deity who has grown slowly out of them. The god is the dead king; the king, as in ancient Egypt, is the living god, and the descendant of gods, his deified ancestors. Indeed, the first-fruits seem sometimes to be offered to the human victim himself, in his deified capacity, and sometimes to the Adonis, or Osiris, who is his crystallised embodiment. Our own harvest festival seems to preserve the offering in a Christianised form.

Finally, I will add that in many cases it looks as though

the divine agriculture-victim were regarded as the king in person, the embodiment of the village or tribal god, and were offered up, himself to himself, at the stone which forms the monument and altar of the primitive deity. Of this idea we shall see examples when we go on to examine the great corn-gods and wine-gods of the Mediterranean region.

CHAPTER XIV.

CORN- AND WINE-GODS.

IN advanced communities, the agricultural gods with whom we dealt in the last chapter come to acquire specific class-names, such as Attis and Adonis; are specialised as corn-gods, wine-gods, gods of the date-palm, or gods of the harvest; and rise to great distinction in the various religions.

I propose to examine at some length the more important of these in the Mediterranean civilisations, where Christianity was first evolved. And I begin with Dionysus.

One of the notable features of the Potraj festival of southern India, which Sir Walter Elliot has minutely described for us, and of which I gave a brief abstract in the previous chapter, is its orgiastic character. As type of the orgiastic god-making ceremonies, with their five-day festival, it well deserves some fuller description. The feast takes place near the temple of the village goddess, who is worshipped in the form of an unshapely stone, stained red with vermillion, the probable representative of the first human foundation-victim. An altar was erected behind this temple to the god who bears the name of Potraj. He is a deity of cultivation. The festival itself was under the charge of the Pariahs, or aboriginal outcasts; it was attended by all the lowest classes, including the dancing girls of the temple and the shepherds or other "non-Aryan" castes. During the festival, these people took temporarily the first place in the village; they appeared to form the court of the temporary king, and to represent the early local worship, whose gods the conquering races are afraid of offending. For since the dead of the conquered race are in possession of the soil, immigrant conquerors everywhere have a superstitious dread of incurring their displeasure. On the first day of the orgy, the low-caste people chose one of themselves as priest or Potraj.

On the second day of the feast, the sacred buffalo, already described as having the character of a theanthropic victim, was thrown down before the goddess; its head was struck off at a single blow, and was placed in front of the shrine, with one leg in its mouth. The carcase, as we saw already, was then cut up, and delivered to the cultivators to bury in their fields. The blood and offal were afterwards collected into a large basket; and the officiating priest, a low-caste man, who bore (like the god) the name of Potraj, taking a live kid, hewed it in pieces over the mess. The basket was then placed on the head of a naked man, of the leather-dresser class, who ran with it round the circuit of the village boundaries, scattering the fragments right and left as he went. The Potraj was armed with a sacred whip, like Osiris; and this whip was itself the object of profound veneration.

On the third and fourth days, many buffaloes and sheep were slaughtered; and on the fourth day, women walked naked to the temple, clad in boughs of trees alone; a common religious exercise of which I have only space here to suggest that St. Elizabeth of Hungary and the Godiva procession at Coventry are surviving relics. (These relations have well been elucidated by Mr. Sidney Hartland.)

On the fifth and last day, the whole community marched with music to the village temple, and offered a concluding sacrifice at the Potraj altar. A lamb was concealed close by. The Potraj, having found it after a pretended search, rendered it insensible by a blow of his whip, or by mesmeric passes—a survival of the idea of the voluntary victim. Then the assistants tied the Potraj's hands behind his back, and the whole party began to dance round him with orgiastic joy. Potraj joined in the excitement, and soon came under the present influence of the deity. He was led up, bound, to the place where the lamb lay motionless. Carried away with divine frenzy, he rushed at it, seized it with his teeth, tore through the skin, and eat into its throat. When it was quite dead, he was lifted up; a dishful of the meat-offering was presented to him; he thrust his blood-stained face into it, and it was then buried with the remains of the lamb beside the altar. After that, his arms were untied, and he fled the place. I may add that as a rule the slaughterer of the god everywhere has to fly from the vengeance of his worshippers, who, after participating in the attack, pretend indignation as soon as the sacrifice is completed.

The rest of the party now adjourned to the front of the temple, where a heap of grain deposited on the first day was divided among all the cultivators, to be sown by each one in the field with his piece of flesh. After this, a distribution was made of the piled-up heads of the buffaloes and sheep slaughtered on the third and fourth days. These were evidently considered as sacred as divine heads generally in all countries and ages. About forty of the sheeps' heads were divided among certain privileged persons; for the remainder, a general scramble took place, men of all castes soon rolling together on the ground in a mess of putrid gore. For the buffaloes' heads, only the Pariahs contended. Whoever was fortunate enough to secure one of either kind carried it off and buried it in his field. Of the special importance of the head in all such sacrifices, Mr. Gomme has collected many apposite examples.

The proceedings were terminated by a procession round the boundaries; the burial of the head of the sacred buffalo close to the shrine of the village goddess; and the outbreak of a perfect orgy, a "rule of misrule," during which the chief musician indulged in unbridled abuse of all the authorities, native or British.

I have given at such length an account of this singular festival, partly because it sheds light upon much that has gone before, but partly also because it helps to explain many elements in the worship of the great corn- and wine-gods. One point of cardinal importance to be noticed here is that the officiating priest, who was at one time also both god and victim, is called Potraj like the deity whom he represents. So, too, in Phrygia the combined Attis-victim and Attis-priest bore the name of Attis; and so in Egypt the annual Osiris-offering bore the name of Osiris, whom he represented.

If I am right, therefore, in the analogy of the two feasts Dionysus was in his origin a corn-god, and later a vine-god, annually slain and buried in order that his blood might fertilise the field or the vineyard. In the Homeric period, he was still a general god of cultivation: only later did he become distinctively the grape-god and wine-deity. There was originally, I believe, a Dionysus in every village; and this divine victim was annually offered, himself to himself, with orgiastic rites like those of Potraj. Mr. Laurence Gomme has already in part pointed out this equation of the Hellenic and the Indian custom. The earliest form of Dionysus-worship, on this hypothesis, would be the one which survived in Chios and Tenedos, where a living human being was orgiastically torn to pieces at the feast of Dionysus. At Orchomenus, the human victim was by custom a woman of the family of the Oleiæ (so that there were women Dionysi): at the annual festival, the priest of Dionysus pursued these women with a drawn sword, and if he caught one, he had the right to slay her. (This is the sacred-chance victim.) In other places, the ceremony had been altered in historical times: thus at Potniæ, in Bœotia, it was once the custom to slay a child as Dionysus; but later on, a goat, which was identified with the god, was substituted for the original human victim. The equivalence of the animal victim with the human god is shown by the fact that at Tenedos the new-born calf sacrificed to Dionysus—or *as* Dionysus—was shod in buskins, while the mother cow was tended like a woman in childbed.

Elsewhere we find other orgiastic rites still more closely resembling the Indian pattern. Among the Cretans, a Dionysus was sacrificed biennially under the form of a bull ; and the worshippers tore the living animal to pieces wildly with their teeth. Indeed, says Mr. Frazer, the rending and devouring of live bulls and calves seems to have been a regular feature of the Dionysiac rites. In some cities, again, the animal that took the place of the human victim was a kid. When the followers of Dionysus tore in pieces a live goat and drank its blood, they believed they were devouring the actual body and blood of the god. This eating and drinking the god is an important point, which will detain us again at a later stage of our enquiry.

I do not desire to dwell too long upon any one deity, or rather class of deities ; therefore I will say briefly here that when Dionysus became the annual or biennial vine-god victim, it was inevitable that his worshippers should have seen his resurrection and embodiment in the vine, and should have regarded the wine it yielded as the blood of the god. In this case, the identification was particularly natural, for could not every worshipper feel the god in the wine ? and did not the divine spirit within it inspire and intoxicate him ? To be "full of the god" was the natural expression for the resulting exhilaration ; the cult of the wine-spirit is thus one of those which stands on the surest and most intimate personal basis.

The death and resurrection of Dionysus are accordingly a physical reality. The god is annually killed in the flesh, as man, bull, or goat ; and he rises again in the vine, to give his blood once more for the good of his votaries. Moreover, he may be used as a fertiliser for many other trees ; and so we find Dionysus has many functions. He is variously adored as Dionysus of the tree, and more particularly of the fruit-bearing fig and apple. His image, like those of other tree-gods already encountered, was often an upright post, without arms, but draped (like the *ashera*) in a mantle, and with a bearded mask to represent the head, while green boughs projecting from it marked his vegetable character. He was the patron of cultivated trees; prayers were offered to him to make trees grow; he was honoured by fruit-growers, who set up an image of him, in the shape of a natural tree-stump, in the midst of their orchards. (Compare that last degraded and utilitarian relic, the modern scarecrow.) For other equally interesting facts, I would refer the reader once more to Mr. Frazer, whose rich store I must not further rifle. It seems to me obvious from his collection of facts that there was originally everywhere a separate local Dionysus, an annual man-god or woman-god victim (for which a beast was later substituted), and that only slowly did the worship of the individual Dionysi pass into the general worship of one great idealised god Dionysus. The great gods are at first classes, not individuals.

Mr. Gomme has further pointed out three interesting points of resemblance between the Dionysiac rites and the Indian Potraj festival. In the first place, Dionysus is sometimes represented to his worshippers by his head only—no doubt a preserved oracular head; and in any case a parallel to the importance of the head in the Indian ceremony. In the second place, the sacrificer of the calf at Tenedos was driven out and stoned after the fulfilment of the rite—a counterpart of the Potraj fleeing from the place after the slaughter of the lamb. And in the third place, the women worshippers of Dionysus attended the rites nude, crowned with garlands, and daubed over with dirt—a counterpart of the naked female votaries surrounded with branches of trees in the Indian festival. All three of these points recur abundantly in similar ceremonies elsewhere.

As a rule, I severely disregard mere myths, as darkeners

of counsel, confining my attention to the purely religious and practical elements of custom and worship. But it is worth while noting here for its illustrative value the Cretan Dionysus-myth, preserved for us in a Romanised form by Firmicus Maternus. Dionysus is there represented as the son of Zeus, a Cretan king; and this legend, dismissed cavalierly by Mr. Frazer as "Euhemeristic," at least encloses the old idea that the Dionysus-victim was at first himself a divine god-king, connected by blood with the supreme god or founder of the community. Hera, the wife of Zeus, was jealous of the child, and lured him into an ambush, where he was set upon by her satellites the Titans, who cut him limb from limb, boiled his body with various herbs, and ate it. Other forms of the myth tell us how his mother Demeter pieced together his mangled remains, and made him young again. More often, however, Dionysus is the son of Semele, and various other versions are given of the mode of his resurrection. It is enough for our purpose that in all of them the wine-god, after having been slain and torn limb from limb, rises again from the dead, and often ascends to his father Zeus in heaven. The resurrection, visibly enacted, formed in many places a part of the rite; though I cannot agree with Mr. Frazer's apparent and (for him) unusual suggestion that the rite grew out of the myth; I hold the exact opposite to have been the order of evolution.

On the whole, then, though I do not deny that the later Greeks envisaged Dionysus as a single supreme god of vegetation, nor that many abstract ideas were finally fathered upon the worship—especially those which identified the death and resurrection of the god with the annual winter sleep and spring revival—I maintain that in his origin the Dionysus was nothing more than the annual corn-victim, afterwards extended into the tree and vine victim, from whose grave sprang the pomegranate, that blood-red fruit, and whose life-juice was expressed as the god-giving wine. At first a yearly human victim, he was afterwards personated by a goat or a bull ; and was therefore represented in art as a bull, or a bull-horned man. Gradually identified with vegetation in general, he was regarded at last as the Flowery Dionysus, the Fig Dionysus, or even, like Attis, the god of the pine-tree. But all these, I believe, were later syncretic additions ; and I consider that in such primitive forms as the orgiastic crop-god of the Indian corn-festival we get the prime original of the Hellenic vine-deity.

I pass on to Osiris, in his secondary or acquired character as corn-god.

I have already expressed the belief, in which I am backed up by Mr. Loftie, that the original Osiris was a real historical early king of This by Abydos. But in the later Egyptian religion, after mystic ideas had begun to be evolved, he came to be regarded as the god of the dead, and every mummy or every justified soul was looked upon as an Osiris. Moreover, it seems probable that in Egypt the name of Osiris was also fitted to the annual slain corn-victim or corn-god. Thus all over Egypt there were many duplicates of Osiris ; notably at Busiris, where the name was attached to an early tomb like the one at Abydos. This identification of the new-made god with the historic ancestor, the dead king, or the tribal deity is quite habitual ; it is parallel to the identification of the officiating Potraj with the Potraj god, of the Attis-priest with Attis, of the Dionysus-victim with the son of Zeus: and it will meet us hereafter in savage parallels. Let us look at the evidence.

As in India, the Osiris festival lasted for five days. (The period is worth noting.) The ceremonies began with ploughing the earth. We do not know for certain that a human victim was immolated ; but many side-analogies would lead us to that conclusion, and suggest that as elsewhere the sacred victim was torn to pieces in the eagerness of the cultivators and worshippers to obtain a fragment of his fertilising body. For in the myth, Typhon cuts up the corpse of the god into fourteen pieces, which he scatters abroad (as the naked leather-dresser scatters the sacred buffalo) : and we know that in the Egyptian ceremonies one chief element was the search for the mangled portions of Osiris, the rejoicings at their discovery, and their solemn burial. On one of the days of the feast, a procession of priests went the round of the temples —or beat the bounds : and the festival closed with the erection of a pillar or stone monument to the Osiris, which, in a bas-relief, the king himself is represented as assisting in raising. I think it is impossible to overlook the general resemblance of these rites to the rites of Potraj.

I ought to add, though I cannot go into that matter fully here, that the many allusions to the flinging of the coffer containing the Osiris into the Nile are clear indications of the rain-charm obtained by throwing the human victim into a spring or river. In this case, however, it must of course be regarded locally as a charm to make the Nile rise in due season.

The character of the later Osiris, or the god-victim identified with him, as a corn and vegetable god, is amply borne out by several other pieces of evidence. Osiris, it is said, was the first to teach men the use of corn. He also introduced the cultivation of the vine. Mr. Frazer notes that in one of the chambers dedicated to Osiris in the great temple of Isis at Philæ, the dead body of Osiris is represented with stalks of corn springing from it, and a priest is watering the stalks from a pitcher which he holds in his hand. That human corn-victims were at least not unknown in Egypt we have on the direct authority of Manetho, who tells us that red-haired men used to be burned, and their ashes scattered with winnowing fans. (Similar cases elsewhere have been previously mentioned.) So, too, the legend tells us that Isis placed the severed limbs of Osiris on a corn-sieve. Red-haired oxen were also sacrificed in Egypt, apparently in order to produce red wheat. This is the analogue of the bull sacrificed as Dionysus.

Again, in the legend of Busiris, and the glosses or comments upon it, we get important evidence, the value of which has not fully been noted, I believe, by Mr. Frazer. The story comes to us in a Greek form; but we can see through it that it represents the myth which accounted for the Osiris sacrifice. The name Busiris means the city of Osiris, which was so called because the grave of an ancient Osiris (either a mummy, or a local chief identified with the great god of Abydos) was situated there. Human sacrifices were said to have been offered at his tomb; just as the Potraj sacrifice is offered at the shrine of the village goddess, and just as the annual victim elsewhere was sacrificed at the Terminus stone or the sacred stone of the foundation-god or goddess. The victims were red-haired men, and strangers. Their ashes were scattered abroad with winnowing fans. They were slain on the harvest-field, and mourned by the reapers (like Adonis and Attis) in the song which through a Greek mistake is known to us as the Maneros. The reapers prayed at the same time that Osiris might revive and return with renewed vigour in the following year. The most interesting point in this account, pieced together from Apollodorus, Diodorus, and Plutarch, is the fact that it shows us how the annual Osiris was identified with the old divine king who lay in his grave hard by; and so brings the case into line with others we have already considered and must still consider. As for the hunting after the pieces of Osiris's body, that is just like the hunting after the mangled pieces of Dionysus by Demeter. I interpret both the resurrection of Osiris, and the story of the fragments being pieced together and growing young again, told of Dionysus, as meaning that the scattered pieces, buried like those of the Khond Meriah, grow up again next year into the living corn for the harvest.

Furthermore, there exists to this day in Egypt an apparent survival of the ancient Osiris rite, in an attenuated form (like the mock mayors in England), which distinctly suggests the identification I am here attempting. In Upper Egypt, Klunzinger tells us, on the first day of the (Egyptian) solar year, when the Nile has usually reached its highest point, the regular government is suspended for three days in each district, and every town chooses its own temporary ruler. This temporary king (a local Osiris, as I believe) wears a conical cap, and a long flaxen beard, and is enveloped in a strange mantle. I say unhesitatingly, the dress of an Osiris, wearing the old royal cap of Upper Egypt. With a wand of office in his hands—like the crook which Osiris carries on the monuments—and attended by men disguised as scribes, executioners, and so forth, he proceeds to the governor's house. The governor allows himself to be deposed; the mock king, mounting the throne, holds a tribunal, to whose decisions even the governor himself must bow. In short, like other temporary kings, he really enjoys royal authority for the moment. After three days, however, the mock king is condemned to death; the envelope or shell in which he is encased is committed to the flames; and from its ashes creeps forth the Fellah who impersonated him. I do not doubt that the case here represents the antique coffer or mummy-case of Osiris.

In this graphic ceremonial, then, I see a survival, with the customary mitigations, of the annual Osiris sacrifice, once actually performed on a human victim. I do not doubt that in Egypt as elsewhere a mock king was formerly chosen in place of the real king to personate the descendant of Osiris, an Osiris himself; and that this substitute was put to death, and torn to pieces or burnt, while his ashes were winnowed and scattered over the land. It may also be worth while to enquire whether the scourge which Osiris holds in the bas-reliefs is not the equivalent of the divine whip of the Potraj, and the other whips which Mr. Gomme has so ingeniously correlated with that very venerable and mystic attribute.

I would suggest, then, that Osiris in his later embodiment was annually renewed as a corn and vine victim. Originally a king of Upper Egypt, or part of it, he was envisaged in later myth as a general culture-god. Isis, his sister and wife, discovered wheat and barley growing wild; and Osiris introduced these grains among his people, who thereupon abandoned cannibalism, and took to grain-growing. An annual victim, most often a stranger, identified with the racial god, was torn to pieces in his place; and Osiris himself was finally merged with the abstract spirit of vegetation, and supposed to be the parent of all trees. Just as the Corinthians, when ordered by an oracle to worship a certain pine tree "equally with the god," cut it down and made two images of Dionysus out of it, with gilt bodies and red-stained faces; so the Egyptians cut down a pine-tree, took out the heart, made an image of Osiris, and then buried it in the hollow of the tree from which it had been taken. Similar rites obtained in Attis-worship; and all alike bear witness to that late and abstract stage of thought where the primitive cultivation-victim has been sublimated and elevated into a generalised god of vegetation in the abstract. But this, which for Mr. Frazer is the starting-point, is for me the goal of the evolution of Osiris.

Let us next look very briefly at the case of Adonis.

The Adon or Lord commonly known as Thammuz was one of the chief elements in Syrian religion. He was closely connected with the namesake river Adonis, which rose by his grave at the sacred spring of Aphaca. We do not actually know, I believe, of a human Adonis-victim; but his death was annually lamented with a bitter wailing, chiefly by women. Images of him were dressed like corpses, and carried out as if for burial, and then thrown into the sea or into springs. This was evidently a rain charm, such as is particularly natural in a dry country like Syria. And I will add incidentally that I attribute to similar circumstances also some portion at least of the sanctity of rivers. In certain places, the resurrection of the Adonis was celebrated on the succeeding day. At Byblos, he also ascended into heaven before the eyes of his worshippers—a point worth notice from its Christian analogies. The blood-red hue of the river Adonis in spring—really due to the discoloration of the tributary torrents by red earth from the mountains—was set down to the blood of the god Adonis; the scarlet anemone sprang from his wounds. But the scholiast on Theocritus expressly explains the Adonis as " the sown corn;" and that he was " seed," like the common corn-victims in India and elsewhere, we can hardly doubt from the repeated stories of his death and resurrection. The so-called " gardens of Adonis," which were mimic representations of a tumulus planted with corn, formed a most noticeable part of the god's ritual. They consisted of baskets or pots, filled with earth, in which wheat, barley, flowers, and so forth were sown and tended by women ; and at the end of eight days they were carried out with the images of the dead Adonis, and flung into the sea or into springs. This was no doubt another case of a rain-charm. Mr. Frazer has collected several interesting examples of similar rites the whole world over.

A few other embodiments of the corn-god may be more hastily treated.

What Adonis was to Syria, Attis was to Phrygia. Originally he seems, according to Professor Ramsay, to have been represented by an annual priest-victim, who slew himself for the people to ensure fertility. This priest-victim himself bore the name of Attis, and was identified with the god whose worship he performed. In later days, instead of killing himself, he merely drew his own blood ; and there is reason to think that a pig was also substituted as duplicate victim, and that this pig was itself regarded as an Attis. Analogies exist with the Paschal lamb ; while the self-mutilation of Attis-worship has also features in common with Jewish circumcision. Moreover, the ceremonies were closely connected, at Pessinus at least, with the ancient sacred stone which bore the name of Cybele, and which was described as the Mother of the Gods ; this connexion exactly recalls that of the Potraj-god in India with the cult of the local village goddess. As I believe the village goddess to be the permanent form of the foundation human sacrifice, I also believe Cybele (gross Euhemerism as it may seem) to be the sacred stone of the original virgin who was sacrificed at the first foundation of Pessinus.

When the sacred stone of Cybele and the cult of Attis were removed to Rome (under circumstances to which I shall refer in a later chapter) the festival consisted of a five days' rite, like that of the Potraj. It took place at the spring equinox, as does our own equivalent festival of Easter. On the first day, a pine-tree was cut down in the woods, and the effigy of a young man was tied to it. This effigy no doubt represented the primitive human sacrifice, and its crucifixion answers exactly to the slaughter of the sacred buffalo in India. The second day yields nothing of importance ; on the third day, the Attis-priest drew blood from his own arms and presented it as an offering ; I would conjecture that this was a substitute for self-immolation, and that the self-immolation was originally performed by mutilation of the genitals. It was perhaps on this night that a mourning took place over the body of Attis, represented by an effigy, which was afterwards solemnly buried. On the fourth day came the Festival of Joy, on which, as Mr. Frazer believes, the resurrection of the god was celebrated. The fifth day closed with a procession to the brook Almo, in which the sacred stone of the goddess and her bullock-cart were bathed as a rain-charm. On the return, the cart was strewn with flowers. I think the close parallelism to the Indian usage is here fairly evident. Indeed, out of consideration for brevity, I have suppressed several other most curious resemblances.

Attis was thus essentially a corn-god. His death and resurrection were annually celebrated at Rome and at Pessinus. An Attis of some sort died yearly. The Attis of Pessinus was both priest and king ; it was perhaps at one time his duty to die at the end of his yearly reign as a corn-god for his people. One epithet of Attis was "very fruitful"; he was addressed as "the reaped yellow ear of corn"; and when an effigy took the place of the annual slain priest-king, this effigy itself was kept for a year, and then burnt as the priest-king himself would have been at an earlier period. It seems to me impossible to resist the cumulative weight of this singular evidence.

For the very curious customs and myths regarding Demeter, Persephone, and other female corn-victims, I must refer the reader once more to Mr. Frazer. It is true, the enquirer will there find the subject treated from the opposite standpoint; he will see the goddesses regarded as first corn-spirits, then animal, finally human: but after the examples I have here given of my own mode of envisaging the facts, I think the reader will see for himself what corrections to make for Mr. Frazer's animism and personal equation. I will only say here that in many countries, from Peru to Africa, a girl or woman seems to have been offered up as a corn-goddess; that this corn-goddess seems to have been sown with the seed, and believed to come to life again with the corn; and that several European harvest customs appear to be mitigations of the old ceremonial, with the usual substitution of an animal or an effigy for the human victim. Regarded in this light, Mr. Frazer's collection of facts about the Corn Baby affords an excellent groundwork for research; but though I could say much on the subject, I will refrain from it here, as I desire only at present to give such an outline as will enable the reader to understand my general principles. The half is often more than the whole; and I fear if I flesh out the framework too much, it may be difficult to follow the main line of my argument.

I cannot, however, refrain from mentioning that the ceremonies of "Carrying out Death" and "Burying the Carnival," which prevail all over Europe, retain many interesting features of the Potraj, Dionysus, and Attis-

Adonis festivals. The figure of Death—that is to say, as I understand it, the image of the dead human god—is often torn to pieces, and the fragments are then buried in the fields to make the crops grow well. But the Death is also drowned or burned; in the first case, like Adonis, in the second, like the Osiris in the modern Egyptian custom. And the analogies of the festivals to those of India and Western Asia must strike every attentive reader of Mr. Frazer's masterwork.

Two or three typical instances must suffice as examples. In Bohemia, the children carry a straw man out of the village, calling it Death, and then burn it, singing,

> Now carry we Death out of the village,
> The new summer into the village;
> Welcome, dear summer,
> Green little corn.

Here the relation of the ceremony to the primitive corn-sacrifice is immediately evident. And the making of the effigy out of straw is significant. At Tabor in Bohemia the image of Death is flung from a high rock into the water, evidently as a rain-charm, with a similar song, praying for "good wheat and rye." (Compare the ceremony of the Tarpeian rock, where the victim was at last a condemned criminal: as also the myths of immolation by jumping into the sea.) In Lower Bavaria the pantomime was more realistic; the *Pfingstl*, as the victim was called, was clad in leaves and flowers, and drenched with water. He waded into a brook up to his middle, while a boy pretended to cut off his head. In Saxony and Thüringen, the Wild Man, who represents the god, is killed in dumb show at Whitsuntide. His captors pretend to shoot him, and he falls as if dead, but is afterwards revived, as in the resurrection of Adonis and Dionysus. Such resurrections form a common episode in the popular corn-drama. I have found a case in Sussex. At Semic in Bohemia we have the further graphic point that the victim is actually described as the King, wears a crown of bark, and carries a wand as a sceptre, like the mock Osiris. Other kings are frequent elsewhere. In the Königgratz district, the King is tried, and, if condemned, is beheaded in pantomime. Near Schömberg, the mock victim used to be known as the Fool, another significant name, and was finally buried under straw and dung, a conjunction of obvious agricultural import. In Rottweil, the Fool is made drunk, and interred in straw amid Adonis-like lamentations. Elsewhere, the Fool, either in person or by a straw effigy, is flung into water. At Schluckenau, realism goes a stage further: the Wild Man wears a bladder filled with blood round his neck; this the executioner stabs, and the blood gushes forth on the ground. Next day, a straw man, made to look as like him as possible, is laid on a bier, and taken to a pool into which it is flung. In all these antique ceremonies it is imposible not to see a now playful survival of the primitive corn-sacrifice. Our own April Fool shows the last stage of degradation in such world-wide customs. Originally sent on a fool's errand to the place of sacrifice, so that he might go voluntarily, he is now merely sent in meaningless derision.

I will only add here that while corn-gods and wine-gods are the most notable members of this strange group of artificial deities, the sacred date-palm has its importance as well in the religions of Mesopotamia; and elsewhere the gods of the maize, the plantain, and the cocoanut rise into special or local prominence. So do the Rice-Spirit, the Oats-Wife, the Mother of the Rye, and the Mother of the Barley (or Demeter). All seem to be modifications of the primitive victim, sacrificed to make a spirit for the crop, or to act as "seed" for the date or the plantain.

CHAPTER XV.

SACRIFICE AND SACRAMENT.

WE have now arrived at a point where we can more fully understand those curious ideas of sacrifice and sacrament which lie at the root of so much that is essential in the Jewish, the Christian, and most other religions.

Mr. Galton tells us that to the Damaras, when he travelled among them, all meat was common property. No one killed an ox except as a sacrifice and on a festal occasion ; and when the ox was killed, the whole community feasted upon it indiscriminately. This is but a single instance of a feeling almost universal among primitive pastoral people. Cattle and other domestic animals, being regarded as sacred, are rarely killed ; and when they are killed, they are eaten at a feast as a social and practically religious rite—in short, sacramentally. I need not give instances of so well-known a principle ; I will content myself with quoting what Dr. Robertson Smith says of a particular race : "Among the early Semites generally, no slaughter was legitimate except for sacrifice."

Barbaric herdsmen, indeed, can hardly conceive of men to whom flesh meat is a daily article of diet. Mr. Galton found the idea very strange to his Damaras. Primitive pastoral races keep their domestic animals mainly for the sake of the milk, or as beasts of burden, or for the wool and hair ; they seldom kill one except for a feast, at which the gods are fellow-partakers. Indeed, it is probable, as the sequel will suggest, that domestic animals were originally kept as totems or ancestor-gods, and that the habit of eating the meat of sheep, goats, and oxen has arisen mainly out of the substitution of such a divine animal-victim for the divine human-victim of earlier usage. Our butchers' shops have their origin in mitigated sacrificial cannibalism.

Sacrifice, regarded merely as offering to the gods, has thus, I believe, two distinct origins. Its earliest, simplest, and most natural form is that whose development we have already traced,—the placing of small articles of food and drink at the graves of ancestors or kings or revered fellow-tribesmen. That from a very early period men have believed the dead to eat and drink, whether as corpse, as mummy, as ghost of buried friend, or as ethereal spirit of cremated chieftain, we have already seen with sufficient frequency. About the origin of these simplest and most primitive sacrifices, I think, there can be little doubt. Savages offer at the graves of their dead precisely those ordinary articles of food which they consumed while living, without any distinction of kind; and they continue to offer them in the same naïve way when the ghost has progressed to the status of one of the great gods of the community.

But there is another mode of sacrifice, superposed upon this, and gradually tending to be more or less identified with it, which yet, if I am right, had a quite different origin in the artificial production of gods about which I have written at considerable length in the last three chapters. The human or animal victim, thus slaughtered in order to make a new god or protecting spirit, came in time to be assimilated in thought to the older type of mere honorific offerings to the dead gods; and so gave rise to those mystic ideas of the god who is sacrificed, himself to himself, of which the sacrament of the Mass is the final and most mysterious outcome. Thus, the foundation-gods, originally killed in order to make a protecting spirit for a house or a tribal god for a city or vilage, came at last to be regarded as victims sacrificed to the Earth Goddess or to the Earth Demons; and thus, too, the Meriahs and other agricultural victims, originally killed in order to make a corn-god or a corn-spirit, came at last to be regarded as sacrifices to the Earth, or to some abstract Dionysus or Attis or Adonis. And since in the last case at least the god and the victim were still called by the same name and recognised as one, there grew up at last in many lands, and in both hemispheres, but especially in the Eastern Mediterranean basin, the mystic theory of the sacrifice of a god, himself to himself, in atonement or expiation, which forms the basis of the Christian Plan of Salvation. It is this secondary and derivative form of sacrifice, I believe, which is mainly considered in Professor Robertson Smith's elaborate and extremely valuable analysis.

I have said that the secondary form of sacrifice, which for brevity's sake I shall henceforth designate as the mystic, is found in most parts of the world and in both hemispheres. This naturally raises the question whether it has a single common origin, and antedates the dispersal of mankind through the hemispheres; or whether it has been independently evolved several times over in many lands by many races. For myself, I have no cut-and-dried answer to this abstruse question, nor do I regard it, indeed, as a really important one. On the one hand, there are many reasons for supposing that certain relatively high traits of thought or art were common property among mankind before the dispersion from the primitive centre, if a primitive centre ever existed. On the other hand, psychologists know well that the human mind acts with extraordinary similarity in given circumstances all the world over, and that identical stages of evolution seem to have been passed through independently by many races, in Egypt and Mexico, in China and Peru; so that we can find nothing inherently improbable in the idea that even these complex conceptions of mystic sacrifice have distinct origins in remote countries. What is certain is the fact that among the Aztecs, as among the Phrygians, the priest who sacrificed, the victim he slew, and the image or great god to whom he slew him, were all identified ; the killer, the killed, and the being in whose honor the killing took place were all one single indivisible deity. Even such details as that the priest clothed himself in the skin of the victim are common to many lands ; they may very well be either a heritage from remote ancestral humanity, or the separate product of the human mind, working along like grooves under identical conditions. In one word they may perhaps be necessary and inevitable corollaries from antecedent conceptions.

I must further premise that no religion as we now know it is by any means primitive. The most savage creeds we find among us have still hundreds of thousands of years behind them. The oldest religions whose records have descended to us, like those of Egypt and of Assyria, are still remote by hundreds of thousands of years from the prime original. Cultivation itself is a very ancient and immemorial art. Few savages, even among those who are commonly described as in the hunting stage, are wholly ignorant of some simple form of seed-sowing and tillage. The few who are now ignorant of those arts show some apparent signs of being rather degenerate than primitive peoples. My own belief or suspicion is that ideas derived from the set of practices in connexion with agriculture detailed in the last two chapters have deeply coloured the life and thought of almost the whole human race, including even those rudest tribes which now know little or nothing of agriculture. But I do not lay stress upon this half-formed conviction, to justify which would lead me too far afield. I shall be content with endeavouring to suggest how far they have coloured the ideas of the greater number of existing nations.

Early pastoral races seldom kill a beast except on great occasions. When they kill it, they devour it in common, all the tribe being invited to the festival. But they also eat it in fellowship with their gods ; every great feast is essentially a Theoxenion, a Lectisternium, a banquet in which the deities participate with mortals. It is this sense of a common feast of gods and men which gave, no doubt, the first step towards the complex idea of the sacramental meal —an idea still further developed at a later stage by the addition of the concept that the worshipper eats and drinks the actual divinity.

My own belief is that all sacrificial feasts of this god-eating character most probably originated in actual cannibalism; and that later an animal victim was substituted for the human meat; but I do not insist on this point, nor attempt, strictly speaking, to prove it. It is hardly more than a deeply grounded suspicion. Nevertheless, I will begin for convenience' sake with the cannibal class of sacrifice, and will come round in time to the familiar slaughter of sheep and oxen, which in many cases is known to have supplanted a human offering.

Acosta's account of the Mexican custom is perhaps the best instance we now possess of the ritual of cannibal mystic sacrifice in its fullest barbarity. "They took a captive," says that racy old author, "at random; and before sacrificing him to their idols, they gave him the name of the idol to whom he should be sacrificed, and dressed him in the same ornaments, identifying him with the god. During the time that the identification lasted, which was for a year in some feasts, six months or less in others, they reverenced and worshipped him in the same manner as the idol itself. Meanwhile, he was allowed to eat, drink, and make merry. When he went through the streets, the people came forth to worship him; and every one brought alms, with children and sick people that he might cure them and bless them. He did as he pleased in everything, except that he had ten or twelve men about him, to prevent him from escaping. In order that he might be reverenced as he passed, he sometimes sounded upon a small flute, to tell the people to worship him. When the feast arrived, and he had grown fat, they killed him, opened him, and making a solemn sacrifice, eat him." There, in the words of a competent authority, we have the simple cannibal feast in its fullest nakedness.

I need hardly point out how much this account recalls the Khond custom of the Meriah. The victim, though not really of royal blood, is made artificially into a divine king; he is treated with all the honours of royalty and godhead, is dressed like the deity with whom he is identified, and is finally killed and eaten. The last point alone differs in any large degree from the case of the Meriah. We have still to enquire, " Why did they eat him ? "

The answer to this enquiry takes us into the very heart and core of the sacramental concept.

It is a common early belief that to eat of any particular animal gives you the qualities of that animal. The Miris of Northern India prize tiger's flesh for men; it gives them strength and courage; but women must not eat it; 'twould make them " too strong-minded." The Namaquas abstain from eating hare; they would become faint-hearted if they swallowed it ; but they eat the meat of the lion or drink the blood of the leopard, in order to gain their strength and courage. Among the Dyaks, young men and warriors must not eat deer ; it would render them cowardly ; but women and very old men are allowed to eat it. Men of the Buro and Aru Islands feed on the flesh of dogs in order to be bold and nimble. Mr. Frazer has collected an immense number of similar instances, which show both how widespread and how deep-seated are such beliefs. Even scrapings of the bones are sufficient to produce the desired result ; in Corea, the bones of tigers fetch a higher price than those of leopards as inspirers of courage. The heart of a lion is also particularly good for this purpose; and the tongues of birds are recommended for eloquence.

Again, on the same analogy, the flesh and blood of brave men are eaten in order to inspire bravery. The Australian Kamilaroi eat the heart and liver of a valiant warrior in order to acquire his courage. The Philippine Islanders drink the blood of their bravest enemies. In the Shire

Highlands of Africa, those who kill a distinguished fighter eat his heart to get his courage. Du Chaillu's negro attendants, we saw, scraped their ancestors' skulls, and drank the powder in water. "Our ancestors were brave," said they; "and by drinking their skulls, we shall be brave as they were." Here again I can only refer the reader for numerous examples to Mr. Frazer's inexhaustible storehouse.

The case of Du Chaillu's warriors, however, takes us with one bound into the heart of the subject. Many savages for similar reasons actually eat their own dead fathers.* We learn from Strabo that the ancient Irish "deemed it honourable to devour the bodies of their parents." So, Herodotus tells us, did the Issedones of Central Asia. The Massagetæ used "from compassion" to club and eat their aged people. The custom was quite recently common among the Battas of Sumatra, who used "religiously and ceremonially to eat their old relations." In Australia, it was usual to eat relatives who died by mischance. Of the Cucumas we read that "as soon as a relation died, these people assembled and eat him roasted or boiled, according as he was thin or fat." The Tarianas and Tucanas, who drink the ashes of their relatives, "believe that thus the virtues of the deceased will be transmitted to the drinkers." The Arawaks think it the highest mark of honour they could pay to the dead to drink their powdered bones mixed in water. Generally speaking, in a large number of cases, the parents or relatives were eaten in order "not to let the life go out of the family"; or to preserve the bodies and souls in a kindred body; or to gain the courage and other qualities of the dead relation. In short, the dead were eaten sacramentally or, as one writer even phrases it, "eucharistically." Mr. Hartland has collected many striking instances.

How this strange custom originates we may guess from

---

* Since this chapter was written, the subject of honorific cannibalism has been far more fully treated by Mr. Sidney Hartland in the chapter on Funeral Rites, in the second volume of *The Legend of Perseus*.

Mr. Wyatt Gill's description of a New Guinea funeral. "The women lacerated their faces and beat their breasts most affectingly," he says; "and then, in the madness of their grief, pressed the matter out of the wounded thigh, and smeared it over their faces and persons, and even licked it up." Of the Koiari corpses he says: "A fire is kept burning day and night at the head and feet for months. The entire skin is removed by means of the thumb and forefinger, and the juices plastered all over the face and body of the operator,—parent, husband, or wife of the deceased. The fire gradually desiccates the flesh, so that little more than the skeleton is left." This naturally leads on to eating the dead, which indeed is practised elsewhere in New Guinea.

But if men eat the bodies of their fathers, who are their family and household gods, they will also naturally eat the bodies of the artificial gods of cultivation, or of the temporary kings who die for the people. By eating the body of a god, you absorb his divinity; he and you become one; he is in you and inspires you. This is the root-idea of sacramental practice; you eat your god by way of complete union; you subsume him in yourself; you and he are one being.

Still, how can you eat your god if you also bury him as a corn-spirit to use him as seed? The Gonds supply us with the answer to that obvious difficulty. For, as we saw, they sprinkle the blood of the victim over the ploughed field or ripe crop, and then they sacramentally devour his body. Such a double use of the artificial god is frequently to be detected, indeed, through the vague words of our authorities. We see it in the Potraj ceremony, where the blood of the lamb is drunk by the officiating priest, while the remainder of the animal is buried beside the altar; we see it in the numerous cases where a portion of the victim is eaten sacramentally, and the rest burned and scattered over the fields, which it is supposed to fertilise. You eat your god in part, so as to imbibe his divinity; but you bury him in part, so as to secure at the same time his fertilising qualities for your corn or your vineyard.

I admit that all this is distinctly mystic; but mystery-mongering and strange reduplication of persons, with marvellous identifications and minute distinctions, have always formed much of the stock-in-trade of religion. If cults were all plain sailing throughout, what room for faith?—there would be less to engage the imagination of the votary.

And now let us return awhile to our Mexican instances.

At the annual feast of the great god Tezcatlipoca, which, like most similar festivals, fell about the same time as the Christian Easter, a young man was chosen to be the representative of the god for a twelvemonth. As in the case of almost all chosen victims, he had to be a person of unblemished body, and he was trained to behave like a god-king with becoming dignity. During his year of godship, he was lapped in luxury; and the actual reigning emperor took care that he should be splendidly attired, regarding him already as a present deity. He was attended by eight pages clad in the royal livery—which shows him to have been a king as well as a god; and wherever he went the people bowed down to him. Twenty days before the festival at which he was to be sacrificed, four noble maidens, bearing the names of four goddesses, were given him to be his brides. The final feast itself, like those of Dionysus, of Attis, and of Potraj, occupied five days—a coincidence between the two hemispheres which almost points to original identity of custom before the dispersion of the races. During these five days the real king remained in his palace —and this circumstance plainly shows that the victim belonged to the common class of substituted and temporary divine king-gods. The whole court, on the other hand, attended the victim. On the last day of the feast, the victim was ferried across the lake in a covered barge to a small temple in the form of a pyramid. On reaching the summit, he was seized and held down on a block of stone,—no doubt an altar of funereal origin,—while the priest cut open his breast with a stone knife, and plucked his heart out. This he offered to the god of the sun. The head was hung up among the skulls of previous victims, no doubt for oracular purposes, and as a permanent god; but the legs and arms were cooked and prepared for the table of the lords, who thus partook of the god sacramentally. His place was immediately filled by another young man, who for a year was treated with the same respect, and at the end of that time was similarly slaughtered.

I do not think I need point out the close resemblance of this ritual to that of the Khond Meriah, of the Potraj, and of the festivals of Dionysus, Osiris, Attis, and Adonis. But I would also call particular attention to the final destination of the skull, and its exact equivalence to the skull of the animal-god in India and elsewhere.

"The idea that the god thus slain in the person of his representative comes to life again immediately," says Mr. Frazer, "was graphically represented in the Mexican ritual by skinning the slain man-god, and clothing in his skin a living man, who thus became the new representative of the godhead." For example, at an annual festival in Mexico, a woman was sacrificed who represented Toci, the Mother of the Gods—a sort of yearly Mexican Cybele. She was dressed in the ornaments and bore the name of the goddess of whom she was believed to be an incarnation. After being feasted for several days, she was taken at midnight to the summit of a temple, and there beheaded. Her body was flayed, and one of the priests, clothing himself in the skin, became the representative of the goddess Toci. The skin of the woman's thigh, however, was separately removed, and a young man who represented the god Cinteotl, the son of Toci, wrapt it round him like a mask. Ceremonies then followed, in which the two men, clad in the woman's skin, enacted the parts of the god and goddess. In all this, there is much that seems to me reminiscent of Isis and Horus, of Cybele and Attis, of Semele and Dionysus, and of several other eastern rituals.

Still more significant is the yearly festival of the god Totec, who was represented in like manner by a priest, clad in the skin of a human victim, and who received offerings of first-fruits and first-flowers, together with bunches of maize which had been kept for seed. Here we have the closest possible analogy to the case of the Meriah. The offering of first-fruits, made sometimes to the king, sometimes to the ancestral spirits, is here made to the human god of cultivation, who represents both in his own person.

Many other cannibal sacrifices are recorded in Mexico: in more than one of them it was customary for the priest to tear out the warm throbbing heart of the victim, and present it to the idol. Whether these sacrifices in each particular case were of the ordinary or of the mystic type it is not always quite easy to decide; probably the worshippers themselves did not accurately discriminate in every instance. But however that may be, we know at least this much: when human sacrifices had been rare, the priests reminded the kings that the gods "were starving with hunger"; war was then made on purpose to take prisoners, "because the gods had asked for something to eat"; and thousands of victims were thus slaughtered annually. The blood of the victims was separately offered; and I may add in this connexion that as a rule both ghosts and gods are rather thirsty than hungry. I take the explanation of this peculiar taste to be that blood and other liquids poured upon the ground of graves or at altar-stones soon sink in, and so seem to have been drunk or sucked up by the ghost or god; whereas meat and solid offerings are seen to be untouched by the deity to whom they are presented. A minor trait in this blood-loving habit of the gods is seen in the fact that the Mexicans also gave the god to drink fresh blood drawn from their own ears, and that the priests likewise drew blood from their legs, and daubed it on the temples. Similar mitigations of self-immolation are seen elsewhere in the Attis-priest drawing blood from his arms for Attis, in the Hebrew Baal-priests "cutting themselves for Baal," and in the familiar Hebrew rite of circumcision. Blood is constantly drawn by survivors or worshippers as an act of homage to the dead or to deities.

I might multiply instances of human sacrifices of the mystic order elsewhere, but I prefer to pass on to the various mitigations which they tend to undergo in various communities. In its fullest form, I take it, the mystic sacrifice ought to be the self-immolation of a divine priest-king, a god and descendant of gods, himself to himself, on the altar of his own divine foundation-ancestor. But in most cases which we can trace, the sacrifice has already assumed the form of an immolation of a willing victim, a temporary king, of the divine stock only by adoption, though sometimes a son or brother of the actual monarch. Further modifications are that the victim becomes a captive taken in war (which indeed is implied in the very etymology of the Latin word *victima*), or a condemned criminal, or an imbecile, who can be more readily induced to undertake the fatal office. Of all of these we have seen hints at least in previous cases. Still more mitigated are the forms in which the victim is allowed to escape actual death by a subterfuge, and those in which an image or effigy is allowed to do duty for the living person. Of these intermediates we get a good instance in the case of the Bhagats, mentioned by Col. Dalton, who "annually make an image of a man in wood, put clothes and ornaments on it, and present it before the altar of a Mahadeo" (or rude stone phallic idol). "The person who officiates as priest on the occasion says, 'O, Mahadeo, we sacrifice this man to you according to ancient customs. Give us rain in due season, and a plentiful harvest.' Then, with one stroke of the axe, the head of the image is struck off, and the body is removed and buried." This strange rite shows us a surviving but much mitigated form of the Khond Meriah practice.

As a rule, however, such bloodless representations do not please the gods ; nor do they succeed in really liberating a ghost or corn-god. They are after all but feeble phantom sacrifices. Blood the gods want, and blood is given them. The most common substitute for the human victim-god is therefore the animal victim-god, of which we have already seen copious examples in the ox and kid of Dionysus, the pig of Attis, and many others. It seems probable that a large number of sacrifices, if not the majority of those in which domestic animals are slain, belong in the last resort to the same category. Thus, indeed, we can most easily explain the theory of the so-called "theanthropic" victim,—the animal which stands for a man and a god,—as well as the point of view of sacrifice so ably elaborated by Dr. Robertson Smith.

According to this theory, the domestic animals were early regarded as of the same kin or blood as the tribe ; and the slaughter of an ox, a goat, or a sheep could only be permitted if it were done, like the slaughter of a king's son, sacrificially and sacramentally. In my own opinion, this scarcely means more than that the sacred domestic animals were early accepted as substitutes for the human victim, and that they were eaten sacrificially and sacramentally as the human victim was also eaten. But I will waive this somewhat controversial point, and content myself with suggesting that the animal victim was habitually treated as in itself divine, and that its blood was treated in the same way as the blood of the original cannibal offering. At the same time, the sacrifice was usually offered at the altar of some older and, so to speak, more constant deity, while the blood of the victim was allowed to flow over the sacred stone. Certainly, both among the Arabs and the Hebrews, all slaughter of domestic animals appears to have been at one time sacrificial ; and even when the slaughter ceased necessarily to involve a formal sacrifice, it was still thought necessary to slay the victim in the name of a god, and to pour out the blood in his honour on the ground. Even in the Græco-Roman world, the mass of butcher's meat was "meat offered to idols." We shall see hereafter that among existing savages the slaughter of domestic animals is still regarded as a sacred rite.

I believe also that as a rule the blood-offering is the earliest and commonest form of slaughter to the gods; and that the victim in the earlier stages was generally consumed by the communicants, as we know the cannibal victim to have been consumed among the Mexicans, and as we saw the theanthropic goat or kid was orgiastically devoured by the worshippers of Dionysus. It is a detail whether the sacred victim happened to be eaten raw or cooked; the one usage prevailed in the earlier and more orgiastic rites, the other in the milder and more civilised ceremonies. But in either case, the animal-god, like the human god, was eaten sacramentally by all his worshippers, who thus took into themselves his divine qualities. The practice of burning the victim, on the other hand, prevailed mainly, I think, among cremationists, like the Tyrians and Hellenes, though it undoubtedly extended also to many burying peoples, like the Hebrews and Egyptians. In most cases even of cremated victims, it would appear, a portion at least of the animal was saved from the fire and sacramentally eaten by the worshippers.

Once more, the victim itself was usually a particular kind of sacred animal. This sacredness of the chosen beast has some more important bearings than we have yet considered. For among various pastoral races, various domesticated animals possess in themselves positive sanctity. We know, for example,, that cows are very holy in the greater part of India, and buffaloes in the Deccan. Among the African peoples of the pastoral tribes, the common food is milk and game; cattle are seldom slaughtered merely to eat, and always on exceptional or sacred occasions—the very occasions which elsewhere demand a human victim—such as the proclamation of a war, a religious festival, a wedding, or the funeral of a great chieftain. In such cases, the feast is public, all blood-relations having a natural right to attend. The cattle-kraal itself is extremely sacred. The herd and its members are treated by their masters with affectionate and almost brotherly regard.

A few further points must also be added. Among early races, to kill and eat wild animals, or to kill and eat enemies, who are not members of the tribe, is not accounted in any way wrong. But to kill a tribesman—to shed kindred blood—is deeply sinful; and so it is sinful to kill and eat the domestic herds. In old age, indeed, or when sick and feeble, you may kill and eat your blood-relation blamelessly; and so you may also kill and eat old or sickly cattle. But as a rule, you only eat them sacramentally and sacrificially, under the same circumstances where you would be justified in killing and eating a human victim. Thus, as a rule, each tribe has its own sacred beast, which is employed as a regular substitute for a man-god. Among the Arabs, this beast was a camel; among the Indian peoples, the bull or the buffalo; among shepherd races, it is the sheep or goat; among the Teutons, the horse; among many settled urban peoples, the pig; and with the Samoyeds and Ostiaks, their one chattel, the reindeer.

Also, as a rule, the cow or other female animal was not usually sacrificed; she was kept for milk-yielding. It was the bull, the ram, the ox, the he-goat that was oftenest offered and eaten sacramentally. Mere utilitarian considerations would soon lead to this use, just as our own butchers kill ram lambs by choice, and spare the ewes for breeding. The custom, once introduced, would tend to become sacred; for whatever our divine ancestors did is itself divine, and should not be lightly or carelessly altered. Hence we can understand that supreme sanctity of the cow, which has made so many races refuse to sacrifice it, while they sacrifice and eat the bull or ox without let or scruple. Thus the Todas have never eaten the flesh of the female buffalo; but the male they eat once a year, sacramentally, all the adult men in the village joining in the ceremony of killing and roasting it.

A remarkable instance of the theanthropic sacrifice of such a sacred animal is given us in Nilus's account of the ceremony performed by the Arabs of his time. A holy camel, chosen as a victim, was bound upon a rude cairn of piled-up stones. In this primitive altar we can hardly fail to recognise the grave of an early tribal chieftain. The leader of the band then led the worshippers thrice round the cairn in a solemn procession, chanting a solemn hymn as they went. As the last words of the hymn were sung, he fell upon the camel (like Potraj on the lamb), wounded it, and hastily drank of the blood that gushed out from it. Forthwith the whole company fell on the victim with their swords, hacked off pieces of the quivering flesh, and devoured them raw with such wild haste that between the rise of the day-star and that of the sun, the entire camel, body and bones, skin, blood, and entrails, was absolutely eaten. I need not point out the close resemblance of this savage rite to those of Potraj and of Dionysus. It is a point, however, to observe that here also the blood falls on the cairn or grave or altar. I may note that the annual sacrifice of the paschal lamb among the shepherd Hebrews is obviously a mere mitigation of this barbarous rite. In that case, as might be expected in a more civilised race, the victim is roasted whole: but it is similarly necessary that every part of it should be hastily eaten. Legend further informs us, in the instance of the Passover, that the lamb was a substitute for a human victim, and that the first-born were sanctified to Jahweh, instead of being sacrificed. Note also that the feast of the paschal lamb occupied the now familiar space of five days: the sacred animal was chosen on the tenth day of the month, and sacrificed on the fourteenth. The whole ceremonial is most illustrative and full of survivals.

Though it breaks for a moment the thread of my argument, I find it impossible not to mention here the curious parallel case of the judicial sacrifice among the Battas of Sumatra, which is the human analogue of the Arabian camel-sacrament. Only in this instance, as in so many others, sacrifice and punishment merge into one another. "With them the adulterer, the night-thief, and those who had treacherously attacked a town, a village, or a particular person, were condemned to be eaten by the people. They were tied to three posts; their legs and their arms were stretched out in the shape of a St. Andrew's cross; and then, when a signal was given, the populace rushed upon the body and cut it into fragments with hatchets or with knives, or perhaps more simply with their nails and their teeth. The strips so torn off were devoured instantly, all raw and bloody; they were merely dipped into a cocoanut bowl containing a sauce prepared beforehand of lemon-juice and salt. In the case of adultery, the outraged husband had the right of choosing first what piece he liked best. The guests invited to the feast performed this work with so much ardour that they often tore and hurt each other." I do not think we can read this account without being struck by its close analogy to many of our previous sacrifices, both of human corn-gods and of sacred animals. The criminal is here nothing more than the substitute for a holy human victim.

And now we must also remember that in most countries the gods were housemates of their worshippers, present at all times in every home, and partakers of every meal, side by side with the living. They lived in the house, as still in New Guinea. Libations to them were poured from every cup; food was offered to their ghosts or skulls or wooden images at every family gathering. The ordinary feasts were thus mere enlarged festal gatherings, at which a victim was sacrificially slain and sacramentally eaten; and the visitors believed they were eating the body and blood of the god to their own salvation. Greater sacrifices, like the hecatombs, or the heroic Indian horse-sacrifice, must have been relatively rare ; but in all of them we see clear proof that the victim was regarded as a sacred animal, that is to say a god, in one of his embodiments.

Clear evidence of this equivalence is seen in the fact that the worshippers often clad themselves in the skin of the victim, as the Mexicans did in the skin of the annual god. Sometimes the hide is even used to deck the idol. In the Cyprian sacrifice of a sheep to the sheep-goddess Aphrodite, the celebrants wore the skin of the sheep ; while the Assyrian Dagon-worshipper offered the fish-sacrifice to the fish-god, clad in a fish-skin. Of similar import is doubtless the ægis or goat-skin of Athena, envisaged as a goat-goddess, and the skins used in the Dionysiac mysteries. I do not hesitate to affiliate all these on a primitive usage like that of the Mexican cannibal sacrifice.

Having reached this point, we can see further that the case where a sacred animal, the representative of a human victim, is slaughtered before the altar of an older god is exactly equivalent to the other known case where a human victim is slaughtered before the foundation-stone of a town or village. In either case, there is a distinct renewal of the divine life; fresh blood, as it were, is instilled by the act into the ancient deity. All the other concomitants are precisely the same. Thus at the Theban sacrifice of a ram to the ram-god Amen, the worshippers bewailed the victim, as the women bewailed Adonis and Attis ; and the image of Amen was finally draped in the skin of the victim, while its body was buried in a sacred coffin. At the Buphonia or sacramental ox-slaying in Athens, there was a regular trial after the victim was slain, everybody throwing the blame on one another, till at last the knife that inflicted the wound was found guilty of murder and cast into the sea. (This casting into the sea of a guilt-bearer for the community will meet us again when we come to consider the doctrine of the atonement.) So we saw that the Potraj fled after the performance of his sanguinary sacrifice ;

and so too the slayer of the Dionysus-calf at Tenedos fled for his life when the ceremony was completed. Indeed, we get many intermediate cases, like that of the goat dressed up as a girl which was offered theanthropically to Artemis Munychia, or that of the Dionysus-calf clad in buskins, whose mother-cow was treated as a woman in child-birth. To me, all these instances are obvious attempts to palm off, as it were, on the gods a sacred animal in place of a genuine human victim. They are little more than divine legal fictions, eked out, no doubt, by the fiction of kinship between the herd and its masters.

As a whole, then, we may venture to say not perhaps that all, but that a great number of sacrifices, and certainly the best-known among historic nations, are slaughters of animal substitutes for human victims; and that the flesh is sacramentally consumed by the worshippers.

There is one special form of this animal sacrifice, however, which I cannot here pass over in complete silence. It is the one of which the harvest-feast is the final relic. Mr. Frazer has fully worked out this theme in his fascinating essay: to detail it here at length would occupy too much space; I can only give the barest outline of his instances. Originally, it would seem, the corn-god or corn-spirit was conceived during the reaping as taking refuge in the last sheaf left standing. Whoever cut that wisp of corn slew the corn-spirit, and was therefore, on the analogy of the slayer of the divine king, himself the corn-spirit. Mr. Frazer does not absolutely assert that this human representative was originally killed and eaten, though all analogy would seem to suggest it; but that he was at least killed is abundantly certain; and killed he still is, in dumb show at any rate, on many modern European corn-fields. More often, however, the corn-spirit is supposed to be embodied in any animal which happens to be found in the last sheaf, where even now small creatures like mice and hedgehogs often take refuge. In earlier times, however, wolves, wild boars, and other large animals seem to have been frequently met with under similar circumstances. However that may be, a great many beasts—generally sacred beasts—are or have been sacramentally eaten as representatives of the corn-god ; while, conversely, the last sheaf is often made up into the image of a man or still more often of a woman, and preserved religiously for a year, like the annual king, till the next harvest. Sometimes a cock is beheaded and eaten at the harvest feast, special importance being here attached to its head, as to the head of the human victim in so many other cases. Sometimes, as with the ancient Prussians, it was the corn-goat whose body was sacramentally eaten. Sometimes, as at Chambéry, an ox is slaughtered, and eaten with special rites by the reapers at supper. Sometimes, it is the old sacred Teutonic animal, the horse, that is believed to inhabit the last wisp of corn. I will add parenthetically here (what I trust in some future work to show) that we have probably in this and kindred ideas the origin of the sacred and oracular heads of horses and oxen attached to temples or built into churches. Sometimes, again, it is a pig that represents the god, and is ceremonially eaten at the harvest festival.

I need hardly mention that all these sacred animals, substitutes for the original human god, find their parallels in the festivals of Dionysus, Attis, Osiris, Demeter, Adonis, Lityerses, and the other great corn and wine gods of the historic civilisations.

But there is yet another and more sublimated form of sacramental feast. Since the corn-god and the wine-god, when slain, undergo resurrection in the corn and the vine, may we not also eat their bodies as bread, and drink their blood as wine or soma?

To people already familiar, first with the honorific cannibal form of god-eating, and then with its gentler animal-victim modification, nothing could be more natural than this slight transference of feeling. Nay, more : whoever eat bread and drank wine from the beginning must have known it was the body and blood of a god he was eating and drinking. Still, there is a certain difference between mere ordinary every-day food and the sacramental feast, to which sacred cannibalism and animal-sacrifice had now familiarised men's minds. Accordingly, we find in many cases that there exists a special *sacramental* eating and drinking of bread and wine, which is more especially regarded as eating the body and drinking the blood of the deity.

Some curious illustrative facts may here be cited. Since straw and corn grow from the slaughtered corn-god, they may be regarded as one of his natural embodiments. Hence, when human sacrifices are prohibited, people sometimes make a straw god do duty for a human one. The Gonds, we saw, used once to kidnap sacred Brahman boys—gods by race, as it were, yet strangers and children—scatter their blood over the fields, and eat their bodies sacramentally. But when the unsympathetic British government interfered with the god-making habits of the Gond people, they took, says Col. Dalton, to making an image of straw instead, which they now similarly sacrifice. So it may be noted in many of the ceremonies of "Burying the Carnival" and the like, which I have already cited, that a straw man is substituted symbolically for the human victim. Indeed, in that singular set of survivals we have every possible substitute—the mock king, the imbecile, the pretended killing, the ceremonial shedding of blood, the animal victim, and the straw man or effigy. I may add that even the making of our modern Guy Fawkes as "a man of straw" is thus no mere accident. But we get a very similar use of corn in the curious practice of fashioning the corn-wife and the corn-baby, so fully detailed by Mr. Frazer. In this attenuated survival of human sacrifice, a sheaf of corn does duty for a human victim, and represents the life of the corn-god or corn-spirit from one year to another. All the existing evidence goes to suggest the idea that at harvest a corn-maiden or corn-wife, after a year of deification, was slain in former times, and that the human victim is now represented by her vegetable analogue or equivalent, the corn in the ear, a sheaf of which does duty in her place, and reigns as corn-queen till the next year's harvest. The corn-baby is thus a temporary queen, made of corn, not of human flesh and blood. We may compare with this case the account of the Sioux girl who was sacrificed by the Pawnees, by being burned over a slow fire, and then shot (like St. Sebastian) with arrows. The chief sacrificer tore out her heart and devoured it, thus eating the goddess in true cannibal fashion. While her flesh was still warm, it was cut up into small pieces and taken to the corn-field. Drops of blood were squeezed from it upon the grains of seed-corn ; after which it was all covered up in the ground to form a crop-raiser. Of such a ghastly goddess-making ceremony, our seemingly innocent harvest comedy of the corn-baby is probably the last surviving relic. Mr. Frazer rightly connects it with the cult of the Athenian Korê, Persephone. I think, indeed, the double form of the name, " the Old Woman " and " the Corn-baby," makes it probable that the pair are the vegetable equivalents of both Demeter and her ravished daughter.

In other cases, however, it is the actual bread and wine themselves, not the straw or the corn in the ear, that represent the god and are sacramentally eaten. We owe to Mr. Frazer most of our existing knowledge of the wide prevalence and religious importance of this singular ritual.

We have seen already that in many countries the first-fruits of the crops are presented either to ancestral ghosts, or to the great gods, or else to the king, who is the living god and present representative of the divine ancestors. Till this is done, it would be unsafe to eat of the new harvest. The god within it would kill you. But in addition to the ceremonial offering of first-fruits to the spirits, many races also " eat the god " in the new corn or rice sacramentally. In Wermland, in Sweden, the farmer's wife uses the grain of the last sheaf (in which, as we saw, the corn-god or corn-spirit is supposed specially to reside), in order to bake a loaf in the shape of a little girl. Here we have the maiden, who was previously sacrificed as a corn-goddess or Persephone, reappearing once more in a bread image. This loaf is divided among all the household and eaten by them. So at La Palisse in France, a man made of dough is hung upon the fir-tree which is carried home to the granary on the last harvest-waggon. The dough man and the tree are taken to the mayor's house till the vintage is over; then a feast takes place, at which the mayor breaks the dough man in pieces, and gives the fragments to the people to eat. Here, the mayor clearly represents the king or chief, while the feast of first-fruits and the sacramental eating are combined, as was perhaps originally the case, in one and the same sacrificial ceremony. No particular mention is made of wine; but as the feast is deferred so as to take place after the vintage, it is probable that the blood of the wine-god as well as the body of the corn-god entered once at least into the primitive ritual.

Many similar feasts survive in Europe; but for the rite of eating the corn-god in its fullest form we must go once more to Mexico, which also supplied us with the best and most thoroughly characteristic examples of the cannibal god-eating. Twice a year, in May and December, an image of the great Mexican god Huitzilopochtli was made of dough, then broken in pieces, and solemnly eaten by his assembled worshippers. Two days before the May feast, says Acosta, the virgins of the temple kneaded beet-seeds with roasted maize, and moulded them with honey into a paste idol, as big as the permanent wooden idol which represented the god, putting in glass beads for eyes, and grains of Indian corn in the place of teeth. The nobles then brought the vegetable god an exquisite and rich garment, like that worn by the wooden idol, and dressed the image up in it. This done, the carried the effigy on a litter on their shoulders, no doubt to mark its royal authority. On the morning of the feast, the virgins of the god dressed themselves in garlands of maize and other festal attire. Young men, similarly caparisoned, carried the image in its ark or litter to the foot of the great pyramid temple. It was drawn up the steps with clanging music of flutes and trumpets—a common accompaniment of god-slaying ceremonies. Flowers were strewed on it, as was usual with all the gods of vegetation, and it was lodged in a little chapel of roses. Certain ceremonies of singing and dancing then took place, by means of which the paste was consecrated into the actual body and bones of the god. Finally, the image was broken up and distributed to the people, first the nobles, and then the commonalty, who received it, men, women, and children, "with such tears, fear, and reverence as if it were sacred, saying they did eat the flesh and bones of God, wherewith they were grieved." I need not point out the close resemblance here to the mourning over the bodies of Attis and Adonis, nor to the rites of Dionysus.

Still more closely does the December feast (which took place, like Christmas, at the winter solstice) recall the cannibal practice; for here an image of the god was made of seeds, kneaded into dough with the blood of children. Such a Massacre of the Innocents occurs often elsewhere in similar connexions: we shall meet with it again on a subsequent occasion. The image was placed on the chief altar of the temple, and on the day of its Epiphany, the king of Mexico offered incense to it. Bambino gods like this are well known in other countries. Next day it was taken down, and a priest flung at it a flint-tipped arrow. This was called "killing the god so that his body might be eaten." One of the priests then cut out the heart of the image and gave it to the actual king to eat, just as in other sacrifices the priest cut out the throbbing heart of the human victim and placed it in the mouth of the cannibal god. The rest of the image was divided into small pieces, which were distributed to all the males of the community, adults or children. The ceremony was called "God is Eaten."

I will not multiply examples of the main principle of eating the corn-god in the shape of little cakes or human images, which have been collected in abundance all the world over. Mr. Frazer's work is a perfect thesaurus of analogous customs. I will rather call attention to one or two special parallels with similar god-eating rites, cannibal or animal, which occur elsewhere. At the close of the rice harvest in Boeroe, in the East Indies, each clan meets at a common sacrificial meal, to which every member of the clan is bound to contribute a little of his new rice from the current season. This is called "eating the soul of the rice." But some of the rice is also set apart and offered to the spirits—that is, I take it, to the ghosts of ancestors. This combination is like the common case of the human victim being offered on the altar-stone of earlier ancestral deities. Amongst the Alfoers of Celebes, again, it is the priest who sows the first rice-seeds, and plucks the first ripe rice in each field. This he roasts and grinds into meal, giving some of it to each member of the family. Here the priest no doubt represents the old tribal priest-king. Several similar practices are reported from India, only one of which need at present detain us. Among the Hindoos of the Deccan there is a magical and sacramental eating of the new rice; but the special point of interest to be noted here is the fact that some of it is offered to the god Ganesa, after which the whole family partake of the produce. Among the Kafirs of Natal and Zululand, however, it is at the king's kraal that the people assemble for their sacramental feast of new fruits, where they dance and perform certain sacred ceremonies. In this case, the king, the living god, seems to take the place of the god, the dead king, in the Indian festival. Various grains are mixed with the flesh of a sacrificed animal, in whom we shall now have perhaps little difficulty in recognising the representative of a human corn-god victim ; and a portion of this mess is placed in the mouth of each man by the king himself, here officiating in his capacity of ancestral priest. By the light of such analogies, I think we need have no hesitation in reconstructing the primitive sacramental feast, where a man was sacrificed as an annual manufactured corn-god ; seeds were mixed with his blood ; his flesh was eaten sacramentally by the people, fed by the king; a part of his body was also eaten by the king himself, and a part was offered to the great gods, or to the tribal god, or the foundation god or goddess of the village or city. After putting together the various survivals already cited, I do not think this is too large an exercise of the constructive faculty.

An interesting mixed case of god-eating, in which the cake was baked, not in the form of a man, but of a divine animal, I have seen myself in the house of Irish emigrants in Canada. The new corn was there made into loaves or buns in the shape of little pigs, with currants for eyes ; and one of these was given to each of the children. Though merely regarded as a playful custom, this instance, I venture to think, has still its own illustrative value.

The practice of kneading sacramental cakes from the blood of infants, which we saw to prevail in the case of a Mexican god, is parallelled in the practice of mixing them with shreds of the flesh from an animal victim in the Zulu ceremony. The cannibal form of the rite must, however, have been very widespread ; as we gather from the fact that a Christian sect, the Paulicians, were accused of it as late as the eighth century. John of Osun, Patriarch of Armenia, wrote a diatribe against these sectaries, in which he mentions the fact that they moulded an image of wheaten flower with the blood of children, and eat therewith their unholy communion. Of course, there could have been no direct intercourse in the ninth century between Armenia and Mexico ; but the accusation shows at least that similar ceremonies were known or remembered in Asia as actual practices. Indeed, the Harranians in the middle ages annually sacrificed an infant, and boiling down its flesh, baked it into cakes, of which every freeman was allowed to partake. In both these cases, we have the two extremes of eating the god combined in one practice—the cannibal rite and the sacramental corn-cake.

Mr. Frazer calls attention to another interesting transitional instance. Loaves made in the shape of men were called at Rome Maniæ; and it appears that such loaves were specially made at Aricia. Now Aricia was also the one place in Italy where a divine priest-king, the Rex Nemoralis, lived on well recognised into the full blaze of the historic period, on the old savage tenure of killing his predecessor. Again, Mania was the name of the Mother or Grandmother of Ghosts. Woollen images, dedicated to this Latin Cybele, were hung out in Rome at the feast of the Compitalia, and were said to be substitutes for human victims. Mr. Frazer suggests that the loaves in human form which were baked at Aricia were sacramental bread; and that in old days, when the Rex Nemoralis was annually slain, loaves were also made in his image as in Mexico, and were eaten sacramentally by his worshippers. I do not hesitate myself to suggest still further that the gingerbread cakes, shaped like a man, and still richly gilt, which are sold at so many fairs in France and Italy, and also sometimes in England, are last dying relics of similar early sacramental images. For fairs are for the most part diminished survivals of religious festivals.

As the theanthropic animal victim represents a man and a god, it is reasonable that a cake shaped as an animal and baked of flour should sometimes do as well as the animal victim. For the corn is after all the embodiment of the corn-god. Hence bakers in the antique world used to keep in stock representations in dough of the various sacrificial animals, for people who were too poor to afford the originals. Oxen and sheep were regularly so represented. When Mithridates besieged Cyzicus, and the people could not get a black cow to sacrifice to Persephone, they made a dough cow and placed it at the altar. At the Athenian festival of the Diasia, cakes shaped like animals were similarly sacrificed ; and at the Osiris festival in Egypt, when the rich offered a real pig, the poor used to present a dough pig as a substitute, like the dough pig of the Irish Canadians.

But in many other rites, the sacramental and sacrificial cake has entirely lost all semblance of a man or animal. The god is then eaten either in the shapeless form of a boiled mess of rice or porridge, or in a round cake or loaf, without image of any sort, or in a wafer stamped with the solar or Christian cross. Instances of this type are familiar to everyone.

More closely related still to primitive cannibalism is the curious ritual of the Sin-Eater, so well elaborated by Mr. Sidney Hartland. In Upper Bavaria, what is called a corpse-cake is kneaded from flour, and placed on the breast of a dead person, in order to absorb the virtues of the departed. This cake is then eaten by the nearest relation. In the Balkan peninsula, a small image of the dead person was made in bread and eaten by the survivors of the family. These are intermediate stages between cannibalism and the well-known practice of sin-eating.

I hope I have now made clear the general affiliation which I am seeking to suggest, if not to establish. My idea is that in the beginning certain races devoured their own parents, or parts of them, so as to absorb the divine souls of their forebears into their own bodies. Later, when artificial god-making became a frequent usage, especially in connexion with agriculture, men eat the god, or part of him, for a similar reason. But they likewise eat him as the corn or yam or rice, sacramentally. When theanthropic victims were substituted for the man-god, they eat the theanthropic victim in like manner. Also they made images in paste of both man and beast, and, treating these as compounded of the god, similarly sacrificed and eat them. And they drank his blood, in the south as wine, in the north as beer, in India as soma. If this line of reconstruction be approximately correct, then sacraments as a whole are in the last resort based upon survival from the cannibal god-feast.

It is a significant fact that in many cases, as at the Potraj festival, the officiating priest drinks the blood of the divine victim, while the laity are only permitted to eat of its body.

CHAPTER XVI.

THE DOCTRINE OF THE ATONEMENT.

One more element of some importance yet remains in the complex conception of the human or animal victim, or slain god, which we must briefly examine before we can proceed with advantage to the evolution of Christianity; I mean the doctrine of piacular sacrifice—or, in other words, of the atonement.

"Without shedding of blood," says the author of one of the earliest Christian tractates, "there is no remission of sin." This is a common theory in all advanced religions; the sacrifice is regarded, not merely as the self-immolation of a willing divine victim or incarnate god, but also as an expiation for crimes committed. "Behold the Lamb of God," says the Baptist in the legend, "which taketh away the sins of the world."

This idea, I take it, is not primitive. Sin must be regarded as a late ethical intruder into the domain of religion. Early man for the most part takes his gods joyously. He is on the best of terms with them. He eats and drinks and carouses in their presence. They join in his phallic and bacchanalian orgies. They are not great moral censors, like the noble creation of the Hebrew prophets, "of purer eyes than to behold iniquity." They are creatures of like passions and failings with himself,— dear ancestors and friends, ever ready to overlook small human frailties like murder or rapine, but exercising a fatherly care for the most part over the lives and fortunes of their descendants or tribesmen. Angry they may be at times, no doubt; but their anger as a rule can be easily assuaged by a human victim, or by the blood of slaughtered goats and bulls. Under normal circumstances, they are familiar housemates. Their skulls or images adorn the hearth. They assist at the family and domestic feasts; and they lick up the offerings of blood or wine made to them with a smiling countenance. In short, they are average members of the tribe, gone before to the spirit-world; and they continue to share without pride or asceticism in the joys and feasts and merry-makings of their relatives.

Thus the idea of expiation, save as a passing appeasement for a temporary tiff, did not probably occur in the very earliest and most primitive religions. It is only later, as ethical ideas begin to obtrude themselves into the sacred cycle, that the notion of sin, which is primarily that of an offence against the established etiquette of the gods, makes itself slowly visible. In many cases, later glosses seem to put a piacular sense upon what was in its origin by obvious analogy a mere practical god-making and god-slaying ceremony. But in more consciously philosophic stages of religion this idea of atonement gains ground so fast that it almost swallows up the earlier conception of communion or feasting together. Sacrifice is then chiefly conceived of as a piacular offering to a justly offended or estranged deity; this is the form of belief which we find almost everywhere meeting us in the hecatombs of the Homeric poems, as in many works of Hellenic and Semitic literature.

In particular, the piacular sacrifice seems to have crystallised and solidified round the sacred person of the artificial deity. "The accumulated misfortunes and sins of the whole people," says Mr. Frazer, "are sometimes laid upon the dying god, who is supposed to bear them away for ever, leaving the people innocent and happy." "Surely he hath borne our griefs and carried our sorrows," says one of the Hebrew poets, whose verses are conjecturally attributed to Isaiah, about one such divine scapegoat; "yet we did esteem him stricken, smitten of God, and afflicted. He was wounded for our transgressions; he was bruised for our iniquities. The chastisement of our peace was upon him, and with his stripes are we healed. Jahweh hath laid upon him the iniquity of us all."

The ideas here expressed in such noble language were common to all the later man-gods of the more advanced and ethical religions.

Mr. Frazer is probably right in connecting the notion of the scapegoat, human or animal, with the popular barbaric idea of the transference of evils. Thus, in popular magic of all nations, diseases of every sort, from serious fevers and plagues, down to headache, toothache, warts, and sores, are transferred by some simple ceremony of witchcraft to animals, rags, or other people. I will quote examples but briefly. Epilepsy is made over to leaves and thrown away in the Malay Archipelago. Toothache is put into a stone in Australia. A Bechuana king gave his illness to an ox, which was drowned in his stead, to secure his recovery. Mr. Gomme quotes a terrible story of a Scotch nobleman who transferred his mortal disease to his brother by a magical ceremony. "Charms" for fever or for warts generally contain some such amiable element of transferring the trouble to a string, a rag, or a piece of paper, which is flung away to carry the evil with it to the person who next touches it. Numerous cases of like implication may be found in the works of Mr. Gomme and Mr. Hartland, to which I would refer enquirers after further evidence.

Closely connected with these notions of transference are also the occasional or periodical ceremonies undertaken for the expulsion of evils from a village or a community. Devils, demons, hostile spirits, diseases, and other misfortunes of every sort are frequently thus expelled with gongs, drums, and other magical instruments. Often the boundaries of the tribe or parish are gone over, a perlustration is performed, and the evil influences are washed out of the territory or forcibly ejected. Our own rite of Beating the Bounds represents on one of its many sides this primitive ceremony. Washings and dippings are frequent accompaniments of the expulsive ritual; in Peru, it was also bound up with that common feature of the corn-god sacrament—a cake kneaded with the blood of living children. The periodical exorcism generally takes place once a year, but is sometimes biennial: it has obvious relations with the sacrifice of the human or animal victim. In Europe, it still survives in many places as the yearly expulsion of witches. The whole subject has been so admirably treated by Mr. Frazer that I have nothing to add to his excellent exposition.

Putting these two cardinal ideas together, we arrive at the compound conception of the scapegoat. A scapegoat is a human or animal victim, chosen to carry off, at first the misfortunes or diseases, later the sin and guilt of the community. The name by which we designate it in English, being taken from the derivative Hebrew usage, has animal implications; but, as in all analogous cases, I do not doubt that the human evil-bearer precedes the animal one.

A good example of this incipient stage in the evolution of the scapegoat occurs at Onitsha, on the Quorra River. Two human beings are there annually sacrificed, "to take away the sins of the land"—though I suspect it would be more true to native ideas to say, "the misfortunes." The number two, as applied to the victims, crops up frequently in this special connexion. The victims here again are "bought with a price"—purchased by public subscription. All persons who during the previous year have committed gross offences against native ethics are expected to contribute to the cost of the victims. Two sickly people are bought with the money, "one for the land and one for the river." The victims are dragged along the ground to the place of execution, face downward. The crowd who accompany them cry, "Wickedness! wickedness!" So in Siam it was customary to choose a broken-down woman of evil life, carry her on a litter through the streets (which is usually a symbol of kingship or godhead) and throw her on a dunghill or hedge of thorns outside the wall, forbidding her ever again to enter the city. In this eastern case, there is mere expulsion, not actual killing.

In other instances, however, the divine character attributed to the human scapegoat is quite unmistakable. Among the Gonds of India, at the festival of the god of the crops, the deity descends on the head of one of the worshippers, who is seized with a fit, and rushes off to the jungle. There, it is believed he would die of himself, if he were not brought back and tenderly treated: but the Gonds, more merciful here than in many other cases, take him back and restore him. The idea is that he is thus singled out to bear the sins of the rest of the village. At Halberstadt in Thuringia an exactly similar custom survived till late in the middle ages. A man was chosen, stained with deadly sin, as the public scapegoat. On the first day of Lent he was dressed in mourning, and expelled from church. For forty days, he wandered about, fed only by the priests, and no one would speak to him. He slept in the street. On the day before Good Friday, however, he was absolved of his sins, and being called Adam, was believed to be now in a state of innocence. This is a mitigated and Christianised form of the human sin-offering.

Again, the Albanians of the Eastern Caucasus kept a number of sacred slaves in the temple of the moon, many of whom were inspired and prophesied. When one of these men exhibited unusual symptoms of inspiration, the high priest had him bound with a sacred chain, and maintained for a year in luxury, like the Mexican corn-god. This fact immediately brings the human scapegoat into line with the annual human gods we have already considered. At the end of a year, he was anointed with unguents (or, so to speak, christed), and led forth to be sacrificed. The sacrifice was accomplished as a purificatory ceremony.

Mr. Frazer, to whom I owe all these examples, connects with such rites the curious ceremony of the expulsion of the Old Mars, the Mamurius Veturius, at Rome. Every year on the 14th of March (near the spring equinox), a man, called by the name of a god, was clad in skins—the significance of which rite we now know—and after being beaten with long white rods, was expelled the city. From one point of view, this personage no doubt represented the god of vegetation of the previous year (for the Mars was originally an annual corn-god). But from another point of view, being now of no further use to the community, he was utilised with true old Roman parsimony as a scapegoat, and sent to carry away the offences of the people. Indeed, there seems to be some reason for believing that he was driven into the territory of the hostile Oscans. In this case we perceive that an annual god is made the sin-offering for the crimes of a nation.

In Greece, we get similar traces of the human scapegoat. At Chæronea in Bœotia, the chief magistrate at the town-hall, and every householder in his own house, as we learn from Plutarch (who was himself a magistrate there) had on a certain day to beat a slave with rods of *agnus castus*, and turn him out of doors, with the formula, "Out, hunger! in, health and wealth!" Elsewhere the custom retained more unpleasant features. At Marseilles, when the colony was ravaged by plague, a man of the poorer classes used voluntarily to offer himself as a sin-offering or scapegoat. Here we have once more the common episode of the willing victim. For a whole year, like other annual gods, he was fed at the public expense, and treated as a gentleman—that is to say, a kingly man-god. At the end of that time, he was dressed in sacred garments —another mark of godship—decked with holy branches, the common insignia of gods of vegetation, and led through the city, while prayers were offered up that the sins of the people might fall on his head. He was then cast out of the colony. The Athenians kept a number of outcasts as public victims at the expense of the town; and when plague, drought, or famine befell, sacrificed two of them (note the number) as human scapegoats. One was said to be a substitute for the men, and one for the women. They were led about the city (like Beating the Bounds again) and then apparently stoned to death without it. Moreover, periodically every year, at the festival of the Thargelia, two victims were stoned to death as scapegoats at Athens, one for the men, and one for the women. I would conjecturally venture to connect this sacred number, not merely with the African practice already noted, but also with the dual kings at Sparta, the two consuls at Rome, and the two suffetes at Carthage and in other Semitic cities. The duality of kings, indeed, is a frequent phenomenon.

I can only add here that the many other ceremonies connected with these human scapegoats have been well expounded and explained by Mannhardt, who shows that they were all of a purificatory character, and that the scourging of the god before putting him to death was a necessary point of divine procedure. Hence the significance of the *agnus castus*.

Briefly, then, the evidence collected by Mannhardt and Frazer suffices to suggest that the human scapegoat was the last term of a god, condemned to death, upon whose head the transgression or misfortunes of the community were laid as substitute. He was the vicarious offering who died for the people.

It is only here and there, however, that the scapegoat retains to historical times his first early form as a human victim. Much more often, in civilised lands at least, we get the usual successive mitigations of the custom. Sometimes, as we have seen already in these cases, the victim is not actually killed, but merely expelled, or even only playfully and ceremonially driven out of the city. In other instances, we get the familiar substitution of the condemned criminal, or the imbecile, as in the Attic Thargelia. The Greeks of Asia Minor used actually to burn their atonement-victim, and cast his ashes into the sea; but the Leucadians merely threw down a condemned prisoner from a cliff, and lightened his fall by fastening live birds to him, while they kept boats below to save him from drowning, and carry him well beyond the frontier. In the vast majority of cases, however, we have the still more common substitution of a sacred animal for a human victim; and this appears to be in large part the origin of that common religious feature, the piacular sacrifice.

Occasionally we get historical or half-historical evidence of the transition from a human victim to a divine or quasi-divine animal. Thus, the people of Nias offer either a red horse or a buffalo to purify the land; but formerly, a man was bound to the same stake with the buffalo, and when the buffalo was killed, the man was driven away, no native daring to receive him or feed him. The sacrificial camel of the ancient Arabs, presumably piacular, is expressly stated to be a substitute for a human victim. The favourite victims of the Saracens were young and beautiful captives: but if such were not to be procured, they contented themselves with a white and faultless camel. The step hence to the habitual immolation or driving forth of a divine animal in place of a divine or quasi-divine man is a very small one. In Malabar, the cow is a sacred beast, and to kill or eat a cow is a crime like murder. Nevertheless, the Brahmans transfer the sins of the people to a cow or cows, which are then driven out wherever the Brahmans appoint. The ancient Egyptians used to sacrifice a bull, and lay upon its head all the evils which might otherwise happen to themselves and their country; then they sold the bull's head to the Greeks, or flung it into the river. (Contrast this effort to get rid of the accursed head with the careful preservation and worship of the sacred one.) The best-known case of all, of course, is the Hebrew scapegoat, which was the sacred animal of a shepherd people, turned out to die of hunger or thirst in the desert, and bearing on its head the sins of the people. (Contrast the scapegoat with the paschal lamb, and compare with the goats and sheep of the last judgment.) When cholera rages among the aboriginal tribes of India, they take a goat or a buffalo—in either case a female, the most sacred sex in Indian sacrifice, and black all over, like Apis and Mnevis; they turn it out of the village, with magical ceremonies, and do not allow it to return within their precincts. In many other similar poojahs, the victim is a goat. Mr. Frazer has collected, here as elsewhere, a vast number of valuable and illustrative instances.

As a rule, the man-god or divine animal selected as a scapegoat is not actually slaughtered, in the fullest form of the rite; he is driven away, or flung into the sea, or left to die of hunger and thirst. Sometimes, however, he is burned as a holocaust: sometimes he is stoned, and sometimes slaughtered. And in later and less perfect forms of piacular animal sacrifice, slaughter was the rule, save where burning had ousted it. Indeed, in many cases, it is difficult to disentangle the various elements of the complex problem. People had got accustomed to certain forms of sacrifice, and mixed them up indiscriminately, so that one and the same rite seems sometimes to be sacramental, sacrificial, and piacular, all at once. Thus Dr. Robertson Smith writes of ancient Egypt: " Bulls were offered on the altar, and part of the flesh eaten in a sacrificial feast; but the sacrifice was only permitted as a piaculum, was preceded by a solemn fast, and was accompanied by public lamentation, as at the death of a kinsman." Compare the annual mourning for Adonis; and also the similar union of sacrifice, sacrament, and atonement in the Mass, which, at the great resurrection-festival of the Christian year, Easter, is equally preceded by a fast, and by the solemn mourning of Good Friday.

Now, I do not pretend to discriminate accurately in

these very mixed cases between one element and another in the compound rite. Often enough, all the various traits of god-slaying, of sacrament, and of public expiation are evidently present. Usually, too, the victim is slain before the altar or sacred stone of some earlier and greater god, and its blood poured forth for him. Thus, in the Hebrew ritual both of the holocaust and the sin-offering, the victim is slain at the altar, "before Jahweh," and the effusion of blood on the sacred slab has a special significance. In the Semitic field, as Dr. Robertson Smith observes (and I would add, in most others), "the fundamental idea of sacrifice is not that of a sacred tribute, but of joint communion between the god and his worshippers, by joint participation in the living flesh and blood of a sacred victim." But the identity of god and victim is often quite clear; thus, as we saw before, the sheep-Aphrodite was worshipped in Cyprus with an annual mystic and piacular sacrifice of a sheep; and the worshippers themselves were clad in sheepskins, a rite whose significance is now abundantly evident to us.

On the whole, then, at the stage we have at last reached, I will not attempt to distinguish in every case between the various superposed ideas in the sacrificial ceremony. Most sacrifices seem in the last resort to be substitutes for human-divine victims. Most seem to be sacramental, and most to be more or less distinctly piacular. I do not even know whether, in reconstructing afresh for others a series of rites the ideas of which have grown slowly clear to my own mind by consideration of numerous mixed examples, I have always placed each particular fact in its best and most effective position for illustration. The elements of the problem are so involved and so closely interosculating. For instance, I do not doubt that the great Phœnician and Carthaginian holocausts of human victims, which I was compelled at first to treat most inadequately, were mainly piacular in intention; nor do I doubt that the Greek hecatomb (or holocaust of a hundred oxen) was a mitigation or attenuation of such gigantic human holocausts as these, or as those attributed to the British Druids. Asclepiades states expressly that every victim was originally regarded as a substitute for human sacrifice ; and so, in the Elohistic account of the origin of burnt sacrifice, a ram is accepted as a substitute for the life of Isaac, the dearly-beloved son whom the chief or king, Abraham, intends to offer as a royal victim to his tribal god. Abraham says that the god himself will provide a victim; and the ram then, as it were, voluntarily offers itself. So at the great temple of Astarte at Eryx, where the victims were drawn from the sacred or divine herds kept at the sanctuary, the chosen beast was believed of its own accord to present itself at the altar. At the Diipolia in like manner a number of bulls were driven together round the holy table ; and the bull was selected which voluntarily approached and eat of the sacred cakes ; thereby not only showing himself to be a willing victim, but also doubly divine, first because he took the food intended for the god, and second because he swallowed the sacred corn, itself the duplicate body of the deity. (Compare, of course, the Hebrew shewbread.) I need not pursue this line of thought any further. It must be obvious that many sacrifices at least are sacramentally-piacular god-slaying ceremonies, and that in most of them the god is slain, himself to himself, in human or animal form, as an expiation of crimes against his own majesty. Nor need I point out how this complex concept lies at the very root of Pauline theology.

I would like to add, however, that the ideas here formulated must give a new meaning to many points we could not at first understand in ceremonies mentioned in our earlier chapters. I will take only one example—that of the place of Samoyed sacrifice which Baron Nordenskiöld saw on Vaygats Island. We can now divine the meaning of the heap of reindeer skulls piled around the rude open-air shrine; for reindeer are the sacred and theanthropic animals of the northern races; while the preservation of their heads at the hypœthral altar of the elder gods or ghosts has its usual holy and oracular meaning. We can also guess why remains of a fireplace could be seen by the side, at which the sacrificial and sacramental meal was habitually prepared; and why the mouths of the idols were smeared with blood, in order to make the older gods or ghosts participators in the festival. Indeed, any reader who has followed me thus far, and who now turns back to the earlier chapters of this book, will find that many details appear to him in quite a different light, and will see why I have insisted beforehand on some minor points which must have seemed to him at the time wholly irrelevant.

Many other curious ceremonies that seem equally meaningless at first in narratives of travel will also come to have a significant meaning when thus regarded. For instance, Mr. Chalmers tells us that among the New Guinea natives of particular districts, " pigs are never killed but in the one place, and then they are offered to the spirit. The blood is poured out there, and the carcase is then carried back to the village, to be divided, cooked, and eaten. Pigs' skulls are kept and hung up in the house. Food for a feast, such as at house-building "—a most pregnant hint—" is placed near the post where the skulls hang, and a prayer is said. When the centre-post is set up, the spirits have wallaby, fish, and bananas presented to them, and they are besought to keep that house always full of food, and that it may not fall when the wind is strong." If we recall other cases elsewhere, we can hardly doubt that the pigs in these instances are killed as sacred victims at the grave of the chief family ancestor; especially when Mr. Chalmers also tells us that "each family has a sacred place where they carry offerings to the spirits of deceased ancestors, whom they greatly fear." When sickness, famine, or scarcity of fish occur, it is these spirits that have to be appeased. And if we recollect once more that in so many cases the central post of the hut is based on a human or animal victim, both in New Guinea and elsewhere, we can hardly doubt that to this household god or foundation-ghost the offerings at the central post are presented. Finally, the skulls of the pigs which are kept in the house and hung on the post remind us on the one hand of the skulls of ancestor-gods similarly preserved, and on the other hand of the skulls of theanthropic victims kept by the people of India at their festivals, or fastened by early Greeks and Romans on their temples. "They cook the heads of their slain enemies," says Mr. Chalmers again, "to secure clean skulls to put on sacred places." Adequately to develop the hints thus suggested, however, would require another book as long as the present one.

Yet here is just one more such hint, from the same author, too pregnant to be omitted.

"When the natives begin planting, they first take a bunch of bananas and sugar-cane, and go to the centre of the plantation, and call over the names of the dead belonging to their family, adding: 'There is your food, your bananas and sugar-cane; let our food grow well, and let it be plentiful. If it does not grow well and plentiful, you all will be full of shame, and so shall we.'

"When they go on trading expeditions, they present their food to the spirits at the centre-post of the house, and ask the spirits to go before them and prepare the people, so that the trading may be prosperous.

"When sickness is in the family, a pig is brought to the sacred place of the great spirit" (probably the chief ancestral ghost), "and killed. The carcase is then taken to the sacred place of the family, and the spirits are asked to accept it. Sins are confessed, such as bananas that are taken, or cocoanuts, and none have been presented, and leave not given to eat them. 'There is a pig; accept, and remove the sickness.' Death follows, and the day of burial arrives. The friends all stand round the open grave, and the chief's sister or cousin" (the primitive priestess) "calls out in a loud voice, 'You have been angry with us for the bananas we have taken (or cocoanuts, as the case may be), and you have, in your anger, taken this child. Now let it suffice, and bury your anger.' The body is then placed in the grave, and covered over with earth."

Here we have in brief a perfect epitome of savage theology, savage ceremonial, and savage atonement. I could enlarge not a little on its numerous implications.

A single quotation from Mr. Savage Landor's work on The Hairy Ainu of Japan will also serve as an excellent summary of such encyclopædic barbaric theology. "If they have any belief at all," he says, "it is an imperfect kind of Totemism, and the central point of that belief is their own descent from the bear. This does not include the smallest reverence for their ancestor. They capture their Totem and keep it in captivity; they speak to it and feed it; but no prayers are offered to it. When the bear is fat, it is taken out of the cage to be ill-treated and baited by all the men present." Like the Khond Meriah and the tortures of martyrs. "It is tied to a stake" or *stauros* or accursed tree, "and a pole is thrust into its mouth; and when the poor beast has been sufficiently tortured, pricked with pointed sticks, shot at with blunted arrows," like St. Sebastian, "bruised with stones," like St. Stephen, "maddened with rage and ill-usage, it is killed outright, and, ancestor as it may be, it makes the chief dish and *raison d'être* of a festival, where all the members of the tribe partake of its flesh. The owner of the hut in which the feast takes place then sticks the skull on to a forked pole, and sets it outside with the others at the east end of his hut. The skin is made into garments, or is spread on the ground to sleep on." Here, I need hardly say, we have sacrifice, sacrament, orientation, the sacred head, the use of the skin as a covering of the worshipper, and all the other traits of theanthropic substitution.

It is more to our purpose now, however, to remember these two cardinal points: first, that a dying god, human or animal, is usually selected as a convenient vehicle for the sins of the people; and second, that "witnout shedding of blood there is no remission of sin." These two doctrines were commonly current all over the world, but especially in that Eastern Mediterranean world where Christianity was first evolved. Indeed, they were there so generally recognised that the writers of the earliest Christian tractates, the Apostolic Epistles, take them for granted as self-evident—as principles of which every intelligent man would at once admit the truth and cogency.

CHAPTER XVII.

THE WORLD BEFORE CHRIST.

CHRISTIANITY grew. It was a natural product. It did not spring, full-fledged, from any one man's brain, as Athene sprang from the head of Zeus. It was not even invented by any little group or school of men, Petrine or Pauline, the apostles or the disciples, the early church of Jerusalem, Antioch, or Alexandria. Christianity grew—slowly. It developed, bit by bit, for three long centuries, taking shape by gradual stages in all the teeming centres of the Roman world; and even after it had assumed a consistent form as the Holy Catholic Church, it still went on growing in the minds of men, with a growth which never ends, but which reveals itself even now in a thousand modes, from a Vatican Council to the last new departure of the last new group of American sectaries.

Christianity grew—in the crowded cosmopolitanised seaports and cities of the Roman empire—in Antioch, Alexandria, Thessalonica, Cyrene, Byzantium, Rome. Its highway was the sea. Though partly Jewish in origin, it yet appears from its earliest days essentially as a universal and international religion. Therefore we may gain some approximate knowledge of its origin and antecedents by considering the religious condition of these various great towns at the time when Christianity began to spring spontaneous in their midst. We can arrive at some idea of the product itself by observing the environment in which it was evolved.

Once more, Christianity grew—for the most part,

among the lower orders of the cosmopolitan seaports. It fashioned itself among the slaves, the freedmen, the Jewish, Syrian, and African immigrants, the Druidical Gauls and Britons of Rome, the petty shopkeepers, the pauperised clients, the babes and sucklings of the populous centres. Hence, while based upon Judaism, it gathered hospitably into itself all those elements of religious thought and religious practice that were common to the whole world, and especially to the Eastern Mediterranean basin. Furthermore, it gathered hospitably into itself in particular those elements which belonged to the older and deeper-seated part of the popular religions, rather than those which belonged to the civilised, Hellenised, and recognised modifications of the state religions. It was a democratic rather than an official product. We have to look, therefore, at the elder far more than the younger stratum of religious thought in the great cities, for the influences which went to mould Christianity. I do not deny, indeed, that the new faith was touched and tinged in all its higher parts by beautiful influences from Neo-Platonism, Alexandrian Judaism, and other half-mystical philosophic systems; but for its essential groundwork we have still to go to the root-stratum of religious practice and belief in Antioch and Alexandria, in Phrygia and Galatia, in Jerusalem and Rome. It based itself above all on sacrament, sacrifice, atonement, and resurrection. Yet again, Christianity originated first of all among the Jewish, Syrian, or Semitic population of these great towns of the empire, at the very moment of its full cosmopolitanisation; it spread rapidly from them, no doubt at first with serious modifications, to the mixed mass of sailors, slaves, freedwomen, and townspeople who formed apparently its earliest adherents. Hence, we must look in it for an intimate blend of Judaism with the central ideas of the popular religions, Aryan or Hamitic, of the Mediterranean basin. We must expect in it much that was common in Syria, Asia Minor, Hellas, and Egypt,—something even from Gaul, Hispania, Carthage. Its first great apostle, if we may believe our authorities, was one Saul or Paul, a half-Hellenised Jew of Semitic and commercial Tarsus in Cilicia, and a Roman citizen. Its first great churches sprang up in the busy ports and marts of the Levant. Its very name of Christian was given to it first in the crowded and cosmopolitan city of Antioch.

It is here, then, in these huge slave-peopled hives of Hellenised and Romanised commerce, that we must look for the mother-ideas of Christianity.

Antioch was quite undoubtedly in the earliest times the principal cradle of the new religion. I do not mean that Jerusalem was not very probably the place where men first began to form a small sect of esoteric Christ-worshippers, or that Galilee was not the region where the Christ himself most largely lived and taught, if indeed such a person ever really existed. In those matters the traditions handed down to us in the relatively late Gospels may be perfectly correct: and again, they may not. But Christianity as we know it, the Christianity of the Pauline epistles and the later writings, such as the Gospels and the works of the Fathers, must have been essentially a cult of wider Syrian and Gentile growth. It embraces in itself elements which doubtless lingered on in secluded corners more or less among the mass of the people even in Judæa itself, though discountenanced by the adherents of the priestly and official Jahweh-worship; but which were integral parts of the popular and even the recognised religion throughout the whole of northern Syria.

Antioch, where Christianity thus took its first feeble steps, was a handsome and bustling commercial city, the capital of the Greek Seleucid kings, and the acknowledged metropolis of the Syrian area. At the time of Paul (if there *was* a Paul), it probably contained half a million people; it was certainly the largest town in Asia, and worthy to be compared with Rome itself in the splendour of its buildings. Many things about its position are deserving of notice. It stood upon the banks of the Orontes, a sacred stream, ensconced in a rich agricultural plain, fourteen miles from the river's mouth. Its Ostia was at Selucia, the harbour whence flowed the entire export trade of Syria and the east towards Hellas and Italy. The Mediterranean in front connected it with Rome, Alexandria, Asia Minor, Greece; the caravan routes across the Syrian desert in the rear put it in communication with the bazars of Mesopotamia and the remoter east. It was thus the main entrepôt of the through trade between two important worlds. The Venice of its time, it lay at the focal point where the highroads of Europe and of Asia converged.

Scholars of repute have pointed out the fact that even earlier than the days of Paul, Buddhist ideas from India seem to have dribbled through and affected the Syrian world, as Zoroastrian ideas a little later dribbled through and affected the thought of Alexandria: and some importance has been attached to this infiltration of motives from the mystical east. Now, I do not care to deny that budding Christianity may have been much influenced on its ritual and still more on its ethical side by floating elements of Buddhist opinion: that the infancy of the Christ may have been nursed by the Magi. But on the whole I think the facts we have just been considering as to the manufacture of artificial human gods and the nature and meaning of piacular sacrifices will suffice to show that Christianity was chiefly a plant of home growth. The native soil contained already every essential element that was needed to feed it—the doctrine of the Incarnation, the death of the Man-God, the atoning power of his Blood, the Resurrection and Ascension. So that, while allowing due weight to this peculiar international position of Antioch, as the double-faced Janus-gate of Europe and Asia, I am not inclined to think that points peculiar to Buddhism need have exercised any predominant influence in the evolution of the new religion. For we must remember that Buddhism itself did but subsume into its own fabric ideas which were common to Peru and Mexico, to Greece and India, to Syria and Egypt, and which came out in fresh forms, surging up from below, in the creed of Christendom. If anything is clear from our previous researches it is this—that the world has never really had more than one religion—"of many names, a single central shape," as the poet phrases it.

The Syrian people, Semites by race and cult, had fallen, like all the rest of the eastern world, under the Hellenic dominion of the successors of Alexander. A quick and subtle folk, very pliable and plastic, they underwent rapid and facile Hellenisation. It was an easy task for them to accept Greek culture and Greek religion. The worshipper of Adonis had little difficulty in renaming his chief god as Dionysus and continuing to practise his old rites and ceremonies to the newly-named deity after the ancestral pattern. The Astarte whom the east had given to Hellas under the alias of Aphrodite, came back again as Aphrodite to Astarte's old sanctuaries. Identifications of gods and cults were but simple matters, where so many gods were after all essentially similar in origin and function. Thus the easy-going Syrian had few scruples about practising his primitive ceremonies under foreign titles, or admitting to the hospitality of his Semitic temples the Hellenic deities of the reigning Antiochi.

The Seleucids, however, did not fare so well in their attempt to impose the alien gods on the fierce Jehovistic zealots of the southern mountains. Antiochus IV. endeavoured in vain to force the cults of intrusive Hellenism on his new kingdom of Palestine. He reckoned without his hosts. The populace of Jerusalem would not away with his "idolatrous" rites—would not permit the worship of Zeus and Pallas, of Artemis and Aphrodite, to usurp a place in the holy city of Jahweh. The rebellion of the Maccabees secured at least the religious independence of Judæa from the early Seleucid period down to the days of Vespasian and Titus. Lower Syria remained true in her arid hills to the exclusive and monotheistic cult of the God of Israel. And at the same time the Jew spread everywhere over the surrounding countries, carrying with him not only his straw and his basket, but also his ingrained and ineradicable prejudices.

In Antioch, then, after the Roman absorption of Syria, a most cosmopolitan religion appears to have existed, containing mingled Semitic and Hellenic elements, half assimilated to one another, in a way that was highly characteristic of the early empire. And among the popular cults of the great city we must certainly place high those of Adonis and Dionysus, of Aphrodite-Astarte, and of the local gods or goddesses, the Baalim and Ashtareth, such as the maiden who, as we learnt from Malalas, was sacrificed at the original foundation of the city, and ever after worshipped as its Tyche or Fortune. In other words, the conception of the human god, of the corn and wine god, of the death of the god, and of his glorious resurrection, must have all been perfectly familiar ideas to the people of Antioch and of Syria in general.

Let us note here, too, that the particular group of Jahweh-worshippers among whom the Christ is said to have found his personal followers, were not people of the priestly type of Jerusalem, but Galilæan peasants of the northern mountains, separated from the most orthodox set of Jews by the intrusive wedge of heretical Samaritans, and closely bordering on the heathen Phœnician seaboard—" the coasts of Tyre and Sidon." Here Judaism and heathenism marched together; here Jahweh had his worshippers among the fishers of the lake, while Hellenism had fixed itself in the statelier villas of Tiberias and Ptolemais.

Alexandria was another of the great cosmopolitan seaport towns where Christianity made its earliest converts, and assumed not a few of its distinctive tenets. Now, in Alexandria, Hellenism and the immemorially ancient Egyptian religion found themselves face to face at very close quarters. It is true, the town in its historical aspect was mainly Greek, founded by the great Macedonian himself, and priding itself on its pure Hellenic culture. But the mass of the lower orders who thronged its alleys must surely have consisted of more or less mongrel Egyptians, still clinging with all the old Egyptian conservatism to the ideas and practices and rites of their fathers. Besides these, we get hints of a large cosmopolitan seafaring population, among whom strange faiths and exotic gods found ready acceptance. Beside the stately forms of the Greek pantheon, and the mummified or animal-headed Egyptian deities, the imported Syrian worship of Adonis had acquired a firm footing; the annual festival of the slaughtered god was one of the principal holidays; and other Syrian or remoter faiths had managed to secure their special following. The hybrid Serapis occupied the stateliest fane of the hybrid city. In that huge and busy hive, indeed, every form of cult found a recognised place, and every creed was tolerated which did not inculcate interference with the equal religious freedom of others.

The Ptolemaic family represents in itself this curious adaptability of the Græco-Egyptian Alexandrian mind. At Alexandria and in the Delta, the kings appear before us as good Hellenes, worshipping their ancestral deities in splendid temples; but in the Thebaid, the god Ptolemy or the goddess Cleopatra erected buildings in honor of Ptah or Khem in precisely the old Egyptian style, and appeared on their propyla in the guise of Pharaohs engaged in worshipping Amen-Ra or Osiris. The great Alexander himself had inaugurated this system when he gave himself out as the son of "Zeus Ammon"; and his indirect representatives carried it on throughout with a curious dualism which excused itself under the veil of arbitrary identifications. Thus Serapis himself was the dead Apis bull, invested with the attributes of an Osiris and of the Hellenic Hades; while Amen-Ra was Zeus in an Egyptian avatar.

The large Jewish colony at Alexandria also prepared the

way for the ultimate admixture of Neo-Platonism in the Christian faith; while the Egyptian belief in Triads of gods formed the groundwork for the future doctrine of the Trinity, so doggedly battled for by the Alexandrian Athanasius. It is true that Ampère and Preller have strenuously denied any Egyptian admixture in the philosophy of Alexandria; and their reasoning may be conclusive enough as to the upper stratum of thought: but it must at least be admitted that popular belief in the city of the Ptolemies must have been deeply coloured by the ideas and creeds of its Egyptian substratum. Now, in the growth of Christianity, it was the people who counted, not the official classes, the learned, or the philosophic. We must not attribute to the population of the East End of London the theology of Pusey or the evolutionism of Herbert Spencer.

Christianity would seem also to have taken part at least of its form in Rome. And as Roman influence extended likewise over every portion of the vast empire, I must say a very few words here about the origin and growth of the Roman religion.

That religion, as it comes upon us in the few glimpses we get of its early Italic and pre-Hellenised form, was one of the rudest and most primitive type, almost savage in its extreme simplicity. It knew hardly any great gods by name: the few deities it possessed, it expressed only for the most part by adjectival names. Few, I say, as to type, for as to number of individuals, their name indeed was legion; they pervaded the whole world in that reckless multiplicity which distinguishes the simple ghosts or spirits of early hunting or pastoral peoples. With the Romans, this multiplicity, ubiquity, and vagueness survived into a relatively settled and civilised agricultural condition. A vast number of small departmental gods, with few or no great ones—that is the first state of the Roman pantheon.

The central point of old Roman religion was clearly the household; the family ghosts or *lares* were the most honoured gods. We may instructively compare Mr. Chalmers's account of the theology of New Guinea. Beside these ancestral shades, or almost identical with them, came the *penates* or practical deities of the store-room, perhaps the representatives of the victims slain as foundation-ghosts at the first erection of the building. Of these two, the Lares were undoubtedly the departed ancestors of the family; they lived near the spot where they were first buried (for the old Romans were buriers), and they still presided over the household as in life, like its fathers and senators. They were worshipped daily with prayers and simple offerings of food and drink; their masks or busts which hung on the wall were perhaps the representatives, or in ancient days the coverings, of the old oracular heads or skulls; for the skulls themselves may have been preserved in wax, as so often elsewhere at an earlier period.* The Penates, which were worshipped with the Lares, seem to have stood for the family spirit in a more generalised way; they represent the continuity and persistence of its Fortune; and therefore, if we may trust the analogy of the Fortune of a town, they are probably the ghosts of the foundation or renewal victims. In judging of all this, we cannot attach too great importance to the analogy of Negritto and Polynesian customs.

Other deities are more public. But most of them seem to belong to the simplest and most immediately ghost-like stratum. They had to do with sowing, reaping, and vintage—in other words, were corn or wine gods. Or else they had to do with the navigable river, the Tiber, and the port of Ostia, which lay at its mouth—in other words, were spring and river gods. Or else they had to do with war and expeditions—in other words were slaughtered campaign gods of the Iphigenia pattern, Bellonas and battle-victims.

* To this use of the oracular head I would venture also to refer the common employment of small masks as amulets: an employment which, as Böttiger rightly remarks, explains " the vast number of such subjects met with in antique gems."

Among this dim crowd of elder manufactured deities, Saturnus, the sowing god, was most likely an annual corn-victim; his adjectival name by itself suggests that conclusion. Terminus, the boundary god, is already familiar to us. About these two at least we can hardly be mistaken. A red-haired man (as in Egypt) no doubt preceded as yearly corn-victim the red-haired puppies still slaughtered for the crops within the ken of Festus. Seia, Segetia, Tutilina, the successive corn-deities, we have already considered. They seem to equate with the successive maidens slain for the corn in other communities, and still commemorated in our midst by the corn-baby and the corn-wife. At each stage of age in the corn, a corresponding stage in the age of the human victim was considered desirable. But how reconcile this idea with the existence of numerous petty functional deities—gods of the door and the hinge?—with the Cunina who guards the child in the cradle, and the Statina who takes care of him when he begins to stand? I answer, all these are but adjectival gods, mere ghosts or spirits, unknown in themselves, but conceived as exercising this particular function. "The god that does so-and-so" is just a convenient expression, no more; it serves its purpose, and that was enough for the practical Roman. How readily they could put up with these rough-and-ready identifications we know in the case of Aius Locutius and of the Deus Rediculus.

Each Terminus and each Silvanus is thus the god or protecting ghost of each boundary stone or each sacred grove—not a proper name, but a class—not a particular god, but a *kind* of spirit. The generalised and abstract gods are later unifications of all the individuals included in each genus. The Janus, I take it, was at first the victim once sacrificed annually before each gate of the city, as he is sacrificed still on the west coast of Africa: as the god of opening, he was slaughtered at the opening of every new year; and the year conversely opened its course with the month sacred to the god of opening. Perhaps he was also slain as fortune at the beginning of each war. The Vesta is the hearth-goddess; and every house had its Vesta; perhaps originally a slaughtered hearth-victim. Every man had in like manner his Genius, an ancestral protecting spirit; the corresponding guardian of the woman was her Juno; they descend to Christianity, especially in its most distinctive Roman form, as the guardian angels. Mars was a corn-spirit; only later was he identified with the expeditionary god. His annual expulsion as the human scapegoat has already been considered. The Jupiter or Jovis was a multiple wine-god, doubtless in every case the annual victim slain, Dionysus-wise, for the benefit of the vineyard. Each village and each farm had once its Jovis, specially worshipped, and, I doubt not, originally slaughtered, at the broaching of the year's first wine-cask in April. But his name shows that, as usual, he was also identified with that very ancient Sky-god who is common to all the Aryan race; the particular Jovis being probably sacrificed, himself to himself, before the old Sky-god's altar, as elsewhere the Dionysus-victim at the shrine of Dionysus.

These identifications, I know, may sound fanciful to mere classical scholars, unacquainted with the recent advances in anthropology, and I would not have ventured to propound them at an earlier stage of our involved argument; but now that we have seen and learned to recognise the extraordinary similarity of all pantheons the whole world over, I think the exact way these deities fall into line with the wall-gods, gate-gods, corn-gods, wine-gods, boundary-gods, forest-gods, fountain-gods, and river-gods everywhere else must surely be allowed some little weight in analogically placing them.

The later Roman religion only widens, if at all, from within its own range, by the inclusion of larger and larger tribal elements. Thus the Deus Fidius, who presided over each separate alliance, I take to be the ghost of the victim slain to form a covenant; just as in Africa to this day, when two tribes have concluded a treaty of peace, they crucify a slave "to ratify the bargain." The nature of such covenant victims has been well illustrated by Professor Robertson Smith, but the growth of the covenant-gods, who finally assumed very wide importance, is a subject which considerations of space prevent me from including in our present purview. The victim, at first no doubt human, became later a theanthropic animal; as did also the Jovis-victim and the representatives of the other adjectival or departmental deities. The Roman Mars and the Sabine Quirinus may readily have been amalgamated into a Mars Quirinus, if we remember that Mars is probably a general name, and that any number of Martes may at any time have been sacrificed. The Jovis of the city of Rome thus comes at last to be the greatest and most powerful Jupiter of them all, and the representative of the Roman union. Under Hellenising influences, however, all these minor gods get elevated at last into generalised deities; and the animal victims offered to them become mere honorific or piacular sacrifices, hardly identified at all with the great images who receive them.

The Hellenising process went so far, indeed, at Rome that the old Roman religion grew completely obscured, and almost disappeared, save in its domestic character. In the home, the Lares still held the first rank. Elsewhere, Bacchus took the place of Liber, while the traits of Hermes were fastened on the adjectival Roman bargain-spirit Mercurius. Yet even so, the Roman retained his primitive belief in corn and wine gods, under the newer guises; his Ceres he saw as one with the Attic Demeter; his rural ceremonies still continued unchanged by the change of attributes that infected and transfigured the city temples. Moreover, the Romans, and later the cosmopolitan population of Rome, borrowed gods and goddesses freely from without in ever increasing numbers. In very early days, they borrowed from Etruria; later, they borrowed Apollo from Greece, and (by an etymological blunder) fixed upon their own Hercules the traits of Heracles. On the occasion of a plague, they publicly summoned Asclepios, the Greek leech-god, from Epidaurus; and at the very crisis of the life-and-death conflict with Hannibal, they fetched the sacred field-stone known as Cybele, the Mother of the Gods, from Pessinus in Phrygia. The people of Pessinus with strange compliance let their goddess go; and the whole orgiastic cult of Attis was thus transported entire to Italian soil. The rites of the great festival were carried on at Rome almost as they had been carried on before in Phrygia; so that an Asiatic worship of the most riotous type found a firm official footing in the centre of the empire. The priest, indeed, was still an Asiatic, or at least not a Roman; but the expulsion of Hannibal from Italy which followed on this adoption of a foreign god, must have greatly increased the prestige and reputation of the alien and orgiastic deity.

The luxurious Aphrodite of Eryx in Sicily arrived in Rome about the same time with Cybele. Originally a Semitic goddess, she combined the Hellenic and oriental ideas, and was identified in Italy with the old Latin Venus.

Later still, yet other gods were imported from without. New deities flowed in from Asia and Africa. The population of the city under the early empire had almost ceased to be Roman, save in the upper strata; a vast number of slaves from all parts of the world formed the lowest layer in the crowded vaults: the middle rank was filled by Syrians, Africans, Greeks, Sicilians, Moors, and freedmen —men of all places and races from Spain or Britain to the Euphrates and the Nile, the steppes and the desert. The Orontes, said Juvenal, had flooded the Tiber. Among this mixed mass of all creeds and colours, subfusk or golden-haired, a curious mixture of religions grew up. Some of these were mere ready-made foreign importations —Isis-worship from Egypt; Jahweh-worship from Judæa; strange eastern or northern or African cults from the remotest parts of Pontus or Mauritania. Others were intermixtures or rationalisations of older religions, such as Christianity, which mingled together Judaism and Adonis or Osiris elements; such as Gnosticism, which, starting from Zoroastrian infiltrations, kneaded all the gods of the world at last into its own supreme mystic and magic-god Abraxas.

Looking a little deeper through the empire in general, we see that from the time of Augustus onward, the need for a new cosmopolitan religion, to fit the new cosmopolitan state, was beginning to be dimly felt and acknowledged. Soldiers, enlisted in one country, took the cult and images of their gods to another. The bull-slaying Mithra (in whom we can hardly fail to see a solar form of the bull-god, who sacrifices a bull, himself to himself, before his own altar) was worshipped here and there, as numerous bas-reliefs show, from Persia to Britain. The Gaul endeavoured to identify his own local war-gods with the Roman Mars, who had been Hellenised in turn into the duplicate presentment of the Greek Ares. The Briton saw his river-gods remodelled in mosaic into images like those of Roman Tiber, or provided with the four horses who drag the Roman Neptune, as Neptune had borrowed the representation at least from the Greek Poseidon. And this was all the easier because everywhere alike horses were sacrificed to sea or river, in lieu of human victims; just as everywhere corn-gods were dressed in green, and everywhere wine-gods wore coronals of vine-leaves on their holy foreheads. Men *felt* the truth I have tried to impress, that everywhere and always there is but one religion. Attributes and origin were so much alike that worship was rapidly undergoing a cosmopolitanisation of name, as it already possessed a similarity of rites and underlying features. Language itself assisted this unifying process. In the west, as Latin spread, Latin names of gods superseded local ones; in the east, as Greek spread, Hellenic deities gave their titles and their beautiful forms to native images. An artificial unity was introduced and fixed by a conventional list of Greek and Roman equivalents; and in the west, as Greek art gained ground and spread, noble Greek representations of the higher gods in ideal human form became everywhere common.

But that was not enough. As the government was one, under a strong centralised despotism, it was but natural that the religion should be one also, under the rule of a similar omnipotent deity. Man makes his heaven in the image of earth; his pantheon answers to his political constitution. The mediæval hall of heaven had an imperial God, like the Othos or the Fredericks, on his regal throne, surrounded by a court of great barons and abbots in the angels and archangels, the saints and martyrs: the new religions, like spiritualism and Theosophy, which spring up in the modern democratic world, are religions of free and independent spirits, hardly even theistic. The Roman empire thus demanded a single religion under a single strong god. It tended to find it, if not in the Genius of Trajan or Antonine, then in some bull-slaying Mithra or some universal Abraxas. Materialists were satisfied with the worship of the Emperor or of the city of Rome: idealists turned rather to Isis or to Christ.

One religion there was which might have answered the turn of the empire: the pure and ideal monotheism of Judæa. But the cult of Jahweh was too local and too national; it never extended beyond the real or adopted sons of Israel. Even so, it gained proselytes of high rank at Rome, especially among women; as regards men, the painful and degrading initiatory ceremony of Judaism must always have stood seriously in the way of converts. Yet in spite of this drawback, there were proselytes in all the cosmopolitan cities where the Jews were settled; men who loved their nation and had built them a synagogue. If Judaism could but get rid of its national exclusiveness, and could incorporate into its god some more of those genial and universal traits which he had too early shuffled off—if it could make itself less austere, less abstract, and at the same time less local—there was a chance that it might rise to be the religion of humanity. The dream of the prophets might still come true and all the world might draw nigh to Zion.

At this critical juncture, an obscure little sect began to appear among the Jews and Galilæans, in Jerusalem and Antioch, which happened to combine in a remarkable degree all the main requirements of a new world-religion. And whatever the cult of Jesus lacked in this respect in its first beginnings, it made up for as it went by absorption and permeation.

It was a Catholic Church: it stood for the world, not for a tribe or a nation. It was a Holy Church: it laid great stress upon the ethical element. It was a Roman Church: it grew and prospered throughout the Roman empire. It made a city what was once a world. Whence it came and how it grew must be our next and final questions.

CHAPTER XVIII.

THE GROWTH OF CHRISTIANITY.

WHILE the world was thus seething and fermenting with new faiths the creed of the Christ made its first appearance on the seaboard of Asia. In spite of certain remarks in my first chapter, I am not such a "gross and crass Euhemerist" as to insist dogmatically on the historical existence of a personal Jesus. Of the Christ himself, if a Christ there were, we know little or nothing. The account of his life which has come down to us in the Gospels is so devoid of authority, and so entirely built up of miraculous fragments, derived from elsewhere, that we may well be excused for gravely doubting whether he is not rather to be numbered with St. George and St. Catherine, with Perseus and Arthur, among the wholly mythical and imaginary figures of legend and religion.

On the other hand, it is quite possible, or even probable, that there really did live in Galilee, at some time about the beginning of our accepted era, a teacher and reformer bearing the Semitic name which is finally Hellenised and Latinised for us as Jesus. If so, it seems not unlikely that this unknown person was crucified (or rather hung on a post) by the Romans at Jerusalem under the Procurator C. Pontius Pilatus; and that after his death he was worshipped more or less as a god by his immediate followers. Such kernel of truth may very well exist in the late and derivative Gospel story; a kernel of truth, but imbedded in a mass of unhistorical myth, which implicitly identifies him with all the familiar corn-gods and wine-gods of the Eastern Mediterranean.

Furthermore, it is even possible that the Christ may have been deliberately put to death, at the instigation of the Jewish rabble, as one of those temporary divine kings whose nature and meaning we have already discussed. If this suggestion seem improbable from the lack of any similar recorded case in the scanty Jewish annals, I would answer that formal histories seldom give us any hint of the similar customs still surviving in civilised European countries; that many popular rites exist unheard of everywhere; and that the Jews were commonly believed through the Middle Ages to crucify Christian boys, like St. Hugh of Lincoln, in certain irregular and unrecognised ethnical ceremonies. Furthermore, lest I should be thought to adduce this instance through an anti-Semite tendency (which I do not in the slightest degree possess), I may add that even among Christians similar customs are believed to exist in rural parts of Italy at the present day,—there are villages where a man dies yearly as the representative of Christ; and that in my opinion the Oberammergau and other Passion Plays are survivals of like representations in which a condemned criminal, the usual substitute, did once actually enact the part of Christ. In short, I do not hesitate to say that god-slaying ceremonies, more or less attenuated, have lingered on everywhere in obscure forms among the folk-rites and folk-customs of the most civilised peoples.

Without doing more than briefly indicate this possibility, however, I pass on to say that if ever there was really a personal Christ, and if his followers began by vaguely believing in his resurrection, the legend, as we get it, is obviously made up of collected fragments from all the god-slaying customs and beliefs we have been considering in detail through the last six or seven chapters. In the Gospel of his later believers, after the sect had spread widely among the Gentiles of the towns, Jesus is conceived of as a corn and wine god, a temporary king, slain on a cross as a piacular atonement, and raised again from the dead after three days, in the manner common to all corn and wine gods. It is possible, of course, that the first believers may have fastened all these ideas on to an accidental condemnation and execution, so to speak; but it is possible too that the Christ may actually have been put to death at the great spring feast of the Passover, in accordance with some obscure and unrecognised folk-rite of the rabble of Jerusalem. I do not even pretend to have an opinion on this subject; I do not assert or deny any historical nucleus of fact: I am satisfied with saying that the story on the whole exhibits the Christ to us entirely in the character of a temporary king, slain with piacular rites as a corn and wine god. In this case at least, I am no dogmatic Euhemerist.

I think it was Professor Freeman who once quaintly described Buddhism as "a blasphemous anticipatory parody of Christianity." The learned historian's idea apparently was that the author of all evil, being aware beforehand of the divine intentions, had invented Buddhism before the advent of Christ, so as to discount the Christian Plan of Salvation by anticipation. If so, we must regard all other religions as similar blasphemous attempts at forestalling God: for we shall see as we proceed that every one of them contains innumerable anticipations of Christianity—or, to put it conversely, that Christianity subsumes them all into itself, in a highly concentrated and etherealised solution.

In the earliest Christian documents, the Pauline and other Apostolic Epistles, we get little information about the history of the real or mythical Christ. Shadowy allusions alone to the crucifixion and the resurrection repay our scrutiny. But through the mist of words we see two or three things clearly. The Christ is described as the son of God—that is to say of the Jewish deity; and he is spoken of continually as slain on a post or tree, the sacred symbol of so many old religions. He dies to save mankind; and salvation is offered in his name to all men. A careful reading of the epistles from this point of view will give in brief an epitome of the earliest and least dogmatic yet very doctrinal Christian theology. Its cardinal points are four —incarnation, death, resurrection, atonement.

The later accounts which we get in the Gospels are far more explicit. The legend by that time had taken form: it had grown clear and consistent. All the elements of the slain and risen corn and wine god are there in perfection. For brevity's sake, I will run all these accounts together, adding to them certain traits of still later origin.

The aspect of Christ as a survival of the corn-god is already clear in Paul's argument in First Corinthians on the resurrection of the body. This argument would strike home at once to every Greek and every Asiatic. "That which you sow is not quickened unless it die. And when you sow, you sow not the body that is to be, but bare grain; it may be wheat or any other grain. But God gives it a shape as pleases him; to every seed its own body." The whole of this fifteenth chapter, the earliest statement of the Christian belief, should be read through in this connexion by any one who wishes to understand the close relation of the idea of sowing to the resurrection. It might have been written by any worshipper of Adonis or Osiris who wished to recommend his special doctrine of a bodily resurrection to a doubtful cremationist, familiar with the cult of Dionysus and of Attis.

The earliest known rite of the Christian church was the sacramental eating and drinking of bread and wine together; which rite was said to commemorate the death of the Lord, and his last supper, when he eat and drank bread and wine with his disciples. The language put into his mouth on this occasion in the Gospels, especially the Fourth, is distinctly that of the corn and wine god. "I am the true vine; ye are the branches." "I am the bread of life." "Take, eat, this is my body." "This is my blood of the new testament." Numberless other touches of like kind are scattered through the speeches. In the parable of the vineyard, God the Father is described as the owner of a vineyard, who sends his only begotten son to receive the fruit of it: and the workers slay him. The first miracle at Cana of Galilee is one where water is turned into wine by the hand of Jesus: and so on through a long series of curious instances, which readers can discover for themselves by inspection.

In early Christian art, as exhibited in the catacombs at Rome, the true vine is most frequently figured; as are also baskets of loaves, with the corresponding miracle of the loaves and fishes. Multiplication of bread and wine are the natural credentials of the corn and wine god. The earliest description we possess of Christ, that of John of Damascus, states that his complexion was "of the colour of wheat"; while in the apocryphal letter of Lentulus to the Roman Senate we read in the same spirit that his hair was "wine-coloured." The Greek description by Epiphanius Monachus says that Christ was six feet high; his hair long and golden-coloured; and in countenance he was ruddy like his father David. All these descriptions are obviously influenced by the identification of the bread and wine of the eucharist with the personal Jesus.

In the usage of the church from very early days, it has been customary to eat the body of Christ in the form of bread, and to drink his blood as wine in the sacrament. In the Catholic church, this continuous ceremony takes place at an altar, containing sacred bones, and is represented as being the offering of God, himself to himself, in the form of a mystic and piacular sacrifice. The priest drinks the wine or blood; the laity eat only the bread or body.

A curious custom which occurs in many churches of Sicily at Easter still further enforces this unity of Christ with the cult of earlier corn and wine gods, like Adonis and Osiris. The women sow wheat, lentils, and canary-seed in plates, which are kept in the dark and watered every second day. The plants soon shoot up; they are then tied together with red ribbons, and the plates containing them are placed on the sepulchres which, with effigies of the dead Christ, are made up in Roman Catholic and Greek churches on Good Friday, "just as the gardens of Adonis," says Mr. Frazer, "were placed on the grave of the dead Adonis." In this curious ceremony we get a survival from the very lowest stratum of corn-god worship; the stratum where an actual human victim is killed, and corn and other crops are sown above his body. Even where the sowing itself no longer survives, the sepulchre remains as a relic of the same antique ritual. Such sepulchres are everywhere common at Easter, as are the cradles of the child-god at the feast of the winter solstice. The Pietà is the final form of this mourning of the corn-god by the holy women.

Passing on to the other aspects of Christ as corn-god and divine-human victim, we see that he is doubly recognised as god and man, like all the similar gods of early races. In the speeches put into his mouth by his biographers, he constantly claims the Jewish god as his father. Moreover, he is a king; and his kingly descent from his ancestor David is insisted upon in the genealogies with some little persistence. He is God incarnate; but also he is the King of the Jews, and the King of Glory. Wise men come from the east to worship him, and bring gifts of gold and myrrh and frankincense to the infant God in his manger cradle. But he is further the Christ, the anointed of God; and, as we saw, anointment is a common element with numerous other divine-human victims.

Once more, he is the King's son; and he is the only begotten son, the dearly beloved son, who is slain as an expiation for the sins of the people. The heavens open, and a voice from them declares, "This is my beloved son in whom I am well pleased." He is affiliated, like all other such victims, on the older and earlier ethnical god, Jahweh; and though he is himself God, and one with the Father, he is offered up, himself to himself, in expiation of the sin committed by men against divine justice. All this would be familiar theology indeed to the worshipper of Osiris, Adonis, and Attis.

The common Hebrew offering was the paschal lamb; therefore Christ is envisaged as the Lamb of God, that taketh away the sins of the world. In the paintings of the catacombs, it is as a lamb that the Saviour of the world is oftenest represented. As a lamb he raises another lamb, Lazarus; as a lamb he turns the water into wine; as a lamb he strikes the living springs from the rock on the spandrils of the sarcophagus of Junius Bassus. But his birth in a manger is also significant: and his vine and his dove are almost as frequent as his lamb in the catacombs.

The Gospel history represents the passion of Christ essentially as the sacrifice of a temporary king, invested with all the familiar elements of that early ritual. Christ enters Jerusalem in royal state, among popular plaudits, like those which always accompany the temporary king, and the Attis or Adonis. He is mounted on an ass, the royal beast of the Semites. The people fling down branches of trees in his path, as they always fling down parts of green trees before the gods of vegetation. On Palm Sunday his churches are still decked with palm-branches or with sprays of willow-catkin. Such rites with green things form an integral part of all the old rituals of the tree-god or the corn-god, and of all the modern European survivals in folk-lore—they are equally found in the Dionysiac festival, and in the Jack-in-the-Green revels on English fair-days. The connexion with trees is also well marked throughout the Gospels; and the miracle of the barren fig-tree is specially mentioned in close connexion with the entry into Jerusalem. The people as he entered cried " Hosanna to the son of David "; and the prophetic words were supposed to be fulfilled, " Behold, thy king cometh unto thee, meek, sitting upon an ass, and a colt, the foal of an ass."

The Christ goes as a willing victim to the cross; he does

not seriously ask that the cup should pass from him. He foretells his own death, and voluntarily submits to it But he is also bought with a price—the thirty pieces of silver paid to Judas. Of all this, we had forecasts in the Khond, the Mexican, and various other rituals.

Furthermore, there is a trial—a double trial, before the high priest, and before Pilate. Such trials, we have seen, are common elements of the mock-king's degradation. Like all other similar victims, the Chrst, after being treated like a monarch, is reviled and spat upon, buffeted and insulted. He is bound with cords, and carried before Pilate. The procurator asks him, "Art thou the King of the Jews?" and the Christ by implication admits the justice of the title. All the subsequent episodes of the painful drama are already familiar to us. The sacred victim is cruelly scourged that his tears may flow. As in other cases he is crowned with flowers or with bark, in order to mark his position as king of vegetation, so here he is crowned with a chaplet of thorns that adds to his ignominy. The sacred blood must flow from the sacred head. But still, he is clothed with purple and saluted with the words, "Hail, King of the Jews!" in solemn irony. He is struck on the head with a reed by the soldiers: yet even as they strike, they bow their knees and worship him. They give him to drink wine, mingled with myrrh; "but he received it not." Then he is crucified at Golgotha, the place of a skull,* on a cross, the old sacred emblem of so many religions; it bears the inscription, "The King of the Jews," by order of the Procurator. After the death of the Christ he is mourned over, like Adonis and Osiris, by the holy women, including his mother. I do not think I need point out in detail the many close resemblances which exist between the Mother of the Gods and the Mother of God—the Theotokos.

* According to mediæval legend, the skull was Adam's, and the sacred blood which fell upon it revived it. In crucifixions, a skull is generally represented at the foot of the cross.

The thieves crucified with the Saviour have their legs broken, like many other sacred victims; but the Christ himself has not a bone broken, like the paschal lamb which was the Jewish substitute for the primitive human victim. Thus both ideas on this subject, the earlier and the later, seem to find an appropriate place in the history. Instead of having his legs broken, however, the Christ has his side pierced; and from it flows the mystic blood of the atonement, in which all Christians are theoretically washed; this baptism of blood (a literal reality in older cults) being already a familiar image at the date of the Apocalypse, where the robes of the elect are washed white in the blood of the lamb that was slain.

After the crucifixion, the Christ is taken down and buried. But, like all other corn and wine gods, he rises again from the dead on the third day—this very period of three days being already a conventional one in similar cases. Every one of the surroundings recalls Osiris and Attis. It is the women once more who see him first; and afterwards the men. Finally, he ascends into heaven, to his Father, before the wondering eyes of his disciples and his mother. In each item of this, there is nothing with which we are not already familiar elsewhere.

I will not pursue the analogy further. To do so would be endless. Indeed, I do not think there is an element in the Gospel story which does not bear out the parallel here suggested. The slight incident of the visit to Herod, for example, is exactly analogous to the visit of the false Osiris in modern Egypt to the governor's house, and the visit of the temporary or mock king in so many other cases to the real king's palace. The episode where Herod and his men of war array the Christ in a gorgeous robe is the equivalent of the episode of the Mexican king arraying the god-victim in royal dress, and is also paralleled in numerous other like dramas elsewhere. The women who prepare spices and ointments for the body recall the Adonis rites; Pilate washing his hands of the guilt of condemnation recalls the frequent episode of the slaughterers of the god laying the blame upon others, or casting it on the knife, or crying out, "We bought you with a price; we are guiltless." Whoever will read carefully through the Gospel accounts, side by side with Mr. Frazer's well-chosen collection of mock-king narratives, will see for himself that endless other minor traits crop up in the story which may be equated with numerous similar incidents in the death and resurrection of the man-god elsewhere.

The very subjects of the parables are in themselves significant: the lord of the vineyard who sends his son, whom the hirers slay; the labourers who come at the eleventh hour: the sower and the good and bad ground: the grain of mustard-seed : the leaven of the Pharisees : the seed growing secretly: the sons in the vineyard. It will be found that almost all of them turn on the key-note subjects of bread and wine, or at least of seed-sowing.

By what precise stages the story of the Galilæan mangod arose and fixed itself around the person of the real or mythical Jesus it would be hard to say. Already in the epistles we may catch stray glimpses, in the germ, of most of it. Already we notice strange hints and foreshadowings. Probably the first Jewish disciples had arrived at the outline of the existing story even before the Gentiles began to add their quotum. And when we look at documents so overloaded with miracle and legend as the Gospels and the Acts of the Apostles, we find it hard indeed to separate any element of historical truth from the enormous accretion of myth and legend. Still, I see no grave reason to doubt the general truth of the idea that the Christian belief and practice arose first among Galilæan Jews, and that from them it spread with comparative rapidity to the people of Syria and Asia Minor. It even seems probable that one Saul or Paul was really the person who first conceived the idea of preaching the new religion throughout the empire, and especially in the great cities, as a faith which might be embraced by both Jew and Gentile.

Certainly, while the young cult contained most of the best features of Judaism, viewed as a possible universal religion,—its monotheism, its purity, its comparative freedom from vile and absurd legends of the gods and their amours—it surpassed the elder faith in acceptability to the world at large, and especially to the people of Syria and western Asia. Every one of them could have said with perfect truth, "Nothing is changed; there is but one god more to worship."

As the church spread, the legend grew apace. To the early account of the death and resurrection of the King of the Jews, later narrators added the story of his miraculous birth from a virgin mother, who conceived directly from the spirit of God wafted down upon her. The wide extent and the origin of this belief about the conception of gods and heroes has been fully examined by Mr. Sidney Hartland in his admirable study of the Legend of Perseus. The new believers further provided their divine leader with a royal genealogy from David downward, and made him by a tolerably circuitous argument be born at Bethlehem, according to the supposed prophecy—though if there ever was really a Jesus at all, it would seem that the one fact of which we could feel tolerably sure about him, was the fact of his being a man of Nazareth. Later writers put into his mouth a high moral teaching for its time, somewhat anticipated by Hillel and other rabbis, and perhaps in part of Buddhist origin; they also made him announce for himself that divine *rôle* of mediator and atoner which they themselves claimed for the Saviour of Mankind. He calls himself the vine, the bread of life, the good shepherd; he is called "the lamb of God that taketh away the sins of the world," by John the Baptist, an enthusiast whose fame has attracted him at last into the Christian legend. Very early, the old rite of water-lustration or baptism, adopted by John, was employed as one of the chief Christian ceremonies, the ceremony of initiation, which replaced with advantage the bloody and dangerous Jewish circumcision.

This allowed for far freer proselytism than Judaism could ever expect; and though no doubt at first the Christians regarded themselves as a sect of the Jews, and though they always adopted entire the Jewish sacred books and the Jewish God, with all the Jewish history, cosmogony, and mythology, yet the new religion was from the beginning a cosmopolitan one, and preached the word unto all nations. Such a faith, coming at such a moment, and telling men precisely what they were ready to believe, was certain beforehand of pretty general acceptance. When Constantine made Christianity the official creed of the empire, it is clear that he did but put an official stamp of approval on a revolution that had long been growing more and more inevitable.

In one word, Christianity triumphed, because it united in itself all the most vital elements of all the religions then current in the world, with little that was local, national, or distasteful; and it added to them all a high ethical note and a social doctrine of human brotherhood especially suited to an age of unification and systematic government.

Occasionally, even in the Gospels themselves, we get strange passing echoes of a mysterious identification of the Christ with the ancient Hebrew ethnical god, not as the Lord of the Universe alone, but vaguely remembered as the sacred stone of the ark, the Rock of Israel. "The stone which the builders rejected, that one has become the head of the corner." "Whosoever shall fall on this stone shall be broken; but on whomsoever it shall fall, it will grind him to powder." And in a speech put into the mouth of Christ, he says to Peter, "Rock thou art, and on this Rock will I build my assembly." *

Sometimes, too, in the epistles the two ideas of the corn-god and the foundation stone-god are worked upon alter-

---

* I can honestly assure the polemical Protestant divine that I am well aware of the difference in gender in this passage—and of its utter unimportance. The name Peter could not well be made feminine to suit a particular play upon words or to anticipate the objections of a particular set of trivial word-twisters.

nately. "I have planted; Apollos watered." "Ye are God's husbandry; ye are God's building." "I have laid the foundation, and another builds thereon. Let every man take care how he builds upon it. For other foundation can no man lay than that which is laid, which is the Christ, Jesus." Or again, "You are built upon the foundation of the apostles and prophets, Jesus, the Christ, being himself the chief corner stone." Whoever rereads the epistles by the light of the analogies suggested in this book will find that they positively teem with similar references to the familiar theology of the various slain man-gods, which must have been known to every one along the shores of the Mediterranean.

The church which was built upon this rock—and that Rock was Christ—has shown its continuity with earlier religions in a thousand ways and by a thousand analogies. Solar and astrological elements have been freely admitted, side by side with those which recall the corn and wine gods. The chief festivals still cling to the solar feasts of the equinoxes and the solstices. Thus every year the church celebrates in mimicry the death and resurrection of the Christ, as the Mediterranean peoples celebrated the death and resurrection of the Attis, the Adonis, the Dionysus, the Osiris. It celebrates the feast at the usual time for most such festivals, the spring equinox. More than that, it chooses for the actual day of the resurrection, commonly called in English Easter, and in the Latin dialects the Paschal feast (or Pâques), a trebly astrological date. The festival must be as near as possible to the spring equinox; but it must be after a full moon, and it must be on the day sacred to the sun. Before the feast, a long fast takes place, at the close of which the Christ is slain in effigy, and solemnly laid in a mimic sepulchre. Good Friday is the anniversary of his piacular death, and the special day of the annual mourning, as for Adonis and Attis. On Easter Sunday, he rises again from the dead, and every good Catholic is bound to communicate—to eat the body of his slaughtered god on the annual spring festival of reviving vegetation. Comparison of the Holy Week ceremonies at Rome with the other annual festivals, from the Mexican corn-feast and the Potraj rite of India to Attis and Adonis, will be found extremely enlightening—I mean, of course, the ceremonies as they were when the Pope, the Priest-King, the representative of the annual Attis at Pessinus, officiated publicly in the Sistine Chapel, with paschal music known as Lamentations, and elevation of the Host amid the blare of trumpets. On this subject, I limit myself to the barest hint. Whoever chooses to follow out so pregnant a clue will find it lead him into curious analogies and almost incredible survivals.

Similarly, the birth of Christ is celebrated at the winter solstice, the well-known date for so many earlier ceremonies of the gods of vegetation. Then the infant god lies unconscious in his cradle. Whoever has read Mr. Frazer's great work will understand the connexion of the holly and the mistletoe, and the Christmas tree, with this second great festival of Christendom, very important in the Teutonic north, though far inferior in the south to the spring-tide feast, when the god is slain and eaten of necessity. I limit myself to saying that the Christmas rites are all of them rites of the birth of the corn-god.

Even the Christian cross, it is now known, was not employed as a symbol of the faith before the days of Constantine, and was borrowed from the solar wheel of the Gaulish sun-god-worshippers who formed the mass of the successful emperor's legionaries.

We are now, therefore, in a very different position for understanding the causes which led to the rise and development of the Christian religion from that which we occupied at the outset of our enquiry. We had then to accept crudely the bare fact that about the first century of our era a certain cult of a Divine Man, Jesus, arose among a fraction of the maritime people of Lower Syria. That fact as we at first received it stood isolated and unrelated in its naked singularity. We can now see that it was but one more example of a universal god-making tendency in human nature, high or low; and in our last chapter we shall find that this universal tendency to worship the dead has ever since persisted as fully as ever, and is in fact the central element in the entire religious instinct of humanity.

The main emotional chord upon which Christianity played in its early days—and indeed the main chord upon which it still plays—is just, I believe, the universal feeling in favour of the deification or beatification of the dead, with the desire for immortality on the part of the individual believer himself in person. Like all other religions, but even more than any other religion at that time in vogue, Christianity appealed to these two allied and deep-seated longings of human nature. It appealed on the one hand to the unselfish emotions and affections of mankind by promising a close, bodily, personal, and speedy re-association of the living believer with his dead relatives and friends. It appealed on the other hand to the selfish wishes and desires of each, by holding forth to every man the sure and certain hope of a glorious resurrection. Like all other creeds, but beyond all other creeds, it was the religion of immortality, of the dead revived, of the new world : in an age of doubt, of scepticism, of the decay of faith, it gave fresh life and a totally new basis to the old beliefs—perhaps the old delusions—of the religious nature.

A necessary consequence of the universal ferment and intermixture of pantheons everywhere during the early days of the Roman empire was a certain amount of floating scepticism about the gods as a whole, which reaches its highest point in the mocking humour of Lucian, or still earlier in the Epicurean atheism of Lucretius and of Roman philosophy in general. But while this nascent scepticism was very real and very widespread, it affected rather current beliefs as to the personality and history of the various gods than the underlying conception of godhead in the abstract. Even those who laughed and those who disbelieved, retained at bottom many superstitions and supernatural ideas. Their scepticism was due, not like that of our own time to fundamental criticism of the very notion of the supernatural, but to the obvious inadequacy of existing gods to satisfy the requirements of educated cosmopolitans. The deities of the time were too coarse, too childish, too gross for their worshippers. The common philosophic attitude of cultivated Rome and cultivated Alexandria might be compared to some extent to that of our own Unitarians, who are not indeed hostile to the conception of theology in its own nature, but who demur to the most miraculous and supernatural part of the popular doctrine.

With the mass, however, the religious unrest showed itself mainly, as it always shows itself at such critical moments, in a general habit of running after new and strange religions, from some one or other of which the anxious enquirer hopes to obtain some divine answer to his doubts and difficulties. When old faiths decay, there is room for new ones. As might have been expected, this tendency was most clearly shown in the great cosmopolitan trading towns, where men of many nations rubbed shoulders together, and where outlandish cults of various sorts had their temples and their adherents. Especially was this the case at Rome, Alexandria, and Antioch, the capitals respectively of the Roman, the Hellenic, and the Semitic worlds. In the Græco-Egyptian metropolis, the worship of Serapis, a composite deity of hybrid origin, grew gradually into the principal cult of the teeming city. At Antioch, Hellenic deities were ousting the Baalim. At Rome, the worship of Isis, of Jahweh, of Syrian and other remoter Eastern gods was carried on by an ever-increasing body of the foreign, native, and servile population. These were the places where Christianity spread. The men of the villages were long, as the world still quaintly phrases it, " pagans."

The strange cults which united in thus gradually crushing out the old local and national pantheons throughout the Roman world, had for the most part two marked attributes in common: they were more or less mystical; and they tended more or less in the direction of monotheism. Solar myth, syncretism, the esoteric priestly interpretations, and the general diffusion of Greek philosophic notions, mixed with subtler oriental and Zoroastrian ideas, had all promoted the rise and growth of the mystic element: while a vague monotheistic movement had long been apparent in the higher thought of Egypt, Greece, Italy, and the East. In the resulting conflict and intermixture of ideas, Judaism, as one of the most mystical and monotheistic of religions, would have stood a good chance of becoming the faith of the world, had it not been for the fatal weight of its strict and obstinate national character. Even as it was, Jewish communities were scattered through all the commercial towns of the Græco-Roman world; a Jewish colony strongly influenced Alexandria; and Jewish teachers made proselytes in Rome in the very bosom of the imperial household.

The ferment which thus existed by the Orontes, the Nile, and the Tiber must also have extended in a somewhat less degree to all the cosmopolitan seaports and trading towns of the great and heterogeneous military empire. What was true of Rome, Alexandria, and Antioch, was true in part, we have every reason to believe, of Damascus, of Byzantium, of Sinope, of Ephesus : of Rhodes, of Cyrene, of Athens, of Carthage; perhaps even of Massilia, of Gades, of Burdigala, of Lugdunum. All around the eastern Mediterranean at least, new faiths were seething, new ideas were brewing, new mysticisms were being evolved, new superstitions were arising, Phœnix-like, out of the dying embers of decaying creeds. Setting aside mere exotic or hybrid cults, like the worship of Serapis at Alexandria and of Isis at Rome, or mere abortive attempts like the short-lived worship of Antinous in

Egypt, we may say that three of these new religions appealed strongly to the wants and desires of the time: and those three were Mithraism, Gnosticism, and Christianity.

All were alike somewhat eclectic in character; and all could lay claim to a certain cosmopolitan and catholic spirit unknown to the cults of the old national pantheons. All came to the Greek and Roman world from the mystic east, the land of the rising sun, whose magic is felt even at the present day by the votaries of Theosophy and of Esoteric Buddhism. Which of the three was to conquer in the end might have seemed at one time extremely doubtful: nor indeed do I believe that the ultimate triumph of Christianity, the least imposing of the three, inevitable as it at last became, was by any means at first a foregone conclusion. The religion of Jesus probably owed quite as much to what we call chance—that is to say, to the play of purely personal and casual circumstances— as to its own essential internal characteristics. If Constantine or any other shrewd military chief had happened to adopt the symbols of Mithra or Abraxas instead of the name of Christ, it is quite conceivable that all the civilised world might now be adoring the mystic divinity of the three hundred and sixty-five emanations, as sedulously as it actually adores the final theological outcome of the old Hebrew Jahweh. But there were certain real advantages as well, which told, I believe, in the very nature of things, in favour of the Christ as against the coinage of Basilides or the far-eastern sun-god. Constantine, in other words, chose his religion wisely. It was the cult exactly adapted to the times: above all others, during the two centuries or so that had passed since its first beginning (for we must place the real evolution of the Christian system considerably later than the life or death of Jesus himself) it had shown itself capable of thoroughly engaging on its own side the profoundest interests and emotions of the religious nature.

We must remember, too, that in all religious crises,

while faith in the actual gods and creeds declines rapidly, no corresponding weakening occurs in the underlying sentiments on which all religions ultimately base themselves. Hence the apparent paradox that periods of doubt are also almost always periods of intense credulity as well. The human mind, cast free from the moorings which have long sufficed for it, drifts about restlessly in search of some new haven in which it may take refuge from the terrors of uncertainty and infidelity. And its new faith is always but a fresh form of the old one. A god or gods, prayer, praise, and sacraments, are essential elements. More especially is it the case that when trust in the great gods begins to fail, a blind groping after necromancy, spiritualism, and ghost-lore in general takes its place for the moment. We have seen this tendency fully exemplified in our own time by the spiritualists and others: nor was it less marked in the tempest of conflicting ideas which broke over the Roman world from the age of the Antonines to the fall of the empire. The fact is, the average man cares but little, after all, for his gods and his goddesses, viewed as individuals. They are but an outlet for his own emotions. He appeals to them for help, as long as he continues to believe in their effective helpfulness: he is ready to cajole them with offerings of blood or to flatter them with homage of praise and prayer, as long as he expects to gain some present or future benefit, bodily or spiritual, in return for his assiduous adulation. But as soon as his faith in their existence and power begins to break down, he puts up with the loss of their godhead, so far as they themselves are concerned, without one qualm of disappointment or inconvenience. It is something far other than *that* that touches him in religion: it is his hopes for his own eternal welfare, and the welfare after death of those that love him.

Hence, a decline of faith in the great gods is immediately followed by a recrudescence of the most barbaric and original element in religion—the cult of the ghost or spirit, necromancy, the direct worship of the dead or intercourse with the dead: a habit of enquiry into the positive chances of human immortality. This necromantic spirit is well marked in Gnostic remains, and in the fragmentary magical literature of the decadent Græco-Roman world. It is precisely the same tendency which produces spiritualism in our own time: and it is due to the desire to find some new and experimental basis for the common human belief in the immortality of the soul or the resurrection of the body.

And here we get the clue to the serious change which Christianity wrought in the religious feeling of the western world: a change whose importance and whose retrograde nature has never yet, I believe, been fully recognised. For Christianity, while from one point of view, as a monotheistic or quasi-monotheistic religion, an immense advance upon the æsthetic paganism of Greece and Italy, was from another point of view, as a religion of resurrection rather than a religion of immortality, a step backward for all Western Europe.

Even among the Jews themselves, however, the new cult must have come with all the force of an "aid to faith" in a sceptical generation. Abroad, among the Jewish Hellenists, Greek philosophy must have undermined much of the fanatical and patriotic enthusiasm for Jahweh which had grown stronger and ever stronger in Judæa itself through the days of the Maccabees and the Asmonæan princes. Scraps of vague Platonic theorising on the nature of the Divine were taking among these exiles the place of the firm old dogmatic belief in the Rock of Israel. At home, the Hellenising tendencies of the house of Herod, and the importance in Jerusalem of the Sadducees "who say there is no resurrection," were striking at the very roots of the hope and faith that pious Jews most tenderly cherished. Instead of Israel converting the world, the world seemed likely to convert Israel. Swamped in the great absorbing and assimilating empire,

Judah might follow in the way of Ephraim. And Israel's work in the world might thus be undone, or rather stultified for ever.

Just at this very moment, when all faiths were tottering visibly to their fall, a tiny band of obscure Galilæan peasants, who perhaps had followed a wild local enthusiast from their native hills up to turbulent Jerusalem, may have been seized with a delusion neither unnatural nor unaccustomed under their peculiar circumstances; but which nevertheless has sufficed to turn or at least to modify profoundly the entire subsequent course of the world's history. Their leader, if we may trust the universal tradition of the sect, as laid down long after in their legendary Gospels, was crucified at Jerusalem under C. Pontius Pilatus. If any fact upon earth about Jesus is true, besides the fact of his residence at Nazareth, it is this fact of the crucifixion, which derives verisimilitude from being always closely connected with the name of that particular Roman official. But three days after, says the legend, the body of Jesus could not be found in the sepulchre where his friends had laid him: and a rumour gradually gained ground that he had risen from the dead, and had been seen abroad by the women who mourned him and by various of his disciples. In short, what was universally believed about all other and elder human gods, was specifically asserted afresh in a newer case about the man Christ Jesus. The idea fitted in with the needs of the time, and the doctrine of the Resurrection of Jesus the Christ became the corner-stone of the new-born Christian religion.

Nothing can be clearer than the fact admitted on all hands, that this event formed the central point of the Apostles' preaching. It was the Resurrection of Jesus, regarded as an earnest of general resurrection for all his followers, that they most insisted upon in their words and writings. It was the resurrection that converted the world of western Europe. "Your faith is flagging," said the early Christians in effect to their pagan fellows: "your gods are half-dead; your ideas about your own future, and the present state of your departed friends, are most vague and shadowy. In opposition to all this, we offer you a sure and certain hope; we tell you a tale of real life, and recent; we preach a god of the familiar pattern, yet very close to you; we present you with a specimen of actual resurrection. We bring you good tidings of Jesus as the Messiah, and him crucified : to the Jews, a stumbling-block ; to the Greeks, foolishness ; but to such as are saved, a plain evidence of the power of the God of Israel. Accept our word: let your dead sleep in Christ in our catacombs, as once they slept in Osiris at Abydos, or rested upon him that rests at Philæ." "If Christ be not risen," says one of the earliest Christian writers in a passionate peroration, "then is our preaching vain, and your faith is vain also: but as it is, Christ is risen from the dead, and has become the first fruits of them that slept." "Else what shall they do," he goes on, touching to the quick that ingrained human desire for communion with the departed, "what shall they do which are baptised for the dead, if the dead rise not at all ? Why are they then baptised for the dead ?" These, in short, apart from the elements common to all creeds, are the three great motors of primitive Christianity: one dogmatic, the resurrection of Jesus: one selfish, the salvation of the individual soul: one altruistic, the desire for reunion with the dead among one's beloved.

Syria and Egypt could easily accept the new doctrine. It involved for them no serious change of front, no wide departure from the ideas and ceremonies which always formed their rounded concept of human existence. There is a representation of the resurrection of Osiris in the little temple on the roof at Denderah which might almost pass for a Christian illustration of the resurrection of Jesus. To Syrian and Egyptian, the resurrection indeed was but a special modern instance of a well-known fact; a fresh basis of evidence upon which to plant firmly the tottering edifice of their old convictions. In its beginnings, in short, Christianity was essentially an oriental religion; it spread fastest in the eastern Mediterranean basin, where Judaism was already well established: at Rome, it seems to have attracted chiefly the oriental population. And it is a significant fact that its official adoption as the public religion of the Roman state was the act of the same prince who deliberately shifted the seat of his government from the Tiber to the Bosphorus, and largely transformed the character of the empire from a Latin to a Græco-Asiatic type. All the new religions which struggled together for the mastery of the world were oriental in origin: the triumph of Christianity was but a single episode in the general triumph of aggressive orientalism over the occidental element in the Roman system.

Egypt in particular, I believe, had far more to do with the dogmatic shaping of early Christianity, and the settlement of Christian symbolism and Christian mysticism, than is generally admitted by the official historians of the primitive church. There, where the idea of resurrection was already so universal, and where every man desired to be "justified by Osiris," Christianity soon made an easy conquest of a people on whose faith it exerted so little change. And Egypt easily made its influence felt on the plastic young creed. It is allowed that the doctrine of the Trinity took shape among the Triad-worshippers on the banks of the Nile, and that the scarcely less important doctrine of the Logos was borrowed from the philosophy of Alexandrian Jews. Nobody can look at the figures of Isis and the infant Horus in any Egyptian museum without being at once struck by the obvious foreshadowing of the Coptic and Byzantine Madonna and Child. The mystery that sprang up about the new doctrines; the strange syncretic union of Father, Son, and Holy Ghost into a single Trinity; the miraculous conception by the Theotokos or mother of God—a clear variant in one aspect on the older idea of Hathor; and the antenatal existence of

Christ in heaven before his incarnation; all are thoroughly Egyptian in character, with a faint superadded dash of Alexandrian Jewish Hellenism. The love of symbols which the young church so early exhibits in the catacombs and elsewhere smacks equally of Ptolemaic reminiscences of Thebes and Memphis. The mummy-form of Lazarus; the fish that makes such a clever alphabetic ideogram for the name and titles of Jesus; the dove that symbolises the Holy Ghost; the animal types of the four evangelists—all these are in large part Egyptian echoes, resonant of the same spirit which produced the hieroglyphics and the symbolism of the great Nilotic temples. At the same time it must be remembered that sacred fish were common in Syria, and that similar identifications of gods with animals have met us at every turn, in our earlier investigation.

Nay, more, the very details themselves of Christian symbolism often go back to early Egyptian models. The central Christian emblem of all, the cross, is holy all the world over: it is the sacred tree: and each race has adapted it to its own preconceived ideas and symbols. But in Coptic Christianity it has obvious affinities with the *crux ansata*. In the Coptic room of the New Museum at Ghizeh is an early Christian monument with a Greek uncial inscription, on which is represented a cross of four equal limbs with expanded flanges, having a *crux ansata* inserted in all its four interstices. At the Coptic church of Abu Sirgeh at Old Cairo occurs a similar cross, also with suggestions of Tau-like origin, but with other equal-limbed crosses substituted for the *cruces ansatæ* in the corners.* How far the Egyptian Christians thus merely transferred their old ideas to the new faith may be gathered from a single curious example. In Mr. Loftie's collection of sacred beetles is a

* Count Goblet d'Alviella's interesting work on *The Migration of Symbols* well illustrates this common syncretism and interchangeability of symbolic signs, which runs parallel with the syncretism of gods and religions.

scarabæus containing a representation of the crucifixion, with two palm branches: and other scarabs have Christian crosses, "some of them," says Mr. Loftie, "very unmistakable." If we remember how extremely sacred the scarab was held in the Egyptian religion, and also that it was regarded as the symbol of the resurrection, we cannot possibly miss the importance of this implication. Indeed, the Alexandrian Father, Epiphanius, speaks of Christ as "the scarabæus of God," a phrase which may be still better understood if I add that in the treatise on hieroglyphs known under the name of Horapollo a scarabæus is said to denote "an only-begotten." Thus "the lamb of God" in the tongue of Israel becomes "the scarabæus of God" in the mouth of an Egyptian speaker. To put it shortly, I believe we may say with truth, in a sense far other than that intended by either prophet or evangelist, "Out of Egypt have I called my son."

In the west, however, the results of the spread of Christianity were far more revolutionary. Indeed, I do not think the cult of Jesus could ever have spread at all in Rome had it not been for the large extent to which the city was peopled in later times by Syrians and Africans. And if Christianity had not spread in Rome, it could never have gained a foothold at all in the Aryan world: for it is not at bottom an Aryan religion in tone and feeling: it has only become possible among Aryan peoples by undergoing at last a considerable change of spirit, though not largely of form, in its westward progress. This change is indicated by the first great schism, which severed the Latin from the Greek communion.

Foremost among the changes which Christianity involved in Italy and the rest of western Europe was the retrograde change from the belief in immortality and the immateriality of the soul, with cremation as its practical outcome, to the belief in the resurrection of the body, with a return to the disused and discredited practice of burial as its normal correlative. The catacombs were the necessary result of this backward movement; and with the catacombs came in the possibility of relic-worship, martyr-worship, and the adoration of saints and their corpses. I shall trace out in my next chapter the remoter effects of this curious revival of the prime element in religion—the cult of the dead—in greater detail: it must suffice here to point out briefly that it resulted as a logcal effect from the belief in the resurrection of Christ, and the consequent restoration of the practice of burial. Moreover, to polytheists, this habit gave a practical opening for the cult of many deities in the midst of nominal monotheism, which the Italians and sundry other essentially polytheistic peoples were not slow to seize upon. Here again the difference between the more monotheistic and syncretic east, which puts a ban upon graven images, and the more polytheistic and separating west, which freely admits the employment of sculpture, is not a little significant. It is true that theoretically the adoration paid to saints and martyrs is never regarded as real worship: but I need hardly say that technical distinctions like these are always a mere part of the artificial theology of scholastic priesthoods, and may be as safely disregarded by the broad anthropological enquirer as may all the other fanciful lumber of metaphysical Brahmans and theologians everywhere. The genuine facts of religion are the facts and rites of the popular cult, which remain in each race for long periods together essentially uniform.

Thus we early get two main forms of Christianity, both official and popular: one eastern—Greek, Coptic, Syrian; more mystical in type, more symbolic, more philosophic, more monotheistic: the other western—Latin, Celtic, Spanish; more Aryan in type, more practical, more material, more polytheistic. And these at a later time are reinforced by a third or northern form,—the Teutonic and Protestant; in which ethical ideas preponderate over religious, and the worship of the Book in its most literal and often foolish interpretation supersedes the earlier worship of Madonna, saints, pictures, statues, and emblems.

At the period when Christianity first begins to emerge from the primitive obscurity of its formative nisus, however, we find it practically compounded of the following elements—which represent the common union of a younger god offered up to an older one with whom he is identified.

First of all, as the implied basis, taken for granted in all the early Hebrew scriptures, there is current Judaism, in the form that Judaism had gradually assumed in the fourth, third, and second centuries before the Christian era. This includes as its main principle the cult of the one god Jahweh, now no longer largely thought of under that personal name, or as a strictly ethnic deity, but rather envisaged as the Lord God who dwells in heaven, very much as Christians of to-day still envisage him. It includes also an undercurrent of belief in a heavenly hierarchy of angels and archangels, the court of the Lord (modifications of an earlier astrological conception, the Host of Heaven), and in a principle of evil, Satan or the devil, dwelling in hell, and similarly surrounded by a crowd of minor or assistant demons. Further, it accepts implicitly from earlier Judaism the resurrection of the dead, the judgment of the good and the wicked, the doctrine of future rewards and punishments (perhaps in its fullest shape a Hellenistic importation from Egypt, though also commonly found in most spontaneous religions), and many other tenets of the current Jewish belief. In short, the very earliest Christians, being probably for the most part Jews, Galilæans, and proselytes, or else Syrians and Africans of Judaising tendencies, did not attempt to get rid of all their preconceived religious opinions when they became Christians, but merely superadded to these as a new item the special cult of the deified Jesus.

On the other hand, as the Gospel spread to the Gentiles, it was not thought necessary to burden the fresh converts with the whole minute ceremonial of Judaism, and especially with the difficult and unpleasant initiatory rite of circumcision. A mere symbolical lustration, known as baptism, was all that was demanded of new adherents to the faith, with abstinence from any participation in "heathen" sacrifices or functions. To this extent the old exclusiveness of Jahweh-worship, the cult of the jealous God, was still allowed to assert itself. And the general authority of the Hebrew scriptures, especially as a historical account of the development of Judaism, from which Christianity sprang, was more or less fully admitted, at first by implication or quotation alone, but afterwards by the deliberate and avowed voice of the whole Christian assembly. The translation of this mixed mass of historical documents, early cosmogonies, ill-reported and Jehovised Jewish traditions, misinterpreted poems, and conscious forgeries, in the Latin version known as the Vulgate, had the effect of endowing Europe for many centuries with a false body of ancient history, which must have largely retarded the development of the race up to our own time, and whose evil effects have hardly yet passed away among the more ignorant and conservative Bibliolatrous classes of modern society.

Superimposed upon this substratum of current Judaism with its worship of Jahweh came the distinctive Jesus-cult, the worship of the particular dead Galilæan peasant. This element was superadded to the cult of the Father, the great god who had slowly and imperceptibly developed out of the sacred stone that the sons of Israel were believed to have brought up with them from the land of Egypt. But how, in a religion pretending to be monotheistic, were these two distinct cults of two such diverse gods to be reconciled or to be explained away? By the familiar doctrine of the incarnation, and the belief in the human god who is sacrificed, himself to himself, as a piacular offering. Jewish tradition and subtler Egyptian mysticism sufficed to smooth over the apparent anomaly. The Jews looked forward to a mysterious deliverer, a new Moses, the Messiah, who was to fulfil the destiny of Israel by uniting all nations under the sceptre of David,

and by bringing the Gentiles to the feet of the God of
Israel. Jesus, said the Christians, had proclaimed himself that very Messiah, the Christ of God; he had often
alluded to the great Hebrew deity as his father; he had
laid claim to the worship of the Lord of heaven. Further
than this, perhaps, the unaided Jewish intelligence would
hardly have gone: it would have been satisfied with
assigning to the slain man-god Jesus a secondary place,
as the only begotten Son of God, who gave himself up as a
willing victim—a position perhaps scarcely more important
than that which Mohammad holds in the system of Islam.
Such, it seems to me, is on the whole the conception which
permeates the synoptic Gospels, representing the ideas of
Syrian Christendom. But here the acute Græco-Egyptian mind came in with its nice distinctions and its mystical
identifications. There was but one god, indeed; yet that
god was at least twofold (to go no further for the present).
He had two persons, the Father and the Son : and the
Second Person, identified with the Alexandrian conception of the Logos, though inferior to the Father as touching his manhood, was equal to the Father as touching his
godhead—after the precise fashion we saw so common in
describing the relations of Osiris and Horus, and the identification of the Attis or Adonis victim with the earlier
and older god he represented. "I and my Father are
one," says the Christ of the Fourth Gospel, the embodiment and incarnation of the Alexandrian Logos. And in
the very forefront of that manifesto of Neo-Platonic
Christianity comes the dogmatic assertion, "In the beginning was the Logos: and the Logos dwelt with God:
and the Logos *was* God."

Even so the basis of the new creed is still incomplete.
The Father and Son give the whole of the compound
deity as the popular mind, everywhere and always, has
commonly apprehended it. But the scholastic and theological intelligence needed a Third Person to complete the
Trinity which to all mankind, as especially to orientals, is

the only perfect and thoroughly rounded figure. In later days, no doubt, the Madonna would have been chosen to fill up the blank, and, on the analogy of Isis, would have filled it most efficiently. As a matter of fact, in the creed of Christendom as the Catholic people know it, the Madonna is really one of the most important personages. But in those early formative times, the cult of the Theotokos had hardly yet assumed its full importance: perhaps, indeed, the Jewish believers would have been shocked at the bare notion of the worship of a woman, the readmission of an Astarte, a Queen of Heaven, into the faith of Israel. Another object of adoration had therefore to be found. It was discovered in that vague essence, the Holy Ghost, or Divine Wisdom, whose gradual development and dissociation from God himself is one of the most curious chapters in all the history of artificial god-making. The "spirit of Jahweh" had frequently been mentioned in Hebrew writings; and with so invisible and unapproachable a deity as the Jewish God, was often made to do duty as a messenger or intermediary where the personal presence of Jahweh himself would have been felt to contravene the first necessities of incorporeal divinity. It was the "spirit of Jahweh" that came upon the prophets: it was the "wisdom of Jahweh" that the poets described, and that grew at last to be detached from the personality of God, and alluded to almost as a living individual. In the early church, this "spirit of God," this "holy spirit," was supposed to be poured forth upon the heads of believers: it descended upon Jesus himself in the visible form of a dove from heaven, and upon the disciples at Pentecost as tongues of fire. Gradually, the conception of a personal Holy Ghost took form and definiteness: an Alexandrian monk insisted on the necessity for a Triad of gods who were yet one God: and by the time the first creeds of the nascent church were committed to writing, the Spirit had come to rank with the Father and the Son as the Third Person in the ever-blessed Trinity.

By this time, too, it is pretty clear that the original manhood of Jesus had got merged in the idea of his eternal godhead; he was regarded as the Logos, come down from heaven, where he had existed before all worlds, and incarnate by the Holy Ghost in the Virgin Mary. The other articles of the Christian faith clustered gradually round these prime elements: the myth gathered force; the mysticism increased; the secondary divine beings or saints grew vastly in numbers; and the element of Judaism disappeared piecemeal, while a new polytheism and a new sacerdotalism took root apace in the Aryan world. I shall strive to show, however, in my concluding chapters, how even to the very end the worship of the dead is still the central force in modern Christianity: how religion, whatever its form, can never wander far from that fundamental reality: and how, whenever by force of circumstances the gods become too remote from human life, so that the doctrine of resurrection or personal immortality is endangered for a time, and reunion with relations in the other world becomes doubtful or insecure, a reaction is sure to set in which takes things back once more to these fundamental concepts, the most persistent and perpetually recurrent element in all religious thinking.

CHAPTER XIX.

SURVIVALS IN CHRISTENDOM.

WE have now travelled far, apparently, from that primitive stage of god-making where the only known gods are the corpses, mummies, skulls, ghosts, or spirits of dead chieftains or dead friends and relations. The God of Christianity, in his fully-evolved form, especially as known to thinkers and theologians, is a being so vast, so abstract, so ubiquitous, so eternal, that he seems to have hardly any points of contact at all with the simple ancestral spirit or sacred stone from which in the last resort he appears to be descended. Yet even here, we must beware of being misled by too personal an outlook. While the higher minds in Christendom undoubtedly conceive of the Christian God in terms of Mansel and Martineau, the lower minds even among ourselves conceive of him in far simpler and more material fashions. A good deal of enquiry among ordinary English people of various classes, not always the poorest, convinces me that to large numbers of them God is envisaged as possessing a material human form, more or less gaseous in composition; that, in spite of the Thirty-nine Articles, he has body, parts, and passions; that he is usually pictured to the mind's eye as about ten or twelve feet high, with head, hands, eyes and mouth, used to see with and speak with in human fashion; and that he sits on a throne, like a king that he is, surrounded by a visible court of angels and archangels. Italian art so invariably represents him, with a frankness unknown to Protestant Christendom. Instead of being in all places at once, pervading and underlying nature, the Deity is conceived of by most of his worshippers as having merely the power of annihilating space, and finding himself wherever he likes at a given moment. His omniscience and omnipotence are readily granted; but his abstractness and immateriality are not really grasped by one out of a thousand of his believers in Britain.

The fact is, so abstract a conception as the highest theological conception of God cannot be realised except symbolically, and then for a few moments only, in complete isolation. The moment God is definitely thought of in connexion with any cosmic activity, still more in connexion with any human need, he is inevitably thought of on human analogies, and more or less completely anthropomorphised in the brain of the believer. Being by origin an offshoot of the mind of man, a great deified human being, he retains necessarily still, for all save a few very mystical or ontological souls, the obvious marks of his ultimate descent from a ghost or spirit. Indeed, on the mental as opposed to the bodily side, he does so for us all; since even theologians freely ascribe to him such human feelings as love, affection, a sense of justice, a spirit of mercy, of truth, of wisdom: knowledge, will, the powers of intellect, all the essential and fundamental human faculties and emotions.

Thus, far as we seem to have travelled from our base in the most exalted concepts of God, we are nearer to it still than most of us imagine. Moreover, in spite of this height to which the highest minds have raised their idea of the Deity, as the creator, sustainer, and mover of the universe, every religion, however monotheistic, still continues to make new minor gods for itself out of the dead as they die, and to worship these gods with even more assiduous worship than it bestows upon the great God of Christendom or the great gods of the central pantheon. And the Christian religion makes such minor deities no less than all others. The fact is, the religious emotion takes its origin from the affection and regard felt for the dead by survivors, mingled with the hope and belief that they may be of some use or advantage, temporal or spiritual, to those who call upon them; and these primitive faiths and feelings remain so ingrained in the very core of humanity that even the most abstract of all religions, like the Protestant schism, cannot wholly choke them, while recrudescences of the original creed and custom spring up from time to time in the form of spiritualism, theosophy, and other vague types of simple ghost-worship.

Most advanced religions, however, and especially Christianity in its central, true, and main form of Catholicism, have found it necessary to keep renewing from time to time the stock of minor gods—here arbitrarily known as saints— much as the older religions found it always necessary from year to year to renew the foundation-gods, the corn and wine gods, and the other special deities of the manufactured order, by a constant supply of theanthropic victims. What I wish more particularly to point out here, however, is that the vast majority of places of worship all the world over are still erected, as at the very beginning, above the body of a dead man or woman; that the chief objects of worship in every shrine are still, as always, such cherished bodies of dead men and women; and that the primitive connexion of Religion with Death has never for a moment been practically severed in the greater part of the world,— not even in Protestant England and America.

Mr. William Simpson was one of the first persons to point out this curious underlying connexion between churches, temples, mosques, or topes, and a tomb or monument. He has proved his point in a very full manner, and I would refer the reader who wishes to pursue this branch of the subject at length to his interesting monographs. In this work, I will confine my attention mainly to the continued presence of this death-element in Christianity; but by way of illustration, I will preface my remarks by a few stray instances picked up at random from the neighbouring and interesting field of Islam.

There is no religion in all the world which professes to be more purely monotheistic in character than Mohammedanism. The unity of God, in the very strictest sense, is the one dogma round which the entire creed of Islam centres. More than any other cult, it represents itself as a distinct reaction against the polytheism and superstition of surrounding faiths. The isolation of Allah is its one great dogma. If, therefore, we find even in this most monotheistic of existing religious systems a large element of practically polytheistic survival—if we find that even here the Worship of the Dead remains, as a chief component in religious practice, if not in religious theory, we shall be fairly entitled to conclude, I think, that such constituents are indeed of the very essence of religious thinking, and we shall be greatly strengthened in the conclusions at which we previously arrived as to a belief in immortality or continued life of the dead being in fact the core and basis of worship and of deity.

Some eight or ten years since, when I first came practically into connexion with Islam in Algeria and Egypt, I was immediately struck by the wide prevalence among the Mahommedan population of forms of worship for which I was little prepared by anything I had previously read or heard as to the nature and practice of that exclusive and ostentatiously monotheistic faith. Two points, indeed, forcibly strike any visitor who for the first time has the opportunity of observing a Mahommedan community in its native surroundings. The first is the universal habit on the part of the women of visiting the cemeteries and mourning or praying over the graves of their relations on Friday, the sacred day of Islam. The second is the frequency of Koubbas, or little whitewashed mosque-tombs erected over the remains of Marabouts, fakeers, or local saints, which form the real centres for the religion and worship of every village. Islam, in practice, is a religion of pilgrimages to the tombs of the dead. In Algeria, every hillside is dotted over with these picturesque little whitewashed domes, each overshadowed by its sacred date-palm, each surrounded by its small walled enclosure or *temenos* of prickly pear or agave, and each attended by its local ministrant, who takes charge of the tomb and of the alms of the faithful. Holy body, sacred stone, tree, well, and priest—not an element of the original cult of the dead is lacking. Numerous pilgrimages are made to these koubbas by the devout: and on Friday evenings the little courtyards are almost invariably thronged by a crowd of eager and devoted worshippers. Within, the bones of the holy man lie preserved in a frame hung about with rosaries, pictures, and other oblations of his ardent disciples, exactly as in the case of Roman Catholic chapels. The saint, in fact, is quite as much an institution of monotheistic Islam as of any other religion with which I am practically acquainted.

These two peculiarities of the cult of Islam strike a stranger immediately on the most casual visit. When he comes to look at the matter more closely, however, he finds also that most of the larger mosques in the principal towns are themselves similarly built to contain and enshrine the bones of saintly personages, more or less revered in their immediate neighbourhood. Some of these are indeed so holy that their bones have been duplicated exactly like the wood of the true cross, and two tombs have been built in separate places where the whole or a portion of the supposed remains are said to be buried. I will only specify as instances of such holy tombs the sacred city of Kerouan in Tunisia, which ranks second to Mecca and Medina alone in the opinion of all devout western Mohammedans. Here, the most revered building is the shrine of "The Companion of the Prophet," who lies within a catafalque covered with palls of black velvet and silver—as funereal a monument as is known to me anywhere. Close by stands the catafalque of an Indian saint:

while other holy tomb-mosques abound in the city. In Algiers town, the holiest place is similarly the mosque-tomb of Sidi Abd-er-Rahman, which contains the shrine and body of that saint, who died in 1471. Around him, so as to share his sacred burial-place (like the Egyptians who wished to be interred with Osiris), lie the bodies of several Deys and Pashas. Lights are kept constantly burning at the saint's tomb, which is hung with variously-coloured drapery, after the old Semitic fashion, while banners and ostrich-eggs, the gifts of the faithful, dangle ostentatiously round it from the decorated ceiling. Still more sacred in its way is the venerable shrine of Sidi Okba near Biskra, one of the most ancient places of worship in the Mahommedan world. The tomb of the great saint stands in a chantry, screened off from the noble mosque which forms the ante-chamber, and is hung round with silk and other dainty offerings. On the front an inscription in very early Cufic characters informs us that " This is the tomb of Okba, son of Nafa: May Allah have mercy upon him." The mosque is a famous place of pilgrimage, and a belief obtains that when the Sidi is rightly invoked, a certain minaret in its front will nod in acceptance of the chosen worshipper. I could multiply instances indefinitely, but refrain on purpose. All the chief mosques at Tlemçen, Constantine, and the other leading North African towns similarly gather over the bodies of saints or *marabouts*, who are invoked in prayer, and to whom every act of worship is offered.

All over Islam we get such holy grave-mosques. The tomb of the Prophet at Medina heads the list: with the equally holy tomb of his daughter Fatima. Among the Shiahs, Ali's grave at Nejef and Hoseyn's grave at Kerbela are as sacred as that of the Prophet at Medina. The shrines of the Imams are much adored in Persia. The graves of the peers in India, the Ziarets of the fakeers in Afghanistan, show the same tendency. In Palestine, says

Major Conder, worship at the tombs of local saints "represents the real religion of the peasant."

I had originally intended, indeed, to include in this work a special chapter on these survivals in Islam, a vast number of which I have collected in various places; but my book has already swelled to so much larger dimensions than I had originally contemplated that I am compelled reluctantly to forego this disquisition.

One word, however, must be given to Egypt, where the cult of the dead was always so marked a feature in the developed religion, and where neither Christianity nor Islam has been able to obscure this primitive tendency. Nothing is more noticeable in the Nile Valley than the extraordinary way in which the habits and ideas as to burial and the preservation of the dead have survived in spite of the double and rapid alteration in religious theory. At Sakkarah and Thebes, one is familiar with the streets and houses of tombs, regularly laid out so as to form in the strictest sense a true Necropolis, or city of the dead. Just outside Cairo, on the edge of the desert, a precisely similar modern Necropolis exists to this day, regularly planned in streets and quarters, with the tomb of each family standing in its own courtyard or enclosure, and often very closely resembling the common round-roofed or domed Egyptian houses. In this town of dead bodies, every distinction of rank and wealth may now be observed. The rich are buried under splendid mausolea of great architectural pretensions; the poor occupy humble tombs just raised above the surface of the desert, and marked at head and foot with rough and simple Egyptian tombstones. Still, the entire aspect of such a cemetery is the aspect of a town. In northern climates, the dead sleep their last sleep under grassy little tumuli, wholly unlike the streets of a city: in Egypt, to this day, the dead occupy, as in life, whole lanes and alleys of eternal houses. Even the spirit which produced the Pyramids and the Tombs of the Kings is conspicuous in modern or mediæval Cairo in the taste which begot those vast domed mosques known as the Tombs of the Khalifs and the Tombs of the Mamelooks. Whatever is biggest in the neighbourhood of ancient Memphis turns out on examination to be the last resting-place of a Dead Man, and a place of worship.

Almost every one of the great mosques of Cairo is either a tomb built for himself by a ruler—and this is the more frequent case—or else the holy shrine of some saint of Islam. It is characteristic of Egypt, however, where king and god have always been so closely combined, that while elsewhere the mosque is usually the prayer-tomb of a holy man, in Cairo it is usually the memorial-temple of a Sultan, an Emeer, a viceroy, or a Khedive. It is interesting to find, too, after all we have seen as to the special sanctity of the oracular head, that perhaps the holiest of all these mosques contains the head of Hoseyn, the grandson of the Prophet. A ceremonial washing is particularly mentioned in the story of its translation. The mosque of Sultan Hassan, with its splendid mausolem, is a peculiarly fine example of the temple-tombs of Cairo.

I will not linger any longer, however, in the precincts of Islam, further than to mention the significant fact that the great central object of worship for the Mahommedan world is the Kaaba at Mecca, which itself, as Mr. William Simpson long ago pointed out, bears obvious traces of being at once a tomb and a sacred altar-stone. Sir Richard Burton's original sketch of this mystic object shows it as a square and undecorated temple-tomb, covered throughout with a tasselled black pall—a most funereal object—the so-called " sacred carpet." It is, in point of fact, a simple catafalque. As the Kaaba was adopted direct by Mohammad from the early Semitic heathenism of Arabia, and as it must always have been treated with the same respect, I do not think we can avoid the obvious conclusion that this very ancient tomb has been funereally draped in the self-same manner, like those of Biskra, Algiers, and Kerouan, from the time of its first erection. This case thus throws light on the draping of the *ashera*, as do also the many-coloured draperies and hangings of saints' catafalques in Algeria and Tunis.

Nor can I resist a passing mention of the Moharram festival, which is said to be the commemoration of the death of Hoseyn, the son of Ali (whose holy head is preserved at Cairo). This is a rude piece of acting, in which the events supposed to be connected with the death of Hoseyn are graphically represented; and it ends with a sacred Adonis-like or Osiris-like procession, in which the body of the saint is carried and mourned over. The funeral is the grand part of the performance; catafalques are constructed for the holy corpse, covered with green and gold tinsel—the green being obviously a last reminiscence of the god of vegetation. In Bombay, after the dead body and shrine have been carried through the streets amid weeping and wailing, they are finally thrown into the sea, like King Carnival. I think we need hardly doubt that here we have an evanescent relic of the rites of the corn-god, ending in a rain-charm, and very closely resembling those of Adonis and Osiris.

But if in Islam the great objects of worship are the Kaaba tomb at Mecca and the Tomb of the Prophet at Medina, so the most holy spot in the world for Christendom is—the Holy Sepulchre. It was for possession of that most sacred place of pilgrimage that Christians fought Moslems through the middle ages; and it is there that while faith in the human Christ was strong and vigorous the vast majority of the most meritorious pilgrimages continued to be directed. To worship at the tomb of the risen Redeemer was the highest hope of the devout mediæval Christian. Imitations of the Holy Sepulchre occur in abundance all over Europe: one exists at S. Stefano in Bologna; another, due to the genius of Alberti, is well known in the Ruccellai chapel at Florence. I need hardly recall the Sacro Monte at Varallo.

For the most part, however, in Christendom, and

especially in those parts of Christendom remote from Palestine, men contented themselves with nearer and more domestic saints. From a very early date we see in the catacombs the growth of this practice of offering up prayer by (or to) the bodies of the Dead who slept in Christ. A chapel or *capella*, as Dean Burgon has pointed out, meant originally an arched sepulchre in the walls of the catacombs, at which prayer was afterwards habitually made: and above-ground chapels were modelled, later on, upon the pattern of these ancient underground shrines. I have alluded briefly in my second chapter to the probable origin of the cruciform church from two galleries of the catacombs crossing one another at right angles; the High Altar stands there over the body or relics of a Dead Saint; and the chapels represent other minor tombs grouped like niches in the catacombs around it. A chapel is thus, as Mr. Herbert Spencer phrases it, "a tomb within a tomb"; and a great cathedral is a serried set of such cumulative tombs, one built beside the other. Sometimes the chapels are actual graves, sometimes they are cenotaphs; but the connexion with death is always equally evident. On this subject, I would refer the reader again to Mr. Spencer's pages.

So long as Christianity was proscribed at Rome and throughout the empire, the worship of the dead must have gone on only silently, and must have centred in the catacombs or by the graves of saints and martyrs—the last-named being practically mere Christian successors of the willing victims of earlier religions. "To be counted worthy to suffer" was the heart's desire of every earnest Christian—as it still is among fresh and living sects like the Salvation Army; and the creed of self-sacrifice, whose very name betrays its human-victim origin, was all but universal. When Christianity had triumphed, however, and gained not only official recognition but official honour, the cult of the martyrs and the other faithful dead became with Christian Rome a perfect passion. The Holy Innocents, St. Stephen Protomartyr, the nameless martyrs of the Ten Persecutions, together with Polycarp, Vivia Perpetua, Felicitas, Ignatius and all the rest, came to receive from the church a form of veneration which only the nice distinctions of the theological mind could enable us to discriminate from actual worship. The great procession of the slain for Christ in the mosaics of Sant' Apollinare Nuovo at Ravenna gives a good comprehensive list of the more important of these earliest saints (at least for Aryan worshippers) headed by St. Martin, St. Clement, St. Justin, St. Lawrence, and St. Hippolytus. Later on came the more mythical and poetic figures, derived apparently from heathen gods—St. Catharine, St. Barbara, St. George, St. Christopher. These form as they go a perfect new pantheon, circling round the figures of Christ himself, and his mother the Madonna, who grows quickly in turn, by absorption of Isis, Astarte, and Artemis, into the Queen of Heaven.

The love-feasts or *agapæ* of the early Christians were usually held, in the catacombs or elsewhere, above the bodies of the martyrs. Subsequently, the remains of the sainted dead were transferred to lordly churches without, like Sant' Agnese and San Paolo, where they were deposited under the altar or sacred stone thus consecrated, from whose top the body and blood of Christ was distributed in the Eucharist. As early as the fourth century, we know that no church was complete without some such relic; and the passion for martyrs spread so greatly from that period onward that at one time no less than 2300 corpses of holy men together were buried at S. Prassede. It is only in Rome itself that the full importance of this martyr-worship can now be sufficiently understood, or the large part which it played in the development of Christianity adequately recognised. Perhaps the easiest way for the Protestant reader to put himself in touch with this side of the subject is to peruse the very interesting and graphic account given in the second volume of Mrs. Jameson's *Sacred and Legendary Art*.

I have room for a few illustrative examples only.

When St. Ambrose founded his new church at Milan, he wished to consecrate it with some holy relics. In a vision, he beheld two young men in shining clothes, and it was revealed to him that these were holy martyrs whose bodies lay near the spot where he lived in the city. He dug for them, accordingly, and found two bodies, which proved to be those of two saints, Gervasius and Protasius, who had suffered for the faith in the reign of Nero. They were installed in the new basilica Ambrose had built at Milan. Churches in their honour now exist all over Christendom, the best known being those at Venice and Paris.

The body of St. Agnes, saint and martyr, who is always represented with that familiar emblem, the lamb which she duplicates, lies in a sarcophagus under the High Altar of Sant' Agnese beyond the Porta Pia, where a basilica was erected over the remains by Constantine the Great, only a few years after the martyrdom of the saint. The body of St. Cecilia lies similarly in the church of Santa Cecilia in Trastevere. In this last-named case, the original house where Cecilia was put to death is said to have been consecrated as a place of worship, after the very early savage fashion, the room where she suffered possessing especial sanctity. Pope Symmachus held a council there in the year 500. This earliest church having fallen into ruins during the troubles of the barbarians, Pope Paschal I., the great patron of relic-hunting, built a new one in honour of the saint in the ninth century. While engaged in the work, he had a dream (of a common pattern), when Cecilia appeared to him and showed him the place in which she lay buried. Search was made, and the body was found in the catacombs of St. Calixtus, wrapped in a shroud of gold tissue, while at her feet lay a linen cloth dipped in the sacred blood of her martyrdom. Near her were deposited the remains of Valerian, Tiburtius, and

Maximus, all of whom are more or less mixed up in her legend. The body was removed to the existing church, the little room where the saint died being preserved as a chapel. In the sixteenth century, the sacred building was again repaired and restored in the atrocious taste of the time; and the sarcophagus was opened before the eyes of several prelates, including Cardinal Baronius. The body was found entire, and was then replaced in the silver shrine in which it still reposes. Almost every church in Rome has thus its entire body of a patron saint, oftenest a martyr of the early persecutions.

In many similar cases, immense importance is attached to the fact that the body remains, as the phrase goes, "uncorrupted"; and I may mention in this connexion that in the frequent representations of the Raising of Lazarus, which occur as "emblems of the resurrection" in the catacombs, the body of Lazarus is represented as a mummy, often enclosed in what seems to be a mummy-case. Indeed, it is most reminiscent of the Egyptian Osiris images.

I pass on to other and more interesting instances of survival in corpse-worship.

The great central temple of the Catholic Church is St. Peter's at Rome. The very body of the crucified saint lies enshrined under the high altar, in a sarcophagus brought from the catacomb near S. Sebastiano. Upon this Rock, St. Peter's and the Catholic Church are founded. Anacletus, the successor of Clement, built a monument over the bones of the blessed Peter; and if Peter be a historical person at all, I see no reason to doubt that his veritable body actually lies there. St. Paul shares with him in the same shrine; but only half the two corpses now repose within the stately Confessio in the Sacristy of the papal basilica: the other portion of St. Peter consecrates the Lateran; the other portion of St. Paul gives sanctity to San Paolo fuori le Murá.

Other much venerated bodies at Rome are those of the Quattro Coronati, in the church of that name; S. Praxedis and St. Pudentiana in their respective churches; St. Cosmo and St. Damian; and many more too numerous to mention. Several of the Roman churches, like San Clemente, stand upon the site of the house of the saint to whom they are dedicated, or whose body they preserve, thus recalling the early New Guinea practice. Others occupy the site of his alleged martyrdom, or enclose the pillar to which he was fastened. The legends of all these Roman saints are full of significant echoes of paganism. The visitor to Rome who goes the round of the churches and catacombs with an unprejudiced mind must be astonished to find how sites, myths, and ceremonies recall at every step familiar heathen holy places or stories. In the single church of San Zaccaria at Venice, again, I found the bodies of St. Zacharias (father of John the Baptist), St. Sabina, St. Tarasius, Sts. Nereus and Achilles, and many other saints too numerous to mention.

How great importance was attached to the possession of the actual corpse or mummy of a saint we see exceptionally well indeed in this case of Venice. The bringing of the corpse or mummy of St. Mark from Alexandria to the lagoons was long considered the most important event in the history of the Republic; the church in which it was housed is the noblest in Christendom, and contains an endless series of records of the connexion of St. Mark with the city and people that so royally received him. The soul, as one may see in Tintoret's famous picture, flitted over sea with the body to Venice, warned the sailors of danger by the way, and ever after protected the hospitable Republic in all its enterprises. One must have lived long in the city of the Lagoons and drunk in its very spirit in order to know how absolutely it identified itself with the Evangelist its patron. "Pax tibi, Marce, evangelista meus," is the motto on its buildings. The lion of St. Mark stood high in the Piazzetta to be seen of all; he recurs in every detail of sculpture or painting in the Doges' Palace and the public edifices of the city. The body that lay under the pall of gold in the great church of the Piazza was a veritable Palladium, a very present help in time of trouble. It was no mere sentiment or fancy to the Venetians; they knew that they possessed in their own soil, and under their own church domes, the body and soul of the second of the evangelists.

Nor was that the only important helper that Venice could boast. She contained also the body of St. George at San Giorgio Maggiore, and the body of St. Nicholas at San Niccolo di Lido. The beautiful legend of the Doge and the Fisherman (immortalised for us by the pencil of Paris Bordone in one of the noblest pictures the world has ever seen) tells us how the three great guardian saints, St. Mark, St. George, and St. Nicholas, took a gondola one day from their respective churches, and rowed out to sea amid a raging storm to circumvent the demons who were coming in a tempest to overwhelm Venice. A fourth saint, of far later date, whom the Venetians also carried off by guile, was St. Roch of Montpelier. This holy man was a very great sanitary precaution against the plague, to which the city was much exposed through its eastern commerce. So the men of Venice simply stole the body by fraud from Montpelier, and built in its honour the exquisite church and Scuola di San Rocco, the great museum of the art of Tintoret. The fact that mere possession of the holy body counts in itself for much could not be better shown than by these forcible abductions.

The corpse of St. Nicholas, who was a highly revered bishop of Myra in Lycia, lies, as I said, under the high altar of San Niccolo di Lido at Venice. But another and more authentic body of the same great saint, the patron of sailors and likewise of schoolboys, lies also under the high altar of the magnificent basilica of San Nicolà at Bari, from which circumstance the holy bishop is generally known as St. Nicolas of Bari. A miraculous fluid, the Manna di Bari, highly prized by the pious, exudes from the remains. A gorgeous cathedral rises over the sepulchre. Such emulous duplication of bodies and relics is extremely common, both in Christendom and in Islam.

I have made a point of visiting the shrines of a vast number of leading saints in various parts of Italy; and could devote a volume to their points of interest. The corpse of St. Augustine, for example, lies at Pavia in a glorious ark, one of the most sumptuous monuments ever erected by the skill of man, as well as one of the loveliest. Padua similarly boasts the body of St. Antony of Padua, locally known as "il Santo," and far more important in his own town than all the rest of the Christian pantheon put together. The many-domed church erected over his remains is considerably larger than St. Mark's at Venice; and the actual body of the saint itself is enclosed in an exquisite marble chapel, designed by Sansovino, and enriched with all the noblest art of the Renaissance. Dominican monks and nuns make pilgrimages to Bologna, in order to venerate the body of St. Dominic, who died in that city, and whose corpse is enclosed in a magnificent sarcophagus in the church dedicated to him, and adorned with exquisite sculpture by various hands from the time of Niccolo Pisano to that of Michael Angelo. Siena has for its special glory St. Catherine the second—the first was the mythical princess of Alexandria; and the house of that ecstatic nun is still preserved intact as an oratory for the prayers of the pious. Her head, laid by in a silver shrine or casket, decorates the altar of her chapel in San Domenico, where the famous frescoes of Sodoma too often usurp the entire attention of northern visitors. Compare the holy head of Hoseyn at Cairo. The great Franciscan church at Assisi, once more, enshrines the remains of the founder of the Franciscans, which formerly reposed under the high altar; the church of Santa Maria degli Angeli below it encloses the little hut which was the first narrow home of the nascent order. I could go on multiplying such instances without number; I hope these few will suffice to make the Protestant reader feel how real is the reverence still paid to the very corpses and houses of the saints in Italy. If ever he was present at Milan on the festa of San Carlo Borromeo, and saw the peasants from neighbouring villages flock in hundreds to kiss the relics of the holy man, as I have seen them, he would not hesitate to connect much current Christianity with the most primitive forms of corpse-worship and mummy-worship.

North of the Alps, again, I cannot refrain from mentioning a few salient instances, which help to enforce principles already enunciated. At Paris, the two great local saints are St. Denis and Ste. Geneviève. St. Denis was the first bishop of Lutetia and of the Parisii: he is said to have been beheaded with his two companions at Montmartre,—Mons Martyrum. He afterwards walked with his head in his hands from that point (now covered by the little church of St. Pierre, next door to the new basilica of the Sacré Cœur), to the spot where he piously desired to be buried. A holy woman named Catulla (note that last echo) performed the final rites for him at the place where the stately abbey-church of St. Denis now preserves his memory. The first cathedral on the spot was erected before the Frankish invasion; the second, built by Dagobert, was consecrated (as a vision showed) by Christ himself, who descended for the purpose from heaven, surrounded by apostles, angels, and St. Denis. The actual head or skull of the saint was long preserved in the basilica in a splendid reliquary of solid silver, the gift of Marguérite de France, just as Hoseyn's head is still preserved at Cairo, and as so many other miraculous or oracular heads are kept by savages or barbarians elsewhere. Indeed, the anthropological enquirer may be inclined to suppose that the severance of the head from the body and its preservation above ground, after the common fashion, gave rise later to the peculiar but by no means unique legend. Compare the bear's head in the Aino superstition, as well as the oracular German and Scandinavian Nithstangs.

As for Ste. Geneviève, she rested first in the church dedicated to her on the site now occupied by the Pantheon, which still in part, though secularised, preserves her memory. Her body (or what remains of it) lies at present in the neighbouring church of St. Etienne du Mont, where every lover of Paris surely pays his devotion to the shrine in the most picturesque and original building which the city holds, whenever he passes through the domain of Ste. Geneviève. How real the devotion of the people still is may be seen on any morning of the working week, and still more during the octave of the saint's fête-day.

As in many other cases, however, the remains of the virgin patroness of Paris have been more than once removed from place to place for safe custody. The body was originally buried in the crypt of the old abbey church of the Holy Apostles on the Ile de la Cité. When the Normans overran the country, the monks carried it away with them in a wooden box to a place of safety. As soon as peace was once more restored, the corpse was enshrined in a splendid *châsse* ; while the empty tomb was still treated with the utmost reverence. At the Revolution, the actual bones, it is said, were destroyed; but the sarcophagus or cenotaph survived the storm, and was transferred to St. Etienne. Throughout the Neuvaine, thousands of the faithful still flock to worship it. The sarcophagus is believed even now to contain some holy portions of the saint's body, saved from the wreck by pious adherents.

Other familiar examples will occur to every one, such as the bones of the Magi or Three Kings, preserved in a reliquary in the Cathedral at Cologne; those of St. Ursula and the 11,000 virgins; those of St. Stephen and St. Lawrence at Rome; those of St. Hubert, disinterred and found uncorrupted, at the town of the same name in the Ardennes; and those of St. Longinus in his chapel at Mantua. All these relics and bodies perform astounding miracles, and all have been the centres of important cults for a considerable period.

In Britain, from the first stages of Christianity, the reverence paid to the bodies of saints was most marked, and the story of their wanderings forms an important part of our early annals. Indeed, I dwell so long upon this point because few northerners of the present day can fully appreciate the large part which the Dead Body plays and has played for many centuries in Christian worship. Only those who, like me, have lived long in thoroughly Catholic countries, have made pilgrimages to numerous famous shrines, and have waded through reams of Anglo-Saxon and other early mediæval documents, can really understand this phase of Christian hagiology. To such people it is abundantly clear that the actual Dead Body of some sainted man or woman has been in many places the chief object of reverence for millions of Christians in successive generations. A good British instance is found in the case of St. Cuthbert's corpse. The tale of its wanderings is too long to be given here in full; it should be read in any good history of Durham. I epitomize briefly. The body of the devoted missionary of the north was first kept for some time at Lindisfarne. When, at the end of eleven years, the saint's tomb was opened, his outer form was found still incorrupt; and so for more than 800 years it was believed to remain. It rested at Lindisfarne till 875, when the piratical Danes invaded Northumbria. The monks, regarding St. Cuthbert as their greatest treasure, fled inland, carrying the holy body with them on their own shoulders. Such translations of sacred corpses are common in Christian and heathen history. After many wanderings, during which it was treated with the utmost care and devotion, the hallowed body found an asylum for a while at Chester-le-Street in 883. In 995, it was transferred to Ripon, where it sanctified the minster by even so short a sojourn; but in the same year it went forth again, on its way north to Lindisfarne. On the way, however, it miraculously signified (by stubborn refusal to move) its desire to rest for ever at Durham—a town whose strong natural position and capacity for defence does honour to the saint's military judgment. Here, enclosed in a costly shrine, it remained working daily miracles till the Reformation. The later grave was opened in 1826, when the coffin was found to enclose another, made in 1104: and this again contained a third, which answered the description of the sarcophagus made in 698, when the saint was raised from his first grave. The innermost case contained, not indeed the uncorrupted body of Cuthbert, but a skeleton, still entire, and wrapped in fine robes of embroidered silk. No story known to me casts more light on corpse-worship than does this one when read with all the graphic details of the original authorities.

But everywhere in Britain we get similar local saints, whose bodies or bones performed marvellous miracles and were zealously guarded against sacrilegious intruders. Bede himself is already full of such holy corpses: and in later days they increased by the hundred. St. Alban at St. Alban's, the protomartyr of Britain; the "white hand" of St. Oswald, that when all else perished remained white and uncorrupted becaused blessed by Aidan; St. Etheldreda at Ely, another remarkable and illustrative instance; Edward the Confessor at Westminster Abbey; these are but a few out of hundreds of examples which will at once occur to students of our history. And I will add that sometimes the legends of these saints link us on unexpectedly to far earlier types of heathen worship; as when we read concerning St. Edmund of East Anglia, the patron of Bury St. Edmund's, that Ingvar the viking took him by force, bound him to a tree, scourged him cruelly, made him a target for the arrows of the pagan Danes, and finally beheaded him. Either, I say, a god-making sacrifice of the northern heathens; or, failing that, a reminiscence, like St. Sebastian, of such god-making rites as preserved in the legends of ancient martyrs. Compare here, once more, the Aino bear-sacrifice.

But during the later middle ages, the sacred Body of Britain, above all others, was undoubtedly that of Thomas A'Becket at Canterbury. Hither, as we know, all England went on pilgrimage; and nothing could more fully show the rapidity of canonisation in such cases than the fact that even the mighty Henry II. had to prostrate himself before his old enemy's body and submit to a public scourging at the shrine of the new-made martyr. For several hundred years after his death there can be no doubt at all that the cult of St. Thomas of Canterbury was much the most real and living worship throughout the whole of England; its only serious rivals in popular favour being the cult of St. Cuthbert to the north of Humber, and that of St. Etheldreda in the Eastern Counties.

Holy heads in particular were common in Britain before the Reformation. A familiar Scottish case is that of the head of St. Fergus, the apostle of Banff and the Pictish Highlands, transferred to and preserved at the royal seat of Scone. "By Sanct Fergus heid at Scone" was the favourite oath of the Scotch monarchs, as "Par Sainct Denys" was that of their French contemporaries.

In almost all these cases, again, and down to the present day, popular appreciation goes long before official Roman canonisation. Miracles are first performed at the tomb, and prayers are answered; an irregular cult precedes the formal one. Even in our own day, only a few weeks after Cardinal Manning's death, advertisements appeared in Catholic papers in London, giving thanks for spiritual and temporal blessings received through the intervention of Our Lady, the saints, "and our beloved Cardinal."

This popular canonisation has often far outrun the regular official acceptance, as in the case of Joan of Arc in France at the present day, or of "Maister John Schorn, that blessed man born," in the Kent of the middle ages. Thus countries like Wales and Cornwall are full of local and patriotic saints, often of doubtful Catholicity, like St. Cadoc, St. Padern, St. Petrock, St. Piran, St. Ruan, and St. Illtyd, not to mention more accepted cases, like St. Asaph and St. David. The fact is, men have everywhere felt the natural desire for a near, a familiar, a recent, and a present god or saint; they have worshipped rather the dead whom they loved and revered themselves than the elder gods and the remoter martyrs who have no body among them, no personal shrine, no local associations, no living memories. "I have seen in Brittany," says a French correspondent of Mr. Herbert Spencer's, "the tomb of a pious and charitable priest covered with garlands: people flocked to it by hundreds to pray of him that he would procure them restoration to health, and guard over their children." There, with the Christian addition of the supreme God, we get once more the root-idea of religion.

I should like to add that beyond such actual veneration of the bodies of saints and martyrs, there has always existed a definite theory in the Roman church that no altar can exist without a relic. The altar, being itself a monumental stone, needs a body or part of a body to justify and consecrate it. Dr. Rock, a high authority, says in his *Hierurgia*, "By the regulations of the Church it is ordained that the Holy Sacrifice of the Mass be offered upon an altar which contains a stone consecrated by a Bishop, enclosing the relics of some saint or martyr; and be covered with three linen cloths that have been blessed for that purpose with an appropriate form of benediction." The consecration of the altar, indeed, is considered even more serious than the consecration of the church itself; for without the stone and its relic, the ceremony of the Mass cannot be performed at all. Even when Mass has to be said in a private house, the priest brings a consecrated stone and its relic along with him; and other such stones were carried in the *retables* or portable altars so common in military expeditions of the middle ages. The church is thus a tomb, with chapel tombs around it; it contains a stone monument covering a dead body or part of a body; and in it is made and exhibited the Body of Christ, in the form of the consecrated and transmuted wafer.

Not only, however, is the altar in this manner a reduced or symbolical tomb, and not only is it often placed above the body of a saint, as at St. Mark's and St. Peter's, but it also sometimes consists itself of a stone sarcophagus. One such sarcophagus exists in the Cathedral at St. Malo; I have seen other coffin-shaped altars in the monastery of La Trappe near Algiers and elsewhere. When, however, the altar stands, like that at St. Peter's, above the actual body of a saint, it does not require to contain a relic ; otherwise it does. That is to say, it must be either a real or else an attenuated and symbolical sarcophagus.

In the eastern church, a sort of relic-bag, called an Antimins, is necessary for the proper performance of the Holy Eucharist. It consists of a square cloth, laid on the altar or wrapped up in its coverings, and figured with a picture representing the burial of Christ by Joseph of Arimathea and the Holy Women. This brings it very near to the Adonis and Hoseyn ceremonies. But it must necessarily contain some saintly relic.

Apart from corpse-worship and relic-worship in the case of saints, Catholic Christendom has long possessed an annual Commemoration of the Dead, the *Jour des Morts*, which links itself on directly to earlier ancestor-worship. It is true, this commemoration is stated officially, and no doubt correctly, to owe its origin (in its recognised form) to a particular historical person, Adam de Saint Victor : but when we consider how universal such commemorations and annual dead-feasts have been in all times and places, we can hardly doubt that the church did but adopt and sanctify a practice which, though perhaps accounted heathenish, had never died out at all among the mass of believers. The very desire to be buried in a church or churchyard, and all that it implies, link on Christian usage here once more to primitive corpse-worship. Compare with the dead who sleep with Osiris. In the middle ages, many people were buried in chapels containing the body (or a relic) of their patron saint.

In short, from first to last, religion never gets far away from these its earliest and profoundest associations. " God and immortality,"—those two are its key-notes. And those two are one; for the god in the last resort is nothing more than the immortal ghost, etherealised and extended.

On the other hand, whenever religion travels too far afield from its emotional and primal base in the cult of the nearer dead, it must either be constantly renewed by fresh and familiar objects of worship, or it tends to dissipate itself into mere vague pantheism. A new god, a new saint, a "revival of religion," is continually necessary. The Sacrifice of the Mass is wisely repeated at frequent intervals; but that alone does not suffice; men want the assurance of a nearer, a more familiar deity. In our own time, and especially in Protestant and sceptical England and America, this need has made itself felt in the rise of spiritualism and kindred beliefs, which are but the doctrine of the ghost or shade in its purified form, apart, as a rule, from the higher conception of a supreme ruler. And what is Positivism itself save the veneration of the mighty dead, just tinged with vague ethical yearnings after the abstract service of living humanity ? I have known many men of intellect, suffering under a severe bereavement—the loss of a wife or a dearly-loved child—take refuge for a time either in spiritualism or Catholicism. The former seems to give them the practical assurance of actual bodily intercourse with the dead, through mediums or table-turning; the latter supplies them with a theory of death which makes reunion a probable future for them. This desire for direct converse with the dead we saw exemplified in a very early or primitive stage in the case of the Mandan wives who talk lovingly to their husbands' skulls; it probably forms the basis for the common habit of keeping the head while burying the body, whose widespread results we have so frequently noticed. I have known two instances of modern spiritualists who similarly had their wives' bodies embalmed, in order that the spirit might return and inhabit them.

Thus the Cult of the Dead, which is the earliest origin of all religion, in the sense of worship, is also the last relic of the religious spirit which survives the gradual decay of faith due to modern scepticism. To this cause I refer on the whole the spiritualistic utterances of so many among our leaders of modern science. They have rejected religion, but they cannot reject the inherited and ingrained religious emotions.

CHAPTER XX.

CONCLUSION.

AND now we have reached at last the end of our long and toilsome disquisition. I need hardly say, to those who have persisted with me so far, that I do not regard a single part of it all as by any means final. There is not a chapter in this book, indeed, which I could not have expanded to double or treble its present length, had I chosen to include in it a tithe of the evidence I have gathered on the subject with which it deals. But for many adequate reasons, compression was imperative. Some of the greatest treatises ever written on this profoundly important and interesting question have met with far less than the attention they deserved because they were so bulky and so overloaded with evidence that the reader could hardly see the wood for the trees; he lost the thread of the argument in the mazes of example. In my own case, I had or believed I had a central idea; and I desired to set that idea forth with such simple brevity as would enable the reader to grasp it and to follow it. I go, as it were, before a Grand Jury only. I do not pretend in any one instance to have proved my points; I am satisfied if I have made out a *prima facie* case for further enquiry.

My object in the present reconstructive treatise has therefore been merely to set forth in as short a form as was consistent with clearness my conception of the steps by which mankind arrived at its idea of its God. I have not tried to produce evidence on each step in full; I have only tried to lay before the general public a rough sketch of a psychological rebuilding, and to suggest at the same time to scholars and anthropologists some inkling of the lines along which evidence in favour of my proposed reconstruction is likeliest to be found. This book is thus no more than a summary of probabilities. Should it succeed in attracting attention and arousing interest in so vast and fundamental a subject, I shall hope to follow it up by others in future, in which the various component elements of my theory will be treated in detail, and original authorities will be copiously quoted with the fullest references. As, however, in this preliminary outline of my views I have dealt with few save well-known facts, and relied for the most part upon familiar collocations of evidence, I have not thought it necessary to encumber my pages with frequent and pedantic footnotes, referring to the passages or persons quoted. The scholar will know well enough where to look for the proofs he needs, while the general reader can only judge my rough foreshadowing of a hypothesis according as he is impressed by its verisimilitude or the contrary.

If, on the other hand, this *avant-courier* of a reasoned system fails to interest the public, I must perforce be content to refrain from going any deeper in print into this fascinating theme, on which I have still an immense number of ideas and facts which I desire the opportunity of publicly ventilating.

I wish also to remark before I close that I do not hold dogmatically to the whole or any part of the elaborate doctrine here tentatively suggested. I have changed my own mind far too often, with regard to these matters, in the course of my personal evolution, ever to think I have reached complete finality. Fifteen or twenty years ago, indeed, I was rash enough to think I had come to anchor, when I first read Mr. Herbert Spencer's sketch of the origin of religion in the opening volume of the *Principles of Sociology*. Ten or twelve years since, doubts and difficulties again obtruded themselves. Six years ago, once more, when *The Golden Bough* appeared, after this book had been planned and in part executed, I was forced to go back entirely upon many cherished former opinions, and to reconsider many questions which I had fondly imagined were long since closed for me. Since that time, new lights have been constantly shed upon me from without, or have occurred to me from within: and I humbly put this sketch forward now for what it may be worth, not with the idea that I have by any means fathomed the whole vast truth, but in the faint hope that I may perhaps have looked down here and there a little deeper into the profound abysses beneath us than has been the lot of most previous investigators. At the same time, I need hardly reiterate my sense of the immense obligations under which I lie to not a few among them, and preeminently to Mr. Spencer, Mr. Frazer, Mr. Hartland, and Dr. Tylor. My only claim is that I may perhaps have set forth a scheme of reconstruction which further evidence will possibly show to be true in parts, and mistaken in others.

On the other hand, by strictly confining my attention to religious features, properly so called, to the exclusion of mythology, ethics, and all other external accretions or accidents, I trust I have been able to demonstrate more clearly than has hitherto been done the intimate connexion which always exists between cults in general and the worship of the Dead God, natural or artificial. Even if I have not quite succeeded in inducing the believer in primitive animism to reconsider his prime dogma of the origin of gods from all-pervading spirits (of which affiliation I can see no proof in the evidence before us), I venture to think I shall at any rate have made him feel that Ancestor-Worship and the Cult of the Dead God have played a far larger and deeper part than he has hitherto been willing to admit in the genesis of the religious emotions. Though I may not have raised the worship of the Dead Man to a supreme and unique place in the god-making process, I have at least, I trust, raised it to a position of higher importance than it has hitherto held, even since the publication of Mr. Herbert Spencer's epoch-making researches. I believe I have made it tolerably clear that the vast mass of existing gods or divine persons, when we come to analyse them, do actually turn out to be dead and deified human beings. In short, it is my hope that I have rehabilitated Euhemerism.

This is not the place, at the very end of so long a disquisition, to examine the theory of primitive animism. I would therefore only say briefly here that I do not deny the actual existence of that profoundly animistic frame of mind which Mr. Im Thurn has so well depicted among the Indians of Guiana; nor that which exists among the Samoyeds of Siberia; nor that which meets us at every turn in historical accounts of the old Roman religion. I am quite ready to admit that, to people at that stage of religious evolution, the world seems simply thronged with spirits on every side, each of whom has often his own special functions and peculiar prerogatives. But I fail to see that any one of these ideas is demonstrably primitive. Most often, we can trace ghosts, spirits, and gods to particular human origins: where spirits exist in abundance and pervade all nature, I still fail to understand why they may not be referred to the one known source and spring of all ghostly beings. It is abundantly clear that no distinction of name or rite habitually demarcates these ubiquitous and uncertain spirits at large from those domestic gods whose origin is perfectly well remembered in the family circle. I make bold to believe, therefore, that in every such case we have to deal with unknown and generalised ghosts,— with ghosts of most varying degrees of antiquity. If any one can show me a race of spirit-believers who do not worship their own ancestral spirits, or can adduce any effective prime differentia between the spirit that was once a living man, and the spirit that never was human at all, I will gladly hear him. Up to date, however, no such race has been pointed out, and no such differentia ever posited.

The truth is, we have now no primitive men at all. Existing men are the descendants of people who have had religions, in all probability, for over a million years. The best we can do, therefore, is to trace what gods we can to their original source, and believe that the rest are of similar development. And whither do we track them?

"So far as I have been able to trace back the origin of the best-known minor provincial deities," says Sir Alfred Lyall, speaking of India in general, "they are usually men of past generations who have earned special promotion and brevet rank among disembodied ghosts. . . . Of the numerous local gods known to have been living men, by far the greater proportion derive from the ordinary canonisation of holy personages. . . . The number of shrines thus raised in Berar alone to these anchorites and persons deceased in the odour of sanctity is large, and it is constantly increasing. Some of them have already attained the rank of temples." We have seen that an acute observer, Erman, came to a similar conclusion about the gods of those very Ostyaks who are often quoted as typical examples of primitive animists. Of late years, all the world over, numerous unprejudiced investigators, like Mr. Duff Macdonald and Captain Henderson, have similarly come to the conclusion that the gods of the natives among whom they worked were all of human origin; while we know that some whole great national creeds, like the Shinto of Japan, recognise no deities at all save living kings and dead ancestral spirits. Under these circumstances, judging the unknown by the known, I hesitate to take the very bold step of positing any new and fanciful source for the small residuum of unresolved gods whose human origin is less certainly known to us.

In one word, I believe that corpse-worship is the protoplasm of religion, while admitting that folk-lore is the protoplasm of mythology, and of its more modern and philosophical offshoot, theology.

INDEX.

A

Adonis, river, and grave of, 151
Adonis-worship, 245, 312; human sacrifice in, 312; rites of, 313
African burial rites, 29
African tribes, religious belief of, 25
Africana, iv
Ainu, The Hairy, 135
Alexander, son of Philip, 6
Alexandria, the Eastern London, 15; state of religion in, 368
Allah, isolation of, in Mohammedanism, 412
American cremationists, early, 55
Amon-Ra, or Zeus Ammon, 6
Ancestor-worship, 182 *et seq.*; in India, 32
Animism, theory of, 437
Antioch, the Venice of its time, 365
Art in primitive Greece, 84
Articles of faith, fresh additions to, 11
Ashera, 135, 189
Athanasius, 7
Atonement, doctrine of, 347; not a primitive idea, 347
Attis, worship of, 313; self-mutilation in, 313; festival of the cult of, 314; parallelism to Indian usage, 314; essentially a corn-god, 314
Aubrey's *Remains of Gentilisme*, 139
Aviella, Goblet d', 401
Aztec cannibal banquets, 110

B

Baptism, 389, 405
Barrows, Long, used for burials, 55; Round, for cremation, 56, 65
Bastian, 134, 139

Baumkultus, Mannhardt's, 138
Beagle, Voyage of the, Darwin's, 143
Belief, Egyptian, summary of, 173
Blood, substitute for, 110
Body, resurrection of the, 43, 54, 63
Buddhism, Freeman on, 380
Builder's Rites and Ceremonies, Speth's, 254
Bull-god, the Hebrew, 191
Bureau of Ethnology, Report of, 106
Burgon, Dean, 418
Burial, cave, 53; dissertation on, 55 *et seq.*; due to fear of ghosts, 56; earlier than burning, 54; Frazer as to, 56; resurrection from practice of, 54; rites, African, 29; sanctity from, sacred well, 152; system, origin of cultivation as adjunct of, 278
Burrough, Stephen (in Hakluyt), 129
Burton, Sir Richard, 416; anecdote of, 27
"Burying the carnival," 338
Busta, 66

C

Cade, Jack (Mortimer), 259
Camel sacrifice, 333; compared with that of Potraj and Dionysus, 333; must be hastily eaten, 333; compare paschal lamb, 333
Cannibal banquets, Aztec, 110
"Carnival, Burying the," 293
Catlin, 50
Cave burial, 53
Ceremonial institution, 200
Ceremonialism, religious, evolution of, 90
Ceremonies for expulsion of evils from communities, 349

440 INDEX.

Chalmers, Mr., 76, 358, 359
Cheyne, Professor, on stone-worship, 120
Christ, a corn-god, 381; a king's son, 383; and Meriah, 292; a temporary king, 379; bought with a price, 385
Christendom, corpse-worship of, at the tomb of Christ, 417; development of God of ancient Hebrews in God of modern, 225; God of, 459
Christian and heathen gods, apotheosis, 235; basis of religion, 226
Christianisation of Megalithic monuments, 115
Christianised form of scapegoat, 351
Christianity, a blend of Judaism with the popular religions of the day, 363; a competitor of Gnosticism, 395; a magma of Mediterranean religious ideas, 244; as standard of reference, 3; a syncretic product, 363; an embodiment of Mediterranean cults, 227; Egyptian influence on, 400 *et seq.;* elements of, 404; growth of, 362; in the West, 403 *et seq.;* in its beginning oriental, 400; least anthropomorphic creed, 18; Mithraism a competitor of, 395; modern worship of dead central force in, 408; origin of, author guided by Frazer and Mannhardt, v; peculiarities of, 17; priesthood not an integral part of early, 11; primitive, three great motors of, 399; reason for triumph of, 389; religion, typical, 15; religion, not a typical, 17; removed from all primitive cults, 17; specially the religion of immortality, 392; two main forms of, 403
Christian Pantheon, 7
Christians a sect of the Jews, 7
Christus, compared with Meriah, 285
Circumcision, baptism substituted for, 405; origin of, 200
Clodd, Mr. Edward, v, 21, 254
Codrington, Dr., 132
Conder, Major, 196, 198, 199, 415

Conway, Sir Martin, 175
Cook, Captain, 132
Corn-god, as seed, 287; Christ a, 381
Corn-god worship and Potraj festival, analogy of, 304
Corn-gods, animal, 289; substitute for human sacrifice, 289; in England, 290, 291
Corn festivals, European, 216
Cornish well-spirits, 152
Corpse, preservation of, 49; value of saintly, as treasure, 422; worship, at Rome, 419; in Britain, 427; in Islam, 413; the protoplasm of religion, 438
Cremationists, early American, Mexicans, 55
Cretan Dionysus myth, 307
Cross, threefold value of, 115
Cultivation, origin of, as adjunct of burial system, 278; paradox of, 273; origin of, 275
Culte du Cyprès, Sur le, Lajard's, 143

D

D'Albertis, 68
D'Alviella, Goblet, 401
Darwin's *Voyage of the Beagle*, 143
Dead, book of the, 170; cult of the, 185, 433; in Egypt, 415; fear of, 53; immortality the basis of worship of, 412; life of, 42; spiritualist belief in, 42; three stages in belief, 43; reappearance in sleep, 48; Roman commemoration of, 431; votive offerings to, 158
Dead bodies, preserving and worship of, 68
Dead god, worship of, universal in cults, 436
Dead man's tomb, the primitive temple, 11
"Death, Carrying out," 293
Death, primitive theories as to, 45, 47; the gate of life, 162; *The Worship of*, 153, 198
Deified man, worship of, 3
Deity, the need of a familiar, 432
De Osiride, Plutarch's, 166

INDEX. 441

Deities, Sir Alfred Lyall on origin of minor provincial, 438
Dii Manes, 9
Dionysus, originally the corn victim, 307; worship, 304, 305; resurrection of, 305; varieties of, 306; resemblance between, and Potraj rites, 306
Divine victim, priest alone drinks blood of, 346; trees in Semitic area, 149
Divinity, abnormal conditions of connection with, 228
Doubt and credulity always coexistent, 396
Du Chaillu, 71

E

Easter compared with other annual festivals, 391
"Eaten with honour," vii
Egypt, evolution of gods in, 155. tombs and caves of, 161, 416
Egyptian Belief, summary of, 178; gods early kings, 176; bestial types of, 173, 175; ophiolatry, Hebrew snake worship parallel with, 192; totems, 168; triads of God's origin of Trinity, 17, 369
Egyptians, true religion of, worship of the dead, and polytheism, 179
Elliot, Sir Walter, 301
Ellis, 68
Emigrants, Irish, in Canada, custom of, 343
Erman, on gods of the Ostyaks, 438
Essay on Scarabs, Loftie's, 167
Ethnology, Report of Bureau of, 106; *in Folklore*, Gomme's, 288, 290
Eucharist, Mexican, 341
Euhemerism, 16

F

Fairs, gingerbread cakes at, significance of, 344
Faith, fresh additions to Articles of, 11
"Feeding the Dead," 299
Fetichism, 97
Flagstone of the kings, 113

Folklore the protoplasm of mythology and theology, 438
Forbes, H. O., 50, 69, 80, 128, 268
Fortnightly Review, viii
Frazer, J. G., v, 56, 87, 91, 138, 142, 174, 175, 191, 228, 230, 231, 232, 233, 235, 237, 238, 239, 241, 242, 245, 246, 248, 252, 270, 279, 280, 283, 286, 287, 288, 291, 294, 297, 305, 306, 307, 309, 310, 312, 314, 315, 316, 336, 338, 342, 344, 348, 349, 350, 352, 353, 355
Freeman, E. A., on Buddhism, 380
Future Life, Hebrew theories as to, 184

G

Galton, Mr., 146, 318
Gentilisme, Remains of, Aubrey's, 139
Ghost theories, 159
Giant's dance, 107
Gill, Wyatt, 69, 329
Gnosticism, a competitor of Christianity, 395
God, boundary, 270; corn-, as seed, 287; development of Holy Ghost from, 407; eating, the, 339; feast, sacraments survival from cannibal, 346; growth of idea of, 19; the Hebrew bull-, 191; human origin of, 3; of Christendom, 409; belief in personality of, 409; as represented by Italian art, 409; cannot be realised except symbolically, 410; of food, making of, 281; manufactured, doctrine of, vi; monotheistic conception of, B. C., 14; of the ancient Hebrews, development of, into God of modern Christendom, 225; of increase, Jahweh a, 195; peculiar story of evolution of God of, 180; resemance between the mother of, and the mother of the gods, 385; sacramental union with a, 322; sacrifice of, in atonement, 320; the, as bread and wine, 337; the Hebrew, 154, 155; worship, development of sentiment from corpse-worship to, 162; Hebrew stone-, 187; of Egypt, the, viii;

442 INDEX.

of the Ostyaks, Erman on, 438; origin of Egyptian triads of, 369; evolution of, 407
God-eating, in Mexico, 327 *et seq.*; sacraments, evolution of, vi
God-making, orgiastic festival of Potraj, 301, 325, 346; for ships, 263; for river, 264; for war, 267
Gods, all primitive, corpses, 91; ancestors as, 86; artificial crop of, 247; bestial types of Egyptian, 173, 175; Egyptian, originally kings, 155; elemental, or nature-gods, 176; superadded factor in Egyptian religion, 177; foundation, 258, 319; framed from abstract conceptions, 174; frequently put to death by their votaries, 233; great, classes rather than individuals, 269; growth of, from ghosts, 71, 72; growth of, spontaneous, 247; importance of antiquity of, in ancient and modern society, 73, 74; in Egypt, evolution of, 155; killing of, a component of many faiths, 234; apotheosis, heathen and Christian, 235; minor, necessity of renewing, 411; new, necessary in religion, 432; of agriculture, 272; of city walls, 251; of towns and villages, 255; Semitic, vagueness of, 205
Golden Bough, The, Frazer's, v, 87, 138, 142, 246, 280, 283, 297
Gomara, 81
Gomme, Lawrence, v, 259, 288, 290, 297, 303, 306, 311, 349
Good qualities, eating, 323, 324
Gould, S. Baring, 248
Graves, food plants on, 281
Grave-stakes and standing-stones or tombstones as objects of worship, 82, 83
Greece, art in primitive, 84
Greek scapegoat, 352
Grote, on Greek worship, 103
Grove, sacred, 93

H

Haggard, H. Rider, 252
Harranians, infant sacrifice among, 344

Hartland, Sidney (note) v, 6, 47, 302, 324, 349, 388
Harvest, first-fruits of, 299
Hebrews, development of God of the ancient, into God of modern Christendom, 225; stone gods, 187; theories as to future life, 184
Heathen sacrifice of a god to himself analogous to Christian sacrifice of the mass, 244
Henderson, Captain, 438
Hierurgia, Dr. Rock's, 430
Holy Ghost, development of, from God, 407
Holy heads, preservation of in Britain, 429
Honorific cannibalism, Sidney Hartland on, 324
Horus, Madonna and Child compared with, 400
Hugh, St., of Lincoln, 379
Huitzilopochtli, image of, in dough, eaten by worshippers, 340
Hunter, Sir William, 31, 32, 143, 144

I

Idea of God, growth of, 19
Idols, 101 *et seq.*, mummy, of Mexicans, 81, 82; wooden-, probable origin of, 69; origin of, 79; supersession of mummy by, 80; wooden, derived from sepulchre head posts, 137
Illustrated London News, 5, 56, 74
Images, multiplication of, 85
Immortality, from practice of burning, 54; and resurrection, viii; of the soul, 43, 54; the basis of, worship of dead, 412
Incarnation, theory of, 229; an ordinary feature of religion in the first century, 233
Iona, black stones of, 116
Irish well-spirits, 152
Isis, Madonna and Child compared with, 400
Israel, evolution of God of, peculiar story of, 180; religion of, originally polytheistic, 201
Italy, shrines of saint, in, 424

INDEX. 443

J

Jahweh, ancestral sacred stone of the people of Israel, 126; a stone god, 197; attempts to make, always incorporeal, 124; destruction of stone, made his worship cosmopolitan, 222; incorporeal Supreme Ruler, 222; dissertation on, 122 *et seq.*; generic conception of pure deity, 223; human sacrifice to, 199; later conception of, 211; Molech-traits of, 212; the value of, 192 *et seq.*; a god of increase, 195; object of portable size, 123; spiritualized into great national deity, 125; the Hebrew god, 154, 155; the Rock of Israel, 125; worship of, astrological additions to, 213
Jameson's, Mrs., *Sacred and Legendary Art*, 420
Japanese totem, 360
Jesus, earliest believers in, 244
Jesus-cult, development of, 405 *et seq.*
Jews, Christians a sect of, 7; polytheists, 181
John the Baptist, 388
Judaism, Christianity a blend of, with the popular religions of the day, 363

K

Kaaba, 114, 186
Kings as gods, 227; as priests, 87; gods, evolution of, 172

L

Lajard's *Sur le Culte du Cyprès*, 143
Landa, 80
Landor, Walter Savage, 135, 360
Lang, Andrew, 23, 108, 114, 171 (note), 176
Lares, 369
Lectures on the Religion of Ancient Egypt, Renouf's, 156
Legend of Perseus, Hartland's, v
Lenormant, M., on ancestorship, 183
Life of the Dead, Three successive stages in, vi
Livingstone, Dr., 147
Loftie, 158, 167, 308, 401
London Stone, 258
Longmans' Magazine, 258
Lundonstone, Henry de, 258
Lyall, Sir Alfred, on origin of minor provincial deities, 438

M

Macdonald, Duff, iv, 24, 25, 27, 29, 30, 73, 74, 77, 96, 143, 247, 438
Madonna and Child, compared with Isis and Horus, 400
Maniæ, 344
Man-god, the death and resurrection of, the keynote to Asian and African religions, 246; types of, 231
Man-gods, importance to welfare of people in early times, 237; necessity of killing them before their powers decayed, 239 *et seq.*
Mannhardt, 138, 353
Man's two halves, 46
Manufactured god, doctrine of, vi
Mariette, M., 162, 168
Martyrdom, 271; the passion for, of early Christians, 419
Maspero, M., 159, 160, 176
Mass developed from Agape feasts, 12
Megalithic monuments, Christianisation of, 115
Men, metamorphosis of, into stones, 107
Meriah, 323; and Christ, 285, 292
Meriahs, 283, 284, 319
Meteorological phenomena, primitive misconception of, 20
Mexican cremationists, early, 55; eucharist, 431
Mexico, god-eating in, 327, *et seq.*
Migration of Symbols, The, 401
Mithraism, a competitor of Christianity, 395
Mock-mayors, 295
Mommsen, Dr., v
Monotheism, origin of, 154; religion reduced to central element, 223; rise of, iv, 204

INDEX.

Monotheistic conception of God, B. C., 14
Mother of the gods, and mother of God, resemblance between, 385
Müller, Max, 23
Mulungu, 25
Mummification, 49
Mummy, idols of Mexicans, 81, 82; worship in Egypt, 157
Mythology, and Religion, relative positions of, 20; essentially theoretical, 23

N

Nature-worship, origin of, v
New ideas of secondary rank, enumeration of, vi
Nordenskiöld, Baron, 357

O

Obelisk, origin of, 105
Oberammergau, 379
Ohio mounds, 55
Osiris, as the god of dead, 308, as a corn-god, 309; legend of Busiris concerning, 310; festival resemblance to rites of Potraj, 308; festivals, customs at, 345; growth of worship of, 167; originally a king, 165; rite, contemporary survival of, in Egypt, 310; rite, annual human victim of, 311; worship of, 107

P

Pandavas, Five, 94, 109, 114
Paris, saints' relics in, 425
Paul, probably first preacher of Christ to the world at large, 387
Paulicians, accusation against, 343
Penates, 370
Petrie, Flinders, vii, 176
Pharaoh, divinity of, 167
Philosophers, Roman, compared with Unitarians, 393
Piacular sacrificial rites, 261, 356
Pilatus, Caius Pontius, 3
Plutarch's *De Osiride*, 166
Polytheism, origin of, Spencer's ghost theory as to, iv; and worship of the dead the true religion of the Egyptians, 179
Potraj, orgiastic god-making festival of, 301, 325, 346
Powell, Professor York, v
"Practical Religion," viii
Prevost, Abbé, 45
Priest, development of, from temple attendant, 89; victim and god, identity of, 320
Priesthood, dual origin of, 86; independent origin of, 88; not integral part of early Christianity, 11
Prophets, enthusiasm of, 219

R

Ramsay, Professor, 245, 313
Reformation, Progress of, in Ireland, 102
Relics, saintly, necessary for the sacrifice of the mass, 430
Religion and mythology, viii; should be separated, 40
Religion, and mythology, relative positions of, 20; as a result of fear, 21; Christian basis of, 226; connection of, with death never severed, 411; demarcation of, from mythology, vi; Egyptian, based on ancestor-worship and totemism, 157; essentially practical, 22, 24; every, continues to make minor gods, 410; Roman, cosmopolitanised under the Empire, 375; Roman, Hellenised, 373; Roman, origin and growth of, 369; solely ceremony, custom, or practice, 32; state of, in Alexandria, 368; worship and sacrifice prime factors of, 40
Religious, belief of African tribes, 25; ceremonialism, evolution of, 90; emotion arises from regard for the dead, 411; sentiment, development of, from corpse- to God-worship, 162; thinking, 400; main schools of, iii; unrest, description of, 394
Renouf, Le Page, 156, 159, 160, 172, 174
Resurrection from practice of burial, 54; immortality and, viii;

of the body, 43, 54, 63; steps to prevent, 57
Revenant, 62
Rex Nemoralis, 344
Rhys, Professor John. v
Rock s, Dr., *Hierurgia*, 430
Rock, Standing, 108
Roden, Earl of, 102
Roman, Catholic mass a survival of the cult of Adonis-worship, 245; scapegoat, 352; ritual, derivation of, 34; scepticism, 392
Rougé, M. de, 157
Royal victims, sacrifice of, 259, 260

S

Sacramental meal, first step toward, 322; union with a god, 325
Sacraments, sacrifice and, 318; survival from cannibal godfeast, 346
Sacred and Legendary Art, Mrs. Jameson's, 420
Sacred books, 13
Sacred objects of the world, 150, 153
"Sacred Stones," viii
Sacred Stones, 93, *et seq.;* attempts to Jehovise, 119, 120; derivation of, from tombs, 116; in Britain, 113; migration of, 111
Sacred trees, 138; among Phœnicians and Canaanites, 150
Sacred well, sanctity from burial, 151, 152
Sacrifice, and sacrament, 318; camel, 333; cannibal mystic, 322; child, to make gods, 261; corn-gods substitute for human, 289; of a god, mystic theory of, 320; heathen, of a god to himself analogous to Christian sacrifice of the mass, 244; human, in Adonis-worship, 312; infant, among Harranians, 344; of God in atonement, 320; of royal victims, 219, 260; piacular, 261, 262; propitiatory annual, in New Guinea, 358; sacramental, involves renewal of divine life, 335; Smith Robertson's view of, 330; theanthropic, 260; two kinds of, 319

Sacrificial, animal, usually male, 333; victim, sanctity of, 331
Saints, intervention of, in Venice, 423; invocation of, 9; preservation of relics of, in Church of Rome, 421; relics in Paris, 425; devotion at the shrines of, 426; shrines of, in Italy, 424
Samoa, Turner's, 99, 111
Samoan collection of Mr. Turner, 97
"Sawing the Old Woman," 294
Sayce, Professor, 33, 173
Scapegoat, belief of transference of evils to, 349; Christianised form of, 351; evolution of, 350; human, 350; Roman and Greek, 352; transition from human to divine animal, 354
Scepticism, Roman, 392
Schoolcraft, 50, 100
Scone stone, 112
Seed-sowing, origin of, as adjunct of burial system, 278
Self-sacrifice, the creed of, 418
Semites, Religion of the, 119, 150, 214
Semitic, gods, vagueness of, 205; stone-cult, 116
Sepolture dei giganti, 94
Simpson, William, v, 40, 74, 271, 411, 416
Sin-eater, ritual of the, 345
Sins, remission of, bloodshed necessary for, 361
Skull, or head, importance of, 51, 66; primitive worship of, 69, 70
Smith, Angus, 101
Smith, Robertson, iv, 21, 32, 91, 117, 118, 136, 145, 152, 153, 185, 189, 209, 214, 215, 255, 256, 260, 262, 318, 320, 330, 355, 356, 373
Smith's, Robertson, view of sacrifice, 330
Snake-worship, Hebrew, parallel with Egyptian ophiolatry, 192
Sociology, Principles of, 34, 63, 74 (note), 99, 435
Soul, Frazer and the, 47; Hartland, Sidney, and the, 47; immortality of the, 63; separate, 47
Spano, Abbate, 101
Spencer, Herbert, iv, 23, 24, 31, 36,

446 INDEX.

47, 49, 50, 52, 68, 70, 74, 76, 79, 81, 82, 99, 110, 134, 146, 173, 174, 200, 279, 418, 430, 435
Speth, 254, 271
Spirit-possessed persons in rude society, 230
Stake, wooden, 93
Stakes, sacred, 127; inferior to stones, 127; derivation of, 128; worship of, 129; evolution into idol, 132
Standard of reference, Christianity as, 3
Stahic, definition of, 249
Statues, an outgrowth of tombstones, 83
Stevenson, R. L., authority on memorial tree-planting, 141
St. Hugh of Lincoln, 379
Stick-worship, 100
Stone-cult, Semitic, 116
Stone-gods, Hebrew, 187
Stonehenge, 93, 112
Stones, sacred, 93 *et seq.*; Sardinian, 101; of the Hebrews, 117 *et seq.*; metamorphosis of men into, 107
Stone worship, Professor Cheyne on, 120
Sun-worship, 105
Swinburne, quoted, 18
Symbolism, never primitive, 209
Syrians, easily Hellenised, 366

T

Taylor, Dr. Isaac, 82
Temenos, cenotaphs if not tombs, 148
Temple, origin of, 74, 75, 76; praying house, origin of, 69; the tomb as a, 159; tombs of Egypt, 416
"The Gods of Egypt," viii
"The Life of the Dead," viii
Theotokos, 9
Theology or mythology essentially theoretical, 23
Thurn, Im, 437
Tombs, of the kings, 142; and caves of Egypt, 161
Tombstones, early, 95, 96
Totem, Japanese, 360; rites and feast at sacrifice of, 360
Totems, Egyptian, 168

Totem-worship, 165; origin of, 174, 175
Totnes Times, 259
Trees, among Phœnicians and Canaanites, sacred, 150; in Semitic area, divine, 149; offering to, 143; sacred, 138
Trinity, Egyptian triads of gods, origin of, 17, 369; evolution of, 407
Turner, Mr., Samoan collection of, 91, 97, 111
Turner, Rev. George, 34, 108, 146, 298
Tylor, Dr., 23, 31, 47, 98, 99, 100, 104, 110, 114, 131, 134, 144, 146, 249, 271, 279

U

Universal Review, viii
Unitarians, Roman philosophers compared with, 393

V

Venice, intervention of saints in, 423
Vesalius, 45
Victims, substituted, 253
Village Community, L. Gomme's 259, 297
Village foundation, ritual of, 257

W

Ward, Lester, 25
Well, sacred, sanctity from burial, 152
Wells, sacred, 151
Well-spirits, Cornish and Irish, 152
Wooden idols, probable origin of, 69
Worship of Death, The, v, 75
Worship, Adonis, 245, 312; ancestor-, 182 *et seq.*, in India, 32; and sacrifice prime factors of religion, 40; corpse, of Christendom, at the tomb of Christ, 417; God, development of sentiment from corpse-worship to, 162; grave-stakes and standing-stones or tombstones as object of, 82, 83; Hebrew snake, paral-

lel with Egyptian ophiolatry, 192; mummy, in Egypt, 157; Nature, origin of, v; of Attis, 313; of corn-god and Potraj festival, analogy of, 304; of dead bodies, 68; of dead god, universal in cults, 436; of deified man, 3; of dead and polytheism the true religion of the Egyptians, 179; of Osiris, growth of, 167; of sacred stakes, 129; of skull, primitive, 69-70; sun, 105; totem, 165; origin of, 174, 175; as proven by monuments, 167

Worshippers, image of Huitzilopochtli, in dough, eaten by, 340

Y

Yarilo, funeral of, 294

Z

Zeus Ammon, or Amon Ra, 6

www.ingramcontent.com/pod-product-compliance
Lightning Source LLC
Chambersburg PA
CBHW032004300426
44117CB00008B/889